Bryan Stotts

D1460710

British Railways

LOCOMOTIVES &

COACHING STOCK

1992

The Complete Guide to all
Locomotives & Coaching Stock
Vehicles of British Railways
(excluding Departmental Stock)

Peter Fox

ISBN 1 872524 37 0

© 1992. Platform 5 Publishing Ltd., Lydgate House, Lydgate Lane,
Sheffield, S10 5FH.

Printed in England by Nuffield Press, Hollow Way, Cowley, Oxford
and Peter Scott Printers, Belshaw Court, Billington Road Industrial
Estate, Burnley.

CONTENTS

This book lists details of all BR locomotives and coaching stock vehicles in service 4th January 1991, together with vehicles on order which may be delivered during 1991. In addition, certain allocation changes which took effect in mid-January have been taken account of. Departmental coaching stock vehicles are excluded. In addition, information is provided on vehicles of light railways and metros (other than London Underground).

1. LOCOMOTIVES

The following notes are applicable to locomotives:

LOCOMOTIVE CLASS DETAILS

Principal details and dimensions are given for each class in metric units. Imperial equivalents are also given for power. Maximum speeds are still quoted in miles per hour since the operating department of BR still uses imperial units. Since the present maximum permissible speed of certain classes of locomotives is different from the design speed, these are now shown separately in class details. In some cases certain low speed limits are arbitrary and may occasionally be raised raised when necessary if a locomotive has to be pressed into passenger service.

Standard abbreviations used are:

BR	British Railways	kW	kilowatts
BREL	British Rail Engineering Ltd.	lbf	pounds force
hp	horse power	mph	miles per hour
kN	kilonewtons	RA	Route availability
kV	kilovolts	t	tonnes

LOCOMOTIVE DETAIL DIFFERENCES

Detail differences which affect the areas and types of train which locos work are shown. Where detail differences occur within a class or part class of locos., these are shown against the individual loco number. Except where shown 'e' or 'y', diesel locomotives have no train heating equipment. Electric or electro-diesel locomotives are assumed to have train heating unless shown 'y'. Standard abbreviations used are:

a	Train air brakes only
c	Cab to shore radio-telephone fitted.
e	Fitted with electric heating apparatus (ETH).
g	Fitted with driver–guard telephone.
p	Fitted with t.d.m. push/pull & multiple working equipment.
r	Fitted with radio electronic token block equipment.
s	Slow speed control fitted (and operable).
t	Fitted with automatic vehicle identification transponders.
v	Train vacuum brakes only.
x	Dual train brakes (air & vacuum).
y	ETH equipped but equipment isolated.
+	Extended range locos with Additional fuel tank capacity compared with others in class.

NAMES AND ALLOCATIONS

All official names are shown as they appear on the locomotive i.e. all upper case or upper & lower case lettering.

(S) denotes stored serviceable and (U) stored unserviceable. Last known allocations of stored locomotives are shown, but readers should note that locomotives may not necessarily be stored at their home depots.

After the locomotive number are shown any notes regarding braking, heating etc.,the livery code (in bold type), the sector code, the depot code and name if any. Locomotives which have been renumbered in recent years show the last number in parentheses after the current number. Where only a few locomotives in a class are named, these are shown in a separate table at the end of the class or sub-class.

Thus the layout is as follows:

No.	Old No.	Notes	Liv.	Sector	Depot	Name
47673	(47593)	†	**IO**	IIHA	IS	Galloway Princess

GENERAL INFORMATION ON BRITISH RAILWAYS'LOCOMOTIVES

CLASSIFICATION & NUMBERING

Initially BR diesel locomotives were allocated numbers in the 1xxxx series, with electrics allotted numbers in the 2xxxx series. Around 1957 diesel locomotives were allocated new four digit numbers with 'D' prefixes. Diesel electric shunters in the 13xxx series had the '1' replaced by a 'D', but diesel mechanical shunters were completely renumbered. Electric locomotives retained their previous numbers but with an 'E' prefix. When all standard gauge steam locomotives had been withdrawn, the prefix letter was removed.

In 1972, the present TOPS numbering system was introduced whereby the loco number consisted of a two-digit class number followed by a serial number. In some cases the last two digits of the former number were generally retained (classes 20, 37, 50), but in other classes this is not the case. In this book former TOPS numbers carried by converted locos. are shown in parentheses. Full renumbering information is to be found in the 'Diesel & Electric loco Register'. This is at present out of print, but a new edition will be published sometime in 1991.

Diesel locomotives are classified as "types" depending on their engine horsepower as follows:

Type	Engine hp.	Old Number Range	Current Classes
1	800–1000	D 8000–D 8999	20
2	1001–1499	D 5000–D 6499/D 7500–D 7999	26, 31.
3	1500–1999	D 6500–D 7499	33, 37.
4	2000–2999	D 1 –D 1999	47, 50.
5	3000+	D 9000–D 9499	56, 58, 59, 60.
Shunter	Under 300	D 2000–D 2999	03.
Shunter	300–799	D 3000–D 4999	08, 09.

Class 14 (650 hp diesel hydraulics) were numbered in the D95xx series.

Electric and electro-diesel locomotives are classified according to their supply system. Locomotives operating on a d.c. system are allocated classes 70–79, whilst a.c. locomotives are allocated classes starting at 80.

Departmental locomotives which remain self propelled or which are likely to move around on a day to day basis are classified 97.

WHEEL ARRANGEMENT

For main line diesel and electric locomotives the system whereby the number of driven axles on a bogie or frame is denoted by a letter (A=1, B=2, C=3 etc.) and the number of undriven axles is noted by a number is used. The letter 'o' after a letter indicates that each axle is individually powered and a + sign indicates that the bogies are intercoupled.

For shunters and steam locomotives the Whyte notation is used. The number of leading wheels are given, followed by the number of driving wheels and then the trailing wheels. Suffix 'T' on a steam locomotive indicates a tank locomotive, and 'PT' a pannier tank loco.

HAULING CAPABILITY OF DIESEL LOCOS

The hauling capability of a diesel locomotive depends basically upon three factors:

1. Its adhesive weight. The greater the weight on its driving wheels, the greater the adhesion and thus more tractive power can be applied before wheel slip occurs.

2. The characteristics of its transmission. In order to start a train the locomotive has to exert a pull at standstill. A direct drive diesel engine cannot do this, hence the need for transmission. This may be mechanical, hydraulic or electric. The current BR standard for locomotives is electric transmission. Here the diesel engine drives a generator or alternator and the current produced is fed to the traction motors. The force produced by each driven wheel depends on the current in its traction motor. In other words the larger the current, the harder it pulls.

As the locomotive speed increases, the current in the traction motors falls hence the *Maximum Tractive Effort* is the maximum force at its wheels that the locomotive can exert at a standstill. The electrical equipment cannot take such high currrents for long without overheating. Hence the *Continuous Tractive Effort* is quoted which represents the current which the equipment can take continuously.

3. The power of its engine. Not all of this power reaches the rail as electrical machines are approximately 90% efficient. As the electrical energy passes through two such machines (the generator/alternator and the traction motors), the *Power At Rail* is about 81% (90% of 90%) of the engine power, less a further amount used for auxiliary equipment such as radiator fans, traction motor cooling fans, air compressors, battery charging, cab heating, ETH, etc. The power of the locomotive is proportional to the tractive effort times the speed. Hence when on full power there is a speed corresponding to the continuous tractive effort.

5

HAULING CAPABILITY OF ELECTRIC LOCOS

Unlike a diesel locomotive, an electric locomotive does not develop its power on board and its performance is determined only by two factors, namely its weight and the characteristics of its electrical equipment. Whereas a diesel locomotive tends to be a constant power machine, the power of an electric locomotive varies considerably. Up to a certain speed it can produce virtually a constant tractive effort. Hence power rises with speed according to the formula given in section 3 above, until a maximum speed is reached at which tractive effort falls, such that the power also falls. Hence the power at the speed corresponding to the maximum tractive effort is lower than the maximum.

BRAKE FORCE

The brake force is a measure of the braking power of a locomotive. This is shown on the locomotive data panels so that railway staff can ensure that sufficient brake power is available on freight trains.

TRAIN HEATING EQUIPMENT

Electric train heating (ETH) is now the standard system in use on BR for loco-hauled trains. Locomotives which were equipped to provide steam heating have had this equipment removed or rendered inoperable (isolated). Electric heat is provided from the locomotive by means of a separate alternator on the loco., except in the case of 47401–18 and classes 33 and 50 which have a d.c. generator. The *ETH Index* is a measure of the electrical power available for train heating. All electrically heated coaches have an ETH index and the total of these in a train must not exceed the ETH power of a locomotive.

ROUTE AVAILABILITY

This is a measure of a railway vehicle's axle load. The higher the axle load of a vehicle, the higher the RA number on a scale 1 to 10. Each route on BR has an RA number and in theory no vehicle with a higher RA number may travel on that route without special clearance. Exceptions are made, however.

MULTIPLE WORKING

Multiple working between diesel locomotives on BR has usually been provided by means of an electro-pneumatic system, with special jumper cables connecting the locos. A coloured symbol is painted on the end of the locomotive to denote which system is in use. Class 47/7 used a time-division multiplex (t.d.m.) system which utilised the existing RCH (an abbreviation for the former railway clearing house, a pre-nationalisation standards organisation) jumper cables which have in the past only been used for train lighting control, and more recently for public address (pa) and driver–guard communication. A new standard t.d.m. system has now been fitted to electric locomotives and other vehicles.

1.1 DIESEL LOCOMOTIVES

CLASS 03   BR SHUNTER   0–6–0

Built: 1960 at BR Doncaster Works (03079) or 1962 at BR Swindon Works (03179).
Engine: Gardner 8L3 of 152 kW (204 hp) at 1200 rpm.
Transmission: Mechanical. Fluidrive type 23 hydraulic coupling to Wilson-Drewry CA5R7 gearbox with SCG type RF11 final drive.
Max. Tractive Effort: 68 kN (15300 lbf).
Brake Force: 13 t.   **Length over Buffers:** 7.92 m.
Weight: 31 t.   **Wheel Diameter:** 1092 mm.
Max. Speed: 28 mph.   **RA:** 1.

Formerly numbered 2079 & 2179 respectively.

03079 v   DCSD   RY | 03179 x **N**   DCSD   RY

CLASS 08   BR SHUNTER   0–6–0

Built: 1953–62 by BR at Crewe, Darlington, Derby, Doncaster or Horwich Works.
Engine: English Electric 6KT of 298 kW (400 hp) at 680 rpm.
Main Generator: English Electric 801.
Traction Motors: Two English Electric 506.
Max. Tractive Effort: 156 kN (35000 lbf).
Cont. Tractive Effort: 49 kN (11100 lbf) at 8.8 mph.
Power At Rail: 194 kW (260 hp).
Brake Force: 19 t.   **Length over Buffers:** 8.92 m.
Weight: 50 t.   **Wheel Diameter:** 1372 mm.
Max. Speed: 15 (20) or 20* mph.   **RA:** 5.
Non standard liveries:

08500 is red lined out in black & white.
08601 is London Midland & Scottish Railway black.
08642 is London & South Western Railway black and also carries its former number D 3809.
08721 is blue with a red & yellow stripe ("Red Star" livery).
08730/867 are BR black.
08793 is London & North Eastern Railway apple green.
08833 is Great Eastern Railway Blue and also carries its former number D4001.
08907 is London & North Western Railway black.
08933 is as 'D' but with two orange cabside stripes.
08938 is grey and red.

n–Waterproofed for working at Oxley Carriage Depot.
z–Fitted with buckeye adaptor at nose end for HST depot shunting.
†–Fitted with yellow flashing light and siren for working between Ipswich Yard and Cliff Quay.
Formerly numbered in series 3000–4192. 08600 was numbered 97800 whilst in departmental use between 1979 and 1989.

CLASS 08/0. Standard Design.

No.					No.				
08308	v		FSCD	DR	08507	a		MSSR	RG
08309	v	F	FSCK	KY	08509	a	F	FSNT	TI
08388	a	F	FSNI	IM	08510	a		FSCD	DR
08389	a		FSNL	NL	08511	a		FSCN	TO
08390	a		FSWL	LE	08512	a	F	FSCB	BL
08393	a	D	MSSS	SF	08514	a		FSCD	DR
08397	a	F	MSNA	AN	08515	a		FSNH	HT
08399	a		MSNC	CD	08516	a	D	FSCK	KY
08401	a	D	FSNI	IM	08517	a		MSNB	BS
08402	a	D	MSNA	AN	08519	a	BS	MSSB	BY
08405	a	D	FSNI	IM	08521	a		MSNA	AN
08407	a	F	MSSS	SF	08523	x		MSSR	RG
08410	a	D	FSWB	BR	08525	x	F	FSCK	KY
08411	a		FSNY	TE	08526	x		MSSS	SF
08413	a	D	MSSS	SF	08527	x	D	MSSS	SF
08414	a*†		MSSS	SF	08528	x	D	MSSM	MR
08415	x		MSNA	AN	08529	x		MSSM	MR
08416	a		FSCN	TO	08530	x	D	MSSS	SF
08417	a	D	MSSS	SF	08531	x	F	MSSS	SF
08418	a	F	FSCD	DR	08532	x		MSNA	AN
08419	a		MSNU	CL	08533	x		MSSS	SF
08421	a		FSCB	BL	08534	x	D	MSNU	CL
08428	a		MSNB	BS	08535	x	D	MSNB	BS
08434	v		FSCE	DY	08536	x		FSCE	DY
08436	v		FSCD	DR	08537	x	FO	MSNX	BS (U)
08441	a		FSCN	TO	08538	x	D	MSSM	MR
08442	a	F	FSCB	BL	08539	x		MSSC	CA
08445	a		FSNI	IM	08540	x	D	MSSM	MR
08447	a		MSNU	CL	08541	x	D	MSSS	SF
08448	a		MSNB	BS	08542	x	F	MSSS	SF
08449	a		FSCN	TO	08543	x	D	MSNB	BS
08451	x		MSSW	WN	08544	x		FSNH	HT
08454	x		MSSO	OC	08561	x		FSSM	ML
08460	a	F	MSSO	OC	08562	x		FSCD	DR
08466	a	FO	MSNB	BS	08565	x		FSSM	ML
08472	a		MSNC	CD	08567	x		MSSB	BY
08480	az		MSSO	OC	08568	x		FSSM	ML
08481	x		FSWK	CF	08569	x		MSNA	AN
08482	a	D	MSNA	AN	08570	x	M	FSSE	ED
08483	a	D	FSWB	BR	08571	xz		FSSE	ED
08484	a	F	MSSB	BY	08573	x		MSSO	OC
08485	a		MSNA	AN	08575	x	BS	FSNY	TE
08489	a	F	MSNA	AN	08576	x		MSSL	LA
08492	a		FSCN	TO	08577	x		FSNH	HT
08493	a		FSWK	CF	08578	x	R	FSNH	HT
08495	x		MSSM	MR	08580	x		MSSM	MR
08498	a		MSSS	SF	08581	x		FSSM	ML
08499	a	F	FSCK	KY	08582	a	D	FSNY	TE
08500	x	O	FSCK	KY	08583	x		FSCK	KY
08506	a		FSNY	TE	08585	x		MSNC	CD

08586	a	F	FSSA	AY	08653	x*		MSSO	OC
08587	x		FSNH	HT	08655	x*	F	MSSS	SF
08588	xz	BS	FSNL	NL	08656	a		MSSB	BY
08589	x		FSWK	CF	08658	a		MSSN	NC
08590	x	BS	FSNH	HT	08661	a		FSNL	NL
08591	x		FSSA	AY	08662	a		FSCK	KY
08593	x		MSSS	SF	08663	a	D	MSSL	LA
08594	x		MSSC	CA	08664	x		FSWK	CF
08595	x		FSCD	DR	08665	x		FSNI	IM
08597	x		FSCN	TO	08666	x		MSNL	LO
08599	x		MSNC	CD	08667	xz		FSNL	NL
08600	a	D	DCSC	AF	08668	x		FSWK	CF
08601		0	MSNB	BS	08670	a		MSSO	OC
08603	x		MSNB	BS	08672	x		MSNB	BS
08604	x	G	MSNB	BS	08673	x	IO	MSNL	LO
08605	x		FSCK	KY	08675	x	F	FSSA	AY
08607	x		FSCN	TO	08676	x		MSNL	LO
08609	x		MSSW	WN	08677	x		MSSW	WN
08610	x		MSNB	BS	08680	x		FSSB	AB
08611	x		MSNL	LO	08682	x		FSCD	DR
08613	x		MSNA	AN	08683	x		MSSW	WN
08614	x		MSSW	WN	08685	x		MSSN	NC
08615	x		MSNA	AN	08689	a		MSSS	SF
08616	x		MSNB	BS	08690	x		MSNU	CL
08617	x		MSSW	WN	08691	x	G	FSNT	TI
08619	x		MSNL	LO	08692	x		MSNC	CD
08620	x		FSSE	ED	08693	x		FSSM	ML
08622	x		FSSM	ML	08694	x		MSNA	AN
08623	x		FSCN	TO	08695	x		MSNC	CD
08624	x		MSNL	LO	08696	a	D	MSSW	WN
08625	x		MSSW	WN	08697	x		FSCE	DY
08627	a		MSSS	SF	08698	x		MSSS	SF
08628	x		MSSB	BY	08699	x		MSNC	CD
08629	x		MSSB	BY	08700	a		MSNB	BS
08630	x		FSSG	GM	08701	x	R	FSNH	HT
08631	x	N	MSSC	CA	08702	x		MSNC	CD
08632	x		FSNI	IM	08703	a		MSNA	AN
08633	x	RX	MSNC	CD	08705	a		MSSM	MR
08634	x		MSSO	OC	08706	x		FSCK	KY
08635	x		MSNC	CD	08707	a		FSCK	KY
08638	x	BS	MSSC	CA	08708	x		MSSS	SF
08641	xz	D	MSSL	LA	08709	x		MSSS	SF
08642	x*	0	DCSD	EH	08710	x		FSSE	ED
08643	xz	D	FSWB	BR	08711	x		MSSC	CA
08644	xz	M	MSSL	LA	08712	x		FSSE	ED
08645	xz	D	MSSL	LA	08713	a		MSSM	MR
08646	x	F	FSWL	LE	08714	x		MSSC	CA
08647	x	G	FSCD	DR	08715	v		MSSS	SF
08648	x*	D	MSSW	WN	08716	x		FSSI	IS
08649	x	D	DCSB	SU	08717	x		FSSE	ED
08651	xz	D	MSSO	OC	08718	x		FSSE	ED
08652	x		FSWK	CF	08720	a	D	FSSE	ED
					08721	x	0	MSNL	LO

9

Reg			Code	
08723	x		FSCN	TO
08724	x		MSSS	SF
08725	x		FSSE	ED
08727	x	F	FSSA	AY
08730	x	O	FSSE	ED
08731	x		FSSG	GM
08732	x		FSSM	ML
08733	x		FSSM	ML
08734	x		MSNB	BS
08735	x		FSSM	ML
08737	x	F	MSNC	CD
08738	x	D	FSSM	ML
08739	x		MSNC	CD
08740	x	F	MSSS	SF
08742	x		MSNC	CD
08743	x		FSNL	NL
08744	x		MSNL	LO
08745	xz	BS	FSNL	NL
08746	x	D	MSNB	BS
08748	x†		MSSS	SF
08749	x		FSNT	TI
08750	x		MSSS	SF
08751	x		MSNB	BS
08752	x		MSSS	SF
08753	x		FSSE	ED
08754	x		FSSI	IS
08755	x		FSSE	ED
08756	x	D	FSWL	LE
08757	x	D	MSSC	CA
08758	x		MSSS	SF
08759	x		MSNB	BS
08760	x*	F	DCSD	EH
08761	x	R	FSSE	ED
08762	x		FSSI	IS
08765	xn	D	MSNB	BS
08766	x		FSNL	NL
08767	x		MSSS	SF
08768	x		MSNU	CL
08770	a	D	FSWK	CF
08771	x		FSNH	HT
08772	x	G	MSSS	SF
08773	x		FSCN	TO
08775	x		MSSS	SF
08776	a	D	FSCK	KY
08778	x	D	FSWK	CF
08780	x		FSWL	LE
08781	x		FSWK	CF
08782	a		FSCK	KY
08783	x		FSCK	KY
08784	x		MSNC	CD
08786	a		FSNY	TE
08788	x		FSCE	DY
08789	a		MSSB	BY
08790	x		MSNL	LO
08791	a	F	FSSE	ED
08792	a		MSSL	LA
08793	a	O	FSSE	ED
08794	xz		FSNL	NL
08795	x	D	FSWK	CF
08798	x		FSWL	LE
08799	x		MSNA	AN
08800	x	I	FSWB	BR
08801	x		MSSL	LA
08802	x		FSNH	HT
08803	x	D	MSSR	RG
08804	x		FSWK	CF
08805	x	FO	MSNB	BS
08806	a	F	FSCK	KY
08807	x		MSSB	BY
08809	x		MSNA	AN
08810	a		MSSN	NC
08811	a*		MSSO	OC
08813	a	D	FSCD	DR
08814	a		FSCE	DY
08815	x		MSNA	AN
08817	x	BS	MSNA	AN
08818	x		FSWK	CF
08819	x	D	MSSL	LA
08821	x		MSSL	LA
08822	x		FSWK	CF
08823	a		MSNC	CD
08824	a	F	FSCD	DR
08825	a		MSSO	OC
08826	a		MSNU	CL
08827	a		MSNU	CL
08828	a		MSSS	SF
08829	a		FSCN	TO
08830	x*		FSWK	CF
08831	x*		DCSD	EH
08832	x	FR	MSNB	BS
08833	x*	O	MSSX	SF (U)
08834	x	F	MSSS	SF
08835	xz		FSWK	CF
08836	x		FSWK	CF
08837	x*	D	MSSO	OC
08839	x		MSSL	LA
08842	x		FSCE	DY
08844	x		MSNU	CL
08845	x*	D	DCSD	EH
08847	x*		DCSD	EH
08848	x		FSWK	CF
08849	x		MSSL	LA
08850	x		MSSR	RG
08853	xr		FSSM	ML

08854	x*		DCSB	SU	08910	x		MSNU	CL
08855	x		FSSB	AB	08911	x	D	MSNU	CL
08856	x		MSNA	AN	08912	x		MSNU	CL
08858	x		MSNA	AN	08913	x	D	MSNA	AN
08859	x		MSSN	NC	08914	x		MSSB	BY
08865	x		MSSC	CA	08915	x	F	MSNL	LO
08866	x		FSCD	DR	08916	x		MSNA	AN
08867	x	O	FSNY	TE	08918	x	D	MSNA	AN
08868	x		MSSN	NC	08919	x		FSNT	TI
08869	x	G	MSSN	NC	08920	x	F	MSNB	BS
08870	x		FSCD	DR	08921	x		MSNC	CD
08872	x	D	MSNA	AN	08922	x	D	DCSC	AF
08873	x	M	MSSS	SF	08923	x	F	MSSS	SF
08874	x	BS	FSNL	NL	08924	x	D	MSSR	RG
08877	x	D	FSCD	DR	08925	x		MSNA	AN
08878	x		MSNB	BS	08926	x		MSSW	WN
08879	x		FSNT	TI	08927	x		MSSB	BY
08880	x		FSNT	TI	08928	x	FR	MSNB	BS
08881	x	D	FSSE	ED	08931	x		FSNH	HT
08882	x		FSSB	AB	08932	x		FSWK	CF
08883	x		FSSE	ED	08933	x*	O	DCSD	EH
08884	x		MSNA	AN	08934	x		MSSW	WN
08885	x		FSCD	DR	08935	x		FSWB	BR
08886	x		FSNH	HT	08936	x		MSSN	NC
08887	x		MSSO	OC	08937	x	D	MSSL	LA
08888	xz	R	FSNH	HT	08938	xr	O	FSSM	ML
08889	x		MSSM	MR	08939	x		MSNA	AN
08890	x	D	MSSW	WN	08940	x		DCSC	AF
08891	x		MSNL	LO	08941	x		MSSL	LA
08892	x*	D	DCSD	EH	08942	x		FSWK	CF
08893	x	D	MSNB	BS	08944	x	D	MSSO	OC
08894	x		MSNA	AN	08945	x		MSSL	LA
08895	x		FSWL	LE	08946	x	D	MSSR	RG
08896	x		FSWL	LE	08947	x		MSSO	OC
08897	x	D	FSWB	BR	08948	x		MSSO	OC
08899	x		FSCE	DY	08949	x		FSWB	BR
08900	x	D	MSNA	AN	08950	x	F	DCSC	AF
08901	xn		MSNB	BS	08951	x	D	MSNA	AN
08902	x		MSNA	AN	08952	x		FSSM	ML
08903	x		FSCD	DR	08953	x	D	MSSL	LA
08904	x		MSSO	OC	08954	x	F	MSSL	LA
08905	x		MSSR	RG	08955	x		MSSL	LA
08906	x		FSNY	TE	08956	x		MSSS	SF
08907	x	O	MSNC	CD	08957	x		MSSS	SF
08908	xz		FSNL	NL	08958	x		MSSS	SF
08909	x		MSSS	SF					

Names:

08562	The Doncaster Postman	08691	ESCAFELD
08578	Libert Dickinson	08701	GATESHEAD TMD 1852–1991
08631	Eagle C.U.R.C.	08772	CAMULODUNUM
08633	The Sorter	08869	The Canary
08647	Crimpsall	08888	Postman's Pride

Class 08/9. Fitted with cut-down cab and headlight for Cwmmawr branch.

08993	(08592)	x	FSWL	LE	ASHBURNHAM
08994	(08462)	a	**FR** FSWL	LE	GWENDRAETH
08995	(08687)	a	**FC** FSWL	LE	KIDWELLY

CLASS 09   BR SHUNTER   0–6–0

Built: 1959–62 by BR at Darlington or Horwich Works.
Engine: English Electric 6KT of 298 kW (400 hp) at 680 rpm.
Main Generator: English Electric 801.
Traction Motors: English Electric 506.
Max. Tractive Effort: 111 kN (25000 lbf).
Cont. Tractive Effort: 39 kN (8800 lbf) at 11.6 mph.
Power At Rail: 201 kW (269 hp).

Brake Force: 19 t.	**Length over Buffers:** 8.92 m.
Weight: 50 t.	**Wheel Diameter:** 1372 mm.
Max. Speed: 27 mph.	**RA:** 5.

Formerly numbered 3665–71, 3719–21, 4099–4114.

09001		FSWK	CF	09014		FSCK	KY
09002		DCSC	AF	09015	**D**	FSWK	CF
09003		DCSB	SU	09016		DCSB	SU
09004		DCSD	EH	09018		DCSC	AF
09005		FSCK	KY	09019	**D**	DCSC	AF
09006		DCSB	SU	09020		DCSB	SU
09007		DCSB	SU	09021		DCSC	AF
09008		FSNT	TI	09022		DCSC	AF
09009	**D**	DCSB	SU	09023		DCSB	SU
09010		DCSB	SU	09024		DCSC	AF
09011	**D**	DCSC	AF	09025		DCSD	EH
09012	**D**	DCSB	SU	09026	**D**	DCSD	EH
09013	**D**	FSNT	TI				

Names:

09008	Sheffield Childrens Hospital	09012	Dick Hardy
09009	Three Bridges C.E.D.	09026	William Pearson

CLASS 20   ENGLISH ELECTRIC TYPE 1   Bo–Bo

Built: 1957–68 by English Electric Company at Vulcan Foundry, Newton le Willows or Robert Stephenson & Hawthorn, Darlington. 20001–128 were originally built with disc indicators whilst 20129–228 were built with four character headcode panels.
Engine: English Electric 8SVT Mk. II of 746 kW (1000 hp) at 850 rpm.

Main Generator: English Electric 819/3C.
Traction Motors: English Electric 526/5D (20001–48) or 526/8D (others).
Max. Tractive Effort: 187 kN (42000 lbf).
Cont. Tractive Effort: 111 kN (25000 lbf) at 11 mph.
Power At Rail: 574 kW (770 hp). **Length over Buffers:** 14.25 m.
Brake Force: 35 t. **Wheel Diameter:** 1092 mm.
Design Speed: 75 mph. **Weight:** 73.5 t.
Max. Speed: 60 mph. **RA:** 5.
Train Brakes: Air & Vacuum.
Multiple Working: Blue Star Coupling Code.

m Fitted with remote control multiple working.
Formerly numbered in series 8007–8198, 8306–8315.

CLASS 20/0. BR-owned Locomotives.

20007 st	FEFN	TO	20121 st		FEFN	TO
20016 st	FEGN	TO	20128 st		FEFN	TO
20032 s	FEFN	TO	20131 st		FEGN	TO
20046	FMTY	TE	20132 st	**FR**	FEGN	TO
20055 st	FEFN	TO	20135 st		FEFN	TO
20057 st	FEFN	TO	20137	**FR**	FMRY	TE
20058 smt	DRTC	TO	20138	**FR**	DRTC	TO
20059 st **FR**	FEGN	TO	20140 st		FEGN	TO
20066	DRTC	TO	20142 st		FEFN	TO
20071 st	FEFN	TO	20143 st		FEFN	TO
20072 st	FEFN	TO	20151 st		FEGN	TO
20073 st	FEGN	TO	20154 st		FEGN	TO
20075 st	FEFN	TO	20163 st **FR**	FEFN	TO
20078 st	FEFN	TO	20165	**FR**	FMRY	TE
20081 st	FEGN	TO	20168 st		FEFN	TO
20082 st	FEFN	TO	20169 st		FEFN	TO
20087 smt	DRTC	TO	20177 st		FEGN	TO
20090 st **FR**	FEGN	TO	20185		FEFN	TO
20092	FMTY	TE	20186 st		FEFN	TO
20094 st	FEGN	TO	20187 st		FEFN	TO
20096	FEFN	TO	20190 st		FEFN	TO
20104 st **FR**	FEFN	TO	20195 s		FEGN	TO
20106 st	FEFN	TO	20196 st		FEGN	TO
20117 st	FEFN	TO	20210 st		FEFN	TO
20118 **FR**	FMRY	TE	20214 st		FEFN	TO
20119	DRTC	TO	20215 st **FR**	FEFN	TO

CLASS 20/9. Privately-owned by Hunslet–Barclay Ltd.

Used on summer weedkilling trains. Stored at Kilmarnock during the winter.
Non-standard Livery: Hunslet–Barclay two-tone grey livery with red lettering.

20901 (20041) t	**0**	CYPD	HB	NANCY
20902 (20060)	**0**	CYPD	HB	LORNA
20903 (20083)	**0**	CYPD	HB	ALISON
20904 (20101)	**0**	CYPD	HB	JANIS
20905 (20225) t	**0**	CYPD	HB	IONA
20906 (20219)	**0**	CYPD	HB	GEORGINA

CLASS 26   BRCW TYPE 2   Bo–Bo

Built: 1958–59 by the Birmingham Rly Carriage & Wagon Co., Smethwick.
Engine: Sulzer 6LDA28 of 870 kW (1160 hp) at 750rpm.
Main Generator: Crompton Parkinson CG391A1.
Traction Motors: Crompton Parkinson C171A1 (26/0), C171D3 (26/1).
Max. Tractive Effort: 187 kN (42000 lbf).
Cont. Tractive Effort: 133 kN (30000 lbf) at 11.25 mph.
Power At Rail: 671 kW (900 hp).   **Length over Buffers:** 15.47 m.
Brake Force: 35 t.   **Wheel Diameter:** 1092 mm.
Design Speed: 80 mph.   **Weight:** 75 t (26/0), 74.5 t (26/1).
Max. Speed: 60 mph.   **RA:** 5 or 6.
Train Brakes: Air & Vacuum.
Multiple Working: Blue Star Coupling Code.
Communication Equipment: This class is in the process of being fitted with cab to shore radio-telephone.
Formerly numbered 5301–43 (except 26007 (5300) & 26028 (5320).

CLASS 26/0. RA6.

				Eastfield				
26001	s	C	DCHA	ED	26007	s	C	DCHA	ED
26002	s	FC	DCHA	ED	26008		FC	DCHA	ED
26003	s	FC	DCHA	ED	26010		FR	DCHB	ED
26004	s	C	DCHA	ED	26011		C	DCHA	ED
26005	s	C	DCHA	ED	26014			DCHB	ED
26006	s	FC	DCHA	ED					

CLASS 26/1. RA5.

26024		DCHB	ED	26037	FR	DCHB	ED
26025	FR	DCHA	ED	26038	FR	DCHA	ED
26026	C	DCHA	ED	26040	FR	DCHA	ED
26027		DXXD	ED (U)	26041	FR	FPAE	ED
26032	FR	DCHA	ED	26042		DCHB	ED
26035	C	DCHA	ED	26043	C	DCHA	ED
26036	C	DCHB	ED				

CLASS 31   BRUSH TYPE 2   A1A–A1A

Built: 1957–62 by Brush Traction at Loughborough. 31102/5–8/10/25/34/44/418/50/61/544 retain two headcode lights. Others have roof-mounted headcode boxes. 31215 has headcode box one end only.
Engine: English Electric 12SVT of 1100 kW (1470 hp) at 850 rpm.
Main Generator: Brush TG160-48.
Traction Motors: Brush TM73-68.
Max. Tractive Effort: 160 kN (35900 lbf) (190 kN (42800 lbf)*).
Cont. Tractive Effort: 83 kN (18700 lbf) at 23.5 mph. (99 kN (22250 lbf) at 19.7 mph *.)
Power At Rail: 872 kW (1170 hp).   **Length over Buffers:** 17.30 m.
Brake Force: 49 t.   **Driving Wheel Diameter:** 1092 mm.
Design Speed: 90 (80*) mph.   **Centre Wheel Diameter:** 1003 mm.
Max. Speed: 60 mph (90 mph 31/4) **Weight:** 107–111 t.
RA: 5 or 6.   **ETH Index (Class 31/4):** 66.

Train Brakes: Air & Vacuum.
Multiple Working: Blue Star Coupling Code.
Communication Equipment: This class is in the process of being fitted with cab to shore radio-telephone.
Non standard liveries:

31101 is BR blue with a red band around the bottom of the cabs and a full height BR logo.
31413 is BR blue with yellow cabsides, a light blue stripe along the bottom of the body and a red band around the bottom of the cabs.

Formerly numbered 5518/20–5862 (not in order).

CLASS 31/1. Standard Design. RA5.

31101	0	DMEA	BS	31181	C	DCAA	SF
31102	C	DCMC	CD	31184	FO	DCEW	IM
31105 *	FR	DCMB	BS	31185	C	DCMB	BS
31106 *		DCMC	CD	31186	C	DCAA	SF
31107	C	DCMB	BS	31187	C	DCAA	SF
31110	C	DCMB	BS	31188	FR	DCMC	CD
31112 *	FR	DCMB	BS	31190	FR	DCAA	SF
31113	D	DCMB	BS	31191	C	DCAA	SF
31116	C	DCMB	BS	31196	C	DCAA	SF
31119	C	DCMB	BS	31199	FP	FPCI	IM
31123		DCMN	BS	31200	FC	FHAC	CD
31125	C	DCMC	CD	31201	FC	FHAC	CD
31126	C	DCMC	BS	31203	C	DCMC	CD
31128	FO	DCMN	BS	31205	FR	DCEW	IM
31130	FC	FHAC	CD	31206	FR	DCMC	CD
31132	FO	DCMN	BS	31207	FP	FPCI	IM
31134	C	DCMB	BS	31209	FA	DCMN	BS
31135	C	DCAA	SF	31210	FO	FPYX	IM (U)
31142	C	DCMC	CD	31215	FO	DCEW	IM
31144	C	DCMC	CD	31217	FC	FHAC	CD
31145	C	DCMB	BS	31219	C	DCAA	SF
31146	C	DCMB	BS	31221		DXXD	IM (U)
31147	C	DCMB	BS	31224	C	DCAA	SF
31149	FR	DCAB	SF	31229	FO	DCAB	SF
31154	FO	DCMB	BS	31230 *	FO	DCEW	IM
31155	FA	DCMN	BS	31232	FR	DCMC	CD
31156		FPYX	IM (U)	31233	FP	FPCI	IM
31158	C	DCMB	BS	31234	FO	DCMN	BS
31159	C	DCMC	CD	31235	C	DCMC	CD
31160	F	DCAB	SF	31237	C	DCMC	CD
31162		DCEW	IM	31238	C	DCMC	CD
31163	C	DCMC	CD	31242	C	DCMC	CD
31164	FO	DCMN	BS	31247	FR	DCEW	IM
31165	G	DCAA	SF	31248	FO	DCMN	BS
31166	C	DCMB	BS	31250	C	DCAA	SF
31171	FO	DCMN	BS	31252	FO	DCMN	BS
31174	C	DCMB	BS	31255	FO	DCMC	CD
31178	FR	DCMB	BS	31263	C	DCAA	SF
31180	FR	DCAB	SF	31268	C	DCAA	SF

31270	**FC**	FHAC	CD		31296	**FA**	DCEW	IM
31271	**FA**	DMEA	BS		31301	**FR**	DCEW	IM
31272	**FR**	DCMC	CD		31302	**FP**	FPCI	IM
31273	**C**	DCMC	CD		31304	**FP**	FPCI	IM
31275	**FC**	FHAC	CD		31306	**C**	DCMC	CD
31276	**FC**	FHAC	CD		31308	**C**	DCMC	CD
31282	**FR**	DCEW	IM		31312	**FC**	FHAC	CD
31285	**FR**	DCMC	CD		31317	**FO**	DCMN	BS
31289		DCMN	BS		31319	**FP**	FPCI	IM
31290	**C**	DCMC	CD		31324	**FC**	FHAC	CD
31294	**FA**	FHAC	CD		31327	**FR**	DCAB	SF

Names:

31102	Cricklewood	31233	Phillips-Imperial
31116	RAIL 1981–1991	31276	Calder Hall Power Station
31165	Stratford Major Depot		

CLASS 31/4. Equipped with Train Heating. RA6.

31402		DMEA	BS	
31403		DMEA	BS	
31405	**M**	DMEA	BS	Mappa Mundi
31407 (31507)	**M**	DMEA	BS	
31408		RXLB	CD	
31410		RXLB	CD	
31413	**O**	RXLB	CD	Severn Valley Railway
31415		DMEA	BS	
31417	**D**	DMEA	BS	
31418		RXLB	CD	
31420 (31172)		DMEA	BS	
31421 (31140)		RXLB	CD	
31422 (31522)	**M**	DMEA	BS	
31423 (31197)	**M**	DMEA	BS	Jerome K. Jerome
31427 (31194)		RXLB	CD	
31432 (31153)		RXLB	CD	
31434 (31258)		DMEA	BS	
31435 (31179)		DMEA	BS	
31438 (31139)		RXLB	CD	
31439 (31239)		RXLB	CD	
31442 (31251)		RXLB	CD	
31450 (31133)		RXLB	CD	
31457 (31169)	**D**	DMEA	BS	
31459 (31256)		DMEA	BS	
31460 (31266)		DMEA	BS	
31461 (31129)	c **D**	DMEA	BS	
31462 (31315)	**D**	DMEA	BS	
31466 (31115)	**D**	DMEA	BS	
31467 (31216)		DMEA	BS	

CLASS 31/5. Dedicated for Civil Engineer's Department Use. Train Heating Equipment isolated. RA6.

31511 (31411)	**D**	DCEW	IM	
31512 (31412)	**C**	DCMB	BS	

31514 (31414)		DCMB	BS	
31516 (31416)	C	DCMB	BS	
31519 (31419)	C	DCMB	BS	
31524 (31424)	C	DCMB	BS	
31526 (31426)		DCMB	BS	
31530 (31430)	C	DCMB	BS	Sister Dora
31531 (31431)	C	DCEA	IM	
31533 (31433)		DCMB	BS	
31537 (31437)		DCMB	BS	
31541 (31441)	C	DCEA	IM	
31544 (31444)		DCEA	IM	Keighley and Worth Valley Railway
31545 (31445)		DCMB	BS	
31546 (31446)		DCMB	BS	
31547 (31447)	C	DCEA	IM	
31548 (31448)		DCMB	BS	
31549 (31449)	C	DCEA	IM	
31551 (31451)	D	DCMB	BS	
31552 (31452)		DCEA	IM	
31553 (31453)	C	DCEA	IM	
31554 (31454)	D	DCMB	BS	
31555 (31455)	D	DCMB	BS	
31556 (31456)	C	DCEA	IM	
31558 (31458)	C	DCEA	IM	
31563 (31463)		DCEA	IM	
31565 (31465)	C	DCMB	BS	
31568 (31468)	C	DCMB	BS	The Enginemen's Fund
31569 (31469)	C	DCEA	IM	

CLASS 33 BRCW TYPE 3 Bo–Bo

Built: 1960–62 by the Birmingham Railway Carriage & Wagon Company, Smethwick.
Engine: Sulzer 8LDA28 of 1160 kW (1550 hp) at 750 rpm.
Main Generator: Crompton Parkinson CG391B1.
Traction Motors: Crompton Parkinson C171C2.
Max. Tractive Effort: 200 kN (45000 lbf).
Cont. Tractive Effort: 116 kN (26000 lbf) at 17.5 mph.
Power At Rail: 906 kW (1215 hp). **Length over Buffers:** 15.47 m.
Brake Force: 35 t. **Wheel Diameter:** 1092 mm.
Design Speed: 85 mph. **Weight:** 77.5 t (78.5 t Class 33/1).
Max. Speed: 60 mph. **RA:** 6.
Train Heating: Electric (y isolated). **ETH Index:** 48.
Train Brakes: Air & Vacuum.
Multiple Working: Blue Star Coupling Code.
Communication Equipment: This class is in the process of being fitted with cab to shore radio-telephone.

Formerly numbered in series 6500–97 but not in order.

Class 33/0. Standard Design.

33002	y	C	DCSM	EH	
33008	y	C	DCSA	EH	Eastleigh

33009 e **C**	DCSM	EH	Walrus
33012 e	DCSW	SL	
33019 e **C**	DCSA	EH	
33020 e	DCSW	SL	
33021 e **FA**	FASB	SL	
33023 e	DCSW	SL	
33025 e **C**	DCSA	EH	Sultan
33026 e **C**	DCSM	EH	Seafire
33029 e	DCSW	SL	
33030 e	DCSA	EH	
33033 e **FA**	DCSW	SL	
33035 e **C**	DCSM	EH	
33040 e	DCSW	SL	
33042 ys **FA**	FASB	SL	
33046 y **C**	DCSM	EH	
33047 ys **C**	DCSM	EH	Spitfire
33048 es	DCSW	SL	
33050 e **FA**	FASB	SL	Isle of Grain
33051 e **FA**	DCSW	SL	Shakespeare Cliff
33052 e	DCSW	SL	Ashford
33053 e **FA**	FASB	SL	
33057 ys **C**	DCSM	EH	Seagull
33063 ys **FA**	FASB	SL	
33064 e **FA**	FASB	SL	
33065 e **C**	DCSM	EH	Sealion

Class 33/1. Fitted with Buckeye Couplings & SR Multiple Working Equipment for use with SR EMUs, TC stock & class 73.

Also fitted with flashing light adaptor for use on Weymouth Quay line.

33101 e	DMSA	EH	
33102 e	NWXB	EH	
33103 e **C**	DCSA	EH	
33108 e **C**	DCSA	EH	
33109 e **D**	DMSA	EH	
33110 e	DCSW	SL	
33113 e	DCSW	SL	
33114 e	NWXB	EH	
33116 e **D**	DMSA	EH	
33117 e	DCSW	SL	
33118 e **C**	DCSA	EH	

Class 33/2. Built to Former Loading Gauge of Hastings Line.

33201 es **C**	DCSM	SL	
33202 ys **C**	DCSM	SL	The Burma Star
33204 es **D**	MDIB	SL	
33205 es **FD**	MDIB	SL	
33206 es **FD**	MDIB	SL	
33207 ys **FA**	FASB	SL	Earl Mountbatten of Burma
33208 e **C**	DCSM	SL	
33211 es **FD**	MDIB	SL	

CLASS 37 ENGLISH ELECTRIC TYPE 3 Co–Co

Built: 1960–5 by English Electric Company at Vulcan Foundry, Newton le Willows or Robert Stephenson & Hawthorn, Darlington. 37003–116/350/1/4/9 with the exception of 37053/065*/072*/073/074/075*/100* (* one end only) retain box-type route indicators, the remainder having central headcode panels/marker lamps.
Engine: English Electric 12CSVT of 1300 kW (1750 hp) at 850 rpm.
Main Generator: English Electric 822/10G.
Traction Motors: English Electric 538/A.
Max. Tractive Effort: 245 kN (55500 lbf).
Cont. Tractive Effort: 156 kN (35000 lbf) at 13.6 mph.
Power At Rail: 932 kW (1250 hp). **Length over Buffers:** 18.75 m.
Brake Force: 50 t. **Wheel Diameter:** 1092 mm.
Design Speed: 90 mph. **RA:** 5 or 7.
Max. Speed: 80 mph. **Weight:** 103–108 t.
Train Heating: Electric (Class 37/4 only). **ETH Index:** 38
Train Brakes: Air & Vacuum.
Multiple Working: Blue Star Coupling Code.
Communication Equipment: This class is in the process of being fitted with cab to shore radio-telephone.
Formerly numbered 6600–8, 6700–6999 (not in order). 37271–4 are the second locos to carry these numbers. They were renumbered to avoid confusion with Class 37/3 locos.

Class 37/0. Unrefurbished Locos. Technical details as above. RA5.

37003	+		DCEA	IM	
37004		FM	FMAK	CF	
37008 (37352)	+	FR	MDTT	TI	
37009	+	FD	MDTT	TI	
37010		C	DCWA	CF	
37012		C	DCWA	CF	
37013	+	F	MDTT	TI	
37015	+	FD	MDTT	TI	
37019		FD	MDST	TI	
37023		C	DCAA	SF	
37025		C	DCHA	ED	
37026 (37320)	+	FD	MDTT	TI	Shap Fell
37029	+	FD	MDTT	TI	
37031	+	FD	MDTT	TI	
37032 (37353)	+	FR	FAXI	IM	
37035		C	DCWA	CF	
37037 (37321)		FM	FMTY	TE	Gartcosh
37038		C	DCWA	CF	
37040		FM	FMGM	ML	
37042	+	FM	FMGM	ML	
37045 (37355)	+	F	MDTT	TI	
37046		C	DCWA	CF	
37047		FD	MDST	TI	
37048		FM	FMTY	TE	
37049		C	DCEA	IM	Imperial

37051		**FM**	FMTY	TE	
37053		**FD**	MDST	TI	
37054		**C**	DCWA	CF	
37055		**FD**	MDST	TI	
37057		**BR**	FPBI	IM	
37058	+	**C**	DCEA	IM	
37059	+	**FD**	MDTT	TI	Port of Tilbury
37063	+	**FD**	MDTT	TI	
37065	+	**FD**	MDTT	TI	
37066	+	**C**	DCEA	IM	
37068 (37356)	+	**FR**	MDTT	TI	Grainflow
37069	+	**F**	FMTY	TE	Thornaby T.M.D.
37070		**FD**	MDST	TI	
37071	+	**D**	DCEA	IM	
37072	+	**D**	FPEK	CF	
37073	+	**FD**	MDTT	TI	Fort William/An Gearasdan
37074		**FD**	MDST	TI	
37075		**F**	MDST	TI	
37077		**FM**	FMGM	ML	
37078	+	**FP**	FMAK	CF	
37079 (37357)	+	**FD**	MDTT	TI	Medite
37080		**FP**	FPAE	ED	
37083	+	**C**	DCEA	IM	
37087		**C**	DCHA	ED	
37088 (37323)		**D**	DCHA	ED	Clydesdale
37092		**C**	DCWA	CF	
37095	+	**D**	DCEA	IM	
37097		**C**	DCWA	CF	
37098	+	**C**	DCWA	CF	
37099 (37324)		**FM**	FMGM	ML	Clydebridge
37100	+	**FM**	FMTY	TE	
37101	+	**FD**	MDTT	TI	
37104		**D**	DCEA	IM	
37106	+	**FM**	FPAE	ED	
37107		**FD**	MDST	TI	
37108 (37325)		**BR**	MDST	TI	Lanarkshire Steel
37109		**FM**	FMTY	TE	
37110		**FM**	FAXI	IM	
37111 (37326)		**FM**	FPAE	ED	Glengarnock
37113		**FD**	MDST	TI	Radio Highland
37114		**FD**	MDST	TI	Dunrobin Castle
37116		**BR**	FPBI	IM	
37128		**BR**	FPCI	IM	
37131	+		FEPE	ED	
37133		**C**	DCWA	CF	
37137 (37312)		**FM**	FMAK	CF	Clyde Iron
37138		**FP**	FMAK	CF	
37139	+	**FC**	FEPE	ED	
37140		**C**	DCAA	SF	
37141		**C**	DCWA	CF	
37142		**C**	DCWA	CF	
37144	r	**FA**	FAXI	IM	

37145 (37313)	**FM**	FMGM	ML	
37146	**C**	DCWA	CF	
37152 (37310)	**BR**	DCHA	ED	
37153	**C**	DCHA	ED	
37154		FPAE	ED	
37156 (37311) r	**C**	DCHA	ED	British Steel Hunterston
37158	**C**	DCWA	CF	
37162 +	**D**	FPEK	CF	
37165 (37374) +	**FC**	FEPE	ED	
37167 +	**FC**	FEPE	ED	
37170 r		DCHA	ED	
37174	**C**	DCWA	CF	
37175	**C**	DCHA	ED	
37178	**FD**	MDST	TI	
37184	**FP**	FPAE	ED	
37185 +	**FD**	MDTT	TI	
37188	**FP**	FPAE	ED	
37190 (37314)	**FM**	FMTY	TE	Dalzell
37191	**C**	DCWA	CF	
37194 +	**FD**	MDTT	TI	British International Freight Association
37196	**C**	DCHA	ED	
37197 +	**C**	DCWA	CF	
37198 +	**FD**	MDTT	TI	
37201	**FM**	FMAK	CF	
37202	**FM**	FPCI	IM	
37203	**FM**	FMTY	TE	
37207	**C**	DCWA	CF	
37209	**BR**	MDST	TI	
37211	**FA**	FAXI	IM	
37212 +	**FC**	FQCK	CF	
37213 +	**FC**	FQCK	CF	
37214 +	**FA**	FALY	TE	
37215	**FP**	FPEK	CF	
37216 r+		DCAA	SF	
37217 +		FEPE	ED	
37218	**FD**	MDST	TI	
37219 r		DCAA	SF	
37220 +	**FP**	FPEK	CF	Westerleigh
37221	**C**	DCEA	IM	
37222 +	**FC**	FQCK	CF	
37223 +	**FC**	FQCK	CF	
37225 +	**FD**	MDTT	TI	
37227 +	**FM**	FMTY	TE	
37229 +	**FC**	FEPE	ED	
37230 +	**C**	DCWA	CF	
37232	**C**	DCHA	ED	The Institution of Railway Signal Engineers
37235 +	**FD**	MDTT	TI	
37238	**FD**	MDST	TI	
37239 +	**FC**	FQCK	CF	The Coal Merchants' Association of Scotland

37240	+	**D**	DCHA	ED	
37241		**FM**	FPYX	TE	
37242	+	**FD**	MDTT	TI	
37244	+	**FD**	MDTT	TI	
37245			DCAA	SF	
37248	+	**FP**	FMAK	CF	
37250	+	**FM**	FMYI	IM	
37251	+	**D**	DCEA	IM	
37252		**FD**	MDST	TI	
37254	+	**C**	DCWA	CF	
37255	+	**FM**	FMYI	IM	
37258	+	**D**	DCWA	CF	
37261		**FD**	MDST	TI	Caithness
37262		**D**	MDST	TI	Dounreay
37263		**C**	DCWA	CF	
37264		**C**	DCWA	CF	
37271 (37303)	+	**FD**	MDTT	TI	
37272 (37304)	+	**FD**	MDTT	TI	
37274 (37308)	+	**FC**	FEPE	ED	
37275	+	**FM**	FMYI	IM	Stainless Pioneer
37278	+	**FC**	FPAE	ED	
37280	+	**FP**	FPEK	CF	
37285	+	**F**	MDTT	TI	
37293	+	**FM**	FMGM	ML	
37294	+	**FP**	FPEK	CF	
37298	+	**FD**	MDTT	TI	

Class 37/3. Unrefurbished locos fitted with regeared (CP7) bogies.
Details as Class 37/0 except:
Max. Tractive Effort: 250 kN (56180 lbf).
Cont. Tractive Effort: 184 kN (41250 lbf) at 11.4 mph.

37350 (37119)	+	**FP**	FPEK	CF	
37351 (37002)		**FR**	FMYI	IM	
37354 (37043)		**FA**	FALY	TE	
37358 (37091)		**BR**	MDRT	TI	P & O Containers
37359 (37118)		**FP**	MDRT	TI	
37370 (37127)		**FR**	FALY	TE	
37371 (37147)	+	**FR**	FPEK	CF	
37372 (37159)		**C**	DCWA	CF	
37373 (37160)		**FR**	FALY	TE	
37375 (37193)	+	**FC**	FEPE	ED	
37376 (37199)	+	**FC**	FEPE	ED	
37377 (37200)	+	**FR**	FMYI	IM	
37378 (37204)	+	**FD**	MDRT	TI	
37379 (37226)		**FR**	FALY	TE	
37380 (37259)		**FC**	FEPE	ED	
37381 (37284)	+	**FM**	FMYI	IM	

Class 37/4. Refurbished locos fitted with train heating. Main generator replaced by alternator. Regeared (CP7) bogies. Details as class 37/0 except:

Main Alternator: Brush BA1005A.
Max. Tractive Effort: 256 kN (57440 lbf).

Cont. Tractive Effort: 184 kN (41250 lbf) at 11.4 mph.
Power At Rail: 935 kW (1254 hp).
All have twin fuel tanks.

37401	(37268)	r **M**	FDTE	ED	Mary Queen of Scots
37402	(37274)	r **M**	FDTE	ED	Oor Wullie
37403	(37307)	r **FD**	FDTE	ED	Glendarroch
37404	(37286)	r **M**	FDTE	ED	Ben Cruachan
37405	(37282)	r **M**	FDTE	ED	Strathclyde Region
37406	(37295)	r **M**	FDTE	ED	The Saltire Society
37407	(37305)	r **M**	FPAE	ED	Loch Long
37408	(37289)	**BR**	FPAE	ED	Loch Rannoch
37409	(37270)	r **M**	FDTE	ED	Loch Awe
37410	(37273)	r **M**	FDTE	ED	Aluminium 100
37411	(37290)	**FD**	MDRL	LA	
37412	(37301)	**FD**	MDRL	LA	
37413	(37276)	r **FD**	FDTE	ED	Loch Eil Outward Bound
37414	(37287)	r **FA**	FABI	IM	
37415	(37277)	r **M**	MDRT	TI	
37416	(37302)	r **M**	PISA	IS	
37417	(37269)	r **M**	MDRL	LA	Highland Region
37418	(37271)	r **FP**	FPBI	IM	Pectinidae
37419	(37291)	**M**	MDRT	TI	
37420	(37297)	r **M**	MDRL	LA	The Scottish Hosteller
37421	(37267)	r **FP**	FPBI	IM	Strombidae
37422	(37266)	r **FA**	FABI	IM	
37423	(37296)	r **M**	FDTE	ED	Sir Murray Morrison 1873–1948
					Pioneer of British Aluminium Industry
37424	(37279)	r **M**	FDTE	ED	Isle of Mull
37425	(37292)	r **FA**	FABI	IM	Sir Robert McAlpine/Concrete Bob
37426	(37299)	r **M**	MDRT	TI	
37427	(37288)	r **FA**	FALY	TE	Bont Y Bermo
37428	(37281)	r **FP**	FPAE	ED	David Lloyd George
37429	(37300)	r **FA**	FALY	TE	Eisteddfod Genedlaethol
37430	(37265)	r **M**	MDRT	TI	Cwmbrân
37431	(37272)	r **M**	FPBI	IM	Bullidae

Class 37/5. Refurbished locos. Main generator replaced by alternator.
Regeared (CP7) bogies. Details as class 37/4 except:

Max. Tractive Effort: 248 kN (55590 lbf).
All have twin fuel tanks.

37501	(37005)	**FM**	FMGM	ML	
37502	(37082)	**FM**	FMGM	ML	
37503	(37017)	**FM**	FMGM	ML	British Steel Shelton
37504	(37039)	**FM**	FMGM	ML	
37505	(37028)	**FM**	FMGM	ML	British Steel Workington
37506	(37007)	**FM**	FMTY	TE	British Steel Skinningrove
37507	(37036)	**FM**	FMTY	TE	Hartlepool Pipe Mill
37508	(37090)	s **FM**	FMTY	TE	
37509	(37093)	**FM**	FMTY	TE	
37510	(37112)	**FM**	FMGM	ML	
37511	(37103)	**FM**	FMTY	TE	Stockton Haulage

37512 (37022)	**FM**	FMTY	TE	Thornaby Demon
37513 (37056)	**FM**	FMTY	TE	
37514 (37115) s **FM**		FMTY	TE	
37515 (37064) s **FM**		FMTY	TE	
37516 (37086) s **FM**		FMTY	TE	
37517 (37018) s **FM**		FMGM	ML	
37518 (37076)	**FM**	FMGM	ML	
37519 (37027)	**FM**	FMGM	ML	
37520 (37041)	**FM**	FMGM	ML	
37521 (37117)	**FP**	FPEK	CF	
37667 (37151) s **FP**		FPEK	CF	
37668 (37257) s **FP**		FPEK	CF	
37669 (37129)	**FD**	MDRL	LA	
37670 (37182)	**FD**	MDRL	LA	
37671 (37247)	**FD**	MDRL	LA	Tre Pol and Pen
37672 (37189) s **FD**		MDRL	LA	Freight Transport Association
37673 (37132)	**FD**	MDRL	LA	
37674 (37169)	**FD**	MDRL	LA	
37675 (37164) s **FD**		MDRL	LA	William Cookworthy
37676 (37126)	**FR**	FABI	IM	
37677 (37121)	**FA**	FABI	IM	
37678 (37256)	**FR**	FABI	IM	
37679 (37123)	**FA**	FABI	IM	
37680 (37224)	**FA**	FABI	IM	
37681 (37130)	**FA**	FABI	IM	
37682 (37236)	**FA**	FABI	IM	
37683 (37187)	**F**	FABI	IM	
37684 (37134)	**FA**	FABI	IM	Peak National Park
37685 (37234)	**FR**	FABI	IM	
37686 (37172)	**FA**	FABI	IM	
37687 (37181)	**FA**	FABI	IM	
37688 (37205)	**FA**	FABI	IM	Great Rocks
37689 (37195) s **FC**		FHBK	CF	
37690 (37171)	**FO**	FEPE	ED	
37691 (37179) s **FO**		FHBK	CF	
37692 (37122) s **FC**		FEPE	ED	
37693 (37210) s **FC**		FEPE	ED	Sir William Arrol
37694 (37192) s **FC**		FEPE	ED	The Lass O' Ballochmyle
37695 (37157) s **FC**		FEPE	ED	
37696 (37228) s **FC**		FEPE	ED	
37697 (37243) s **FC**		FHBK	CF	
37698 (37246) s **FC**		FHBK	CF	Coedbach
37699 (37253)	**FC**	FHBK	CF	

Class 37/7. Refurbished locos. Main generator replaced by alternator. Regeared (CP7) bogies. Ballast weights added.
Details as class 37/4 except:
Main Alternator: GEC G564AZ (37796–803) Brush BA1005A (others).
Max. Tractive Effort: 276 kN (62000 lbf).
Weight: 120 t.   **RA:** 7.
All have twin fuel tanks.

37701 (37030) s **FO**		FEKK	CF	

37702	(37020)	s **FC**	FEKK	CF	Taff Merthyr
37703	(37067)	s **FC**	FEKK	CF	
37704	(37034)	s **FC**	FEKK	CF	
37705	(37060)	**FP**	FPFR	IM	
37706	(37016)	**FP**	FPBI	IM	Conidae
37707	(37001)	**FP**	FPCI	IM	
37708	(37089)	**FP**	FPCI	IM	
37709	(37014)	**FP**	FPFR	IM	
37710	(37044)	**FM**	FMHK	CF	
37711	(37085)	**FM**	FMHK	CF	Tremorfa Steel Works
37712	(37102)	**FM**	FMHK	CF	The Cardiff Rod Mill
37713	(37052)	**FM**	FMTY	TE	
37714	(37024)	**FM**	FMTY	TE	
37715	(37021)	**FM**	FMTY	TE	
37716	(37094)	**FM**	FMTY	TE	
37717	(37050)	**FM**	FMTY	TE	
37718	(37084)	**FM**	FMTY	TE	
37719	(37033)	**FM**	FMTY	TE	
37796	(37105)	s **FC**	FEKK	CF	
37797	(37081)	s **FC**	FEKK	CF	
37798	(37006)	s **FC**	FEKK	CF	
37799	(37061)	s **FC**	FEKK	CF	Sir Dyfed/County of Dyfed
37800	(37143)	s **FC**	FEKK	CF	Glo Cymru
37801	(37173)	s **FC**	FEKK	CF	Aberthaw/Aberddawan
37802	(37163)	s **FO**	FEKK	CF	
37803	(37208)	s **FC**	FEKK	CF	
37883	(37176)	**FM**	FMTY	TE	
37884	(37183)	**FM**	FMHK	CF	
37885	(37177)	**FM**	FMHK	CF	
37886	(37180)	**FM**	FMHK	CF	
37887	(37120)	s **FP**	FEKK	CF	
37888	(37135)	**FP**	FPFR	IM	Petrolea
37889	(37233)	**FP**	FEKK	CF	
37890	(37168)	**FP**	FPFR	IM	
37891	(37166)	**FP**	FPCI	IM	
37892	(37149)	**FP**	FPFR	IM	Ripple Lane
37893	(37237)	**FP**	FPFR	IM	
37894	(37124)	s **FC**	FEKK	CF	
37895	(37283)	s **FC**	FEKK	CF	
37896	(37231)	s **FC**	FEKK	CF	
37897	(37155)	s **FC**	FEKK	CF	
37898	(37069)	s **FO**	FEKK	CF	
37899	(37161)	s **FC**	FEKK	CF	County of West Glamorgan/ Sir Gorllewin Morgannwg

Class 37/9. Refurbished Locos. Fitted with manufacturers prototype power units and ballast weights. Main generator replaced by alternator. Details as class 37/0 except:

Engine: Mirrlees MB275T of 1340 kW (1800 hp) at 1000 rpm (37901–4), Ruston RK270T of 1340 kW (1800 hp) at 900 rpm (37905–6).
Main Alternator: Brush BA1005A (GEC G564, 37905/6).
Max. Tractive Effort: 279 kN (62680 lbf).

Cont. Tractive Effort: 184 kN (41250 lbf) at 11.4 mph.
Weight: 120 t.   **RA:** 7.
All have twin fuel tanks.

37901 (37150)	**FM**	FMHK	CF	Mirrlees Pioneer
37902 (37148)	**FM**	FMHK	CF	British Steel Llanwern
37903 (37249)	**FM**	FMHK	CF	
37904 (37125)	**FM**	FMHK	CF	
37905 (37136) s	**FM**	FMHK	CF	Vulcan Enterprise
37906 (37206) s	**FM**	FMHK	CF	

CLASS 43   HST POWER CAR   Bo–Bo

Built: 1976–82 by BREL Crewe Works. Formerly numbered as coaching stock but now classified as locomotives. Include luggage compartment.
Engine: Paxman Valenta 12RP200L of 1680 kW (2250 hp) at 1500 rpm. (Mirrlees MB190 of 1680 kW (2250 hp)*.
Main Alternator: Brush BA1001B.
Traction Motors: Brush TMH68–46 or GEC G417AZ (43124–151/180). Frame mounted.
Max. Tractive Effort: 80 kN (17980 lbf).
Cont. Tractive Effort: 46 kN (10340 lbf) at 64.5 mph.
Power At Rail: 1320 kW (1770 hp). **ETH:** Non standard 3-phase system.
Brake Force: **Length over Buffers:** 17.79 m.
Weight: 70 t.   **Wheel Diameter:** 1020 mm.
Max. Speed: 125 mph.   **RA:** 5.
Train Brakes: Air.
Multiple Working: With one other similar vehicle.
Communication Equipment: All equipped with driver–guard telephone and cab to shore radio-telephone.

§ Modified to be able to remotely control a class 91 locomotive and to be remotely controlled by a class 91 locomotive.

43002	I	IWRP	PM	Top of the Pops
43003	I	IWRP	PM	
43004	I	IWRP	PM	Swan Hunter
43005	I	IWRP	PM	
43006	I	IWRP	LA	
43007	I	IWRP	LA	
43008	I	IWRP	LA	
43009	I	IWRP	PM	
43010	I	IWRP	PM	TSW Today
43011	I	IWRP	PM	
43012	I	IWRP	PM	
43013 §	I	ICCS	EC	
43014 §	I	ICCS	EC	
43015	I	IWRP	PM	
43016	I	IWRP	PM	
43017	I	IWRP	PM	
43018	I	IWRP	PM	
43019	I	IWRP	PM	Dinas Abertawe/City of Swansea
43020	I	IWRP	LA	

43021	I	IWRP	LA	
43022	I	IWRP	LA	
43023	I	IWRP	LA	County of Cornwall
43024	I	IWRP	LA	
43025	I	IWRP	LA	
43026	I	IWRP	LA	City of Westminster
43027	I	IWRP	LA	
43028	I	IWRP	LA	
43029	I	IWRP	LA	
43030	I	IWRP	PM	
43031	I	IWRP	PM	
43032	I	IWRP	PM	The Royal Regiment of Wales
43033	I	IWRP	PM	
43034	I	IWRP	PM	
43035	I	ICCP	PM	
43036	I	ICCP	PM	
43037	I	ICCP	PM	
43038	I	IECP	NL	National Railway Museum The First Ten Years 1975–1985
43039	I	IECP	NL	
43040	I	ICCP	PM	Granite City
43041	I	ICCP	PM	City of Discovery
43042	I	ICCP	PM	
43043	I	IMLP	NL	
43044	I	IMLP	NL	
43045	I	IMLP	NL	The Grammar School Doncaster AD 1350
43046	I	IMLP	NL	
43047	I	IMLP	NL	Rotherham Enterprise
43048	I	IMLP	NL	
43049	I	IMLP	NL	Neville Hill
43050	I	IMLP	NL	
43051	I	IMLP	NL	The Duke & Duchess of York
43052	I	IMLP	NL	City of Peterborough
43053	I	IMLP	NL	County of Humberside
43054	I	IMLP	NL	
43055	I	IMLP	NL	
43056	I	IMLP	NL	
43057	I	IMLP	NL	Bounds Green
43058	I	IMLP	NL	
43059	IO	IMLP	NL	
43060	I	IMLP	NL	County of Leicestershire
43061	I	IMLP	NL	City of Lincoln
43062	I	ICCS	EC	
43063	I	ICCS	EC	
43064	I	IMLP	NL	City of York
43065 §	I	ICCS	EC	
43066	I	IMLP	NL	
43067 §	I	ICCS	EC	
43068 §	I	ICCS	EC	
43069	IO	ICCS	EC	
43070	I	ICCS	EC	
43071	I	ICCS	EC	

43072	I	IMLP	NL	
43073	I	IMLP	NL	
43074	I	IMLP	NL	
43075	I	IMLP	NL	
43076	I	IMLP	NL	BBC East Midlands Today
43077	I	IMLP	NL	County of Nottingham
43078	I	ICCS	EC	
43079	I	ICCS	EC	
43080 §	I	ICCS	EC	
43081	I	IMLP	NL	
43082	I	IMLP	NL	
43083	I	IMLP	NL	
43084 §	I	ICCS	EC	County of Derbyshire
43085	I	IMLP	NL	
43086	I	ICCP	PM	
43087	I0	ICCP	PM	
43088	I	IWCP	LA	XIII Commonwealth Games Scotland 1986
43089	I	IWCP	LA	
43090	I	ICCS	EC	
43091	I	ICCS	EC	
43092	I	ICCS	EC	
43093	I	ICCS	EC	York Festival '88
43094	I	ICCS	EC	
43095	I	IECP	NL	
43096	I	IECP	NL	
43097	I	ICCS	EC	
43098	I	ICCS	EC	
43099	I	ICCS	EC	
43100	I	ICCS	EC	Craigentinny
43101	I	IWCP	LA	
43102	I	IWCP	LA	
43103	I	IWCP	LA	John Wesley
43104	I	IECP	NL	
43105	I	IECP	NL	
43106	I	IECP	NL	Songs of Praise
43107	I	IECP	NL	
43108	I	IECP	NL	
43109	I	IECP	NL	Yorkshire Evening Press
43110	I	IECP	NL	Darlington
43111	I	IECP	NL	
43112	I	IECP	NL	
43113	I	IECP	NL	
43114	I	IECP	NL	National Garden Festival Gateshead 1990
43115	I	IECP	NL	Yorkshire Cricket Academy
43116	I	IECP	NL	City of Kingston Upon Hull
43117	I	IECP	NL	
43118	I	IECP	NL	Charles Wesley
43119	I	IECP	NL	
43120	I	IECP	NL	
43121	I	IECP	NL	West Yorkshire Metropolitan County
43122	I	IECP	NL	South Yorkshire Metropolitan County
43123 §	I	ICCS	EC	

43124	I	IWRP	PM	
43125	I	IWRP	PM	
43126	I	ICCP	PM	City of Bristol
43127	I	ICCP	PM	
43128	I	IWRP	PM	
43129	I	IWRP	PM	
43130	I	IWRP	PM	
43131	I	IWRP	PM	
43132	I	IWRP	PM	Worshipful Company of Carmen
43133	I	IWRP	PM	
43134	I	IWRP	PM	
43135	I	IWRP	PM	
43136	I	IWRP	PM	
43137	IO	IWRP	PM	
43138	I	IWRP	PM	
43139	I	IWRP	PM	
43140	I	IWRP	OO	
43141	I	IWRP	OO	
43142	I	IWRP	OO	
43143	IO	IWCP	LA	
43144	I	IWRP	OO	
43145	I	IWRP	OO	
43146	I	IWRP	OO	
43147	I	IWRP	OO	The Red Cross
43148	I	IWRP	OO	
43149	I	IWRP	PM	B.B.C. Wales Today
43150	I	IWRP	PM	Bristol Evening Post
43151	I	IWRP	PM	
43152	I	IWRP	LA	St. Peters School York AD 627
43153	I	IECP	NL	University of Durham
43154	I	IWRP	LA	
43155	I	IECP	NL	B.B.C. Look North
43156	IO	IWRP	LA	
43157	I	IWRP	LA	Yorkshire Evening Post
43158	I	IWRP	LA	
43159	IO	IWRP	LA	
43160	I	IWRP	LA	Storm Force
43161	I	IWRP	LA	Reading Evening Post
43162	I	IWRP	LA	Borough of Stevenage
43163	I	IWRP	LA	
43164	I	ICCP	LA	
43165	I	ICCP	LA	
43166	I	ICCP	LA	
43167 *	I	IWRP	PM	
43168 *	I	IWRP	PM	
43169 *	I	ICCP	PM	The National Trust
43170 *	I	ICCP	PM	
43171	I	ICCP	LA	
43172	I	ICCP	LA	
43173	IO	ICCP	LA	
43174	I	ICCP	LA	
43175	I	ICCP	LA	

43176	**I0**	IWRP	LA	
43177	**I0**	IWRP	LA	
43178	**I**	ICCP	LA	
43179	**I**	ICCP	LA	Pride of Laira
43180	**I**	ICCP	PM	
43181	**I0**	IWRP	LA	
43182	**I0**	IWRP	LA	
43183	**I0**	IWRP	LA	
43184	**I0**	ICCP	LA	
43185	**I**	ICCP	LA	
43186	**I**	ICCP	LA	Sir Francis Drake
43187	**I**	IWRP	LA	
43188	**I**	IWRP	LA	City of Plymouth
43189	**I**	IWRP	LA	
43190	**I**	IWRP	LA	
43191	**I**	IWRP	LA	Seahawk
43192	**I**	IWRP	LA	City of Truro
43193	**I0**	IWRP	LA	Yorkshire Post
43194	**I**	IWRP	LA	
43195	**I**	IWRP	LA	
43196	**I**	IWRP	LA	The Newspaper Society Founded 1836
43197	**I**	IWRP	LA	
43198	**I**	IWRP	LA	

CLASS 47   BRUSH TYPE 4   Co–Co

Built: 1963–67 by Brush Traction, Loughborough or BR Crewe Works.
Engine: Sulzer 12LDA28C of 1920 kW (2580 hp) at 750 rpm.
Main Generator: Brush TG160-60 Mk2, TG 160-60 Mk4 or TM172-50 Mk1.
Traction Motors: Brush TM64-68 Mk1 or Mk1A (axle hung).
Max. Tractive Effort: 267 kN (60000 lbf).(245 kN (55000 lbf) 47401–18)
Cont. Tractive Effort: 133 kN (30000 lbf) at 26 mph.
Power At Rail: 1550 kW (2080 hp).**Length over Buffers:** 19.38 m.
Brake Force: 61 t.   **Wheel Diameter:** 1143 mm.
Design Speed: 95 mph.   **Weight:** 120.5–125 t.
Max. Speed: various.   **RA:** 6 or 7.
Train Brakes: Air & Vacuum.
Multiple Working: Not equipped (Blue Star Coupling Code*).
ETH Index (47/4 & 47/7): 66 (75†).
Train Brakes: Air & Vacuum.
Communication Equipment: Cab to shore radio-telephone.
Non-standard Livery:

47401 is in BR two-tone green and also carries its original number D 1500.

Formerly numbered 1100–11, 1500–1999 not in order. 47299 was also previously 47216.

Class 47/0. Built with train heating boiler. RA6. Max Speed 75 mph.

47004	**FA**	DCWW	OC
47010	**FP**	FPCI	IM
47016	**F0**	DCMA	CD
47019	**F0**	DCWA	OC

47033	+**FD**	MDDT	TI
47049	**FD**	MDAT	TI
47050	+**FD**	MDDT	TI
47051	**FD**	MDAT	TI
47052	**FD**	MDCT	TI
47053	+**FD**	MDDT	TI
47054	+**FP**	FPBI	IM	Xancidae
47060	**FD**	MDCT	TI	Halewood Silver Jubilee 1988
47063	**FA**	FAME	ED
47079	**FD**	MDAT	TI
47085	+**FD**	MDDT	TI
47094	**FP**	FPCI	IM
47095	+**FD**	MDDT	TI
47105		DCWW	OC
47108		DCWW	OC
47114	**FA**	FAME	ED
47119	**FP**	FPCI	IM
47121		DCWW	OC
47125	**FP**	MDAT	TI
47142	**FR**	MDAT	TI	The Sapper
47144	**FD**	MDCT	TI
47145		MDAT	TI
47146		MDAT	TI
47147	**FD**	MDAT	TI
47150	**FD**	MDAT	TI
47152	**FD**	MDCT	TI
47156	**FD**	MDAT	TI
47157	**FD**	MDAT	TI
47186	**FD**	MDAT	TI
47187	**FD**	MDAT	TI
47188	**FD**	MDAT	TI
47190	**FP**	MDAT	TI
47193	**FP**	FPBI	IM	Lucinidae
47194	+**FD**	MDDT	TI
47196	**FP**	MDAT	TI
47197	**FP**	FPEK	CF
47200	**FD**	MDCT	TI
47201	**FD**	MDCT	TI
47204	**FD**	MDAT	TI
47205	**FD**	MDAT	TI
47206	**FD**	MDAT	TI
47207	**FD**	MDAT	TI	Bulmers of Hereford
47209	**FD**	MDAT	TI	Herbert Austin
47210	**FA**	FAME	ED	Blue Circle Cement
47211	**FD**	MDAT	TI
47212	+**FP**	FPCI	IM
47213	**FD**	MDAT	TI
47214	**FD**	MDAT	TI	Distillers MG
47217		MDAT	TI
47218	**FD**	MDAT	TI	United Transport Europe
47219	**FD**	MDCT	TI	Arnold Kunzler
47220	**FO**	MDAT	TI

47221	+FP	FPCI	IM	
47222	+FD	MDDT	TI	
47223	+FP	FPFR	IM	British Petroleum
47224	+FP	FPBI	IM	Arcidae
47225	FD	MDCT	TI	
47226		MDAT	TI	
47227	FR	MDAT	TI	
47228	FD	MDAT	TI	
47229	+	MDDT	TI	
47231	FD	MDAT	TI	The Silcock Express
47234	+FD	MDDT	TI	
47236	FD	MDAT	TI	
47237	FD	MDCT	TI	
47238	FD	MDAT	TI	Bescot Yard
47241	FD	MDAT	TI	
47245	FD	MDAT	TI	
47249	FR	MDAT	TI	
47256	FD	MDAT	TI	
47258	FD	MDAT	TI	
47270		MDAT	TI	
47276	+FP	FPCI	IM	
47277	FP	FPEK	CF	
47278	FP	FPBI	IM	Vasidae
47279	FD	MDAT	TI	
47280	FD	MDAT	TI	Pedigree
47281	FD	MDCT	TI	
47283	FD	MDAT	TI	Johnnie Walker
47284	FD	MDCT	TI	
47285	FD	MDAT	TI	
47286	+FD	MDDT	TI	
47287	FD	MDAT	TI	
47288	FD	MDAT	TI	
47289	FD	MDAT	TI	
47290	F	MDAT	TI	
47291	FD	MDCT	TI	The Port of Felixstowe
47292	FD	MDAT	TI	
47293	FD	MDAT	TI	
47294	+FP	FPFR	IM	
47295	+FP	FPFR	IM	
47296	FD	MDAT	TI	
47297	FD	MDAT	TI	
47298	FD	MDAT	TI	Pegasus
47299	+	MDDT	TI	

Class 47/3. Built without Train Heat. RA6. Max Speed 75 mph. All equipped with slow speed control.

47301	FR	MDAT	TI
47302	FR	MDAT	TI
47303	F	MDAT	TI
47304	FD	MDAT	TI
47305	FP	MDAT	TI
47306	FD	MDAT	TI

Trainload Construction

Trainload Coal

Trainload Metals

Trainload Petroleum

Railfreight Distribution

Trainload Freight and Railfreight Distribution sub-sector markings as used on locomotives.

Class 03 shunter No. 03079 in BR blue livery with an assortment of wagons at Sandown, Isle of Wight on 1st September 1990. *John Auguston*

▲ Class 08 shunter No. 08675 at Ayr depot on 6th July 1991. The locomotive in Railfreight livery without sub-sector markings (code 'F'). *Brian Morris*

▼ Class 09 shunter No. 09025 at Hamworthy on 14th August 1990. *Paul Shannon*

▲ Class 20s Nos. 20169 and 20210 are seen arriving at Willington Power Station with an MGR from Denby Colliery on 7th September 1991. *A O Wynn*

▼ Class 26 No. 26040 in old Railfreight livery is seen at Workington on 29th September 1989 with a freight for Carlisle consisting of a single TEA sulphuric acid tanker. *Dave McAlone*

▲ Class 31/4 No. 31462 in departmental grey livery at Bamber Bridge on 12th April 1990.   *Paul D Shannon*

▼ Class 33/0 No. 33053 in Trainload Construction livery (Code 'FA') comes off the Strood line at Paddock Wood with the 11.18 Hoo Junction–Tonbridge engineer train.   *Nic Joynson*

A pair of 33/0s in Civil Engineer's livery Nos. 33025 'Sultan' and 33026 (now named 'Seafire') descend Acton bank with 6V96, the 09.38 Tonbridge–Meldon Quarry.

Paul D Shannon

▲ Class 37s Nos. 37128 and 37209 in revised blue livery pass Hartlepool with the Sunderland South Dock–Lindsey empties. *John Augustson*

▼ Re-engined Class 37/9 No. 37902 'British Steel Llanwern' at Gloucester depot on 4th August 1991. This loco is in Trainload Metals livery (code 'FM') *Norman Preedy*

Class 43 HST power car No. 43143 in old InterCity livery at the head of a Penzance–Paddington working are Bolitho Viaduct, Liskeard on 3rd April 1991.

Michael J Collins

▲ Class 47/0 No. 47207 in Railfreight Distribution livery (code 'F') in Wembley Yard.
Brian Morrison

▼ Class 47/4 No. 47594 'Resourceful' in Rail Express Systems livery at Crewe diesel depot on 12th October 1991.
John Augustor

Class 50 No. 50029 'Renown' is seen just past Tisbury with the 08.55 Waterloo–Yeovil on 12th May 1991. The loco is in the distinctive Network SouthEast livery.

Mike Goodfield

Class 56 No. 56057 approaches March station with an empty aggregates working heading for Mountsorrel, Leicester-

Class 58 No. 58039 'Rugeley Power Station' in Trainload Coal livery hurries an MGR coal train for Didcot Power Station through Oxford.

John Augustson

The complete fleet of Foster-Yeoman Class 59/0 locomotives at Merehead on 25th May 1991. 59002 'YEOMAN

Class 60 No. 60026 'William Caxton' in Trainload Petroleum livery passes Hasland, just south of Chesterfield with 6M14, Peak Forest–Washwood Heath roadstone train on 20th August 1991.

Ian N Lyall

▲ Class 73/1 No. 73101 'Brighton Evening Argus' has been specially painted Pullman umber and cream. It was to have been repainted into Civil Engineer livery, but retains its Pullman colours by popular demand. It is seen at Selhurst o 20th September 1991. *Colin J Marsde*

▼ Class 86/4 No. 86425 at Crewe on 28th July 1991 on the 08.59 Liverpool–Pa dington. The loco is in parcels livery. *Brian Morriso*

Class 87 No. 87028 'Lord. President' in Mainline livery (but with 'INTERCITY' branding) arrives at Carlisle on 29th March 1991 with the 11.25 Euston–Glasgow.
Dave McAlone

The Solitary Class 89 No. 89001 'Avocet' is now stored. It is seen at Doncaster 16th September 1989. The livery is InterCity.
John Auguston

▲ Class 90 No. 90028 in Mainline livery. *Brian Morris*

▼ Class 91 No. 91012 at the head of a King's Cross–Leeds service at Helpsto Junction, Peterborough in May 1991. *Michael J Collin*

47307		MDAT	TI
47308	F	MDAT	TI
47309	FD	MDAT	TI	The Halewood Transmission
47310	FD	MDCT	TI	Henry Ford
47312	FD	MDAT	TI
47313	FD	MDCT	TI
47314	FD	MDCT	TI	Transmark
47315	C	DCWA	OC
47316	+FD	MDDT	TI
47317	FD	MDAT	TI	Willesden Yard
47318	FO	DCMA	CD
47319	+FP	FPCI	IM	Norsk Hydro
47320	FO	MDAT	TI
47321	FD	MDAT	TI
47322	FR	MDAT	TI
47323	FD	MDAT	TI
47324	FP	FPBI	IM	Glossidae
47325	FO	MDAT	TI
47326	FD	MDAT	TI
47327	FO	FPCI	IM
47328	FA	FAME	ED
47329	C	DCMA	CD
47330	FD	MDAT	TI	Amlwch Freighter/Trên Nwyddau Amlwch
47331	FO	DCEA	IM
47332	C	DCEA	IM
47333	C	DCMA	CD	Civil Link
47334	C	DCWA	OC
47335	FD	MDAT	TI
47336	+FP	FPBI	IM
47337	FO	MDAT	TI
47338	FD	MDAT	TI
47339	C	MDAT	TI
47340	C	DCMA	CD
47341	C	DCMA	CD
47343	C	DCMA	CD
47344		MDAT	TI
47345	FR	MDAT	TI
47346	C	DCEA	IM
47347	M	MDAT	TI
47348	FO	DCEA	IM	St. Christopher's Railway Home
47349	FD	MDAT	TI
47350	FO	MDAT	TI
47351	FD	MDAT	TI
47352	D	DCEA	IM
47353	C	DCMA	CD
47354	FD	MDAT	TI
47355	FD	MDAT	TI
47356	FO	DCMA	CD
47357	C	DCMA	CD
47358	FO	DCMA	CD
47359	FD	MDAT	TI
47360	FD	MDAT	TI

47361	**FD**	MDAT	TI	Wilton Endeavour
47362	+**FO**	MDDT	TI	
47363	+**FD**	MDDT	TI	Billingham Enterprise
47364	**C**	DCWA	OC	
47365	**FO**	MDAT	TI	ICI Diamond Jubilee
47366	**FO**	DCWA	OC	
47367	**FR**	MDAT	TI	
47368	**FP**	FPBI	IM	Neritidae
47369	**FP**	FPFR	IM	
47370	**FO**	MDAT	TI	
47371	**FO**	MDAT	TI	
47372	**C**	DCMA	CD	
47373	+**FP**	FPYX	IM (U)	
47374	+**FP**	FPCI	IM	
47375	**FD**	MDAT	TI	Tinsley Traction Depot (Quality Approved)
47376		MDAT	TI	
47377	**FD**	MDAT	TI	
47378	**FD**	MDAT	TI	
47379	+**FP**	FPFR	IM	Total Energy
47380	+**FP**	FPCI	IM	Immingham
47381	**FP**	FPBI	IM	

Class 47/4. Equipped with train heating. RA7. Max Speed 95 (75†) mph.

47401	**0**	FPCI	IM	Star of the East
47402		FPYX	IM (U)	
47417		FPYX	IM (U)	
47423		NWRA	OC	
47425		NWRA	OC	
47426	**BR**	NWRA	OC	
47430	**FA**	NWRA	OC	
47431	**BR**	NWRA	OC	
47432	**BR**	IXXS	BR (S)	
47433	**BR**	RXLC	CD	
47438	**BR**	NWRA	OC	
47439	**BR**	RXLC	CD	
47441	**BR**	NWRA	OC	
47442	**BR**	RXLC	CD	
47443	**BR**	RXLC	CD	North Eastern
47446	**BR**	NWRA	OC	
47449	**BR**	NWRA	OC	
47453	**BR**	NWRA	OC	
47457	**BR**	NWRA	OC	
47458	**R**	RXLC	CD	County of Cambridgeshire
47459	**BR**	RXLC	CD	
47460	**BR**	RXLC	CD	
47462	**R**	RXLC	CD	Cambridge Traction & Rolling Stock Depot
47463		RXLC	CD	
47467	**BR**	RXLC	CD	
47468	**BR**	RXLC	CD	
47471	**I0**	RXLC	CD	Norman Tunna G.C.
47473	**BR**	RXLC	CD	
47474	**R**	RXLC	CD	Sir Rowland Hill

47475	**P**	RXLC	CD	
47476	**R**	RXLC	CD	Night Mail
47477		RXLC	CD	
47478		IXXS	BR (S)	
47479	**R**	RXLC	CD	Track 29
47481	**BR**	RXLC	CD	
47482	**BR**	RXLC	CD	
47483	**M**	IXXS	IM (S)	
47484	**G**	DCWW	OC	ISAMBARD KINGDOM BRUNEL
47485	**BR**	RXLC	CD	
47488	**BR**	RXLC	CD	Rail Riders
47489	**R**	RXLC	CD	Crewe Diesel Depot
47490	**IO**	RXLC	CD	
47491		RXLC	CD	Horwich Enterprise
47492	**IO**	RXLC	CD	The Enterprising Scot
47500	**G**	IEDA	IM	
47501	**R**	RXLC	CD	Craftsman
47503	**BR**	RXLC	CD	
47508	**M**	IXXS	BR (S)	S.S. Great Britain
47509	**I**	ICDA	CD	Albion
47513	**R**	RXLC	CD	Severn
47517	**BR**	RXLC	CD	Andrew Carnegie
47519	**BR**	IEDA	IM	
47520	**M**	ICDA	CD	
47521	**N**	NWRA	OC	
47522	**R**	RXLC	CD	Doncaster Enterprise
47523	**M**	RXLC	CD	
47524	**M**	RXLC	CD	
47525	**IO**	IXXS	BR (S)	
47526	**BR**	NWRA	OC	
47527	**M**	IXXS	BR (S)	Kettering
47528	**M**	RXLC	CD	The Queen's Own Mercian Yeomanry
47530	**N**	RXLC	CD	
47532	**BR**	PISA	IS	
47535	**R**	RXLC	CD	University of Leicester
47536	**BR**	RXLC	CD	
47537	**BR**	RXLC	CD	Sir Gwynedd – County of Gwynedd
47539	**BR**	RXLC	CD	Rochdale Pioneers
47543	**R**	RXLC	CD	
47547	**N**	NWRA	OC	University of Oxford
47550	**M**	ICDA	CD	University of Dundee
47555 (47126)	**IO**	IXXS	BR (U)	The Commonwealth Spirit
47557 (47024)	**M**	RXLC	CD	
47558 (47027)	**M**	RXLC	CD	Mayflower
47559 (47028)	**RX**	RXLC	CD	Sir Joshua Reynolds
47564 (47038)	**BR**	RXLC	CD	
47565 (47039)	**M**	RXLC	CD	
47566 (47043)	**M**	RXLC	CD	
47567 (47044)	**M**	RXLC	CD	Red Star
47568 (47045)	**M**	RXLC	CD	Royal Engineers Postal & Courier Services
47569 (47047)	**R**	RXLC	CD	The Gloucestershire Regiment

47572	(47168)	**R**	RXLC	CD	Ely Cathedral
47573	(47173)	**N**	RXLC	CD	THE LONDON STANDARD
47574	(47174)	**R**	RXLC	CD	Benjamin Gimbert G.C.
47575	(47175)	**R**	RXLC	CD	City of Hereford
47576	(47176)	**N**	RXLC	CD	King's Lynn
47579	(47183)	**N**	NTWE	OC	James Nightall G.C.
47580	(47167)	**BR**	RXLC	CD	County of Essex
47581	(47169)	**N**	NWRA	OC	
47582	(47170)	**R**	RXLC	CD	County of Norfolk
47583	(47172)	**N**	NWRA	OC	County of Hertfordshire
47584	(47180)	**M**	RXLC	CD	County of Suffolk
47585	(47184)	**BR**	RXLD	CD (U)	
47587	(47263)	**N**	NWRA	OC	Ruskin College Oxford
47588	(47178)	**F**	RXLC	CD	
47592	(47171)	**BR**	RXLC	CD	County of Avon
47594	(47035)	**RX**	RXLC	CD	Resourceful
47596	(47255)	**N**	RXLC	CD	Aldeburgh Festival
47597	(47026)	**RX**	RXLC	CD	Resilient
47598	(47182)	**N**	RXLC	CD	
47599	(47177)	**F**	RXLC	CD	
47600	(47250)	**F**	RXLC	CD	
47603	(47267)	**BR**	RXLC	CD	County of Somerset
47605	(47160)	**F**	RXLC	CD	
47615	(47252)	**F**	RXLC	CD	Castell Caerffili/Caerphilly Castle
47624	(47087)	**M**	RXLC	CD	
47625	(47076)	**RX**	RXLC	CD	Resplendent
47626	(47082)	**M**	RXLC	CD	ATLAS
47627	(47273)	**M**	RXLC	CD	City of Oxford
47628	(47078)	**M**	RXLC	CD	
47630	(47041)	**BR**	RXLC	CD	
47631	(47059)	**BR**	RXLC	CD	
47634	(47158)	**R**	RXLC	CD	Holbeck
47635	(47029)	**R**	RXLC	CD	
47636	(47243)	**BR**	NWRA	OC	Sir John de Graeme
47640	(47244)	**R**	RXLC	CD	University of Strathclyde
47642	(47040)	**IO**	RXLC	CD	Strathisla
47671	(47616)	**† BR**	IIHA	IS	Y Ddraig Goch/The Red Dragon
47672	(47562)	**† M**	IXXS	IS (S)	Sir William Burrell
47673	(47593)	**† IO**	IIHA	IS	Galloway Princess
47674	(47604)	**† BR**	IXXS	IS (S)	Women's Royal Voluntary Service
47675	(47595)	**† M**	IIHA	IS	Confederation of British Industry
47676	(47586)	**† I**	IIHA	IS	Northamptonshire
47677	(47617)	**† I**	IIHA	IS	University of Stirling

Class 47/7. TDM fitted. RA6. Max speed. 100 mph.

47701	(47493)	**N**	NTWE	OC	Old Oak Common Traction & Rolling
47702	(47504)	**N**	NTWE	OC	Saint Cuthbert [Stock Depot
47703	(47514)	**R**	NTWE	OC	The Queen Mother
47704	(47495)	**RX**	RXLC	CD	
47705	(47554)	**N**	NTWE	OC	
47706	(47494)	**PS**	NTWE	OC	
47707	(47506)	**N**	NTWE	OC	Holyrood

47708 (47516)	**N**	NTWE	OC	Templecombe
47709 (47499)	**N**	NTWE	OC	
47710 (47496)	**N**	NTWE	OC	Capital Radio's Help a London Child
47711 (47498)	**N**	NTWE	OC	
47712 (47505)	**R**	NTWE	OC	Lady Diana Spencer
47714 (47511)	**N**	NTWE	OC	
47715 (47502)	**N**	NTWE	OC	Haymarket
47716 (47507)	**N**	NTWE	OC	Duke of Edinburgh's Award
47717 (47497)	**R**	NTWE	OC	

Class 47/4 continued.

47801 (47551)	**BR**	NWRA	OC	
47802 (47552)	**I**	IBRA	BR	
47803 (47553)	**IO**	ICDA	CD	Woman's Guild
47804 (47591)	**I**	ILRA	BR	
47805 (47650)	**I**	ILRA	BR	Bristol Bath Road
47806 (47651)	**I**	ILRA	BR	
47807 (47652)	**I**	ILRA	BR	
47808 (47653)	**I**	ILRA	BR	
47809 (47654)	**I**	ILRA	BR	Finsbury Park
47810 (47655)	**I**	ILRA	BR	
47811 (47656)	**I**	ILRA	BR	
47812 (47657)	**I**	ILRA	BR	
47813 (47658)	**I**	ILRA	BR	
47814 (47659)	**I**	ILRA	BR	
47815 (47660)	**I**	ILRA	BR	
47816 (47661)	**I**	ILRA	BR	
47817 (47662)	**I**	ICDA	CD	
47818 (47663)	**M**	ILRA	BR	
47819 (47664)	**I**	ICDA	CD	
47820 (47665)	**BR**	IBRA	BR	
47821 (47607)	**I**	ILRA	BR	Royal Worcester
47822 (47571)	**I**	ILRA	BR	
47823 (47610)	**I**	ILRA	BR	
47824 (47602)	**M**	ILRA	BR	Glorious Devon
47825 (47590)	**M**	ILRA	BR	Thomas Telford
47826 (47637)	**I**	ILRA	BR	
47827 (47589)	**I**	ILRA	BR	
47828 (47629)	**I**	ILRA	BR	
47829 (47619)	**M**	IERA	CD	
47830 (47649)	**I**	ICDA	CD	
47831 (47563)	**M**	IERA	CD	Bolton Wanderer
47832 (47560)	**M**	ILRA	BR	Tamar
47833 (47608)	**I**	ILRA	BR	
47834 (47609)	**I**	ILRA	BR	FIRE FLY
47835 (47620)	**I**	ILRA	BR	Windsor Castle
47836 (47618)	**I**	IERA	CD	
47837 (47611)	**I**	RXXA	CD	
47838 (47612)	**I**	IERA	CD	
47839 (47621)	**I**	IERA	CD	
47840 (47613)	**I**	IERA	CD	NORTH STAR
47841 (47622)	**I**	IERA	CD	The Institution of Mechanical Engineers

47842	(47606)	**I**	IERA	CD	
47843	(47623)	**I**	IERA	CD	
47844	(47556)	**I**	IERA	CD	Derby & Derbyshire Chamber of Commerce & Industry
47845	(47638)	**I**	IERA	CD	County of Kent
47846	(47647)	**I**	IERA	CD	THOR
47847	(47577)	**I**	IERA	CD	
47848	(47632)	**I**	IERA	CD	
47849	(47570)	**M**	IERA	CD	
47850	(47648)	**I**	IERA	CD	
47851	(47639)	**I**	IERA	CD	
47852	(47646)	**BR**	RXLC	CD	
47853	(47614)	**M**	IERA	CD	
47971	(97480)	* **BR**	DRTC	CD	Robin Hood
47972	(97545)	**BR**	DRTC	CD	
47973	(97561)	**M**	DRTC	CD	Derby Evening Telegraph
47974	(47531)	* **C**	DCQA	CD	The Permanent Way Institution
47975	(47540)	* **C**	DCQA	CD	Institution of Civil Engineers
47976	(47546)	* **C**	DCQA	CD	Aviemore Centre

CLASS 50   ENGLISH ELECTRIC TYPE 4   Co–Co

Built: 1967–68 by English Electric Co. at Vulcan Foundry, Newton le Willows.
Engine: English Electric 16CVST of 2010 kW (2700 hp) at 850 rpm.
Main Generator: English Electric 840/4B.
Traction Motors: English Electric 538/5A.
Max. Tractive Effort: 216 kN (48500 lbf).
Cont. Tractive Effort: 147 kN (33000 lbf) at 23.5 mph.
Power At Rail: 1540 kW (2070 hp).**Length over Buffers:** 20.88 m.
Brake Force: 59 t.   **Wheel Diameter:** 1092 mm.
Design Speed: 105 mph.   **Weight:** 117 t.
Max. Speed: 100 mph.   **RA:** 6.
Train Heating: Electric. **ETH Index:** 61.
Train Brakes: Air & Vacuum.
Multiple Working: Orange Square coupling code. (Within class only).
Communication Equipment: Cab to shore radio-telephone.
All equipped with slow speed control.

Formerly numbered 408–446, 400.

50008		DCQA	LA	(U)Thunderer
50015	**C**	DCQA	LA	(U)Valiant
50029	**N**	NWXA	LA	Renown
50030	**N**	NWXA	LA	Repulse
50033	**N**	NWXA	LA	Glorious
50046	**BR**	NWXA	LA	Ajax
50050		NWXA	LA	

CLASS 56   BRUSH TYPE 5   Co–Co

Built: 1976–84 by Electroputere at Craiova, Romania (as sub contractors for Brush) or BREL at Doncaster or Crewe Works.

Engine: Ruston Paxman 16RK3CT of 2460 kW (3250 hp) at 900 rpm.
Main Alternator: Brush BA1101A.
Traction Motors: Brush TM73-62.
Max. Tractive Effort: 275 kN (61800 lbf).
Cont. Tractive Effort: 240 kN (53950 lbf) at 16.8 mph.
Power At Rail: 1790 kW (2400 hp). **Length over Buffers:** 19.36 m.
Brake Force: 60 t. **Wheel Diameter:** 1143 mm.
Design Speed: 80 mph. **Weight:** 125 t.
Max. Speed: 80 mph. **RA:** 7.
Train Brakes: Air.
Multiple Working: Red Diamond coupling code.
Communication Equipment: Cab to shore radio-telephone.
All equipped with slow speed control.

† Derated to 1790 kW (2400 hp).
* Derated to 2060 kW (2800 hp).

56001	**FA**	FASB	SL	Whatley
56002	**FC**	FEXX	TO (U)	
56003	**F**	FECN	TO	
56004		FECN	TO	
56005	**FC**	FECN	TO	
56006	**FC**	FECN	TO	
56007	**FC**	FECN	TO	
56008		FECN	TO	
56009	**FC**	FECN	TO	
56010	**FC**	FECN	TO	
56011	**FR**	FECN	TO	
56012	**FC**	FECN	TO	Maltby Colliery
56013	**FC**	FECN	TO	
56014	**FC**	FECN	TO	
56015	**FC**	FECN	TO	
56016	**FC**	FECN	TO	
56017	**FC**	FEXX	TO (U)	
56018	**FC**	FECN	TO	
56019	**FR**	FECN	TO	
56020		FECN	TO	
56021	**FC**	FECN	TO	
56022		FEDN	TO	
56023	**FC**	FECN	TO	
56024	**FO**	FECN	TO	
56025	**FC**	FECN	TO	
56026		FECN	TO	
56027	**FC**	FECN	TO	
56028	**FC**	FECN	TO	West Burton Power Station
56029	**FC**	FEDN	TO	
56030	**FC**	FEDN	TO	Eggborough Power Station
56031	**FA**	FASB	SL	Merehead
56032	**FM**	FMCK	CF	Sir De Morgannwg/ County of South Glamorgan
56033	**FA**	FXXC	SL	
56034	**FA**	FASB	SL	Castell Ogwr/Ogmore Castle
56035	**FA**	FAXN	TO	
56036	**FA**	FAXN	TO	

56037	**FA**	FASB	SL	Richard Trevithick
56038	**FM**	FMCK	CF	Western Mail
56039	**FA**	FASB	SL	
56040	**FM**	FMCK	CF	
56041	**FA**	FASB	SL	
56043	**FA**	FASB	SL	
56044	**FM**	FMCK	CF	Cardiff Canton
56045	**FA**	FAXN	TO	
56046	**FA**	FMCK	CF	
56047	**FC**	FEDN	TO	
56048	**FR**	FAXN	TO	
56049	**FR**	FAXN	TO	
56050	**FA**	FASB	SL	
56051	**FA**	FASB	SL	
56052	**FA**	FASB	SL	
56053	**FA**	FASB	SL	Sir Morgannwg Ganol/ County of Mid Glamorgan
56054	**FC**	FAXN	TO	
56055	**FA**	FASB	SL	
56056	**FA**	FASB	SL	
56057	**FO**	FAXN	TO	
56058	**FA**	FAXN	TO	
56059	**FA**	FAXN	TO	
56060	**FA**	FAXN	TO	
56061	**F**	FAXN	TO	
56062	**FA**	FAXN	TO	Mountsorrel
56063	**FA**	FAXN	TO	Bardon Hill
56064	**FA**	FAXN	TO	
56065	**FA**	FAXN	TO	
56066	**FC**	FEDN	TO	
56067	**FC**	FEDN	TO	
56068	**FC**	FEDN	TO	
56069 †	**FC**	FEDN	TO	
56070	**FA**	FAXN	TO	
56071	**FC**	FEDN	TO	
56072	**FC**	FEDN	TO	
56073	**FC**	FEDN	TO	
56074	**FC**	FEDN	TO	Kellingley Colliery
56075	**FC**	FEDN	TO	West Yorkshire Enterprise
56076	**FC**	FEDN	TO	
56077 †	**FC**	FEDN	TO	Thorpe Marsh Power Station
56078	**FA**	FAXN	TO	
56079	**FC**	FEDN	TO	
56080	**FC**	FEDN	TO	Selby Coalfield
56081	**FC**	FEDN	TO	
56082	**FC**	FECN	TO	
56083 *	**FC**	FEDN	TO	
56084 *	**FC**	FEDN	TO	
56085	**FC**	FEDN	TO	
56086 *	**FC**	FEDN	TO	
56087	**FC**	FEDN	TO	
56088	**FC**	FEDN	TO	

56089	**FC**	FEDN	TO	Ferrybridge C Power Station
56090	**FC**	FEDN	TO	
56091	**FC**	FEDN	TO	Castle Donington Power Station
56092	**FC**	FEDN	TO	
56093	**FC**	FEDN	TO	The Institution of Mining Engineers
56094	**FC**	FECN	TO	
56095	**FC**	FEDN	TO	Harworth Colliery
56096	**FC**	FEDN	TO	
56097	**FC**	FEDN	TO	
56098	**FC**	FEDN	TO	
56099	**FC**	FEDN	TO	Fiddlers Ferry Power Station
56100	**FC**	FEDN	TO	
56101	**FC**	FEDN	TO	Mutual Improvement
56102	**FC**	FEDN	TO	Scunthorpe Steel Centenary
56103	**FA**	FAXN	TO	
56104	**FC**	FEDN	TO	
56105	**FA**	FAXN	TO	
56106	**FC**	FEDN	TO	
56107 † **FC**		FEDN	TO	
56108	**FR**	FEDN	TO	
56109	**FC**	FEDN	TO	
56110	**FA**	FAXN	TO	
56111	**FC**	FEDN	TO	
56112	**BR**	FEDN	TO	
56113	**F**	FEEN	TO	
56114	**BR**	FEEN	TO	
56115	**F**	FEEN	TO	
56116	**FC**	FASN	TO	
56117	**BR**	FEEN	TO	
56118	**FC**	FEEN	TO	
56119	**BR**	FEEN	TO	
56120	**BR**	FEEN	TO	
56121	**FC**	FEEN	TO	
56122	**FC**	FEEN	TO	Wilton–Coalpower
56123	**FC**	FEDN	TO	Drax Power Station
56124	**BR**	FEEN	TO	
56125	**FC**	FEEN	TO	
56126	**BR**	FEEN	TO	
56127	**FC**	FEEN	TO	
56128	**FC**	FEEN	TO	
56129	**FC**	FEEN	TO	
56130	**FC**	FEEN	TO	Wardley Opencast
56131	**FC**	FEEN	TO	Ellington Colliery
56132	**FC**	FEEN	TO	
56133	**FC**	FEEN	TO	Crewe Locomotive Works
56134	**FC**	FEEN	TO	Blyth Power
56135	**FC**	FEEN	TO	Port of Tyne Authority

CLASS 58   BREL TYPE 5   Co–Co

Built: 1983–87 by BREL at Doncaster Works.
Engine: Ruston Paxman RK3ACT of 2460 kW (3300 hp) at 1000 rpm.

Main Alternator: Brush BA1101B.
Traction Motors: Brush TM73-62.
Max. Tractive Effort: 275 kN (61800 lbf).
Cont. Tractive Effort: 240 kN (53950 lbf) at 17.4 mph.
Power At Rail: 1780 kW (2387 hp).**Length over Buffers:** 19.13 m.
Brake Force: 62 t.   **Wheel Diameter:** 1120 mm.
Design Speed: 80 mph.   **Weight:** 130 t.
Max. Speed: 80 mph.   **RA:** 7.
Train Brakes: Air.
Multiple Working: Red Diamond coupling code.
Communication Equipment: Cab to shore radio-telephone.
All equipped with slow speed control.

58001	FC	FEAN	TO	
58002	FC	FEAN	TO	Daw Mill Colliery
58003	FC	FEAN	TO	Markham Colliery
58004	FC	FEAN	TO	
58005	FC	FEAN	TO	
58006	FC	FEAN	TO	
58007	FC	FEAN	TO	Drakelow Power Station
58008	FC	FEBN	TO	
58009	FC	FEAN	TO	
58010	FC	FEAN	TO	
58011	FC	FEAN	TO	
58012	FC	FEBN	TO	
58013	FC	FEBN	TO	
58014	FC	FEBN	TO	Didcot Power Station
58015	FC	FEBN	TO	
58016	FC	FEBN	TO	
58017	FC	FEBN	TO	
58018	FC	FEBN	TO	High Marnham Power Station
58019	FC	FEBN	TO	Shirebrook Colliery
58020	FC	FEBN	TO	Doncaster Works
58021	FC	FEBN	TO	
58022	FC	FEBN	TO	
58023	FC	FEBN	TO	
58024	FC	FEBN	TO	
58025	FC	FEBN	TO	
58026	FC	FEBN	TO	
58027	FC	FEBN	TO	
58028	FC	FEBN	TO	
58029	FC	FEBN	TO	
58030	FC	FEBN	TO	
58031	FC	FEBN	TO	
58032	FC	FEBN	TO	
58033	FC	FEBN	TO	
58034	FC	FEBN	TO	Bassetlaw
58035	FC	FEBN	TO	
58036	FC	FEBN	TO	
58037	FC	FEBN	TO	
58038	FC	FEBN	TO	
58039	FC	FEBN	TO	Rugeley Power Station

58040	FC	FEBN	TO	Cottam Power Station
58041	FC	FEBN	TO	Ratcliffe Power Station
58042	FC	FEBN	TO	Ironbridge Power Station
58043	FC	FEBN	TO	
58044	FC	FEBN	TO	
58045	FC	FEBN	TO	
58046	FC	FEBN	TO	Thoresby Colliery
58047	FC	FEBN	TO	
58048	FC	FEBN	TO	Coventry Colliery
58049	FC	FEBN	TO	Littleton Colliery
58050	FC	FEBN	TO	Toton Traction Depot

CLASS 59   GENERAL MOTORS TYPE 5   Co–Co

Built: 1985 (59001-4), 1989 (59005) by General Motors, La Grange, Illinois, U.S.A. or 1990 (59101-4) by General Motors, London, Ontario, Canada.
Engine: General Motors 645E3C two stroke of 2460 kW (3300 hp) at 900 rpm.
Main Alternator: General Motors AR11 MLD-D14A.
Traction Motors: General Motors D77B.
Max. Tractive Effort: 506 kN (113 550 lbf).
Cont. Tractive Effort: 291 kN (65 300 lbf) at 14.3 mph.
Power At Rail: 1889 kW (2533 hp).**Length over Buffers:** 21.35 m.
Brake Force: 69 t. **Wheel Diameter:** 1067 mm.
Design Speed: 60 mph. **Weight:** 121 t.
Max. Speed: 60 mph. **RA:** 7.

Class 59/0. Owned by Foster-Yeoman Ltd. Blue/silver/blue livery with white lettering and cast numberplates.

59001	0	CYPO	FY	YEOMAN ENDEAVOUR
59002	0	CYPO	FY	YEOMAN ENTERPRISE
59003	0	CYPO	FY	YEOMAN HIGHLANDER
59004	0	CYPO	FY	YEOMAN CHALLENGER
59005	0	CYPO	FY	KENNETH J. PAINTER

Class 59/1. Owned by ARC Limited. Yellow/grey with grey lettering.

59101	0	CYPA	AR	Village of Whatley
59102	0	CYPA	AR	Village of Chantry
59103	0	CYPA	AR	Village of Mells
59104	0	CYPA	AR	Village of Great Elm

CLASS 60   BRUSH TYPE 5   Co–Co

Built: 1989 onwards by Brush Traction.
Engine: Mirrlees MB275T of 2310 kW (3100 hp) at 1000 rpm.
Main Alternator: Brush .
Traction Motors: Brush separately excited.
Max. Tractive Effort: 500 kN (106500 lbf).
Cont. Tractive Effort: 336 kN (71570 lbf) at 17.4 mph.
Power At Rail: 1800 kW (2415 hp).**Length over Buffers:** 21.34 m.
Brake Force: 74 t. **Wheel Diameter:** 1118 mm.
Design Speed: 62 mph. **Weight:** 129 t.
Max. Speed: 60 mph. **RA:** 7.

Multiple Working: Within class.
Communication Equipment: Cab to shore radio-telephone.
All equipped with slow speed control.

60001	**FA**	FASB	SL	Steadfast
60002	**FP**			Capability Brown
60003	**FP**			Christopher Wren
60004	**FC**	FENN	TO	Lochnagar
60005	**FA**	FPEK	CF	Skiddaw
60006	**FA**	FAXN	TO	Great Gable
60007	**FP**			Robert Adam
60008	**FM**			Moel Fammau
60009	**FA**			Carnedd Dafydd
60010	**FA**	FAXN	TO	Pumlumon Plynlimon
60011	**FA**	FAXN	TO	Cader Idris
60012	**FA**	FAXN	TO	Glyder Fawr
60013	**FP**	F		Robert Boyle
60014	**FP**	F		Alexander Fleming
60015	**FA**	F		Bow Fell
60016	**FA**	F		Langdale Pikes
60017	**FA**	FASB	SL	Arenig Fawr
60018	**FA**	FASB	SL	Moel Siabod
60019	**FA**	FASB	SL	Wild Boar Fell
60020	**FM**	FMHK	CF	Great Whernside
60021	**FM**	FMMY	TE	Pen-y-Ghent
60022	**FM**	FMMY	TE	Ingleborough
60023	**FM**	FMMY	TE	The Cheviot
60024	**FP**	FPEK	CF	Elizabeth Fry
60025	**FP**	FPEK	CF	Joseph Lister
60026	**FP**	FPDI	IM	William Caxton
60027	**FP**	FPDI	IM	Joseph Banks
60028	**FP**	FPDI	IM	John Flamsteed
60029	**FM**	FMHK	CF	Ben Nevis
60030	**FM**	FMMY	TE	Cir Mhor
60031	**FM**	FMMY	TE	Ben Lui
60032	**FC**	FEHN	TO	William Booth
60033	**FP**	FPEK	CF	Anthony Ashley Cooper
60034	**FM**	FMHK	CF	Carnedd Llewelyn
60035	**FM**	FMMY	TE	Florence Nightingale
60036	**FM**	FMMY	TE	Sgurr Na Ciche
60037	**FM**	FMMY	TE	Helvellyn
60038	**FM**	FMMY	TE	Bidean Nam Bian
60039	**FA**	FPDI	IM	Glastonbury Tor
60040	**FA**			Brecon Beacons
60041	**FA**	FASB	SL	High Willhays
60042	**FA**	FASB	SL	Dunkery Beacon
60043	**FA**	FASB	SL	Yes Tor
60044	**FM**	FMMY	TE	Ailsa Craig
60045	**FC**	FEHN	TO	Josephine Butler
60046	**FC**	FABI	IM	William Wilberforce
60047	**FC**	FASB	SL	Robert Owen
60048	**FA**	FAXN	TO	Saddleback

60049	**FM**	FMMY	TE	Scafell
60050	**FM**	FMMY	TE	Roseberry Topping
60051	**FP**	FPEK	CF	Mary Somerville
60052	**FM**	FMMY	TE	Goat Fell
60053	**FP**	FPDI	IM	John Reith
60054	**FP**	FPDI	IM	Charles Babbage
60055	**FC**	FEHN	TO	Thomas Barnardo
60056	**FC**	FABI	IM	William Beveridge
60057	**FC**	FEHN	TO	Adam Smith
60058	**FC**	FABI	IM	John Howard
60059	**FC**	FMMY	TE	Samuel Plimsoll
60060	**FC**	FEHN	TO	James Watt
60061	**FC**	FENN	TO	Alexander Graham Bell
60062	**FP**	FPEK	CF	Samuel Johnson
60063	**FP**	FPEK	CF	James Murray
60064	**FP**	FPDI	IM	Back Tor
60065	**FP**	FPEK	CF	Kinder Low
60066	**FC**	FEJN	TO	John Logie Baird
60067	**FC**	FPDI	IM	James Clerk-Maxwell
60068	**FC**	FXXB	TO	Charles Darwin
60069	**FC**	FENN	TO	Humphry Davy
60070	**FC**	FENN	TO	John Loudon McAdam
60071	**FC**	FENN	TO	Dorothy Garrod
60072	**FC**	FENN	TO	Cairn Toul
60073	**FC**	FENN	TO	Cairn Gorm
60074	**FC**	FENN	TO	Braeriach
60075	**FC**	FEJN	TO	Liathach
60076	**FC**	FEHN	TO	Suilven
60077	**FC**	FENN	TO	Canisp
60078	**FC**	FPDI	IM	Stac Pollaidh
60079	**FC**	FXXB		Foinaven
60080	**FM**	FABI	IM	Kinder Scout
60081	**FM**	FPDI	IM	Bleaklow Hill
60082	**FM**	FPDI	IM	Mam Tor
60083	**FM**	FXXB		Shining Tor
60084	**FM**			Cross Fell
60085	**FM**	FABI	IM	Axe Edge
60086	**FC**	FXXB		Schiehallion
60087	**FC**	FEJN	TO	Slioch
60088	**FC**			Buachaille Etive Mor
60089	**FC**	FXXB		Arcuil
60090	**FC**	F		Quinag
60091	**FC**	F		An Teallach
60092	**FC**	F		
60093	**FC**	F		
60094	**FA**	F		Tryfan
60095	**FA**	F		Crib Goch
60096	**FA**	F		Ben Macdui
60097	**FA**	F		Pillar
60098	**FA**	F		Charles Francis Brush
60099	**FA**	F		Ben More Assynt
60100	**FA**	F		Boar of Badenoch

1.2 D.C. ELECTRIC LOCOMOTIVES

Supply System: 660–850 V d.c. from third rail.

CLASS 73/0   ELECTRO–DIESEL   Bo–Bo

Built: 1962 by BR at Eastleigh Works.
Engine: English Electric 4SRKT of 447 kW (600 hp) at 850 rpm.
Main Generator: English Electric 824/3D (73/0), 824/5D (73/1).
Traction Motors: English Electric 542A (73/0), 546/1B (73/1).
Max. Tractive Effort: Electric 187 kN (42000 lbf). Diesel 152 kN (34100 lbf).
Continuous Rating: Electric 1060 kW (1420 hp) giving a tractive effort of 43 kN (9600 lbf) at 55.5 mph.
Cont. Tractive Effort: Diesel 72 kN (16100 lbf) at 10 mph.
Maximum Rail Power: Electric 1830 kW (2450 hp) at 37 mph.

Brake Force: 31 t.	**Length over Buffers:** 16.36 m.
Design Speed: 80 mph.	**Weight:** 76.5 t.
Max. Speed: 60 mph.	**RA:** 6.
Wheel Diameter: 1016 mm.	**ETH Index (Elec. power):** 66

Train Brakes: Air, Vacuum and electro-pneumatic.
Multiple Working: Within each sub-class and with Class 33/1 and also various SR EMUs.
Communication Equipment: All equipped with driver–guard telephone.
Couplings: Drop-head buckeye.
Formerly numbered E 6001–26/28–49 (not in order).

Non-standard Livery: 73005 is Network SouthEast blue.

73001		DCSW	SL
73002	**BR**	DCSW	SL
73003	**BR**	DCSW	SL
73005	**O**	DCSW	SL Mid Hants WATERCRESS LINE
73006	**BR**	DMSB	SL

CLASS 73/1 & 73/2   ELECTRO–DIESEL   Bo–Bo

Built: 1965–67 by English Electric Co. at Vulcan Foundry, Newton le Willows.
Max. Tractive Effort: Electric 179 kN (40000 lbf). Diesel 160 kN (36000 lbf).
Continuous Rating: Electric 1060 kW (1420 hp) giving a tractive effort of 35 kN (7800 lbf) at 68 mph.
Cont. Tractive Effort: Diesel 60 kN (13600 lbf) at 11.5 mph.
Maximum Rail Power: Electric 2350 kW (3150 hp) at 42 mph.
Engine: English Electric 4SRKT of 447 kW (600 hp) at 850 rpm.
Main Generator: English Electric 824/3D (73/0), 824/5D (73/1).
Traction Motors: English Electric 542A (73/0), 546/1B (73/1).

Brake Force: 31 t.	**Length over Buffers:** 16.36 m.
Design Speed: 90 mph.	**Weight:** 77 t.
Max. Speed: 60 (90*) mph.	**RA:** 6.
Wheel Diameter: 1016 mm.	**ETH Index (Elec. power):** 66

Train Brakes: Air, Vacuum and electro-pneumatic.
Multiple Working: Within each sub-class and with Class 33/1 and also various SR EMUs.

Communication Equipment: All equipped with driver–guard telephone.
Couplings: Drop-head buckeye.

Non-standard Livery: 73101 is Pullman umber & Cream.
Formerly numbered E 6001–26/28–49 (not in order).

Class 73/2 are locos dedicated to InterCity and Network SouthEast services.

73101	**O** DCSA	SL	Brighton Evening Argus
73103	**IO** DCSA	SL	
73104	**IO** DMSA	SL	
73105	**C** DCSA	SL	
73106	**D** DMSA	SL	
73107	**C** DCSA	SL	
73108	**C** DCSA	SL	
73109	* **N** NWXB	SL	Battle of Britain 50th Anniversary
73110	**C** DCSA	SL	
73112	**N** DMSA	SL	University of Kent at Canterbury
73114	**IO** DCSA	SL	
73117	**IO** DCSA	SL	University of Surrey
73118	**IO** DCSA	SL	The Romney Hythe and Dymchurch Railway
73119	**C** DCSA	SL	Kentish Mercury
73126	**N** DCSA	SL	Kent & East Sussex Railway
73128	**C** DCSA	SL	OVS BULLIED C.B.E. 1937 C.M.E. SOUTHERN RAILWAY 1949
73129	**C** DCSA	SL	City of Winchester
73130	**M** DCSA	SL	City of Portsmouth
73131	**C** DCSA	SL	County of Surrey
73132	**IO** DCSA	SL	
73133	**C** DCSA	SL	The Bluebell Railway
73134	**IO** DCSA	SL	Woking Homes 1885–1985
73136	**D** DMSA	SL	
73138	**C** DCSA	SL	
73139	**IO** DCSW	SL	
73140	**IO** DCSW	SL	
73141	**IO** DCSW	SL	
73201 (73142)	* **M** IVGA	SL	Broadlands
73202 (73137)	* **I** IVGA	SL	Royal Observer Corps
73203 (73127)	* **I** IVGA	SL	
73204 (73125)	* **IO** IVGA	SL	Stewarts Lane 1860–1985
73205 (73124)	* **M** IVGA	SL	London Chamber of Commerce
73206 (73123)	* **I** IVGA	SL	Gatwick Express
73207 (73122)	* **I** IVGA	SL	County of East Sussex
73208 (73121)	* **IO** IVGA	SL	Croydon 1883–1983
73209 (73120)	* **I** IVGA	SL	
73210 (73116)	* **I** IVGA	SL	Selhurst
73211 (73113)	* **I** IVGA	SL	
73212 (73102)	* **I** IVGA	SL	Airtour Suisse
73235 (73135)	* **I** IVGA	SL	

1.3. A.C. ELECTRIC LOCOMOTIVES

Supply System: 25 kV a.c. from overhead equipment.

CLASS 86/1   BR DESIGN   Bo–Bo

Built: 1965–66 by English Electric Co. at Vulcan Foundry, Newton le Willows or BR at Doncaster Works. Rebuilt with Class 87 type bogies and motors.
Traction Motors: GEC G412AZ frame mounted.
Max. Tractive Effort: 258 kN (58000 lbf).
Continuous Rating: 3730 kW (5000 hp) giving a tractive effort of 95 kN (21300 lbf) at 87 mph.
Maximum Rail Power: 5860 kW (7860 hp) at ?? mph.
Brake Force: 40 t.   **Length over Buffers:** 17.83 m.
Design Speed: 110 mph.   **Weight:** 87 t.
Max. Speed: 110 mph.   **RA:** 6.
ETH Index: 74   **Wheel Diameter:** 1150 mm.
Train Brakes: Air & Vacuum.   **Electric Brake:** Rheostatic.
Communication Equipment: Driver–guard telephone and cab to shore radio- telephone.
Note: Class 86 were formerly numbered E 3101–3200 (not in order).

86101 (86201)	**M** IWPA	WN	Sir William A Stanier FRS
86102 (86202)	**I0** IWPA	WN	Robert A Riddles
86103 (86203)	**I0** IWPA	WN	Andre´ Chapelon

CLASS 86/2   BR DESIGN   Bo–Bo

Built: 1965–66 by English Electric Co. at Vulcan Foundry, Newton le Willows or BR at Doncaster Works. Later rebuilt with resilient wheels and flexicoil suspension.
Traction Motors: AEI 282BZ.
Max. Tractive Effort: 207 kN (46500 lbf).
Continuous Rating: 3010 kW (4040 hp) giving a tractive effort of 85 kN (19200 lbf) at 77.5 mph.
Maximum Rail Power: 4550 kW (6100 hp) at 49.5 mph.
Brake Force: 40 t.   **Length over Buffers:** 17.83 m.
Design Speed: 125 mph.   **Weight:** 85 t–86 t.
Max. Speed: 100 (110§) mph.   **RA:** 6.
ETH Index: 74   **Wheel Diameter:** 1156 mm.
Train Brakes: Air & Vacuum.   **Electric Brake:** Rheostatic.
Communication Equipment: Driver–guard telephone and cab to shore radio- telephone.
Multiple Working: Time division multiplex system.

86204	**I** IWPA	WN	City of Carlisle
86205 (86503)	**I** ICCA	LG	City of Lancaster
86206	**M** ICCA	LG	City of Stoke on Trent
86207	**M** IWPA	WN	City of Lichfield
86208	**I** IWPA	WN	City of Chester
86209	§ **M** IWPA	WN	City of Coventry
86210	**I** IWPA	WN	City of Edinburgh

86212	**M**	ICCA	LG	Preston Guild
86213	**IO**	IWPA	WN	Lancashire Witch
86214	**M**	ICCA	LG	Sans Pareil
86215	**M**	IANA	NC	Joseph Chamberlain
86216	**I**	ICCA	LG	Meteor
86217 (86504)	**I**	IANA	NC	Halley's Comet
86218	**I**	IANA	NC	Planet
86219	**I**	IWPA	WN	Phoenix
86220	**I**	IANA	NC	The Round Tabler
86221	**M**	IANA	NC	B.B.C. Look East
86222 (86502)	**I**	ICCA	LG	LLOYD'S LIST 250th ANNIVERSARY
86223	**I**	IANA	NC	Norwich Union
86224	**§ IO**	IWPA	WN	Caledonian
86225	**§ M**	IWPA	WN	Hardwicke
86226	**M**	IWPA	WN	Royal Mail Midlands
86227	**M**	ICCA	LG	Sir Henry Johnson
86228	**M**	ICCA	LG	Vulcan Heritage
86229	**M**	ICCA	LG	Sir John Betjeman
86230	**M**	IANA	NC	The Duke of Wellington
86231	**§ I**	IWPA	WN	Starlight Express
86232	**I**	IANA	NC	Norwich Festival
86233 (86506)	**I**	ICCA	LG	Laurence Olivier
86234	**I**	ICCA	LG	J B Priestley OM
86235	**I**	IANA	NC	Harold Macmillan
86236	**I**	IWPA	WN	Josiah Wedgwood MASTER POTTER 1736–1795
86237	**I**	IANA	NC	Sir Charles Halle'
86238	**I**	IANA	NC	European Community
86239 (86507)	**R**	RXLE	CE	L S Lowry
86240	**M**	IWPA	WN	Bishop Eric Treacy
86241 (86508)	**R**	RXLE	CE	Glenfiddich
86242	**M**	IWPA	WN	James Kennedy GC
86243	**IO**	RXLE	CE	The Boys' Brigade
86244	**I**	ICCA	LG	The Royal British Legion
86245	**IO**	IWPA	WN	Dudley Castle
86246 (86505)	**I**	IANA	NC	Royal Anglian Regiment
86247	**I**	IWPA	WN	Abraham Darby
86248	**I**	IWPA	WN	Sir Clwyd/County of Clwyd
86249	**M**	IWPA	WN	County of Merseyside
86250	**M**	IANA	NC	The Glasgow Herald
86251	**M**	IWPA	WN	The Birmingham Post
86252	**IO**	ICCA	LG	The Liverpool Daily Post
86253 (86044)	**I**	IWPA	WN	The Manchester Guardian
86254 (86047)	**M**	RXLE	CE	William Webb Ellis
86255 (86042)	**I**	ICCA	LG	Penrith Beacon
86256 (86040)	**M**	ICCA	LG	Pebble Mill
86257 (86043)	**I**	IWPA	WN	Snowdon
86258 (86501)	**I**	IWPA	WN	Talyllyn–The First Preserved Railway
86259 (86045)	**I**	ICCA	LG	Peter Pan
86260 (86048)	**I**	ICCA	LG	Driver Wallace Oakes G.C.
86261 (86041)	**M**	RXLE	CE	Driver John Axon G.C.

CLASS 86/4 & 86/6   BR DESIGN   Bo–Bo

Built: 1965–66 by English Electric Co. at Vulcan Foundry, Newton le Willows or BR at Doncaster Works. Later rebuilt with resilient wheels and flexicoil suspension.
Traction Motors: AEI 282AZ.
Max. Tractive Effort: 258 kN (58000 lbf).
Continuous Rating: 2680 kW (3600 hp) giving a tractive effort of 89 kN (20000 lbf) at 67 mph.
Maximum Rail Power: 4400 kW (5900 hp) at 38 mph.
Brake Force: 40 t. **Length over Buffers:** 17.83 m.
Design Speed: 100 mph. **Weight:** 83 t–84 t.
Max. Speed: 100 (75*) mph. **RA:** 6.
ETH Index: 74 **Wheel Diameter:** 1156 mm.
Train Brakes: Air & Vacuum. **Electric Brake:** Rheostatic.
Multiple Working: Time division multiplex system. Note: All Class 86/4, 86/6 and 87 locos are also fitted with an older system of multiple working and can work in multiple with one another.
Communication Equipment: Driver–guard telephone and cab to shore radio- telephone.

Class 86/4. ETH equipment operative.

86401 (86001)	**RX** RXLE	CE	
86416 (86316)	**M** RXLE	CE	Wigan Pier
86417 (86317)	**M** RXLE	CE	The Kingsman
86419 (86319)	**R** RXLE	CE	Post Haste 150 YEARS OF TRAVELLING POST OFFICES
86424 (86324)	**R** RXLE	CE	
86425 (86325)	**R** RXLE	CE	
86426 (86326)	**M** RXLE	CE	
86430 (86030)	**RX** RXLE	CE	Scottish National Orchestra

Class 86/6. ETH equipment isolated.

86602 (86402)	* **FD** MDNC	CE	
86603 (86403)	* **FD** MDNC	CE	
86604 (86404)	* **FD** MDNC	CE	
86605 (86405)	* **FD** MDNC	CE	Intercontainer
86606 (86406)	* **M** MDNC	CE	
86607 (86407)	* **M** MDNC	CE	The Institution of Electrical Engineers
86608 (86408)	* **FD** MDNC	CE	St. John Ambulance
86609 (86409)	* **M** MDNC	CE	
86610 (86410)	* **FD** MDNC	CE	
86611 (86411)	* **FD** MDNC	CE	Airey Neave
86612 (86412)	* **M** MDNC	CE	Elizabeth Garrett Anderson
86613 (86413)	* **FD** MDNC	CE	County of Lancashire
86614 (86414)	* **FD** MDNC	CE	Frank Hornby
86615 (86415)	* **FD** MDNC	CE	Rotary International
86618 (86418)	* **FD** MDNC	CE	
86620 (86420)	* **M** MDNC	CE	
86621 (86421)	* **M** MDNC	CE	London School of Economics

86622	(86422)	* **FD** MDNC	CE	
86623	(86423)	* **FD** MDNC	CE	
86627	(86427)	* **FD** MDNC	CE	The Industrial Society
86628	(86428)	* **FD** MDNC	CE	Aldaniti
86631	(86431)	* **FD** MDNC	CE	
86632	(86432)	* **FD** MDNC	CE	Brookside
86633	(86433)	* **FD** MDNC	CE	Wulfruna
86634	(86434)	* **FD** MDNC	CE	University of London
86635	(86435)	* **FD** MDNC	CE	
86636	(86436)	* **FD** MDNC	CE	
86637	(86437)	* **FD** MDNC	CE	
86638	(86438)	* **FD** MDNC	CE	
86639	(86439)	* **FD** MDNC	CE	

CLASS 87   BR DESIGN   Bo–Bo

Built: 1973–75 by BREL at Crewe Works. Class 87/1 has thyristor control instead of HT tap changing.
Supply System: 25 kV a.c. from overhead equipment.
Traction Motors: GEC G412AZ frame mounted (87/0), G412BZ (87/1).
Max. Tractive Effort: 258 kN (58000 lbf).
Continuous Rating: 3730 kW (5000 hp) giving a tractive effort of 95 kN (21300 lbf) at 87 mph (Class 87/0), 3620 kW (4850 hp) giving a tractive effort of 96 kN (21600 lbf) at 84 mph (Class 87/1).
Maximum Rail Power: 5860 kW (7860 hp) at ?? mph.

Brake Force: 40 t.	**Length over Buffers:** 17.83 m.
Design Speed: 110 mph	**Weight:** 83.5 t.
Max. Speed: 110 (75*) mph.	**RA:** 6.
ETH Index: 74	**Wheel Diameter:** 1150 mm.
Train Brakes: Air.	**Electric Brake:** Rheostatic.

Multiple Working: Time division multiplex system. Note: All Class 86/4, 86/6 and 87 locos are also fitted with an older system of multiple working and can work in multiple with one another.
Communication Equipment: All equipped with driver–guard telephone and cab to shore radio-telephone.

Class 87/0. Standard Design. Tap Changer Control.

87001	**M**	IWCA	WN	Royal Scot
87002	**I**	IWCA	WN	Royal Sovereign
87003	**I**	IWCA	WN	Patriot
87004	**M**	IWCA	WN	Britannia
87005	**M**	IWCA	WN	City of London
87006	**I0**	IWCA	WN	City of Glasgow
87007	**I0**	IWCA	WN	City of Manchester
87008	**I0**	IWCA	WN	City of Liverpool
87009	**M**	IWCA	WN	City of Birmingham
87010	**M**	IWCA	WN	King Arthur
87011	**M**	IWCA	WN	The Black Prince
87012	**M**	IWCA	WN	The Royal Bank of Scotland
87013	**M**	IWCA	WN	John O' Gaunt
87014	**M**	IWCA	WN	Knight of the Thistle
87015	**I0**	IWCA	WN	Howard of Effingham

87016	**I**	IWCA	WN	
87017	**IO**	IWCA	WN	Iron Duke
87018	**M**	IWCA	WN	Lord Nelson
87019	**IO**	IWCA	WN	Sir Winston Churchill
87020	**IO**	IWCA	WN	North Briton
87021	**IO**	IWCA	WN	Robert the Bruce
87022	**M**	IWCA	WN	Cock o' the North
87023	**IO**	IWCA	WN	Velocity
87024	**IO**	IWCA	WN	Lord of the Isles
87025	**IO**	IWCA	WN	County of Cheshire
87026	**IO**	IWCA	WN	Sir Richard Arkwright
87027	**IO**	IWCA	WN	Wolf of Badenoch
87028	**M**	IWCA	WN	Lord President
87029	**IO**	IWCA	WN	Earl Marischal
87030	**IO**	IWCA	WN	Black Douglas
87031	**M**	IWCA	WN	Hal o' the Wynd
87032	**IO**	IWCA	WN	Kenilworth
87033	**M**	IWCA	WN	Thane of Fife
87034	**IO**	IWCA	WN	William Shakespeare
87035	**M**	IWCA	WN	Robert Burns

Class 87/1. Thyristor Control.

87101	* **FD**	MDNC	CE	STEPHENSON

CLASS 89　　　　　BRUSH DESIGN　　　　Co–Co

Built: 1986 by BREL at Crewe Works (under sub-contract for Brush Traction, Loughborough).
Supply System: 25 kV a.c. from overhead equipment.
Traction Motors: Brush TM2201A.
Max. Tractive Effort: 205 kN (46100 lbf).
Continuous Rating: 4350 kW (5850 hp) giving a tractive effort of 105 kN (23540 lbf) at 92 mph.
Maximum Rail Power: 5860 kW (7860 hp) at ?? mph.
Brake Force: 50 t.   **Length over Buffers:** 19.80 m.
Design Speed: 125 mph.   **Weight:** 104 t.
Max. Speed: 125 mph.   **RA:** 6.
ETH Index: 95   **Wheel Diameter:** 1150 mm.
Train Brakes: Air.   **Electric Brake:** Rheostatic.
Multiple Working: Time division multiplex system.
Communication Equipment: Equipped with driver–guard telephone and cab to shore radio-telephone.

89001	**I**	IXXA	BN (U)Avocet

CLASS 90　　　　　GEC DESIGN　　　　Bo–Bo

Built: 1987–90 by BREL at Crewe Works. Thyristor control.
Supply System: 25 kV a.c. from overhead equipment.
Traction Motors: GEC G412CY separately excited frame mounted.
Max. Tractive Effort: 192 kN (43150 lbf).

Continuous Rating: 3730 kW (5000 hp) giving a tractive effort of 95 kN (21300 lbf) at 87 mph.
Maximum Rail Power: 5860 kW (7860 hp) at ?? mph.
Brake Force: 40 t.　　　　　　　　　　**Length over Buffers**: 18.80 m.
Design Speed: 110 mph.　　　　　　　　**Weight**: 84.5 t.
Max. Speed: 110 (75*) mph.　　　　　　**RA**: 7.
ETH Index: 74　　　　　　　　　　　　**Wheel Diameter**: 1156 mm.
Train Brakes: Air.　　　　　　　　　　**Electric Brake**: Rheostatic.
Couplings: Drop-head buckeye.
Multiple Working: Time division multiplex system.
Communication Equipment: Driver–guard telephone and cab to shore radio- telephone.

Class 90/0. As built.

90001	I	IWCA	WN	BBC Midlands Today
90002	I	IWCA	WN	
90003	I	IWCA	WN	
90004	I	IWCA	WN	The D' Oyly Carte Opera Company
90005	I	IWCA	WN	Financial Times
90006	I	IWCA	WN	
90007	I	IWCA	WN	
90008	I	IWCA	WN	The Birmingham Royal Ballet
90009	I	IWCA	WN	Royal Show
90010	I	IWCA	WN	275 Railway Squadron (Volunteers)
90011	I	IWCA	WN	The Chartered Institute of Transport
90012	I	IWCA	WN	Glasgow 1990 Cultural Capital of Europe
90013	I	IWCA	WN	
90014	I	IWCA	WN	The Liverpool Phil
90015	I	IWCA	WN	BBC North West
90016	I	RXLE	CE	
90017	I	RXLE	CE	
90018	I	RXLE	CE	
90019	I	RXLE	CE	Penny Black
90020	RX	RXLE	CE	Colonel Bill Cockburn CBE TD
90021	I	MDLC	CE	
90022	I	MDLC	CE	
90023	I	MDLC	CE	
90024	I	MDLC	CE	
90025	I	MDLC	CE	

Class 90/1. ETH equipment isolated.

90126	*	M	MDMC	CE
90127	*	M	MDMC	CE
90128	*	M	MDMC	CE
90129	*	M	MDMC	CE
90130	*	M	MDMC	CE
90131	*	M	MDMC	CE
90132	*	M	MDMC	CE
90133	*	M	MDMC	CE
90134	*	M	MDMC	CE
90135	*	M	MDMC	CE
90136	*	M	MDMC	CE

```
90137 *  FD  MDMC     CE
90138 *  FD  MDMC     CE
90139 *  FD  MDMC     CE
90140 *  FD  MDMC     CE
90141 *  FD  MDMC     CE
90142 *  FD  MDMC     CE
90143 *  FD  MDMC     CE
90144 *  FD  MDMC     CE
90145 *  FD  MDMC     CE
90146 *  FD  MDMC     CE
90147 *  FD  MDMC     CE
90148 *  FD  MDMC     CE
90149 *  FD  MDMC     CE
90150 *  FD  MDMC     CE
```

CLASS 91   GEC DESIGN   Bo–Bo

Built: 1988 onwards by BREL at Crewe Works. Thyristor control.
Supply System: 25 kV a.c. from overhead equipment.
Traction Motors: GEC G426AZ.
Max. Tractive Effort: .
Continuous Rating: 4540 kW (6090 hp).
Maximum Rail Power: 4700 kW (6300 hp).

Brake Force: 45 t.	**Length over Buffers:** 19.40 m.
Design Speed: 140 mph.	**Weight:** 84 t.
Max. Speed: 140 mph.	**RA:** 7.
ETH Index: 95	**Wheel Diameter:** 1000 mm.
Train Brakes: Air.	**Electric Brake:** Rheostatic.

Couplings: Drop-head buckeye.
Multiple Working: Time division multiplex system.
Communication Equipment: Driver–guard telephone and cab to shore radio- telephone.

```
91001   I   IECA     BN    Swallow
91002   I   IECA     BN
91003   I   IECA     BN
91004   I   IECA     BN    The Red Arrows
91005   I   IECA     BN
91006   I   IECA     BN
91007   I   IECA     BN
91008   I   IECA     BN    Thomas Cook
91009   I   IECA     BN
91010   I   IECA     BN
91011   I   IECA     BN    Terence Cuneo
91012   I   IECA     BN
91013   I   IECA     BN    Michael Faraday
91014   I   IECA     BN
91015   I   IECA     BN
91016   I   IECA     BN
91017   I   IECA     BN
91018   I   IECA     BN
91019   I   IECA     BN    Scottish Enterprise
91020   I   IECA     BN
```

91021	I	IECA	BN	
91022	I	IECA	BN	
91023	I	IECA	BN	
91024	I	IECA	BN	
91025	I	IECA	BN	
91026	I	IECA	BN	
91027	I	IECA	BN	
91028	I	IECA	BN	Guide Dog
91029	I	IECA	BN	Queen Elizabeth II
91030	I	IECA	BN	Palace of Holyroodhouse
91031	I	IECA	BN	Sir Henry Royce

1.4 DEPARTMENTAL LOCOMOTIVES

CLASS 97/2   BR TYPE 2   Bo–Bo

Built: 1966 by Beyer Peacock, Manchester (97251), BR at Derby Loco Works (97252). Converted to ETH generator vehicles (non self-propelled) to work with steam locomotives.
Engine: Sulzer 6LDA28-B of 930 kW (1250 hp) at 750 rpm.
Main Generator: AEI RTB 15656.
Brake Force: 38 t.   **Length over Buffers:** 15.39 m.
Weight: 71.7 t.   **Wheel Diameters:** 1143 mm.
Max. Speed: 90 mph.   **RA:** 5.
ETH Index: 66.

97251 (25305)	**M**	IXXA	CL(S)
97252 (25314)	**M**	IXXA	OC(S)

CLASS 97/6   RUSTON SHUNTER   0–6–0

Built: 1959 by Ruston & Hornsby at Lincoln.
Engine: Ruston 6VPH of 123 kW (165 hp).
Main Generator: British Thomson Houston RTB6034.
Traction Motor: One British Thomson Houston RTA5041.
Max. Tractive Effort: 75 kN (17000 lbf).
Brake Force: 16t.   **Length over Buffers:** 7.62 m.
Weight: 31t.   **Wheel Diameter:** 978 mm.
Max. Speed: 20 mph.   **RA:** 1.
Train Brakes: Vacuum.

Non-Standard Livery: Departmental Yellow.

97651	(PWM 651)	v	**O**	DCWC	CF
97653	(PWM 653)	v	**O**	DCWC	CF
97654	(PWM 654)	v	**O**	DCWC	RG

CLASS 97/7   BATTERY LOCOS   Bo–Bo

Built: 1973–80 by BREL at Doncaster and Wolverton Works. Converted from class 501 EMU cars.
Supply System: 750 volts dc third rail or 320 volts dc batteries.
Traction Motors: GEC WT344A.
Max. Tractive Effort: 73 kN (16400 lbf).
Brake Force: 45 t.   **Length over Buffers:** 18.44 m.
Weight: 59 t.   **Wheel Diameter:** 1071 mm.
Max. Speed: 25 mph.   **RA:** 4.
Multiple Working: Work in pairs.
Non-Standard Livery: Bright blue with yellow stripe.

97701	(61136) a	**O**	DMEC	BD	97706	(61189) a		DMEC	HE
97702	(61139) a	**O**	DMEC	BD	97707	(61166) a	**N**	DMEC	HE
97703	(61182) a		DMEC	HE	97708	(61173) a	**N**	DMEC	HE
97704	(61185) a		DMEC	HE	97709	(61172) a		DMEC	HE (S)
97705	(61184) a		DMEC	HE	97710	(61175) a		DMEC	HE (S)

Note: 97701/2 carry DB 977363/2 in error.

CLASS 97/8   SHUNTER   0–6–0

For details see Class 09. Severn Tunnel emergency train locomotive.

Non-Standard Livery: BR blue with grey cab.

97806   (09017) xo **O** DOPA CF   Normally kept at Sudbrook.

TRAINING LOCOS

The following locomotives are normally used for staff training purposes.

20001   x   DMEX TO
20188   xs   DMEX IL

DB 968xxx SERIES

This number series was introduced in 1969 and is for former capital stock locomotives which no longer operate under their own power.

Non-standard Livery: 968021 is British Rail Research red/blue/white.

ADB 968021 (84009) x CE   Mobile load bank.
TDB 968030 (33018) x   Moreton-in-Marsh training loco.

2. LOCO-HAULED COACHING STOCK

This section contains full details of all BR loco-hauled coaching stock. Coaches are listed in batches, according to their class, with lot number information for the various batches being shown above the listings. Where a coach has been renumbered, the former number is shown in parentheses. If the coach has been renumbered more than once, the original number is shown in parentheses, with the intermediate numbers being given in the text. Where the old number of a coach due to be converted or renumbered is known and the conversion or renumbering has not yet taken place, the coach is listed both under its old number with its depot allocation, and under its new number without an allocation

NUMBERING SYSTEMS

Six different numbering systems were in use on BR. These were the BR series, the four pre-nationalisation companies' series' and the Pullman Car Company's series. Only BR number series loco-hauled coaches now exist in stock.

All coaching stock vehicles have now been given depot allocations, regional prefixes not now being used.

DETAILED INFORMATION AND CODES

After the heading, the following details are shown:

(1) Diagram code. This consists of the first three characters of the TOPS code followed by two numbers which relate to the particular design of vehicle.
(2) 'Mark' of coach (see below).
(3) Number of first class seats , standard class seats and lavatory compartments shown as nF nS nL respectively.
(4) Bogie type (see below).
(5) Brake type. (see below).
(6) Heating type. (see below).
(7) Additional features.
(8) ETH Index.

BOGIE TYPES

BR Mk 1 (BR1). Standard double bolster leaf spring bogie. Generally 90 m.p.h. but certain vehicles were allowed to run at 100 m.p.h. with special maintenance. Weight: 6.1 t.
BR Mk 1 (heavy duty). Similar to above. Weight 6.5 t.
BR Mk 2 (BR2). Later variant of BR Mark 1 used on certain vans.
COMMONWEALTH (C). Heavy, cast steel soil spring bogie. 100 m.p.h. Weight: 6.75 t.
B4. Coil spring fabricated bogie for 100 m.p.h. Certain BGs (classified NHA) are allowed to run at 110 m.p.h. with special maintenance. Weight: 5.2 t.
B5. Heavy duty version of B4. 100 m.p.h. Weight: 5.3 t.
BT10. A fabricated bogie designed for 125 m.p.h. Air suspension.
T4. The latest 125 m.p.h. bogie from BREL.
The new Mark 4 vehicles are fitted with bogie from the Swiss firm of SIG.

BRAKE TYPE CODES.

a   Air braked.
v   Vacuum braked.
x   Dual braked (air and vacuum).

HEATING TYPE CODES.

d   Dual heated (steam & electric).
e   electric heated
o   No heating apparatus.

r   Steam piped & electric wired.
u   UIC/BR electric heat.
y   Electric wired.

Note: All BR train heating nowadays is electric, but dual heated vehicles still often retain the steam heating equipment, albeit isolated.

ADDITIONAL FEATURE CODES.

f   Facelifted or fluorescent lighting provided.
k   Composition brake blocks (instead of cast iron).
n   Day/night lighting.
p   Fitted with public telephone.
pa   Public address speakers installed.
pg   Public address transmission and driver–guard communication.
pt   Public address transmission and speakers.
q   Fitted with catering staff to shore telephone.
s   Short swing links (see page 79)
to   Public address transmission only.
w   Fitted with wheelchair space.
z   Fitted with wheelchair space and disabled persons' toilet.

NOTES ON ETH INDICES.

The sum of ETH indices in a train must not be more than that of the locomotive. Suffix 'S' was used to denote SR 750 V heaters, the usual voltage on BR being 1000, and suffix 'X' denotes 600 amp wiring instead of 400 amp. Trains whose ETH index comes to more than 66 must be formed completely with 600 amp wired stock. There are now no loco-hauled vehicles in BR capital stock with SR heaters.

TOPS CODES

TOPS (Total operations processing system) codes are allocated to all coaching stock. For passenger stock the code consists of:

(1) Two letters denoting the layout of the vehicle as follows:

AA Gangwayed Corridor
AB Gangwayed Corridor Brake
AC Gangwayed Open (2 + 2 seating)
AD Gangwayed Open (2 + 1 seating)
AE Gangwayed Open Brake
AF Gangwayed Driving Open Brake
AG Micro-Buffet
AH Brake Micro-Buffet
AI As 'AC' but fitted with drop-head buckeye and no gangway at one end.
AJ Restaurant Buffet with Kitchen
AK Kitchen Car
AL As 'AC' but with disabled person's toilet (Mark 4 only)
AN Miniature Buffet
AO Privately-owned
AS Sleeping Car
AT Royal Train Coach
AU Sleepi

(2) A digit for the class of passenger accommodation:

1   first
2   standard (formerly 'second')
3   Composite
4   Unclassified
5   None

(3) A suffix relating to the build of coach.

| 1 Mark 1 | A Mark 2A | C Mark 2C | E Mark 2E | G Mark 3 or | H Mark 3B |
| Z Mark 2 | B Mark 2B | D Mark 2D | F Mark 2F | Mark 3A | J Mark 4 |

For non-passenger carrying coaching stock, the suffix denotes the brake type:

A   Air braked
V   Vacuum braked
X   Dual braked

OPERATOR CODES

The normal operator codes are given in brackets after the TOPS codes. These are as follows:

F   First
S   standard (formerly known as 'second')
C   Composite
B   Brake
O   Open
K   Side corridor with lavatory

Various other letters are in use and the meaning of these can be ascertained by referring to the titles at the head of each class.

ABBREVIATIONS:

DMU	Diesel multiple unit
GER	Great Eastern Railway
GWR	Great Western Railway
LMS	London Midland and Scottish Railway
LNER	London & North Eastern Railway
LNWR	London & North Western Railway

THE DEVELOPMENT OF BR STANDARD COACHES

The standard BR coach built from 1951 to 1963 is the mark 1. This has a separate underframe and body. The underframe is normally 64'6" long, but certain vehicles were built on short (57') frames. Tungsten lighting is standard and until 1961, BR mark 1 bogies were generally provided. In 1959 TSOs to lot No. 30525 appeared with fluorescent lighting and melamine interior panels and from 1961 onwards Commonwealth bogies were fitted in an attempt to improve the quality of ride which became very poor when the tyre profiles on the wheels of the Mark 1 bogies became worn. The further batches of TSOs and BSOs retained the features of lot 30525, but the BSKs, SKs, BCKs and CKs, whilst utilising melamine panelling in standard class, still retained tungsten lighting. Wooden interior finish was retained in first class compartments. The FOs had fluorescent lighting with wooden panelling except for lot No. 30648 which had tungsten lighting. In later years many mark 1s had their mark 1 bogies replaced by B4s.

In 1964, a new train was introduced. Known as "XP64", it featured new seat designs, pressure ventilation, aluminium compartment doors and corridor partitions, foot pedal operated toilets, and B4 bogies. The vehicles were on standard mark 1 underframes. Folding doors were fitted but these proved troublesome and were later replaced with hinged doors. All XP64 coaches have now been withdrawn, but some have been preserved.

The prototype mark 2 vehicle (W 13252) was produced in 1963. This was an FK of semi-integral construction and was pressure ventilated. Tungsten lighting was provided and B4 bogies. This vehicle has been preserved by the National Railway Museum. The production build was similar, but wider windows were used. The standard class open vehicles used the new seat design similar to that in the XP64 and fluorescent lighting was provided. Interior finish reverted to wood. MK 2s were built from 1964–66.

The mark 2As, built 1967–68, incorporated the rest of the novel features first used in the XP64 set, i.e. foot pedal operated toilets (except BSOs), new first class seat design, aluminium compartment doors and partitions together with fluorescent lighting in first class compartments. Folding gangway doors (lime green coloured) were used instead of the traditional variety. The following list summarises the changes made in the later Mk 2 variants:

Mk 2B: Wide wrap round doors, no centre doors, slightly longer body. In standard class, one toilet at each end instead of two at one end as previously . Red gangway doors.
Mk 2C: Lowered ceiling with twin strips of fluorescent lighting, ducting for air conditioning, but no air conditioning.
Mk 2D: Air conditioning. No opening lights in windows.
Mk 2E: Smaller toilets with luggage racks opposite. Fawn gangway doors.
Mk 2F: Plastic interior panels. Inter-City 70 seats. Modified air conditioning system.

The Mark 3 coach has BT10 bogies, is 75′ long and is of fully integral construction with Inter-City 70 seats. Gangway doors are yellow (red in RFB), Loco-hauled coaches are classified Mark 3A, Mark 3 being reserved for HST trailers. A new batch of FOs and BFOs classified Mark 3B was built in 1985 with APT style seating and revised lighting. The last vehicles in the Mark 3 series are the driving brake vehicles (officially called driving van trailers) which have been built for West Coast Main Line services.

The Mark 4 coach built by Metro-Cammell for the East Coast Main Line electrification scheme features a body profile suitable for tilting trains, although tilt is not fitted, and is not intended to be. They are suitable for 140 m.p.h. running, although initially they will be restricted to 125 m.p.h. pending the installation of automatic train protection (ATP) on the East Coast Main Line.

SWING-LINKS ON BT10 BOGIES

In order for Mark 3 coaches (including HST trailers) to work on third-rail electrified lines, the bogies must have short-swing links. There are two types of swing-links as shown in the photographs below. Long swing links are stirrup-shaped as shown in the top photograph, whereas the short swing links are a wire rope sling. This can just be ascertained in the bottom photograph.

In this book, those coaches known to be fitted with short swing-links are shown with an 's'. If this is not shown, the coach may or may not be fitted. BR has yet not completed the survey as to which coaches have which type.

Long swing-link bogie   *M.A. King*

Short swing-link bogie   *M.A. King*

2.1. LOCO-HAULED PASSENGER STOCK

AJ1F(RFB) — BUFFET OPEN FIRST

Dia. AJ104 (AJ106*). Mark 2F. Air conditioned. Converted 1988–9/91 at BREL, Derby from Mark 2F FOs. 1200/1/3/6/11/14–17/20/21/50/2/5/6/9 have Stones equipment, others have Temperature Ltd. 26F 1L. B4 bogies. ae. pt. payphone. ETH 6X.

1200/3/6/11/14/16/20/52/5/6. Lot No. 30845 Derby 1973. 33 t.
1201/4/5/7/8/10/12/13/15/17–9/21/50/1/4/7/9. Lot No. 30859 Derby 1973–4. 33 t.
1202/9/53/8. Lot No. 30873 Derby 1974–5. 33 t.

Note: 1200–2/5/7/9/10/10/2/4/7/20 were also numbered 6459/45/56/38/22/57/62/53/33/44/32 respectively when declassified prior to conversion.

1200	(3287)	I	ICCX	PC	1216	(3302)	I	ICCX	PC
1201	(3361)	I	ICCX	PC	1217	(3357)	I	ICCX	PC
1202	(3436)	I	ICCX	PC	1218	(3332)	I	ICCX	MA
1203	(3291)	I	ICCX	MA	1219	(3418)	I	ICCX	MA
1204	(3401)	I	ICCX	PC	1220	(3315)	I	ICCX	PC
1205	(3329)	I	ICCX	PC	1221	(3371)	I	ICCX	MA
1206	(3319)	I	ICCX	PC	1250	(3372)	I	ICCX	MA
1207	(3328)	I	ICCX	PC	1251	(3383)	I	ICCX	MA
1208	(3393)	I	ICCX	PC	1252	(3280)	I	ICCX	MA
1209	(3437)	I	ICCX	PC	1253	(3432)	I	ICCX	MA
1210	(3405)	I	ICCX	PC	1254	(3391)	I	ICCX	MA
1211	(3305)	I	ICCX	PC	1255	(3284)	I	ICCX	MA
1212	(3427)	I	ICCX	PC	1256	(3296)	I	ICCX	MA
1213	(3419)	I	ICCX	PC	1258	(3322)	I	ICCX	MA
1214	(3317)	I	ICCX	MA	1259	(3439)	I	ICCX	MA
1215	(3377)	I	ICCX	PC	1260	(3378)	I	ICCX	MA

AJ41 (RBR) — RESTAURANT BUFFET

Dia. AJ403. Mark 1. Gas cooking. Built with 23 loose chairs (dia. AJ402). All remaining vehicles refurbished with 23 (21 w) fixed polypropylene chairs and fluorescent lighting. Commonwealth bogies. pt. ETH 2 (2X*).

Coaches with suffix 'R' in sector code have been further refurbished. 21 chairs, payphone, wheelchair space and carpets (Dia. AJ417).

Lot No. 30628 Pressed Steel 1960–61. d. 39 t.

1644	a	I	ICHV	BN	1653	aw	I	ICHH	OM
1645	a	I	ICHV	BN	1655	a	I	ICHH	CL
1646	a	I	ICHH	OM	1658	a	I	ICCL	DY
1647	a	I	IANR	NC	1659	a	I	ICHV	OM
1649	aw	I	ICHH	BN	1663	x*	I	ICHH	BN
1650	aw	I	ICHH	BN	1666	x*	I	ICCL	DY
1651	aw	I	IXXZ	NC	1667	x	I	ICHV	BN
1652	aw	I	ICHH	BN	1670	x*w		ICHH	BN

1671	x* p	I	IANR	NC		1686	a p	I	IANR	NC
1672	x*	I	ICHV	BN		1688	aw		ICCL	DY
1673	aw		ICHH	BN		1689	a p	I	IANR	NC
1674	a	I	ICHV	BN		1691	a p	I	IANR	NC
1675	x*	I	ICHV	BN		1692	a p	I	IANR	NC
1678	x*	I	ICHV	BN		1693	x*	I	ICHV	BN
1679	a	I	ICHV	BN		1696	a p	I	IANR	NC
1680	x*w	M	ICHL	BN		1697	a p	I	IANR	NC
1683	a p	I	IANR	NC		1698	a	I	ICHV	OM
1684	x*		ICHH	BN		1699	a p	I	IANR	NC

AN21 (RMB)   MINIATURE BUFFET CAR

Dia. AN203. Mark 1. Gas cooking. 44S 2L. These vehicles are basically an open standard with two full window spaces removed to accommodate a buffet counter, and four seats removed to for a stock cupboard. All remaining vehicles now have fluorescent lighting. All vehicles have Commonwealth bogies except 1850 (B5). d. ETH 3 (3X*).

1813–1833. Lot No. 30520 Wolverton 1960. 38 t.
1842–1850. Lot No. 30507 Wolverton 1960. 37 t (1850 is 36 t).
1853–1864. Lot No. 30670 Wolverton 1961–2. 38 t.
1865–1876. Lot No. 30702 Wolverton 1962. 38 t.

1842/50/71 have been been refurbished and are fitted with a microwave oven and payphone. Dia. AN208.

1813	x*pt	I	ICHH	CL		1857	x pt		IXXH	IS
1832	x	I	ICHS	LL		1860	x	I	ICHH	CL
1833	x*	I	PISX	IS		1863	x pt		ICHH	CL
1842	x pt	I	ICCL	PC		1864	x pt		PXXZ	IS
1845	x		IXXH	PM		1865	v p	N	PXXZ	IS
1850	v pt	I	ICCR	DY		1871	x pt	I	ICCL	PC
1853	x	I	ICHS	LL		1876	a	I	ICHH	CL
1854	x pt	I	PXXZ	IS						

AJ41 (RBR)   RESTAURANT BUFFET

Dia. AJ414. Mark 1. Gas cooking. These vehicles were built as unclassified restaurant (RU). All remaining vehicles were rebuilt with buffet counter and 21 fixed polypropylene chairs (RBS). They were then further refurbished by fitting fluorescent lighting and reclassified RBR. ad. w pt. ETH 2 (2X*).

1954. Lot No. 30575 Ashford/Eastleigh 1960. B4/B5 bogies. 36.5 t.
1959–1984. Lot No. 30632 Ashford/Eastleigh 1960–61. Commonwealth bogies. 39 t.

1954		IXXZ	NC		1970		IXXZ	BN	
1959	I	IXXZ	OM		1971	I	IXXZ	BN	
1961	I	IXXH	NC		1972		IXXZ	BN	
1966	I	ICCL	DY		1984		IXXZ	BN	
1969	I	IXXZ	NC						

AU51 CHARTER TRAIN STAFF COACHES

Dia. AU501. Mark 1. Converted from BCKs. ETH 2.

Lot No. 30732 Derby 1964. Commonwealth bogies. ae. 37 t.

| 2833 | (21270) | I | ICHV | | BN | | 2834 | (21267) | I | ICHV | | BN |

AT5 ROYAL SALOONS

Non-standard livery: All Royal vehicles are in Royal purple.

AT51. Royal Saloon (Royal family or household).

Dia AT501. Mark 1. This vehicle is a side corridor with a lounge, four bedrooms and a bathroom. Air conditioned. Converted 1977 from vs to ae and B5 bogies. Lot No. 30130 Wolverton 1955. ETH 5X. 42 t.

2900 **0**   ICHX   ZN

AT51. Royal Saloon (Private secretary and Royal household).

Dia AT503. Mark 1. This vehicle is a side corridor with an attendant's compartment, three bedrooms two bathrooms and a lounge/office compartment. Air conditioned. Converted 1977 from vs to ae and B5 bogies.

Lot No. 30131 Wolverton 1957. ETH 5X. 42 t.

2901 **0**   ICHX   ZN

AT5G. The Queen's Saloon.

Dia. AT525. Mark 3. Converted from a mark 3 FO built 1972. Consists of a lounge, bedroom and bathroom for the Queen, and a combined bedroom and bathroom for the Queen's dresser. One entrance vestibule has double doors. Air conditioned. ae. BT10 bogies. Lot No. 30886 Wolverton 1977. ETH 9X. 36 t.

2903 (11001) **0**   ICHX   ZN

AT5G. The Duke of Edinburgh's Saloon.

Dia. AT526. Mark 3. Converted from a mark 3 TSO built 1972. Consists of a combined lounge/dining room, a bedroom and a shower room for the Duke, a kitchen and a valet's bedroom and bathroom. Air conditioned. ae. BT10 bogies. Lot No. 30887 Wolverton 1977. ETH 15X. 36 t.

2904 (12001) **0**   ICHX   ZN

AT5B. Staff Couchette/Power Brake.

Dia. AT527. Mark 2B. Converted from a Mk. 2B BFK built 1969. Consists of luggage accommodation, guard's compartment, 350 kW diesel generator and Staff sleeping accommodation. Pressure ventilated. ae. B5 bogies. Lot No. 30888 Wolverton 1977. ETH 5X. 46 t.

2905 (14105) **0**   ICHX   ZN

AT5B. Staff Couchette.

Dia. AT528. Mark 2B. Converted from a Mk. 2B BFK built 1969. Pressure ventilated. ae. B5 bogies. Lot No. 30889 Wolverton 1977. ETH 4X. 35.5 t.

2906 (14112) **0**   ICHX   ZN

AT51 (RF). First Class Restaurant.

Dia. AT517. Mark 1. Gas cooking. 24F. B5 bogies. ETH 2. Lot No. 30633 Swindon 1961. 41 t.

2907 (325) **0**   ICHX   ZN

AT5G. Royal Train Staff Sleeping Cars.

Dia. AT531. Mark 3A Details as for 10646–732 except that controlled emission toilets are not fitted. Lot No. 31002 Derby/Wolverton 1985. 42.5 t.

2914   **0**   ICHX   ZN |2915   **0**   ICHX   ZN

AT5G Royal Dining Car.

Lot No. 31059 Wolverton 1986. Dia. AT537.

2916 (40512) **0**   ICHX   ZN

AT5G New Royal Vehicles. Full details not available.

Lot Nos. 31083/4/5 Wolverton 1989. Dias. AT539/8/40 respectively.

2917 (40514) **0**   ICHX   ZN |2919 (40518) **0**   ICHX   ZN
2918 (40515) **0**   ICHX   ZN

AT5B. Royal Staff Vehicles. Full details not available. 2920 is a staff/generator vehicle.

Lot Nos. 31034/86 Wolverton 1986/90. Dia. AT536/41.

2920 (17109) **0**   ICHX   ZN |2921 (17107) **0**   ICHX   ZN

AT5G. Royal Sleeping Car.

Lot No. 31035 Derby/Wolverton 1987. Dia. AT534.

2922 **0**   ICHX   ZN

AT5G. The Prince of Wales's Saloon.

Lot No. 31036 Derby/Wolverton 1987. Dia. AT535.

2923 **0**   ICHX   ZN

AD11 (FO)   OPEN FIRST

Dia. AD103. Mark 1. 42F 2L. ETH 3. d. Now fitted with table lights for use in first class charter trains. pa.

Lot No. 30576 BRCW 1959. B4 bogies. 33 t.

3097 a **I** ICHV   BN |3100 x **I** ICHV   BN
3098 a **I** ICHV   BN

Later design with fluorescent lighting, aluminium window frames and Commonwealth bogies. pa.

3107–3127. Lot No. 30697 Swindon 1962–3. 36 t.
3131–3150. Lot No. 30717 Swindon 1963. 36 t.

Note: 3136/41/3/4/6/7/8 were renumbered 1060/3/5/6/8/9/70 when reclassified RUO, then 3605/8/9/2/6/4/10 when declassified, but have now regained their original numbers.

Note: 3131–3 are on loan to Flying Scotsman Services.

3107	x	I	ICHV	BN	3133	x	**M** ICHL	BN
3111	x	I	ICHV	BN	3134	x	I ICHV	BN
3114	x	I	ICHV	BN	3136	a	I ICHV	BN
3115	x	I	ICHV	BN	3140	x	I ICHV	BN
3118	x	I	ICHV	BN	3141	a	I ICHV	BN
3119	x	I	ICHV	BN	3143	a	I ICHV	BN
3120	x	I	ICHV	BN	3144	a	I ICHV	BN
3121	a	I	ICHV	BN	3146	a	I ICHV	BN
3123	a	I	ICHV	BN	3147	a	I ICHV	BN
3124	a	I	ICHV	BN	3148	a	I ICHV	BN
3127	a	I	ICHV	BN	3149	a	I ICHV	BN
3131	x	**M**	ICHL	BN	3150	a	I ICHV	BN
3132	x	**M**	ICHL	BN				

AD1D (FO)   OPEN FIRST

Dia. AD105. Mark 2D. Air conditioned. 3172–88 have Stones equipment. 3192/3202 have Temperature Ltd and require at least 800 V train heating supply. 42F 2L. B4 bogies. ae. pa. ETH 5.

Lot No. 30821 Derby 1971–2. 32.5 t.

3172	I	ICHH	CL	3186	I	ICCL	PC
3174	I	ICHH	CL	3187	I	ICHH	CL
3178	I	ICHV	OM	3188	I	ICHH	CL
3181	I	ICHV	BN	3192	I	ICHV	OM
3182	I	ICCL	PC	3202	I	ICHH	CL

AD1E (FO)   OPEN FIRST

Dia. AD106. Mark 2E. Air conditioned. Stones equipment. Require at least 800 V train heating supply. 42F 2L (41F 2L w). B4 bogies. ae. pa. ETH 5.

† Fitted with power supply for Mk. 1 RBR.

Lot No. 30843 Derby 1972–3. 32.5 t.

3221	w	I	IANR	NC	3230		I	IWRL	OM
3223	n	I	ICHX	BN	3231		I	ICHV	OM
3224		I	ICCX	DY	3232	w	I	IANX	NC
3225		I	IXXZ	DY	3233			ICHX	BN
3226		I	IWRL	OM	3234	w	I	IANX	NC
3227		I	ICHV	OM	3235	†	I	IANX	NC
3228		I	IANR	NC	3236		I	ICCX	PC
3229		I	IANX	NC	3237		I	ICHV	OM

3238	I	ICCX	PC	3257	wtI	IANX	PC
3239	I	IANX	NC	3258	n I	IXXT	NC
3240	I	ICCX	DY	3259	wtI	IANX	NC
3241	I	IANX	NC	3261	w I	IANX	NC
3242	wtI	IANX	NC	3262	I	IANX	NC
3244	w I	IANR	NC	3263	I	ICHV	OM
3245	I	ICCX	DY	3264	I	ICHV	OM
3246	w I	IANX	NC	3265	I	ICHV	OM
3247	I	IMLX	DY	3266	† I	IANX	NC
3248	I	IMLX	DY	3267	I	ICHX	BN
3249	† I	IANX	NC	3268	I	IWRL	OM
3250	w I	IANX	NC	3269	I	ICCX	DY
3251	wtI	IANX	NC	3270	I	ICHV	OM
3252	w I	ICCX	DY	3271	I	IWRX	OM
3253	I	IWRX	OM	3272	I	ICHV	OM
3254	I	ICCX	PC	3273	I	IMLX	DY
3255	n I	IWRX	OM	3275	I	ICHV	OM
3256	w I	ICCX	DY				

AD1F (FO) OPEN FIRST

Dia. AD107. Mark 2F. Air conditioned. 3277–3318/58–81 have Stones equipment, others have Temperature Ltd. 42F 2L. B4 bogies. ae. pa. ETH 5X.

3277–3318. Lot No. 30845 Derby 1973. 33 t.
3325–3428. Lot No. 30859 Derby 1973–4. 33 t.
3429–3438. Lot No. 30873 Derby 1974–5. 33 t.

Refurbished vehicles have power-operated vestibule doors, new panels and seat trim. These are denoted by the "R" suffix in the sector code.

3277	I	IWCR	OY	3334	I	IANR	NC
3278	I	IWCR	MA	3336	I	IANR	NC
3279	I	IANR	NC	3337	I	IWCR	OY
3285	I	IWCR	OY	3338	I	IANR	NC
3290	I	IWCR	OY	3340	I	IWCR	OY
3292	I	IWCR	OY	3344	I	IWCR	MA
3293	I	IWCR	MA	3345	I	IWCR	OY
3295	I	IWCR	OY	3348	I	IWCR	OY
3299	I	IWCR	OY	3350	I	IWCR	MA
3300	I	IWCR	OY	3351	I	IWCR	OY
3303	I	IANR	NC	3352	I	IWCR	MA
3304	I	IWCR	OY	3353	I	IWCX	OY
3309	I	IWCR	MA	3354	I	IWCR	OY
3312	I	IWCR	MA	3356	I	IWCR	MA
3313	I	IWCR	OY	3358	I	IWCR	MA
3314	I	IWCR	MA	3359	I	IWCR	MA
3318	I	IWCR	OY	3360	I	IWCX	OY
3325	I	IWCR	OY	3362	I	IWCX	OY
3326	I	IWCR	OY	3363	I	IWCR	OY
3330	I	IWCR	OY	3364	I	IWCR	MA
3331	I	IWCR	OY	3366	I	IWCR	OY
3333	I	IWCR	OY	3368	I	IWCR	OY

3369	I	IWCR	OY	3400	I	IWCR	OY
3373	I	IWCR	MA	3402	I	IWCR	OY
3374	I	IWCR	MA	3403	I	IWCR	OY
3375	I	IWCR	OY	3408	I	IWCR	MA
3379	I	IANR	NC	3411	I	IWCR	OY
3381	I	IWCR	OY	3414	I	IWCR	OY
3384	I	IWCR	OY	3416	I	IWCR	OY
3385	I	IWCR	OY	3417	I	IWCR	OY
3386	I	IWCR	OY	3424	I	IWCR	OY
3387	I	IWCR	OY	3425	I	IWCR	OY
3388	I	IWCR	MA	3426	I	IWCX	MA
3389	I	IWCR	OY	3428 n	I	IWCR	OY
3390	I	IWCR	MA	3429	I	IWCR	OY
3392	I	IWCR	MA	3431	I	IWCR	OY
3395	I	IWCR	OY	3433	I	IWCR	OY
3397	I	IWCR	OY	3434	I	IWCR	OY
3399	I	IANR	NC	3438	I	IWCR	OY

AG1F (FO)   OPEN FIRST (TROLLEY)

Dia. Ag101. Mark 2F. Air conditioned. to be converted from FO. 36F 1L. B4 bogies. ae. pa. ETH 5X.

3520	3523
3521	3524
3522	3525

AC21 (TSO)   OPEN STANDARD

Dia. AC204. Mark 1. These vehicles have 2+2 seating and are classified TSO ('Tourist second open'–a former LNER designation). TSOs numbered below 4098 have narrower seats than later vehicles. These narrow seats are also fitted to the later batch adjacent to the vestibule end doors. 64S 2L. BR1 bogies. ETH 4.

3769/71. Lot No. 30079 York 1953. 32.5 t.
3958/61. Lot No. 30086 Ashford/Eastleigh 1954–5. 33 t.
4420. Lot No. 30226 BRCW 1956–7. 33 t.

3769	vd	PHTX	HT	3961	vd	PHTX	HT
3771	vd	PHTX	HT	4420	vd	PHTX	HT
3958	vd	PHTX	HT				

AD21 (SO)   OPEN STANDARD

Dia. AD201. Mark 1. This vehicle has 2+1 seating. Vehicles of this type were often used as second class dining cars when new. 48S 2L. BR1 bogies. ETH 4.

Lot No. 30376 York 1957. 33 t.

4809	vd	PPCX	PC

AC21 (TSO) OPEN STANDARD

Dia. AC201. Mark 1. Development of dia. AC204 with fluorescent lighting and modified design of seat headrest. Built with BR1 bogies but most rebuilt with B4 bogies. 64S 2L. ETH 4.

Note: 4860, 5032/5 are on loan to Flying Scotsman Services and 4856 is on loan to the SRPS at Bo'ness.

Lot No. 30506 Wolverton 1959. xd. Commonwealth bogies. pa. 35 t.

| 4830 | | **N** NWRX | OM | |

Lot No. 30525 Wolverton 1959–60. d. B4 bogies except where otherwise stated. 33 t. (35 t BR1).

4842	x	ICHS	LL	4869	x	**I** ICHS	LL
4849	v pa	**N** NWRX	OM	4873	v pa	**N** NWRX	OM
4854	v pa	**N** NWRX	OM	4875	v pa	**N** NWRX	OM
4856	x	ICHL	BO	4876	v pa	**N** NWRX	OM
4858	x	**I** ICHS	LL	4880	v pa	**N** NWRX	OM
4860	x	**M** ICHL	BN	4884	v pa	**N** NWRX	OM
4862	v pa	**N** NWRX	OM	4891	v	**N** NWRX	OM
4864	vBR1	PPCX	PC	4895	v pa	**N** NWRX	OM
4866	v pa	**N** NWRX	OM	4899	v pa	**N** NWRX	OM
4867	v pa	**N** NWRX	OM				

Lot No. 30646 Wolverton 1961. Built with Commonwealth bogies, but BR1 bogies substituted by the SR. Most now re-rebogied. BR1 bogies except where stated otherwise. d. 35 t. (34 t B4, 36 t C).

4901	v C	**N** NWRX	OM	4909	x B4	**I** ICHS	LL
4902	x B4	**I** ICHS	LL	4910	vCpa	**N** NWRX	OM
4903	v	PHTX	HT	4913	vCpa	**N** NWRX	OM
4904	v	PHTX	HT	4915	x B4	**I** ICHS	BN
4905	vCpa	**N** NWRX	OM	4916	x B4	**I** ICHS	LL
4906	v	PHTX	HT	4917	vCpa	**N** PDYX	DY

Lot No. 30690 Wolverton 1961–2. Commonwealth bogies and aluminium window frames. d. 37 t.

f–Facelifted with new laminate, new diffusers etc.

4919	afpa	**I** ICHD	LL	4946	afpa	**I** ICHD	LL
4923	v pa	**N** NWRX	OM	4949	a pa	**I** ICHD	LL
4925	a pa	**I** ICHD	LL	4951	v pa	**N** NWRX	OM
4927	afpa	**I** ICHD	LL	4955	v pa	**N** NWRX	OM
4930	afpa	**I** ICHD	LL	4956	a pa	**I** ICHD	LL
4931	v	**N** NWRX	OM	4959	a pa	**I** ICHD	LL
4933	v	**N** NWRX	OM	4960	v	**E** ICHS	BN
4936	v pa	**N** NWRX	OM	4961	afpa	**I** ICHD	LL
4938	a pa	**I** ICHD	LL	4963	a pa	**I** ICHD	LL
4939	a pa	**I** ICHD	LL	4966	afpa	**I** ICHD	LL
4940	v pa	**N** NWRX	OM	4973	v pa	**N** NWRX	OM
4943	v	**N** NWRX	OM	4974	v	PLLX	LL
4945	v pa	**N** NWRX	OM	4977	a pa	**I** ICHD	LL

4979	afpa	**I**	ICHD	LL
4980	v pa	**N**	NWRX	OM
4984	v	**E**	ICHS	BN
4986	a pa	**I**	ICHD	LL
4990	v pa	**N**	NWRX	OM
4991	a pa	**I**	ICHD	LL
4992	v pa	**N**	NWRX	OM
4993	a pa	**I**	ICHD	LL
4994	v pa	**N**	NWRX	OM
4996	afpa	**I**	ICHD	LL
4998	a pa	**I**	ICHD	LL
4999	a pa	**I**	ICHD	LL
5000	v pa	**N**	NWRX	OM
5001	afpa	**I**	ICHD	LL
5002	a pa	**I**	ICHD	LL
5003	v pa	**N**	NWRX	OM
5005	a pa	**I**	ICHD	LL
5007	a pa	**I**	ICHD	LL
5008	afpa	**I**	ICHD	LL
5009	a pa	**I**	ICHD	LL
5010	a pa	**I**	ICHD	LL
5023	a pa	**I**	ICHD	LL
5024	v pa	**N**	NWRX	OM
5025	a pa	**I**	ICHD	LL
5027	a pa	**I**	ICHD	LL
5028	x		ICHL	PH
5029	a pa	**I**	ICHD	LL
5030	a pa	**I**	ICHD	LL
5032	x	**M**	ICHL	BN
5033	a pa	**I**	ICHD	LL
5035	x	**M**	ICHL	BN
5037	a pa	**I**	ICHD	LL
5038	x	**I**	ICHS	LL
5039	v pa	**N**	PDYX	DY
5040	x	**I**	ICHS	LL
5041	a pa	**I**	ICHD	LL
5042	x	**I**	ICHS	LL
5044	a pa	**I**	ICHD	LL

AC2Z (TSO) OPEN STANDARD

Dia. AC205. Mark 2. Pressure ventilated. 64S 2L. B4 bogies. vd. ETH 4.

*–Air braked by means of disc brakes.

Lot No. 30751 Derby 1965–7. 32 t.

5085		**N**	NWRX	OM
5090		**N**	NWRX	OM
5104		**N**	NWRX	OM
5105		**N**	NWRX	OM
5113		**N**	NWRX	OM
5132	pa	**E**	PISX	IS
5133			PISX	IS
5135			PISX	IS
5136		**N**	NWRX	OM
5138		**N**	PDYX	DY
5139	pa	**E**	PISX	IS
5140		**N**	NWRX	OM
5141		**N**	NWRX	OM
5145	pa		PISX	IS
5147	*	**P**	PHTX	HT
5148	pa		PISX	IS
5149	pa		PISX	IS
5150		**N**	PDYX	DY
5152	* pa	**PS**	PXXZ	EC
5154	pa	**E**	PISX	IS
5156	pa		PISX	IS
5157		**RS**	PISX	IS
5158		**N**	PDYX	DY
5159		**RS**	PISX	IS
5161		**NS**	PISX	IS
5162		**N**	NWRX	OM
5163			PISX	IS
5166	pa	**E**	PISX	IS
5167		**NS**	PISX	IS
5171		**N**	NWRX	OM
5173		**NS**	PISX	IS
5174	pa	**RS**	PISX	IS
5175		**N**	NWRX	OM
5177		**NS**	PISX	IS
5179		**RS**	PISX	IS
5180		**N**	PDYX	DY
5181		**N**	NWRX	OM
5183		**NS**	PISX	IS
5184		**RS**	PISX	IS
5186		**NS**	PISX	IS
5191	pa	**E**	PISX	IS
5193	pa	**E**	PISX	IS
5194		**NS**	PISX	IS
5198		**NS**	PISX	IS
5199		**N**	NWRX	OM
5200		**N**	NWRX	OM
5204		**N**	NWRX	OM
5207	pa		PISX	IS
5209		**NS**	PISX	IS
5210		**N**	PDYX	DY

5211		N	NWRX	OM	5220	N	NWRX	OM

5211		**N**	NWRX	OM	5220		**N**	NWRX	OM
5212	pa	**E**	PISX	IS	5221	pa		PISX	IS
5213		**N**	PDYX	DY	5222		**N**	NWRX	OM
5215		**N**	NWRX	OM	5225		**NS**	PISX	IS
5216		**N**	NWRX	OM	5226		**NS**	PISX	IS
5219		**N**	NWRX	OM	5228		**N**	PXXZ	LL

Named vehicles:

5132	CLAN MUNRO	5191	CLAN DONALD
5139	CLAN ?	5193	CLAN MACLEOD
5154	CLAN FRASER	5212	CAPERKAILZIE
5166	CLAN MACKENZIE		

AD2Z (SO) OPEN STANDARD

Dia. AD203. Mark 2. Pressure ventilated. 48S 2L. B4 bogies. Originally used as restaurant cars. d. ETH 4. (5251–6 are pa fitted).

Note: 5230 has been converted to an SO(T), seats 40S 1L and is named CORRIEMOILLIE.

Lot No. 30752 Derby 1966.

5230	v	**E**	PISX	IS	5246	a		PDYX	DY
5232	v		PXXZ	IS	5251	a		PNCX	NC
5233	v		PISX	IS	5255	a		PNCX	NC
5234	v		PISX	IS	5256	a	**N**	PNCX	NC

AC2A (TSO) OPEN STANDARD

Dia. AC206. Mark 2A. Pressure ventilated. 64S 2L. B4 bogies. ad. ETH 4.

5257–5345. Lot No. 30776 Derby 1967–8. 32 t.
5349–5433. Lot No. 30787 Derby 1968. 32 t.

5259			PDYX	DY	5301		**P**	PDYX	DY
5261	pa	**N**	NWXX	OM	5304		**P**	PLLX	LL
5264		**N**	PNCX	NC	5307	pa		PDYX	DY
5265	pa	**N**	NWXX	OM	5309		**N**	NWXX	OM
5266		**P**	PLLX	LL	5311		**P**	PDYX	DY
5267		**P**	PLLX	LL	5314			PDYX	DY
5270	pa		PNCX	NC	5316		**P**	PLLX	LL
5271	pa	**P**	PLLX	LL	5322		**N**	NWXX	EH
5272	pa		PDYX	DY	5323		**P**	PDYX	DY
5275		**N**	NWXX	OM	5331	pa	**N**	NWXX	OM
5276	pa	**N**	NWXX	OM	5335		**N**	NWXX	EH
5278	pa	**N**	NWXX	OM	5336	pa	**N**	NWXX	OM
5279	pa		PDYX	DY	5337			PDYX	DY
5282	pa	**P**	PLLX	LL	5341		**N**	PLLX	LL
5290	pa	**N**	NWXX	OM	5345	pa	**N**	NWXX	OM
5291		**P**	PDYX	DY	5349			PDYX	DY
5292	pa		PDYX	DY	5350	pa	**N**	NWXX	OM
5293		**N**	NWXX	OM	5353	pa	**P**	PLLX	LL
5300	pa		PDYX	DY	5354		**P**	PLLX	LL

5362	**N**	PNCX	NC	5396	**P**	PLLX	LL
5364		PLLX	LL	5398	pa **N**	NWXX	OM
5365	**P**	PDYX	DY	5401	pa **P**	PLLX	LL
5366	**P**	PLLX	LL	5402		PDYX	DY
5372		IXXZ	MA	5404	pa **N**	NWXX	OM
5373	**N**	NWXX	OM	5406	**P**	PDYX	DY
5376	**N**	NWXX	OM	5408	pa **N**	NWXX	EH
5378	**N**	NWXX	OM	5410	**N**	NWXX	EH
5379	**P**	PDYX	DY	5412	**N**	NWXX	OM
5381	pa **N**	NWXX	OM	5414	**P**	PDYX	DY
5382	**N**	PNCX	NC	5416		PDYX	DY
5384	pa **N**	NWXX	OM	5418	**N**	NWXX	EH
5385	**P**	PLLX	LL	5419	pa **N**	NWXX	EH
5386	**P**	PLLX	LL	5420	pa **N**	NWXX	OM
5389	pa **N**	NWXX	OM	5429		PDYX	DY
5391	**P**	PDYX	DY	5432	**P**	PLLX	LL
5392	pa	PDYX	DY	5433	pa **N**	NWXX	OM
5393	pa **P**	PLLX	LL				

AC2B (TSO)   OPEN STANDARD

Dia. AC207. Mark 2B. Pressure ventilated. 62S 2L. B4 bogies. ad. ETH 4.
Lot No. 30791 Derby 1969. 32 t.

5435	pa **N**	NWXX	OM	5465	pa **N**	NWXX	OM
5436	pa **N**	NWXX	EH	5468	pa **N**	NWXX	OM
5439	**N**	NWXX	EH	5470	pa **N**	NWXX	OM
5443	**N**	NWXX	EH	5471	**N**	NWXX	EH
5444	pa **N**	NWXX	OM	5472	pa **N**	NWXX	OM
5446	pa **N**	NWXX	OM	5474	pa **N**	NWXX	OM
5447	pa **N**	NWXX	OM	5475	pa **N**	NWXX	OM
5448	pa **N**	NWXX	OM	5478		PDYX	DY
5449	pa **N**	NWXX	OM	5480	pa **N**	NWXX	OM
5450	pa **N**	NWXX	OM	5482	pa **N**	NWXX	OM
5451	pa **N**	NWXX	OM	5484	**N**	NWXX	EH
5452	**N**	PNCX	NC	5486		PXXZ	DY
5454	pa **N**	NWXX	OM	5487		PDYX	DY
5455	**N**	NWXX	OM	5488		PXXZ	EC
5456	pa **N**	NWXX	OM	5491	**P**	PLLX	LL
5458	**N**	NWXX	EH	5492	pa **N**	NWXX	OM
5459		PDYX	DY	5494	pa **N**	NWXX	OM
5462	pa **N**	NWXX	OM	5495	pa **N**	NWXX	OM
5463	**P**	PDYX	DY	5497	pa **N**	NWXX	OM
5464	pa **N**	NWXX	EH				

AC2C (TSO)   OPEN STANDARD

Dia. AC208. Mark 2C. Pressure Ventilated. 62S 2L. B4 bogies. ad. pa. ETH 5.
Lot No. 30795 Derby 1969–70. 32.4 t.

5505	**P**	PLLX	LL	5520	**P**	PNCX	NC
5509		PNCX	NC	5554		PLLX	LL

5557		PDYX	DY	5605		PXXZ	DY
5569		PDYX	DY	5614	P	PDYX	DY
5586		PNCX	NC				

AC2D (TSO)   OPEN STANDARD

Dia. AC209. Mark 2D. Air conditioned. Stones (5653 has Temperature Ltd.) equipment. 62S 2L. B4 bogies. ae. pa. ETH 5.

Lot No. 30822 Derby 1971. 33 t.

5616	I	IANX	NC	5669	I	IANR	NC
5617	I	ICCL	PC	5671	I	ICCR	PC
5618	I	ICCR	PC	5672	I	IWCL	WB
5619	I	IANR	NC	5673	I	ICCR	PC
5620	I	ICCR	PC	5674	I	IXXT	DY
5621	I	IANX	NC	5675	I	ICCL	PC
5623	I	ICCR	PC	5676	I	ICCR	PC
5624	I	ICCR	PC	5678	I	ICCL	PC
5625	I	IWCX	WB	5679	I	IANR	NC
5626	I	ICCR	PC	5681	I	ICCL	PC
5628	I	IANR	NC	5682	I	ICCR	PC
5629	I	IANR	NC	5684	I	ICCL	PC
5630	I	ICCL	PC	5685	I	ICCR	PC
5631	I	ICCR	PC	5686	I	ICCR	PC
5632	I	ICCR	PC	5687	I	NWXX	OM
5633	I	ICCL	PC	5689	I	IANX	NC
5634	I	ICCR	PC	5690	I	ICCR	PC
5636	I	ICCR	PC	5692	I	ICCR	PC
5637	I	ICCL	PC	5693	I	IANR	NC
5638	I	ICCR	PC	5694	I	IXXT	DY
5639	I	IWCX	WB	5695	I	IANR	NC
5640	I	IXXT	WB	5699	I	IXXT	WB
5643	I	IXXT	DY	5700	I	ICCR	PC
5646	I	ICCR	PC	5701	I	IXXT	DY
5647	I	IWRL	OM	5703	I	ICCR	PC
5648	I	ICCL	PC	5705	I	IWCX	WB
5650	I	ICCR	PC	5706	I	IXXT	DY
5651	I	ICCR	PC	5707	I	IXXT	MA
5652	I	ICCR	PC	5708	I	IXXT	DY
5653	I	ICCR	PC	5710	I	ICCR	PC
5654	I	IANR	NC	5711	I	ICCR	PC
5657	I	ICCR	PC	5713	I	IANX	NC
5658	I	ICCR	PC	5715	I	ICCR	PC
5659	I	ICCR	PC	5716	I	IXXT	DY
5660	I	IWCL	WB	5717	I	NWXX	OM
5661	I	IXXT	MA	5718	I	IANX	NC
5662	I	ICCR	PC	5719	I	ICCL	PC
5663	I	ICCX	PC	5722	I	ICCL	PC
5665	I	ICCR	PC	5723	I	ICCR	PC
5666	I	IXXZ	DY	5724	I	ICCR	PC
5667	I	IXXT	DY	5726	I	ICCR	PC
5668	I	IXXZ	NC	5727	I	IXXZ	WB

5728	I	IANR	NC		5735	I	IANX	NC
5729	I	IWCX	WB		5737	I	IANX	NC
5730	I	ICCR	PC		5738	I	ICCX	DY
5731	I	IXXT	NC		5739	I	IANX	NC
5732	I	IANX	NC		5740	I	ICCR	PC
5734	I	IWCL	WB		5743	I	IANR	NC

AC2E (TSO)   OPEN STANDARD

Dia. AC210. Mark 2E. Air conditioned. Stones equipment. 64S 2L (62S 2L w).
B4 bogies. Require at least 800 V train heat supply. ae. pa. ETH 5.

5744–5803. Lot No. 30837 Derby 1972. 33.5 t.
5810–5907. Lot No. 30844 Derby 1972–3. 33.5 t.

5744		I	ICCX	MA		5784		I	ICCR	PC
5745		I	ICCX	DY		5785		I	ICCX	PC
5746		I	ICCR	PC		5786		I	ICCX	PC
5747		I	ICCX	PC		5787		I	ICCX	PC
5748		I	ICCR	PC		5788	w	I	ICCX	MA
5750		I	ICCX	MA		5789		I	ICCR	PC
5751	w	I	ICCR	PC		5791	w	I	ICCR	PC
5752	w	I	ICCX	MA		5792		I	ICCR	PC
5753	w	I	IXXT	MA		5793		I	ICCR	PC
5754	w	I	ICCR	PC		5794		I	ICCR	PC
5755		I	ICCX	PC		5795		I	NWXX	OM
5756		I	IXXZ	WB		5796		I	ICCR	PC
5757		I	IXXT	MA		5797		I	ICCR	PC
5758		I	IXXT	MA		5798		I	IXXT	MA
5759		I	ICCX	PC		5799		I	ICCX	WB
5760		I	ICCR	PC		5800		I	ICCX	MA
5761		I	ICCX	MA		5801		I	ICCR	PC
5762		I	ICCX	PC		5802		I	IXXT	MA
5763		I	NWXX	OM		5803		I	ICCX	MA
5764		I	ICCX	MA		5810		I	NWXX	OM
5766		I	ICCX	MA		5811		I	ICCX	MA
5767	w	I	IXXT	PC		5812	w	I	ICCR	PC
5768		I	ICCX	PC		5813		I	ICCX	PC
5769		I	ICCR	PC		5814		I	ICCR	PC
5770		I	ICCX	MA		5815		I	IWCL	WB
5771		I	IXXT	PC		5816		I	ICCR	PC
5772	w	I	ICCR	PC		5818		I	ICCX	MA
5773		I	ICCX	PC		5820		I	ICCX	MA
5774		I	ICCX	PC		5821		I	ICCR	PC
5775		I	ICCX	MA		5822		I	ICCX	MA
5776		I	ICCR	PC		5823		I	IXXT	MA
5777		I	ICCX	MA		5824		I	ICCR	PC
5778		I	ICCR	PC		5826		I	ICCR	PC
5779		I	ICCX	MA		5827	w	I	ICCX	MA
5780		I	ICCR	PC		5828	w	I	ICCX	MA
5781	w	I	ICCX	MA		5829		I	ICCX	MA
5782		I	IXXT	MA		5831		I	ICCX	MA
5783		I	IXXT	PC		5833		I	ICCX	MA

5834	I	IXXT	MA	5870	I	ICCX	PC
5835	I	ICCX	MA	5871	I	ICCX	MA
5836	I	ICCX	MA	5872	n	IWCX	WB
5837	I	ICCX	MA	5873	I	ICCX	MA
5838	I	IXXT	MA	5874 w	I	ICCX	MA
5839	I	IXXT	MA	5875	I	ICCX	MA
5840	I	ICCX	MA	5876	I	ICCR	PC
5841	I	NWXX	OM	5878	I	ICCX	MA
5842 w	I	ICCX	MA	5879	I	ICCX	MA
5843 w	I	ICCR	PC	5880	I	IXXT	MA
5844	I	IWCL	WB	5881	I	ICCX	PC
5845 w	I	ICCX	MA	5883	I	NWXX	OM
5846	I	NWXX	OM	5884	I	IWCL	WB
5847	I	ICCR	PC	5885	I	ICCX	PC
5849	I	IXXT	MA	5886	I	ICCX	PC
5850	I	ICCL	PC	5887	I	ICCR	PC
5851	I	ICCX	MA	5888 w	I	ICCR	PC
5852	I	ICCX	MA	5889	I	ICCR	PC
5853	I	ICCX	MA	5890	I	ICCX	MA
5854	I	ICCX	MA	5891	I	ICCX	MA
5857	I	IXXT	MA	5892	I	ICCR	PC
5858	I	ICCX	PC	5893	I	ICCR	PC
5859	I	ICCX	MA	5897	I	ICCR	PC
5860 w	I	ICCX	PC	5899	I	ICCR	PC
5861	I	ICCX	MA	5900	I	ICCR	PC
5862	I	IXXT	MA	5901	I	IXXT	MA
5863	I	ICCX	PC	5902	I	ICCX	MA
5864	I	IXXT	MA	5903	I	ICCX	MA
5866	I	ICCX	MA	5904	I	ICCX	PC
5867	I	IXXT	MA	5905	I	ICCR	PC
5868	I	ICCR	PC	5906	I	ICCR	PC
5869	I	ICCR	PC	5907	I	ICCX	PC

AC2F (TSO)   OPEN STANDARD

Dia. AC211. Mark 2F. Air conditioned. Temperature Ltd. equipment. 64S 2L (62S 1L w). B4 bogies. ae. pa. ETH 5X. Inter-City 70 seats.

*–Early Mark 2 style seats.
Refurbished vehicles have power-operated vestibule doors, new panels and seat trim. These are denoted by the "R" suffix in the sector code.

5908–5958. Lot No. 30846 Derby 1973. 33 t.
5959–6170. Lot No. 30860 Derby 1973–4. 33 t.
6171–6184. Lot No. 30874 Derby 1974–5. 33 t.

5908	I	IWCR	OY	5916 w	I	ICCR	DY
5910 w	I	IWCR	OY	5917	I	ICCR	MA
5911	I	IWCR	OY	5918 w	I	ICCX	DY
5912	I	IWCR	OY	5919	I	IWCR	MA
5913	I	IWCR	OY	5920	I	IWCR	OY
5914	I	IWCR	MA	5921	I	IANR	NC
5915	I	IWCR	OY	5922	I	IWCR	MA

No.			Code	Reg	No.			Code	Reg
5924		I	IANR	NC	5983		I	ICCR	MA
5925		I	ICCR	MA	5984	*	I	IWCR	OY
5926		I	IWCR	MA	5985		I	IWCR	OY
5927		I	IANR	NC	5986		I	IWCR	OY
5928		I	IANR	NC	5987	*	I	IWCR	OY
5929		I	IANR	NC	5988	w	I	IWCR	MA
5930		I	ICCR	MA	5989	w	I	ICCR	MA
5931	w	I	IWCR	MA	5991		I	ICCR	DY
5932		I	IWCR	MA	5993	*w	I	ICCR	MA
5933		I	IWCR	OY	5994	*	I	ICCR	MA
5934		I	IWCR	MA	5995		I	ICCR	DY
5935		I	IWCR	MA	5996		I	IWCR	MA
5936		I	IANR	NC	5997		I	IWCR	OY
5937		I	IWCR	OY	5998		I	IANR	NC
5939		I	IWCR	OY	5999		I	ICCR	MA
5940	w	I	IWCR	MA	6000		I	IWCR	OY
5941		I	IWCR	OY	6001	w	I	IWCR	OY
5943	w	I	IWCR	OY	6002		I	IWCR	OY
5944	w	I	IWCR	OY	6005	*	I	ICCR	MA
5945	w	I	IWCR	MA	6006		I	IWCR	MA
5946		I	IWCR	OY	6008		I	IWCR	MA
5947		I	ICCR	MA	6009		I	IWCR	OY
5948	w	I	IWCR	OY	6010	n	I	ICCR	MA
5949	w	I	IWCR	MA	6011		I	ICCR	MA
5950		I	IANR	NC	6012	*	I	IWCR	OY
5951		I	ICCR	MA	6013	*	I	IANR	NC
5952		I	IWCR	MA	6014		I	ICCR	MA
5953		I	IWCR	MA	6015		I	ICCR	DY
5954		I	IANR	NC	6016		I	IWCR	MA
5955		I	IWCR	OY	6018	*	I	IWCR	MA
5956		I	IANR	NC	6021		I	IWCR	MA
5957		I	IWCR	MA	6022	w	I	ICCR	DY
5958		I	IWCR	OY	6024		I	IWCR	OY
5959	n	I	IANR	NC	6025	*	I	ICCR	MA
5960		I	IWCR	MA	6026	*	I	IWCR	OY
5961		I	ICCR	MA	6027	w	I	IWCR	OY
5962		I	ICCR	DY	6028		I	IWCR	OY
5963		I	IWCR	OY	6029		I	IWCR	OY
5964		I	IANR	NC	6030		I	IWCR	OY
5965	w	I	ICCR	DY	6031		I	IWCR	OY
5966		I	IANR	NC	6034		I	IWCR	OY
5967		I	ICCR	MA	6035	w	I	ICCR	DY
5968		I	IANR	NC	6036	*	I	IANR	NC
5969	w	I	IWCR	OY	6037		I	IWCR	MA
5971		I	ICCR	DY	6038		I	IWCR	MA
5973		I	IANR	NC	6041		I	IWCR	MA
5975	*n	I	ICCR	DY	6042		I	IWCR	MA
5976		I	ICCX	DY	6043		I	IWCR	MA
5977		I	IWCR	MA	6045	w	I	IWCR	OY
5978	*	I	IWCR	MA	6046		I	IWCR	MA
5980		I	IWCR	OY	6047	*n	I	IWCR	MA
5981		I	IWCR	OY	6049		I	IWCR	MA

6050		I	ICCR	MA	6138	I	IWCR	MA
6051	*	I	IWCR	OY	6139	*n I	IANR	NC
6052	w	I	IWCR	OY	6141	w I	IWCR	OY
6053	*	I	IANR	NC	6142	* I	IWCR	MA
6054		I	IWCR	OY	6144	* I	IWCR	MA
6055		I	IWCR	OY	6145	* I	ICCX	MA
6056		I	IWCR	OY	6146	* I	IWCR	OY
6057		I	IWCR	OY	6147	* I	IWCR	OY
6059		I	ICCR	MA	6148	* I	ICCR	DY
6060	*	I	IWCR	OY	6149	*w I	IWCR	OY
6061	*	I	IWCR	MA	6150	* I	ICCR	DY
6062	*	I	IWCR	OY	6151	* I	IWCR	OY
6063	w	I	IWCR	OY	6152	* I	IANR	NC
6064		I	IWCR	OY	6153	* I	IWCR	MA
6065		I	IWCR	OY	6154	* I	IWCR	OY
6066		I	IWCR	OY	6155	* I	IANR	NC
6067		I	IWCR	OY	6157	* I	ICCR	MA
6073		I	ICCR	DY	6158	* I	IWCR	OY
6100	*	I	IWCR	MA	6159	*n I	ICCR	MA
6101		I	IWCR	OY	6160	* I	IANR	NC
6102		I	IWCR	MA	6161	* I	IWCR	OY
6103		I	IANR	NC	6162	I	IWCR	OY
6104		I	IWCR	OY	6163	I	IWCR	MA
6105		I	IWCR	OY	6164	I	IWCR	OY
6106		I	IWCR	MA	6165	I	IWCR	MA
6107		I	IWCR	MA	6166	I	IANR	NC
6110	w	I	IWCR	MA	6167	I	IANR	NC
6111		I	IWCR	OY	6168	I	ICCR	DY
6112		I	ICCR	MA	6170	I	IWCR	OY
6113		I	IWCR	OY	6171	I	IWCR	OY
6115		I	IWCR	MA	6172	I	ICCR	MA
6116		I	IWCR	OY	6173	I	IWCR	OY
6117		I	IWCR	OY	6174	I	IANR	NC
6119		I	ICCR	DY	6175	I	IWCR	OY
6120		I	ICCR	MA	6176	w I	IWCR	OY
6121		I	IWCR	MA	6177	I	IWCR	OY
6122		I	IWCR	OY	6178	w I	IWCR	OY
6123		I	IANR	NC	6179	I	IWCR	MA
6124		I	IWCR	OY	6180	w I	IWCR	MA
6134		I	IWCR	MA	6181	wn I	IWCR	MA
6135		I	ICCR	DY	6182	I	ICCR	DY
6136		I	IWCR	MA	6183	I	ICCR	DY
6137		I	ICWR	OY	6184	* I	ICCR	MA

AC2D (TSO)   OPEN STANDARD

Dia. AC217. Mark 2D. Air conditioned. Stones. 58S 2L. B4 bogies. ae. pa.
ETH 5X. Rebuilt from FO with new style 2+2 seats.

Lot No. 30821 Derby 1971–2. 33.5 t.

6200	(3198)	I	IWRX	OM	6202	(3191)	I	IWCX	WB
6201	(3210)	I	IWCX	WB	6203	(3180)	I	IWCX	WB

6204	(3216)	I	ICHX	BN	6220	(3175)	I	IWCX	WB
6205	(3193)	I	ICHX	BN	6221	(3173)	I	IWCX	WB
6206	(3183)	I	ICHX	OM	6222	(3171)	I	IWCX	WB
6207	(3204)	I	IWCX	WB	6223	(3194)	I	ICHX	BN
6208	(3205)	I	IWCX	WB	6224	(3195)	I	IWCX	WB
6209	(3177)	I	ICHX	BN	6225	(3200)	I	ICHX	BN
6210	(3196)	I	IWCX	WB	6226	(3203)	I	IWRX	OM
6211	(3215)	I	IWCX	WB	6227	(3197)	I	IWCL	WB
6212	(3176)	I	IWCX	WB	6228	(3201)	I	IWCX	WB
6213	(3208)	I	IWRX	OM	6229	(3212)	I	IWCX	WB
6214	(3211)	I	IWCX	WB	6230	(3185)	n I	IWCL	WB
6215	(3170)	I	ICHX	BN	6231	(3189)	I	ICHX	BN
6216	(3179)	I	IWCX	WB	6232	(3199)	I	IWCX	WB
6217	(3184)	I	IWCX	WB	6233	(3206)	I	ICHX	BN
6218	(3209)	I	IWCX	WB	6234	(3207)	I	IWCX	WB
6219	(3213)	I	IWCX	WB	6235	(3190)	I	ICHX	BN

AD4Z (OC)   OBSERVATION CAR

Dia.AD401. Converted 1987 from DMU DTCL. DMU bogies. 42U 1L. v. pa.

Lot No. 30468 Metro-Cammell 1958. 25.5 t.

6300 (56356)   E   PISX   IS   HEBRIDEAN

GX51   GENERATOR VAN

Dia. GX501. Renumbered 1989 from BR departmental series. Three-phase supply generator van for use with HST trailers. Often used at times of low availability of HST power cars. Rebuilt from NDA 81448. B5 bogies.

Lot No. 30400 Pressed Steel 1958.   t.

6310 (ADB 975325)   I   IWRR   PM

AZ5Z   SPECIAL SALOON

Dia. AZ501. Renumbered 1989 from LMR departmental series. Formerly the LMR General Manager's saloon. Rebuilt from LMS period 1 BFK M 5033 M to dia. 1654 and mounted on the underframe of BR suburban BS M 43232. B5 bogies. This vehicle has a maximum speed of 100 mph, but is restricted to 60 mph when carrying passengers with screw coupling operative.

LMS Lot No. 326 Derby 1927.   t.

6320 (TDM 395707)   I   ICHV   BN

GS51 (GS5A†)(HSBV)   HST BARRIER VEHICLE

Various diagrams. Renumbered from departmental stock, or converted from BG. Various original types and characteristics. ae. B4 bogies (Commonwealth bogies *).

6330/9. Lot No. 30786 Derby 1968. 32 t.
6332/43. Lot No. 30795 Derby 1969/70. 32 t.

6334. Lot No. 30400 Pressed Steel 1957–8. 31.5 t.
6335. Lot No. 30775 Derby 1967–8. 32 t.
6336/8. Lot No. 30715 Gloucester 1962. 31 t.
6340. Lot No. 30669 Swindon 1962. 36 t.
6341/2. Lot No. 30632 Ashford/Swindon 1961. 38 t.
6343. Lot No. 30091 Doncaster 1954. 33 t.
6344. Lot No. 30163 Pressed Steel 1957. 31.5 t.
6345. Lot No. 30796 Derby 1970. 32.5 t.
6346. Lot No. 30777 Derby 1967. 31.5 t.
6347. Lot No. 30787 Derby 1968. 31.5 t.

6330 (14084, ADB 975629)	GS503		IWRG	OO
6332 (5594)	GS508	I	IECG	EC
6334 (92128)	GS507	I	IECG	NL
6335 (14065, ADB 975655)	GS503	I	IECG	EC
6336 (92185)	GS507	I	IECG	BN
6338 (92180)	GS507	I	IWRG	PM
6339 (14078, ADB 975666)	GS503	I	IWRG	PM
6340 (21251, ADB 975678)	GS504*	I	IWRG	LA
6341 (1967, ADB 975980)	GS505*	I	IWRG	OO
6342 (1983, ADB 975981)	GS505*	I	IWRG	LA
6343 (5522)	GS508	I	IECG	NL
6344 (92080)	GS507	I	IECG	HT
6345 (17137)	GS510	I	IECG	BN
6346 (9422)	GS511	I	IECG	NL
6347 (5395)	GS509	I	IWRG	PM

GF51 (HSBV) MARK 4 BARRIER VEHICLE

Various diagrams. Renumbered from departmental stock, or converted from
FK or BSO. Various original types and characteristics. ae. B4 bogies.
6350. Lot No. 30472 BRCW 1959. 33 t.
6351. Lot No. 30091 Doncaster 1954. 33 t.
6352/3. Lot No. 30774 Derby 1968. 33 t.
6354–6. Lot No. 30820 Derby 1970. 32 t.
6357. Lot No. 30798 Derby 1970. 32 t.
6358–9. Lot No. 30788 Derby 1968. 31.5 t.

6350 (3088, ADB 977434)	AV501	I	IECG	BN
6351 (3050, ADB 977435)	AV501	I	IECG	EC
6352 (19465)	AV502		IECG	BN
6353 (19478)	AV503		IECG	EC
6354 (9459)	AV504	I	IECG	BN
6355 (9477)	AV504		IECG	BN
6356 (9455)	AV504		IECG	BN
6357 (9443)	AV504		IECG	BN
6358 (9432)	AV505		IECG	BN
6359 (9429)	AV505		IECG	BN

AG2C (TSOT) OPEN STANDARD (TROLLEY)

Dia. AG201. Mark 2C. Converted from TSO by removal of one seating bay and replacing this by a counter with a space for a trolley. Adjacent toilet removed and converted to steward's washing area/store. Pressure ventilated. 54S 1L. B4 bogies. ad. pa. ETH 4.

Lot No. 30795 Derby 1969–70. 32.5 t.

6500	(5603)	pt**N**	NWXX	OM	6518	(5503)	pt PDYX	DY
6501	(5547)	pt**N**	NWXX	OM	6521	(5558)	**N** NWXX	OM
6502	(5602)	pt**N**	NWXX	OM	6522	(5611)	pt**N** PNCX	NC
6503	(5510)	pt**N**	NWXX	OM	6523	(5568)	PDYX	DY
6508	(5511)		PDYX	DY	6524	(5564)	PDYX	DY
6510	(5518)	pt	PNCX	NC	6527	(5563)	pt**N** NWXX	OM
6513	(5538)	pt**N**	NWXX	OM	6528	(5592)	PDYX	DY
6517	(5499)	pt**N**	NWXX	OM	6529	(5579)	PDYX	DY

AG2D (TSOT) OPEN STANDARD (TROLLEY)

Dia. AG202. Mark 2D. Converted from TSO by removal of one seating bay and replacing this by a counter with a space for a trolley. Adjacent toilet removed and converted to steward's washing area/store. Air conditioned. Stones equipment. 54S 1L. B4 bogies. ae. pa. ETH 5.

Lot No. 30822 Derby 1971. 33 t.

6601	(5697)	I	IANX	NC	6609	(5698)	I IWRL	OM
6603	(5691)	I	IXXZ	PC	6613	(5702)	I IXXT	PC
6605	(5741)	I	NWXX	OM	6614	(5725)	I NWXX	OM
6607	(5635)	I	IANX	NC	6617	(5733)	I IXXT	NC
6608	(5696)	I	IANX	NC	6619	(5655)	I NWXX	OM

AN2D (RMBT) MINIATURE BUFFET CAR

Dia. AN207. Mark 2D. Converted from TSOT by the removal of another seating bay and fitting a proper buffet counter with boiler and microwave oven. Air conditioned. Stones equipment. 46S 1L. B4 bogies. ae. pa. ETH 5.

Lot No. 30822 Derby 1971. 33 t.

Note: Original numbers shown in parentheses. These vehicles carried 6602/10–2/5 when they were TSOTs.

6652	(5622)	I	ICCX	DY	6662	(5641)	I IWRL	OM
6660	(5627)	I	IWRL	OM	6665	(5721)	I IWRL	OM
6661	(5736)	I	ICCX	DY				

AN1F (RLO) SLEEPER RECEPTION CAR

Dia. AN101 (AN102*). Mark 2F. Converted from FO, these vehicles consist of pantry, microwave cooking facilities, seating area for passengers, telephone booth and staff toilet. 6703–8 also have a bar. Converted at RTC, Derby (6700), Ilford (6701–5) and Derby (6706–8). Air conditioned. ae. B4 bogies.

Fitted with payphone. 26F 1L.

6701–2/4/8. Lot No. 30859 Derby 1973–4. 33.5 t.
6703/5–7. Lot No. 30845 Derby 1973. 33.5 t.

Note: 6705–7 were also numbered 6430/21/18 when declassified prior to conversion.

6700	(3347)	I	IWCX	PC	6705	(3310)	I	IWCX	PC
6701	(3346)	* I	IWCX	PC	6706	(3283)	I	IWCX	PC
6702	(3421)	* I	IWCX	PC	6707	(3276)	I	IWCX	PC
6703	(3308)	I	IWCX	PC	6708	(3370)	I	IWCX	PC
6704	(3341)	I	IWCX	PC					

AC2F (TSO)   OPEN STANDARD

Dia. AC224. Mark 2F. Renumbered 1985–6 from FO. Converted 1990 to TSO with mainly unidirectional seating and power-operated sliding doors. Air conditioned. B4 bogies. 74S 2L + one tip-up seat. 6800–14 were converted by BREL Derby and have Temperature Ltd. air conditioning. 6815–29 were converted by RFS Industries Doncaster and have Stones air conditioning. ae. pa. ETH 5X.

The coaches were also numbered 6435/42/39/43/9/36/40/52/4/5/1/37/48/63/65 and 6420/61/31/27/46/34/58/47/24/29/60/25/8/64/23 respectively.

6800–07. 6810–12. 6813–14. 6819/22/28. Lot No. 30859 Derby 1973–4. 33 t.
6808–6809. Lot No. 30873 Derby 1974–5. 33.5 t.
6815–18. 6820–21. 6823–27. 6829. Lot No. 30845 Derby 1973. 33 t.

6800	(3323)	I	IANR	NC	6815	(3282)	I	IANR	NC
6801	(3349)	I	IANR	NC	6816	(3316)	I	IANR	NC
6802	(3339)	I	IANR	NC	6817	(3311)	I	IANR	NC
6803	(3355)	I	IANR	NC	6818	(3298)	I	IANR	NC
6804	(3396)	I	IANR	NC	6819	(3365)	I	IANR	NC
6805	(3324)	I	IANR	NC	6820	(3320)	I	IANR	NC
6806	(3342)	I	IANR	NC	6821	(3281)	I	IANR	NC
6807	(3423)	I	IANR	NC	6822	(3376)	I	IANR	NC
6808	(3430)	I	IANR	NC	6823	(3289)	I	IANR	NC
6809	(3435)	I	IANR	NC	6824	(3307)	I	IANR	NC
6810	(3404)	I	IMLX	DY	6825	(3301)	I	IMLX	DY
6811	(3327)	I	IMLX	DY	6826	(3294)	I	IMLX	DY
6812	(3394)	I	IMLX	DY	6827	(3306)	I	IMLX	DY
6813	(3410)	I	IMLX	DY	6828	(3380)	I	IMLX	DY
6814	(3422)	I	IMLX	DY	6829	(3288)	I	IMLX	DY

AA31 (CK)   CORRIDOR COMPOSITE

Mark 1. There are two variants: those built for the Eastern, London Midland, North Eastern or Scottish regions which have 6-seater standard class compartments with armrests (24F 18S 2L. Dia. AA301) and those built for the Southern and Western regions which have 8-seater standard class compartments without armrests (24F 24S 2L. dia AA302). All vehicles are assumed to seat 24F 18S, unless marked * (24F 24S). vd. All remaining vehicles were renumbered from the 16xxx series, with the 16 being replaced by a 7 and were built with Commonwealth bogies, metal window frames and melamine finish in the standard class sections. ETH 4.

7153–7190. Lot No. 30665 Derby 1961. 37 t.
7212–7213. Lot No. 30666 Derby 1961. 37 t.
7232–7235. Lot No. 30729 Derby 1963. 37 t.

f–Facelifted with fluorescent lighting, wide mirrors, blinds removed.

7153	**N**	NWRX	OM		7172	**N**	NWRX	OM
7156	**N**	NWRX	OM		7190	**N**	NWRX	OM
7158	**N**	NWRX	OM		7212	*f **N**	NWRX	OM
7165	**N**	NWRX	OM		7213	*f **N**	NWRX	OM
7166	**N**	NWRX	OM		7232	pa **N**	NWRX	OM
7167	**N**	NWRX	OM		7235	pa **N**	NWRX	OM
7168	**N**	NWRX	OM					

AA3C (CK)　　　　CORRIDOR COMPOSITE

Dia. AA304. Mark 2C. Declassified 1985 from FK. Pressure ventilated. 18F 24S 2L. B4 bogies. ad. pa. ETH 4.

Lot No. 30797 Derby 1969–70. 33.5 t.

7550　(13550)　　PDYX　　DY

AH2Z (BSOT)　　OPEN BRAKE STANDARD (MICRO-BUFFET)

Dia. AH203. Mark 2. Converted from BSO by removal of one seating bay and replacing this by a counter with a space for a trolley. Adjacent toilet removed and converted to a steward's washing area/store. 23S 0L. ETH 4.

Lot No. 30757 Derby 1966.

9100	(9405)		PISX	IS		9105 (9404) pt	PISX	IS
9101	(9398)		PISX	IS				

AE2Z (BSO)　　　　OPEN BRAKE STANDARD

Dia. AE203. Mark 2. These vehicles use the same body shell as the mark 2 BFK and have first class seat spacing and wider tables. Pressure ventilated. 31S 1L. B4 bogies. vd. pt. ETH 4.
*–Air braked by means of disc brakes.

Lot No. 30757 Derby 1966. 31.5t (33.5t*).

9382	**N**	NWRX	OM		9391	**N**	NWRX	OM
9384	**N**	NWRX	OM		9396	**N**	NWRX	OM
9385		PISX	IS		9409	**N**	NWRX	OM
9388	**E**	PISX	IS		9412	* **P**	PHTX	HT
9390	**N**	NWRX	OM		9414	**E**	PISX	IS

Named vehicles:

9385 BALMACARA		9414 BRAHAN SEER
9388 BAILECHAUL		

AE2A (BSO)   OPEN BRAKE STANDARD

Dia. AE204. Mark 2A. These vehicles use the same body shell as the mark 2A BFK and have first class seat spacing and wider tables. Pressure ventilated. 31S 1L. B4 bogies. ad. ETH 4.

9417–9424. Lot No. 30777 Derby 1967. 31.5 t.
9428–9438. Lot No. 30788 Derby 1968. 31.5 t.

9417		PLLX	LL	9428	pt	PDYX	DY
9418	pt	PDYX	DY	9431	pt P	PDYX	DY
9419	P	PLLX	LL	9434	pt	PNCX	NC
9420		PDYX	DY	9435	P	PLLX	LL
9421	P	PLLX	LL	9438	I	PDYX	DY
9424	pt P	PLLX	LL				

AE2C (BSO)   OPEN BRAKE STANDARD

Dia. AE205. Mark 2C. Pressure ventilated. 31S 1L. B4 bogies. ad. ETH 4.

9440–9448. Lot No. 30798 Derby 1970. 32 t.
9449–9467. Lot No. 30820 Derby 1970. 32 t.

9440	pt	PDYX	DY	9454	pt	ILAG	LA
9444	pt	PNCX	NC	9458	P	PLLX	LL
9448		PNCX	NC	9460	pt	PDYX	DY
9449		PXXZ	IS	9465	I	IXXH	PM
9451	pt	PLAX	LA	9467		PDYX	DY
9453	pt	ILAG	LA				

AE2D (BSO)   OPEN BRAKE STANDARD

Dia. AE206. Mark 2D. Air conditioned (Stones). 31S 1L. B4 bogies. ae. pg. ETH 5.

Lot No. 30824 Derby 1971. 33 t.

9479	I	IXXT	MA	9488	I	ICCL	PC
9480	I	ICCL	PC	9489	I	IXXT	PC
9481	I	IWRX	OM	9490	I	ICCL	PC
9482	I	IXXT	DY	9492	I	IWRX	OM
9483	I	IMLX	DY	9493	I	ICCL	PC
9484	I	IXXT	PC	9494	I	IXXT	OM
9485	I	ICCX	DY	9495	I	IXXT	WB
9486	I	IMLX	DY				

AE2E (BSO)   OPEN BRAKE STANDARD

Dia. AE207. Mark 2E. Air conditioned (Stones). 32S 1L. B4 bogies. ae. pg. ETH 5.

Lot No. 30838 Derby 1972. 33 t.

9496	I	NWXX	OM	9498	I	IWRL	OM
9497	I	IXXT	PC	9499	I	IXXT	DY

9500	I	IMLX	DY	9505	I	IMLX	DY
9501	I	IWRX	OM	9506	I	ICCX	DY
9502	I	NWXX	OM	9507	I	IXXT	DY
9503	I	IMLX	DY	9508	I	IXXT	DY
9504	I	IXXT	PC	9509	I	ICCX	DY

AE2F (BSO)   OPEN BRAKE STANDARD

Dia. AE208. Mark 2F. Air conditioned (Temperature Ltd.). 32S 1L. B4 bogies. ae. pg. ETH 5X.

Refurbished vehicles have power-operated vestibule doors, new panels and seat trim. These are denoted by the "R" suffix in the sector code.

Lot No. 30861 Derby 1974. 34 t.

9513		I	IWCR	WB	9526	n I	IWCR	WB
9516	n I		IWCR	WB	9527	I	IWCR	WB
9520	n I		IWCR	WB	9529	I	IWCR	WB
9521		I	ICCX	DY	9531	I	IWCR	WB
9522		I	IWCR	WB	9533	I	IWCR	WB
9523		I	IWCR	WB	9537	n I	ICCR	DY
9524	n I		IWCR	WB	9538	I	IWCR	WB
9525		I	IWCX	WB	9539	I	ICCR	DY

AF2F (DBSO)   DRIVING OPEN BRAKE STANDARD

Dia. AF201. Mark 2F. Air conditioned (Temperature Ltd.). Push & pull (t.d.m. system). Converted from BSO, these vehicles originally had half cabs at the brake end. They have since been refurbished and have had their cabs widened and the outer gangways removed. Fitted with cowcatchers. 32S 0L. B4 bogies. ae. pg. Cab to shore communication. BR Cellnet phone and data transmitter. ETH 5X.

9701–9710. Lot No. 30861 Derby 1974. Converted 1979. Disc brakes. 34 t.
9711–9713. Lot No. 30861 Derby 1974. Converted Glasgow 1985. 34 t.
9714. Lot No. 30861 Derby 1974. Converted Glasgow 1986. Disc brakes. 34 t.

9701	(9528)	I	IANR	NC	9709	(9515)	I	IANR	NC
9702	(9510)	I	IANR	NC	9710	(9518)	I	IANR	NC
9703	(9517)	I	IANR	NC	9711	(9532)	I	IANR	NC
9704	(9512)	I	IANR	NC	9712	(9534)	I	IANR	NC
9705	(9519)	I	IANR	NC	9713	(9535)	I	IANR	NC
9707	(9511)	I	IANR	NC	9714	(9536)	I	IANR	NC
9708	(9530)	I	IANR	NC					

AJ1G (RFM)   RESTAURANT BUFFET FIRST (MODULAR)

Dia. AJ103 (10200/1 are Dia. AJ101). Mark 3A. Air conditioned. Converted from HST TRFKs, RFBs and FOs. 22F (24F*). BT10 bogies. ae. pt. Fitted with payphone. ETH 14X.

10200–10211. Lot No. 30884 Derby 1977.
10212–10229. Lot No. 30878 Derby 1975–6. 39.80 t.
10230–10260. Lot No. 30890 Derby 1979. 39.80 t.

10200 (40519) *	I	IWCX	WB	10229 (11059)	I	IWCX	MA
10201 (40520) *	I	IWCX	WB	10230 (10021)	I	IWCX	WB
10202 (40504) s	I	IWCX	MA	10231 (10016)	I	IWCX	WB
10203 (40506)	I	IWCX	MA	10232 (10027)	I	IWCX	OY
10204 (40502)	I	IWCX	OY	10233 (10013)	I	IWCX	MA
10205 (40503)	I	IWCX	OY	10234 (10004)	I	IWCX	WB
10206 (40507)	I	IWCX	OY	10235 (10015)	I	IWCX	WB
10207 (40516) s	I	IWCX	MA	10236 (10018)	I	IWCX	WB
10208 (40517)	I	IWCX	WB	10237 (10022)	I	IWCX	WB
10209 (40508)	I	IWCX	OY	10238 (10017)	I	IWCX	WB
10210 (40509)	I	IWCX	WB	10240 (10003)	I	IWCX	OY
10211 (40510)	I	IWCX	WB	10241 (10009)	I	IWCX	WB
10212 (11049)	I	IWCX	WB	10242 (10002)	I	IWCX	WB
10213 (11050)	I	IWCX	MA	10245 (10019)	I	IWCX	WB
10214 (11034)	I	IWCX	OY	10246 (10014)	I	IWCX	MA
10215 (11032)	I	IWCX	WB	10247 (10011) s	I	IWCX	MA
10216 (11041)	I	IWCX	OY	10248 (10005)	I	IWCX	WB
10217 (11051)	I	IWCX	MA	10249 (10012)	I	IWCX	OY
10218 (11053)	I	IWCX	WB	10250 (10020)	I	IWCX	OY
10219 (11047)	I	IWCX	OY	10251 (10024)	I	IWCX	WB
10220 (11056)	I	IWCX	OY	10252 (10008)	I	IWCX	WB
10221 (11012)	I	IWCX	WB	10253 (10026)	I	IWCX	WB
10222 (11063)	I	IWCX	MA	10254 (10006)	I	IWCX	WB
10223 (11043) s	I	IWCX	MA	10255 (10010)	I	IWCX	OY
10224 (11062)	I	IWCX	MA	10256 (10028)	I	IWCX	MA
10225 (11014)	I	IWCX	WB	10257 (10007) s	I	IWCX	WB
10226 (11015) s	I	IWCX	MA	10258 (10023)	I	IWCX	WB
10227 (11057)	I	IWCX	MA	10259 (10025)	I	IWCX	WB
10228 (11035)	I	IWCX	OY	10260 (10001) s	I	IWCX	WB

AJ1J (RFM)   RESTAURANT BUFFET FIRST (MODULAR)

Dia. AJ105. Mark 4. Air conditioned. 20F 1L. SIG bogies (BT41). ae. pt. ETH X.

Lot No. 31045 Metro-Cammell 1989 onwards. 45.5 t.

10300	I	IECX	BN	10316	I	IECX	BN
10301	I	IECX	BN	10317	I	IECX	BN
10302	I	IECX	BN	10318	I	IECX	BN
10303	I	IECX	BN	10319	I	IECX	BN
10304	I	IECX	BN	10320	I	IECX	BN
10305	I	IECX	BN	10321	I	IECX	BN
10306 q	I	IECX	BN	10322	I	IECX	BN
10307	I	IECX	BN	10323	I	IECX	BN
10308	I	IECX	BN	10324	I	IECX	BN
10309	I	IECX	BN	10325	I	IECX	BN
10310	I	IECX	BN	10326	I	IECX	BN
10311	I	IECX	BN	10327	I	IECX	BN
10312	I	IECX	BN	10328	I	IECX	BN
10313	I	IECX	BN	10329	I	IECX	BN
10314	I	IECX	BN	10330	I	IECX	BN
10315	I	IECX	BN	10331	I	IECX	BN

10332	I	IECX	BN	10333	I IECX	BN

AU4G (SLEP)   SLEEPING CAR WITH PANTRY

Dia. AU401. Mark 3A. Air conditioned. 12 compartments with a fixed lower berth and a hinged upper berth, plus an attendants compartment with 2L (controlled emission). BT10 bogies. ae. ETH 7X.

(S) Stored at MoD Bicester.

Lot No. 30960 Derby 1981–3.

10500	I	ICHV	BN	10544 s	I	IWCR	PC
10501 s	I	IWCR	PC	10545 s	I	IXXH	EC
10502	I	IWCR	PC	10546 s	I	ICCR	PC
10503	I	ICHV	BN	10547 s	I	IWCR	PC
10504 s	I	IWCR	PC	10548	I	IWCR	PC
10506	I	IWCX	WB	10549 s	I	ICCX	PC
10507	I	IWCR	PC	10550 s	I	IWRX	LA
10508	I	IWCR	PC	10551 s	I	IWCR	PC
10509		IXXZ	S	10552		IWCD	ZN
10510	I	IWCR	PC	10553	I	IWCR	PC
10511		IXXZ	S	10554 s	I	ICCR	PC
10512 s	I	IWCR	PC	10555 s	I	IWCR	PC
10513	I	IWCR	PC	10556	I	IWRX	LA
10514	I	ICHV	BN	10557 s	I	IWCX	WB
10515	I	IWCR	PC	10558	I	IWRX	LA
10516	I	IWCR	PC	10559	I	IWCR	PC
10517		IXXZ	S	10560	I	IWRX	LA
10518		IXXZ	S	10561	I	IWCR	PC
10519	I	IWCR	PC	10562		IWCR	PC
10520 s	I	IWCR	PC	10563	I	ICCR	PC
10521		IXXZ	S	10564	I	IXXZ	LA
10522	I	IWCR	PC	10565	I	IWCR	PC
10523	I	IWCR	PC	10566 s	I	ICCX	PC
10525		IXXZ	S	10567	I	IXXH	WB
10526 s	I	IWCR	PC	10568	I	IXXZ	LA
10527 s	I	IWCR	PC	10569 s	I	IWCX	WB
10529	I	IWCR	PC	10570	I	IXXH	WB
10530	I	IWCR	PC	10571	I	IWCX	WB
10531 s	I	ICCR	PC	10572 s	I	ICCR	PC
10532 s	I	ICCR	PC	10573	I	IWRX	LA
10533	I	IXXH	WB	10574 s	I	ICHV	BN
10534 s	I	IWCR	PC	10575	I	ICHV	BN
10535 s	I	IWCR	PC	10576 s		IXXX	ZA
10536	I	IWCR	PC	10577 s		IXXX	ZA
10537 s	I	ICCR	PC	10578 s	I	IWCX	WB
10538	I	IWRX	LA	10579 s		IXXH	WB
10539 s	I	IWCX	WB	10580 s	I	ICCR	PC
10540	I	IWRX	LA	10581 s		IXXX	ZA
10541 s	I	IWCX	WB	10582 s	I	IWCX	WB
10542	I	IWCR	PC	10583	I	IWCX	WB
10543 s	I	IWCR	PC	10584 s	I	IWCR	PC

10585	I	IXXZ	LA	10602 s	I	IWCX	PC
10586	I	IWRX	LA	10603	I	IWRX	LA
10587	I	IXXZ	LA	10604	I	IWRX	LA
10588 s	I	IWCR	PC	10605	I	IWCR	PC
10589 s	I	IWCR	PC	10606	I	IXXH	WB
10590 s	I	IWCR	PC	10607 s	I	IWCR	PC
10591 s	I	IXXH	WB	10609 s	I	IXXH	WB
10592 s	I	ICCX	PC	10610 s	I	IWCR	PC
10593 s	I	IWCX	WB	10611	I	IXXZ	S
10594 s	I	ICCR	PC	10612 s	I	IWCR	PC
10595 s	I	IXXH	WB	10613 s	I	IWCR	PC
10596	I	IWCR	PC	10614 s	I	IWCR	PC
10597 s	I	IWCR	PC	10615 s	I	IXXZ	DY
10598	I	IWCR	PC	10616 s	I	IXXH	PC
10599	I	IXXH	WB	10617 s	I	IWCR	PC
10600	I	IWCR	PC	10618	I	IXXZ	S
10601 s	I	ICCR	PC	10619	I	IXXZ	S

AS4G (SLE)   SLEEPING CAR

Dia. AS403. Mark 3A. Air conditioned. 13 compartments with a fixed lower berth and a hinged upper berth. 2L (controlled emission). BT10 bogies. ae. ETH 6X.

Lot No. 30961 Derby 1980–4.

10646 s	I	ICHV	BN	10680	I	IWCR	PC
10647	I	IWCR	PC	10682 s	I	IWCR	PC
10648	I	IWCR	PC	10683	I	IWCR	PC
10649 s	I	IWCR	PC	10684		IXXH	PC
10650 s	I	IWCR	PC	10685 s	I	IWCR	PC
10651	I	IWCR	PC	10686	I	IWCR	PC
10653	I	IWCR	PC	10687 s	I	IWCR	PC
10654	I	IWCR	PC	10688	I	IWCR	PC
10655	I	IWCR	PC	10689 s	I	IWCR	PC
10656 s	I	IXXH	PC	10690	I	IWCR	PC
10657	I	IWCR	PC	10691	I	IWCR	PC
10658	I	IWCR	PC	10692 s	I	IWCR	PC
10660	I	IWCR	PC	10693 s	I	IWCR	PC
10661	I	ICHV	BN	10696	I	IWCR	PC
10662	I	ICHV	BN	10697 s	I	IWCR	PC
10663	I	IWCR	PC	10699 s	I	IWCR	PC
10665	I	IXXX	ZA	10700		IXXH	WB
10666	I	IWCR	PC	10701	I	IWCR	PC
10668	I	IWCR	PC	10702 s	I	IWCX	PC
10670	I	IWCX	PC	10703 s	I	IWCR	PC
10671	I	IXXH	EC	10704	I	IXXH	LA
10672 s	I	IWCR	PC	10705	I	IXXH	EC
10673		IXXX	ZA	10706	I	IWCR	PC
10674 s	I	IWCR	PC	10707 s	I	IWCX	PC
10675 s	I	IWCR	PC	10708 s	I	IWCR	PC
10678		IXXH	PC	10709	I	IWCR	PC
10679		IXXX	ZA	10710		IWCR	PC

10711	I	IWCR	PC	10723	I	IWCR	PC
10712	s	I IWCR	PC	10724	I	ICHV	BN
10713	I	IXXH	EC	10725	I	ICHV	BN
10714	I	IWCR	PC	10726	I	ICHV	BN
10715	I	IXXH	WB	10727	I	ICHV	BN
10716	s	I IWCR	PC	10728	I	ICHV	BN
10717	s	I IWCR	PC	10729	I	ICHV	BN
10718	I	IWCR	PC	10730	s	I IWCR	PC
10719	s	I IWCR	PC	10731	I	IWCR	PC
10720	I	IXXH	WB	10732		IWCR	PC
10722	I	IWCR	PC				

AD1G (FO)   OPEN FIRST

Dia. AD108. Mark 3A. Air conditioned. 48F 2L. BT10 bogies (BT15*). ae. pa. ETH 6X. All now facelifted with new upholstery, carpets etc. 11005–7 have regained their original numbers, having being converted back from open composites 11905–7. all now refurbished.

Lot No. 30878 Derby 1975–6. 34.30 t.

11005	I	IWCX	WB	11031	I	IWCX	WB
11006	I	IWCX	WB	11033	I	IWCX	WB
11007	I	IWCX	WB	11036	I	IWCX	WB
11011	zs	I IWCX	WB	11037	I	IWCX	WB
11013	I	IWCX	WB	11038	I	IWCX	WB
11016	I	IWCX	WB	11039	I	IWCX	WB
11017	I	IWCX	WB	11040	I	IWCX	WB
11018	I	IWCX	WB	11042	I	IWCX	WB
11019	I	IWCX	WB	11044	I	IWCX	WB
11020	I	IWCX	WB	11045	I	IWCX	WB
11021	I	IWCX	WB	11046	I	IWCX	WB
11023	I	IWCX	WB	11048	I	IWCX	WB
11024	I	IWCX	WB	11052	I	IWCX	WB
11026	I	IWCX	WB	11054	I	IWCX	WB
11027	I	IWCX	WB	11055	I	IWCX	WB
11028	I	IWCX	WB	11058	I	IWCX	WB
11029	I	IWCX	WB	11060	I	IWCX	WB
11030	I	IWCX	WB				

AD1H (FO)   OPEN FIRST

Dia. AD109. Mark 3B. Air conditioned. 48F 2L. BT10 bogies. ae. pa. ETH 6X. Inter-City 80 seats. Some of these coaches were named, but the names are now being removed.

Lot No. 30982 Derby 1985. 36.46 t.

11064	I	IWCX	WB	11070	s	I IWCX	MA
11065	s	I IWCX	MA	11071	I	IWCX	WB
11066	s	I IWCX	MA	11072	I	IWCX	WB
11067	I	IWCX	WB	11073	s	I IWCX	MA
11068	I	IWCX	WB	11074	s	I IWCX	WB
11069	I	IWCX	MA	11075	I	IWCX	WB

11076	I	IWCX	MA	11089 ps I	IWCX	WB
11077	I	IWCX	WB	11090 p I	IWCX	WB
11078	I	IWCX	WB	11091 p I	IWCX	MA
11079	I	IWCX	WB	11092 p I	IWCX	WB
11080 s	I	IWCX	WB	11093 p I	IWCX	MA
11081	I	IWCX	WB	11094 ps I	IWCX	MA
11082	I	IWCX	WB	11095 p I	IWCX	WB
11083 p	I	IWCX	WB	11096 p I	IWCX	MA
11084 ps	I	IWCX	WB	11097 ps I	IWCX	WB
11085 p	I	IWCX	MA	11098 ps I	IWCX	WB
11086 p	I	IWCX	WB	11099 p I	IWCX	WB
11087 ps	I	IWCX	WB	11100 ps I	IWCX	MA
11088 p	I	IWCX	WB	11101 p I	IWCX	MA

AD1J (FO) OPEN FIRST

Dia. AD111. Mark 4. Air conditioned. Known as 'Pullman open' by BR. 46F 1L. SIG bogies (BT41). ae. pa. ETH 6.

Lot No. 31046 Metro-Cammell 1989 onwards. 39.70 t.

11200	I	IECX	BN	11232	I	IECX	BN
11201 p	I	IECX	BN	11233 p	I	IECX	BN
11202	I	IECX	BN	11234	I	IECX	BN
11203 p	I	IECX	BN	11235 p	I	IECX	BN
11204 p	I	IECX	BN	11236	I	IECX	BN
11205	I	IECX	BN	11237 p	I	IECX	BN
11206	I	IECX	BN	11238	I	IECX	BN
11207 p	I	IECX	BN	11239 p	I	IECX	BN
11208	I	IECX	BN	11240	I	IECX	BN
11209	I	IECX	BN	11241	I	IECX	BN
11210	I	IECX	BN	11242 p	I	IECX	BN
11211 p	I	IECX	BN	11243 p	I	IECX	BN
11212	I	IECX	BN	11244	I	IECX	BN
11213 p	I	IECX	BN	11245 p	I	IECX	BN
11214 p	I	IECX	BN	11246 p	I	IECX	BN
11215	I	IECX	BN	11247	I	IECX	BN
11216	I	IECX	BN	11248	I	IECX	BN
11217 p	I	IECX	BN	11249 p	I	IECX	BN
11218	I	IECX	BN	11250	I	IECX	BN
11219 p	I	IECX	BN	11251 p	I	IECX	BN
11220	I	IECX	BN	11252	I	IECX	BN
11221 p	I	IECX	BN	11253 p	I	IECX	BN
11222	I	IECX	BN	11254	I	IECX	BN
11223	I	IECX	BN	11255 p	I	IECX	BN
11224	I	IECX	BN	11256	I	IECX	BN
11225	I	IECX	BN	11257 p	I	IECX	BN
11226	I	IECX	BN	11258	I	IECX	BN
11227	I	IECX	BN	11259 p	I	IECX	BN
11228	I	IECX	BN	11260	I	IECX	BN
11229	I	IECX	BN	11261 p	I	IECX	BN
11230	I	IECX	BN	11262	I	IECX	BN
11231	I	IECX	BN	11263 p	I	IECX	BN

11264		11271
11265		11272
11266		11273
11267		11274
11268		11275
11269		11276
11270		

AC2G (TSO)   OPEN STANDARD

Dia. AC213 (AC220 z). Mark 3A. Air conditioned. All now refurbished with modified seat backs and new layout. 76S 2L (74S 2L z). BT10 (BREL T4*) bogies. ae. pa. ETH 6X. 12169–72 have been converted from open composites 11908–10/22, which in turn were converted from FOs 11008–10/22.

Lot No. 30877 Derby 1975–7. 34.30 t.

12004	I	IWCX	WB	12043	I	IWCX	WB
12005	I	IWCX	WB	12044	I	IWCX	WB
12007	I	IWCX	WB	12045	I	IWCX	WB
12008	I	IWCX	WB	12046	I	IWCX	WB
12009	I	IWCX	WB	12047 z	I	IWCX	WB
12010	I	IWCX	WB	12048	I	IWCX	WB
12011	I	IWCX	WB	12049	I	IWCX	WB
12012	I	IWCX	WB	12050	I	IWCX	WB
12013	I	IWCX	WB	12051	I	IWCX	WB
12014	I	IWCX	WB	12052	I	IWCX	WB
12015	I	IWCX	WB	12053	I	IWCX	WB
12016	I	IWCX	WB	12054	I	IWCX	WB
12017	I	IWCX	WB	12055	I	IWCX	WB
12019	I	IWCX	WB	12056	I	IWCX	MA
12020	I	IWCX	WB	12057	I	IWCX	WB
12021	I	IWCX	WB	12058	I	IWCX	WB
12022	I	IWCX	WB	12059	I	IWCX	WB
12023	I	IWCX	WB	12060	I	IWCX	MA
12024	I	IWCX	WB	12061	I	IWCX	WB
12025	I	IWCX	WB	12062	I	IWCX	MA
12026	I	IWCX	WB	12063	I	IWCX	WB
12027	I	IWCX	WB	12064	I	IWCX	WB
12028	I	IWCX	WB	12065	I	IWCX	WB
12029	I	IWCX	WB	12066	I	IWCX	WB
12030	I	IWCX	WB	12067	I	IWCX	WB
12031	I	IWCX	WB	12068.	I	IWCX	WB
12032	I	IWCX	WB	12069	I	IWCX	WB
12033 z	I	IWCX	WB	12070	I	IWCX	WB
12034	I	IWCX	MA	12071	I	IWCX	WB
12035	I	IWCX	WB	12072	I	IWCX	WB
12036 s	I	IWCX	MA	12073	I	IWCX	WB
12037	I	IWCX	WB	12075	I	IWCX	WB
12038	I	IWCX	MA	12076	I	IWCX	WB
12040	I	IWCX	WB	12077	I	IWCX	WB
12041	I	IWCX	WB	12078	I	IWCX	WB
12042	I	IWCX	WB	12079	I	IWCX	WB

12080	I	IWCX	WB	12127	I	IWCX	WB
12081	I	IWCX	WB	12128	I	IWCX	MA
12082	I	IWCX	WB	12129	I	IWCX	WB
12083	I	IWCX	WB	12130	I	IWCX	WB
12084	I	IWCX	WB	12131	I	IWCX	WB
12085	I	IWCX	WB	12132	I	IWCX	WB
12086	I	IWCX	WB	12133	I	IWCX	WB
12087	I	IWCX	WB	12133	I	IMLR	NL
12088 z	I	IWCX	WB	12134	I	IWCX	WB
12089	I	IWCX	MA	12135	I	IWCX	WB
12090	I	IWCX	WB	12136	I	IWCX	WB
12091	I	IWCX	WB	12137	I	IWCX	MA
12092	I	IWCX	WB	12138	I	IWCX	WB
12093	I	IWCX	WB	12139	I	IWCX	MA
12094	I	IWCX	WB	12140 *z	I	IWCX	WB
12095	I	IWCX	WB	12141	I	IWCX	WB
12096	I	IWCX	WB	12142 z	I	IWCX	WB
12097	I	IWCX	WB	12143	I	IWCX	WB
12098	I	IWCX	WB	12144 z	I	IWCX	WB
12099	I	IWCX	WB	12145	I	IWCX	WB
12100 z	I	IWCX	WB	12146	I	IWCX	MA
12101	I	IWCX	WB	12147	I	IWCX	WB
12102	I	IWCX	WB	12148	I	IWCX	WB
12103 z	I	IWCX	WB	12149	I	IWCX	WB
12104	I	IWCX	WB	12150	I	IWCX	WB
12105	I	IWCX	MA	12151	I	IWCX	WB
12106	I	IWCX	WB	12152	I	IWCX	WB
12107	I	IWCX	MA	12153	I	IWCX	WB
12108	I	IWCX	WB	12154	I	IWCX	MA
12109 s	I	IWCX	MA	12155	I	IWCX	WB
12110	I	IWCX	MA	12156	I	IWCX	MA
12111	I	IWCX	WB	12157	I	IWCX	WB
12112 z	I	IWCX	WB	12158	I	IWCX	WB
12113	I	IWCX	WB	12159	I	IWCX	MA
12114	I	IWCX	WB	12160 s	I	IWCX	MA
12115	I	IWCX	WB	12161 z	I	IWCX	WB
12116	I	IWCX	WB	12163	I	IWCX	WB
12117	I	IWCX	WB	12164	I	IWCX	WB
12118	I	IWCX	WB	12165	I	IWCX	WB
12119	I	IWCX	WB	12166	I	IWCX	WB
12120	I	IWCX	MA	12167	I	IWCX	MA
12121	I	IWCX	WB	12168	I	IWCX	WB
12122 z	I	IWCX	WB	12169 z	I	IWCX	WB
12123	I	IWCX	WB	12170 z	I	IWCX	WB
12124	I	IWCX	WB	12171 z	I	IWCX	WB
12125	I	IWCX	MA	12172 z	I	IWCX	WB
12126	I	IWCX	WB				

AI2J (TSOE) OPEN STANDARD (END)

Dia. AI201. Mark 4. Air conditioned. 74S 2L. SIG bogies (BT41). ae. pa. ETH 6.

Note: 12232 was converted from 12405 and is now renumbered as 12204.

Lot No. 31047 Metro-Cammell 1989 onwards. 39.5 t.

12200	I	IECX	BN	12216	I	IECX	BN
12201	I	IECX	BN	12217	I	IECX	BN
12202	I	IECX	BN	12218	I	IECX	BN
12203	I	IECX	BN	12219	I	IECX	BN
12204	I	IECX	BN	12220	I	IECX	BN
12205	I	IECX	BN	12221			
12206	I	IECX	BN	12222	I	IECX	BN
12207	I	IECX	BN	12223	I	IECX	BN
12208	I	IECX	BN	12224	I	IECX	BN
12209	I	IECX	BN	12225	I	IECX	BN
12210	I	IECX	BN	12226	I	IECX	BN
12211	I	IECX	BN	12227	I	IECX	BN
12212	I	IECX	BN	12228	I	IECX	BN
12213	I	IECX	BN	12229	I	IECX	BN
12214	I	IECX	BN	12230	I	IECX	BN
12215	I	IECX	BN	12231	I	IECX	BN

AL2J (TSOD) OPEN STANDARD (DISABLED ACCESS)

Dia. AL201. Mark 4. Air conditioned. 72S + wheelchair space 1L (suitable for a disabled person). SIG bogies (BT41). ae. pa. p. ETH 6.

Lot No. 31048 Metro-Cammell 1989 onwards. 39.4 t.

12300	I	IECX	BN	12316	I	IECX	BN
12301	I	IECX	BN	12317	I	IECX	BN
12302	I	IECX	BN	12318	I	IECX	BN
12303	I	IECX	BN	12319	I	IECX	BN
12304	I	IECX	BN	12320	I	IECX	BN
12305	I	IECX	BN	12321	I	IECX	BN
12306	I	IECX	BN	12322	I	IECX	BN
12307	I	IECX	BN	12323	I	IECX	BN
12308	I	IECX	BN	12324	I	IECX	BN
12309	I	IECX	BN	12325	I	IECX	BN
12310	I	IECX	BN	12326	I	IECX	BN
12311	I	IECX	BN	12327	I	IECX	BN
12312	I	IECX	BN	12328	I	IECX	BN
12313	I	IECX	BN	12329	I	IECX	BN
12314	I	IECX	BN	12330	I	IECX	BN
12315	I	IECX	BN				

AC2J (TSO)   OPEN STANDARD

Dia. AC214. Mark 4. Air conditioned. 74S 2L. SIG bogies (BT41). ae. pa. ETH 6.

Note: 12405 has been converted from 12204.

Lot No. 31049 Metro-Cammell 1989 onwards. 39.9 t.

12400	I	IECX	BN	12452	I	IECX	BN
12401	I	IECX	BN	12453	I	IECX	BN
12402	I	IECX	BN	12454	I	IECX	BN
12403	I	IECX	BN	12455	I	IECX	BN
12404	I	IECX	BN	12456	I	IECX	BN
12405	I	IECX	BN	12457	I	IECX	BN
12406	I	IECX	BN	12458	I	IECX	BN
12407	I	IECX	BN	12459	I	IECX	BN
12408	I	IECX	BN	12460	I	IECX	BN
12409	I	IECX	BN	12461	I	IECX	BN
12410	I	IECX	BN	12462	I	IECX	BN
12411	I	IECX	BN	12463	I	IECX	BN
12412	I	IECX	BN	12464	I	IECX	BN
12413	I	IECX	BN	12465	I	IECX	BN
12414	I	IECX	BN	12466	I	IECX	BN
12415	I	IECX	BN	12467	I	IECX	BN
12416	I	IECX	BN	12468	I	IECX	BN
12417	I	IECX	BN	12469	I	IECX	BN
12418	I	IECX	BN	12470	I	IECX	BN
12419	I	IECX	BN	12471	I	IECX	BN
12420	I	IECX	BN	12472	I	IECX	BN
12421	I	IECX	BN	12473	I	IECX	BN
12422	I	IECX	BN	12474	I	IECX	BN
12423	I	IECX	BN	12475	I	IECX	BN
12424	I	IECX	BN	12476	I	IECX	BN
12425	I	IECX	BN	12477	I	IECX	BN
12426	I	IECX	BN	12478	I	IECX	BN
12427	I	IECX	BN	12479	I	IECX	BN
12428	I	IECX	BN	12480	I	IECX	BN
12429	I	IECX	BN	12481	I	IECX	BN
12430	I	IECX	BN	12482	I	IECX	BN
12431	I	IECX	BN	12483	I	IECX	BN
12432	I	IECX	BN	12484	I	IECX	BN
12433	I	IECX	BN	12485	I	IECX	BN
12434	I	IECX	BN	12486	I	IECX	BN
12435	I	IECX	BN	12487	I	IECX	BN
12436	I	IECX	BN	12488	I	IECX	BN
12437	I	IECX	BN	12489	I	IECX	BN
12438	I	IECX	BN	12490			
12439	I	IECX	BN	12491			
12440	I	IECX	BN	12492			
12441	I	IECX	BN	12493			
12442	I	IECX	BN	12494			
12443	I	IECX	BN	12495			
12444	I	IECX	BN	12496			
12445	I	IECX	BN	12497			
12446	I	IECX	BN	12498			
12447	I	IECX	BN	12499			
12448	I	IECX	BN	12500			
12449				12501			
12450	I	IECX	BN	12502			
12451	I	IECX	BN	12503			

12504–13450

12504				12522	I		
12505				12523	I		
12506				12524	I	IECX	BN
12507				12525	I	IECX	BN
12508				12526	I	IECX	BN
12509				12527	I	IECX	BN
12510				12528	I	IECX	BN
12511				12529	I	IECX	BN
12512				12530	I	IECX	BN
12513	I	IECX	BN	12531	I	IECX	BN
12514	I	IECX	BN	12532	I	IECX	BN
12515	I	IECX	BN	12533	I	IECX	BN
12516	I	IECX	BN	12534	I	IECX	BN
12517	I	IECX	BN	12535	I		
12518	I			12536	I		
12519	I			12537	I		
12520	I	IECX	BN	12538	I		
12521	I	IECX	BN				

AA11 (FK)   CORRIDOR FIRST

Dia. AA101. Mark 1. 42F 2L. ETH 3. d.

Note: 13233/6/7, 13303/14/6/26/35/41 are on loan to the Humberside Loco Preservation Group at Hull Dairycoates and 13230 is on loan to the SRPS at Bo'ness.

13225–13237. Lot No. 30381 Ashford/Eastleigh 1959. B4 bogies. 33 t.
13303–13344. Lot No. 30667 Swindon 1962. Commonwealth bogies. 36 t.

13225	xk	I	ICHH	DY	13318	a pal	ICHV	BN
13227	xk	I	ICHH	DY	13324	vf	**N** NWRX	OM
13230	xk	I	ICHL	BO	13326	v	ICHL	HD
13233	vk	**M**	ICHL	HD	13328	vf	**N** NWRX	OM
13236	vk	I	ICHL	HD	13329	vf	**N** NWRX	OM
13237	vk	I	ICHL	HD	13331	vf	**N** NWRX	OM
13303	v	**M**	ICHL	HD	13335	v	ICHL	HD
13306	v		ICHH	CL	13341	vf	I	ICHL	HD
13314	vk	**M**	ICHL	HD	13344	vf	ICHL	CL
13316	v		ICHL	HD				

AA1A (FK)   CORRIDOR FIRST

Dia. AA106. Mark 2A. Pressure ventilated. 42F 2L. B4 bogies. d. ETH 4.

13435–13462. Lot No. 30774 Derby 1968. 33 t.
13467–13475. Lot No. 30785 Derby 1968. 33 t.

13462/73 carried 19462/73 when previously declassified.

13435	v	**N**	NWRX	OM	13444	v	**N** NWRX	OM
13436	v	**N**	NWRX	OM	13446	v	**N** NWRX	OM
13437	v	**N**	NWRX	OM	13447	v	**N** NWRX	OM
13440	v	**N**	NWRX	OM	13450	v	**N** NWRX	OM

112

Royal train staff/generator vehicle No. 2920 at Carlisle on 3rd May 1991 in the distinctive Royal train livery.   Dave McAlone

▲**Mark 1 Stock.** RBR No. 1670 is one of the few such vehicles still carrying blue and grey livery. It was seen at York on 19th July 1990.   *John Augusts*

▼ TSO 4999 at Gloucester on 4th August 1991 in InterCity livery.   *John Augusts*

Open first 3118 in InterCity livery passes Ocean Dock in the formation of the 10.15 Southampton Eastern Docks–Waterloo boat train on 29th June 1991.

John Augustson

▲ Open first 13328 in Network SouthEast livery at Oxford on 30th August 1990.
John Augusts

▼ One of the few remaining brake composite (BCK) vehicles No. 21274 at Y○
on 30th September 1990.
John Augusts

Mark 2 Stock. BSO No. 9391 at Oxford on 30th August 1990.

John Augustson

TSO No. 5226 at the rear of the 15.24 Aberdeen–Inverness on 18th July 1991. is vehicle was in Network SouthEast livery, but has had the red stripe replaced th a dark grey stripe and is branded 'SCOTRAIL'. *Norman Barrington*

▲**Mark 2A Stock.** Brake first (BFK) No. 17079 stabled at Eastleigh on 7th June 1991.   *Brian Dent*

▼**Mark 2B Stock.** TSO No. 5453 in provincial livery.   *Brian Morris*

Mark 2C Stock. Open second with trolley space (TSOT) No. 6521 at ~~~singstoke on 14th January 1989. *Brain Denton*

Mark 2D Stock. Air conditioned corridor firsts are now finding their way into ~~~aterloo–Exeter sets, e.g. 13575 seen here in blue and grey livery. *Chris Wilson*

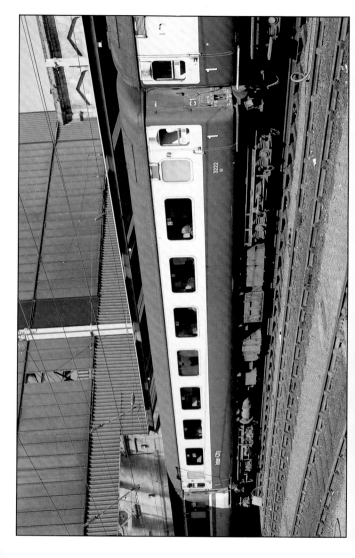

Mark 2F Stock. 1260 is the last of the buffet firsts (RFB) converted from FOs. s seen at BREL Ltd's Derby Carriage Works on 27th March 1991.   *Colin J Marsden*

Refurbished FO No. 3400 at Coventry on 20th July 1990.   *John Augustson*

▲**Mark 3 Stock.** HST trailer buffet first No. 40717 passing through Middlesbrough on 14th July 1991. *John Augustso*

▼**Mark 3A Stock.** Modular restaurant buffet first (RFM) No. 10213 (converted from FO) at Crewe on 19th July 1990. *John Augustso*

Sleeping car with pantry (SLEP) No. 10574 at Newcastle on 9th May 1989.
John Augustson

Mark 4 Stock. TSO No. 12227 at Newcastle on 24th July 1991.
John Augustson

▲ Non-passenger-carrying Coaching Stock. Courier Van No. 80208 in r
livery at Workington on 8th July 1990.   *Dave McAlo*

▼ Post Office Sorting van in red livery with the latest TPO branding at Carlisle
6th September 1991.   *Colin J Marsd*

Mark 3 DVT 82124 at the head of the 11.15 Glasgow Central–London Euston ('The Royal Scot') at Carlingill in the Lune Gorge on 19th October 1991.

Hugh Ballantyne

▲ Mark 4 DVT No. 82228 approaches Durham at the head of the 15.35 Newcastl London Kings Cross on 21st September 1991.   *John Augusts*

▼ NEA No. 92078 in blue and grey livery at Carlisle on 26th May 1989.
                                                                John Augusts

NJX (GUV) No. 93852 in Network SouthEast livery at Southampton Queen Elizabeth II terminal on 27th June 1991.   *John Augustson*

Airline container van (NRX) No. 95400 in Rail Express Systems livery at Crewe on 12th October 1991.   *John Augustson*

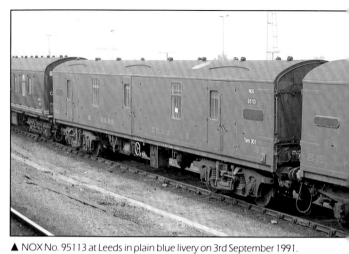

▲ NOX No. 95113 at Leeds in plain blue livery on 3rd September 1991.

John Augustsc

▼ Motorail van (NXA) No. 96112 at Carlisle on 20th July 1991.   *John Augustsc*

13459 a	**N** NWXX	EH		13473 a	**N** NWXX	EH
13462 a	**N** NWXX	EH		13474 v	**N** NWRX	OM
13467 a	**N** NWXX	EH		13475 v	**N** NWRX	OM
13470 v	**N** NWRX	OM				

AA1B (FK)   CORRIDOR FIRST

Dia. AA107. Mark 2B. Pressure ventilated. 42F 2L. B4 bogies. ad. ETH 4.

13479/507/13 carried 19479/507/13 when previously declassified.

Lot No. 30789 Derby 1969. 33 t.

13479	**N** NWXX	EH	13499	**N** NWXX	EH
13482	**N** NWXX	EH	13507	**N** NWXX	EH
13493	**N** NWXX	EH	13513	**N** NWXX	EH

AA1C (FK)   CORRIDOR FIRST

Dia. AA108. Mark 2C. Pressure ventilated. 42F 2L. B4 bogies. ad. pa. ETH 4.

Lot No. 30797 Derby 1969–70. 33.5 t.

13525	**N** NWXX	EH	13526 pa	**N** NWXX	EH

AA1D (FK)   CORRIDOR FIRST

Dia. AA109. Mark 2D. Air conditioned (Stones). 42F 2L. B4 bogies. ae. pa. ETH 5. 13585–13610 require at least 800 V train heat supply.

Lot No. 30825 Derby 1971–2. 34.5 t.

13563		NWXX	OM	13592	**I** IXXX	DY
13567	**I**	IXXZ	OM	13593	**I** IXXX	PC
13575	**N**	NWXX	OM	13594	**I** IWRL	OM
13581	**I**	IXXX	DY	13595	**I** IXXX	DY
13582	**I**	ICHH	CL	13596	**I** IXXX	DY
13583	**I**	IXXX	PC	13603	**I** IXXX	DY
13585	**I**	ICHV	BN	13604	**I** ICHV	BN
13586	**I**	IWRL	OM	13607	**I** ICHH	CL
13589	**I**	IWRL	OM			

SPECIAL NOTE: All BFKs were formerly numbered in the 14xxx series. Subtract 3000 from present number to obtain former number.

AB11 (BFK)   CORRIDOR BRAKE FIRST

Dia. AB101. Mark 1. 24F 1L. vd. ETH 2.

17015. Lot No. 30668 Swindon 1961. Commonwealth bogies. 36 t.
17023. Lot No. 30718 Swindon 1963. Commonwealth bogies and metal window frames. 36 t.

17015 x	**I** ICHV	BN	17023 x	**I** ICHV	BN

AB1Z (BFK)   CORRIDOR BRAKE FIRST

Dia. AB102. Mark 2. Pressure ventilated. 24F 1L. B4 bogies. d. ETH 4.

Lot No. 30756 Derby 1966 31.5 t.

| 17039 v | **RS**PISX | IS | | 17042 a | | PLLX | LL |

AB1A (BFK)   CORRIDOR BRAKE FIRST

Dia. AB103. Mark 2A. Pressure ventilated. 24F 1L. B4 bogies. d. ETH 4.

17056–17077. Lot No. 30775 Derby 1967–8. 32 t.
17079–17099. Lot No. 30786 Derby 1968. 32 t.

17056 a pt	**N** NWXX	OM		17081 a pt	**N** NWXX	EH
17057 a pt	**N** NWXX	OM		17082 a pt	**N** NWXX	OM
17058 a	**N** NWXX	EH		17086 a pt	**N** NWXX	OM
17063 a pt	**N** NWXX	OM		17088 a pt	**N** NWXX	OM
17064 v	**NS**PISX	IS		17089 v	**NS**PISX	IS
17069 a pt	**N** NWXX	OM		17090 v	**N** PXXZ	LL
17073 a pt	**N** NWXX	OM		17091 v	**NS**PISX	IS
17075 a	**I** PXXZ	LL		17096 a pt	**N** NWXX	OM
17076 a pt	**N** NWXX	OM		17097 a pt	**N** NWXX	OM
17077 a	**N** NWXX	OM		17098 a	**I** PXXZ	LL
17079 a	**N** NWXX	EH		17099 v	PISX	IS
17080 a pt	**N** NWXX	OM				

AB1C (BFK)   CORRIDOR BRAKE FIRST

Dia. AB105. Mark 2C. Pressure ventilated. 24F 1L. B4 Bogies. ad. ETH 4.

Lot No. 30796 Derby 1969–70. 32.5 t.

17115 pt	**N** NWXX	OM		17128	**P** PLLX	LL
17118	**P** PLLX	LL		17129 pt	**I** IXXZ	LL
17120 pt	**N** NWXX	OM		17130 pt	**I** PXXZ	LL
17121 pt	**N** NWXX	OM		17132 pt	**N** NWXX	EH
17122 pt	**I** PLLX	LL		17133 k pt	**N** NWXX	EH
17123 pt	**P** PLLX	LL		17136	PDYX	DY
17125 pt	PLLX	LL		17138 pt	**I** PLLX	LL

AB1D (BFK)   CORRIDOR BRAKE FIRST

Dia. AB106. Mark 2D. Air conditioned (Stones equipment). 24F 1L. B4 Bogies. 17162–17172 require at least 800 V train heat supply. ae. pt. ETH 5.

Lot No. 30823 Derby 1971–2. 33.5 t.

17139 pg **I**	IXXT	PC		17145 pg **I**	IXXT	DY
17140 pg **I**	IXXT	PC		17146 pg **I**	ICHD	LL
17141 pg **I**	ICHV	OM		17147 pg **I**	ICHD	LL
17142 pg **I**	IWRL	OM		17148 pg **I**	NWXX	OM
17143 pg **I**	IXXT	DY		17149 pg **I**	IXXT	MA
17144 **I**	ICHD	LL		17150 pg **I**	IXXT	PC

17151 pg I	ICHD	LL
17152 pg I	ICCX	PC
17153 pg I	ICHV	OM
17154 pg I	IWRL	OM
17155 I	IXXT	LL
17156 I	ICHD	LL
17157 pg I	IXXT	MA
17158 pg I	ICHD	LL
17159 pg I	ICHD	LL
17160 pg I	IXXT	MA
17161 pg I	IWRL	OM

17162 pg I	IXXT	PC
17163 I	NWXX	OM
17164 pg I	ICHX	BN
17165 I	ICHD	LL
17166 pg I	IXXT	MA
17167 pg I	ICCX	PC
17169 pg I	ICHD	LL
17170 pg I	ICHX	BN
17171 pg I	ICHD	LL
17172 pg I	ICCX	PC

AE1G (BFO)   OPEN BRAKE FIRST

Dia. AE101. Mark 3B. Air conditioned. 36F 1L. BT10 bogies. ae. pg. ETH 5X. Fitted with hydraulic handbrake.

Lot No. 30990 Derby 1986. 35.81 t.

| 17173 I | IWCX | WB | 17175 s I | IWCX | WB |
| 17174 s I | IWCX | WB |

AA21 (SK)   CORRIDOR STANDARD

Dia. AA201 (AA202*). Mark 1. As with CKs there were two variants depending on whether the compartments have armrests. Each vehicle has eight compartments. 48S 2L (64S 2L*). ETH 4.

NOTE: Although three SKs are still shown in stock, all three are out of use. Thus the type of loco-hauled coach which was once the most numerous on BR is now effectively extinct.

Lot No. 30686 Derby 1962. Commonwealth bogies, metal window frames and melamine interior panelling. Formerly numbered 25945/58. Facelifted with fluorescent lighting and wide mirrors. Blinds removed. vd. 36 t.

| 18945 * N PXXZ | LL | 18958 * N PXXZ | LL |

AB31 (BCK)   CORRIDOR BRAKE COMPOSITE

Dia.AB301 (AB302*). Mark 1. As with the CKs there are two variants depending upon whether the standard class compartments have armrests. Each vehicle has two first class and three standard class compartments. 12F 18S 2L (12F 24S 2L*). ETH 2.

21241–21247. Lot No. 30669 Swindon 1961–2. Commonwealth bogies. 36 t.
21265–21274. Lot No. 30732 Derby 1964. Commonwealth bogies. 37 t.

21241 vd	E ICHS	BN	21266 *ae I	ICHV	BN
21242 vd	E ICHH	CL	21268 *ae I	ICHV	BN
21246 xd	I ICHH	BN	21269 *ad I	ICHV	BN
21247 vd	ICHH	BN	21274 *ae I	ICHV	BN
21265 *ae	ICHH	CL

AA21 (SK)   CORRIDOR STANDARD

Dia. AA201. Class continued from 18958. BR1 bogies. vd.

Lot No. 30153 Derby 1955–6. 33 t. vd.

24895	PXXZ	PC	

AB21 (BSK)   CORRIDOR BRAKE STANDARD

Dia. AB201 (AB202*). Mark 1. As with other compartment vehicles there are two variants depending upon whether the compartments have armrests. each vehicle has four compartments. 24S 1L (32S 1L*). ETH 2.

Lot No. 30156 Wolverton 1955. BR1 bogies. vd. 34 t.

34681	PXXZ	HT	

The following lots of BSK all have metal window frames and melamine interior panelling: (all vd).

35284–35290. Lot No. 30573 Gloucester 1960. B4 bogies. 33 t.
35309–35329. Lot No. 30699 Wolverton 1962–3. Commonwealth bogies. 37 t.
35447. Lot No. 30728 Wolverton 1963. Commonwealth bogies. 37 t.
35452–35482. Lot No. 30721 Wolverton 1963. Commonwealth bogies. 37 t.

f–Facelifted with fluorescent lighting.
g–Converted to ETH generator vehicle for Flying Scotsman Services. Still in BR stock. May be renumbered in 63xx series.

35284		PLAX	LA	35455	**N**	NWRX	OM
35290	pt **N**	NWRX	OM	35457		PHTX	HT
35309	**N**	NWRX	OM	35465	f **I**	ICHS	BN
35317	pt **N**	NWRX	OM	35469	g **M**	ICHP	BN
35329	**N**	NWRX	OM	35474	**N**	PHTX	HT
35447	pt **N**	NWRX	OM	35479	pt **N**	NWRX	OM
35452	pt **N**	NWRX	OM	35482	*f	PXXZ	LL
35453		PLLX	LL				

AB2A (BSK)   CORRIDOR BRAKE STANDARD

Dia. AB204. Mark 2A. Pressure ventilated. Renumbered from BFK in 1985/6. 24S 1L. B4 bogies. vd. ETH 4.

Lot No. 30786 Derby 1968. 32 t.

35500 (17094)	**N**		PDYX	DY

2.2. HIGH SPEED TRAIN TRAILER CARS

HSTs run in formations of 7 or 8 trailer cars with a driving motor brake (power car) at each end. All vehicles are classified mark 3. All trailer cars have BT10 bogies with disc brakes. Heating is by a three-phase supply and vehicles have air conditioning. Max. Speed is 125 mph.

GN4G (TRB)   TRAILER BUFFET FIRST

Dia. GN401. Converted from TRSB by fitting first class seats. Renumbered from 404xx series by subtracting 200. pt. 23F.

40204–40228. Lot No. 30883 Derby 1976–7. 36.12 t.
40231–40233. Lot No. 30899 Derby 1978–9. 36.12 t.

40204	I	IWRR	PM	40212	I	ICCT	LA
40205	I	IWRR	PM	40213	I	IWRR	LA
40206 s	I	IWRR	PM	40221 p	I	ICCT	PM
40207	I	IWRR	PM	40228 s	I	IWRR	PM
40208	I	IWRR	PM	40231 p	I	IWRR	LA
40209	I	IWRR	PM	40232 p	I	ICCT	PM
40210 s	I	IWRR	PM	40233	I	ICCT	LA
40211 s	I	IWRR	PM				

GK2G (TRSB)   TRAILER BUFFET STANDARD

Dia. GK202. pt. Renumbered from 400xx series by adding 400. 35S.

40401–40427. Lot No. 30883 Derby 1976–7. 36.12 t.
40429–40437. Lot No. 30899 Derby 1978–9. 36.12 t.

40401 ps	I	ICCE	EC	40423 s	I	ICCE	EC
40402 ps	I	ICCE	EC	40424 ps	I	ICCT	LA
40403 ps	I	ICCT	PM	40425 p	I	ICCT	PM
40414 ps	I	ICCT	PM	40426 p	I	ICCT	LA
40415 p	I	ICCT	PM	40427 ps	I	ICCE	EC
40416 qs	I	ICCE	EC	40429 ps	I	ICCE	EC
40417 q	I	ICCT	LA	40430 ps	I	ICCE	EC
40418 q	I	ICCT	LA	40434 pqs	I	ICCT	LA
40419 qs	I	ICCE	EC	40435 pqs	I	ICCE	EC
40420 ps	I	ICCE	EC	40436 q	I	ICCT	LA
40422 pqs	I	ICCE	EC	40437 pqs	I	ICCE	EC

GL1G (TRFK)   TRAILER KITCHEN FIRST

Dia. GL101. pt. Reclassified from TRUK. Used in "Pullman" sets and as replacements for out of service TRFBs. pt. 24F.

*–Converted to lounge first seating 16F 1L. Dia. GM101.
Lot No. 30884 Derby 1976–7. 37 t.

40501	I	ICHL	NL	40511 s	I	IWRR	OO
40505 s	I	IECD	NL	40513 *	I	IXXH	NL

GK1G (TRFM)   TRAILER MODULAR BUFFET FIRST

Dia. GK102. Converted to modular catering from 40719. pt. 17F.

Lot No. 30921 Derby 1978–9. 38.16 t.

40619 ps	I	IMLR	NL	

GK1G (TRFB)   TRAILER BUFFET FIRST

Dia. GK101. These vehicles have larger kitchens than the 402xx and 404xx series vehicles, and are used in trains where full meal service is required. They have been renumbered from the 403xx series (in which the seats were unclassified) by adding 400 to previous number. pt. 17F.

40700–40721. Lot No. 30921 Derby 1978–9. 38.16 t.
40722–40735. Lot No. 30940 Derby 1979–80. 38.16 t.
40736–40753. Lot No. 30948 Derby 1980–1. 38.16 t.
40754–40757. Lot No. 30966 Derby 1982. 38.16 t.

40700	p	I	IMLR	NL		40730	psd	I	IMLR	NL
40701	p	I	IMLR	NL		40731	qs	I	IWRR	LA
40702	ps	I	IMLR	NL		40732	q	I	IWRR	LA
40703	ps	I	IWRR	LA		40733	ps	I	IWRR	LA
40704	p	I	IECD	EC		40734	ps	I	IWRR	LA
40705	p	I	IECD	EC		40735	p	I	IECD	NL
40706	ps	I	IECD	EC		40736	p	I	IWRR	LA
40707	p	I	IWCW	LA		40737	p	I	IECD	NL
40708	p	I	IMLR	NL		40738	p	I	IWCW	LA
40709	p	I	IWCW	LA		40739	p	I	IWRR	PM
40710	p	I	IWRR	LA		40740		I	IECD	EC
40711	ps	I	IECD	EC		40741	p	I	IMLR	NL
40712	p	I	IWRR	LA		40742	ps	I	IWRR	LA
40713	ps	I	IWRR	LA		40743	ps	I	IECD	NL
40714	qs	I	IECD	EC		40744	pq	I	IWRR	PM
40715	p	I	IWRR	PM		40745	ps	I	IWRR	PM
40716	p	I	IWRR	PM		40746	p	I	IMLR	NL
40717	p	I	IWRR	PM		40747	pq	I	IWRR	PM
40718	p	I	IWRR	LA		40748	p	I	IECD	NL
40720	p	I	IECD	EC		40749	ps	I	IMLR	NL
40721	ps	I	IWRR	LA		40750	p	I	IECD	EC
40722	q	I	IWRR	LA		40751	p	I	IMLR	NL
40723	q	I	IWRR	LA		40752	pq	I	IWRR	PM
40724	qs	I	IWRR	LA		40753	p	I	IMLR	NL
40725	q	I	IWRR	LA		40754	ps	I	IMLR	NL
40726	qs	I	IWRR	LA		40755	qs	I	IWRR	LA
40727	qs	I	IWRR	LA		40756	ps	I	IMLR	NL
40728	ps	I	IMLR	NL		40757	q	I	IWRR	LA
40729	ps	I	IMLR	NL						

GH1G (TF)   TRAILER FIRST

Dia. GH102. pa. 48F 2L.

41003–41056. Lot No. 30881 Derby 1976–7. 33.66 t.
41057–41120. Lot No. 30896 Derby 1977–8. 33.66 t.
41121–41148. Lot No. 30938 Derby 1979–80. 33.66 t.
41149–41166. Lot No. 30947 Derby 1980. 33.66 t.
41167–41169. Lot No. 30963 Derby 1982. 33.66 t.
41170–41174. Lot No. 30967 Derby 1982. Ex prototype vehicles. 33.66 t.
41175–41176. Lot No. 30897 Derby 1977. Converted 1982 from TS. 33.66 t.

41170–4 were converted from prototype vehicles.
41175–6 were converted from TS.

41003	ps	I	IWRR	PM	41040	s	I	IECD	NL
41004		I	IWRR	PM	41041	ps	I	IECD	NL
41005	p	I	IWRR	PM	41042		I	IWRR	PM
41006		I	IWRR	PM	41043		I	IECD	NL
41007	p	I	IWRR	PM	41044		I	IECD	NL
41008		I	IWRR	PM	41045	s	I	IWCW	LA
41009	p	I	IWRR	PM	41046		I	IMLR	NL
41010		I	IWRR	PM	41049	s	I	IWRR	PM
41011	p	I	IWRR	PM	41050	s	I	IWRR	PM
41012		I	IWRR	PM	41051		I	IWRR	LA
41013	ps	I	IWRR	PM	41052		I	IWRR	LA
41014		I	IWRR	PM	41055	s	I	IWCW	LA
41015	p	I	IWRR	PM	41056		I	IWCW	LA
41016		I	IWRR	PM	41057	s	I	IMLR	NL
41017	p	I	IWRR	PM	41058		I	IMLR	NL
41018	s	I	IWRR	PM	41059	s	I	ICCE	EC
41019	p	I	IWRR	PM	41060		I	IECD	EC
41020		I	IWRR	PM	41061	s	I	IMLR	NL
41021	p	I	IWRR	PM	41062	s	I	IMLR	NL
41022		I	IWRR	PM	41063	s	I	IMLR	NL
41023	p	I	IWRR	LA	41064	s	I	IMLR	NL
41024		I	IWRR	LA	41065	s	I	IWCW	LA
41025	p	I	IWRR	LA	41066	p	I	IECD	NL
41026		I	IWRR	LA	41067	s	I	IMLR	NL
41027	p	I	IWRR	LA	41068	s	I	IMLR	NL
41028		I	IWRR	LA	41069	s	I	IMLR	NL
41029	ps	I	IWRR	LA	41070	s	I	IMLR	NL
41030	s	I	IWRR	LA	41071		I	IMLR	NL
41031	ps	I	IWRR	LA	41072		I	IMLR	NL
41032	s	I	IWRR	LA	41075	s	I	IMLR	NL
41033	ps	I	IWRR	LA	41076		I	IMLR	NL
41034	s	I	IWRR	LA	41077		I	IMLR	NL
41035	p	I	IWRR	LA	41078		I	IMLR	NL
41036		I	IWRR	LA	41079		I	IMLR	NL
41037	p	I	IWRR	LA	41080		I	IMLR	NL
41038		I	IWRR	LA	41081	s	I	ICCE	EC
41039		I	IECD	NL	41082		I	IMLR	NL

41083	s	I	IMLR	NL		41130		I	IWRR	PM
41084	s	I	IMLR	NL		41131	p	I	IWRR	LA
41085	s	I	ICCE	EC		41132		I	IWRR	LA
41086	s	I	ICCE	EC		41133	ps	I	IWRR	LA
41087		I	IECD	EC		41134	s	I	IWRR	LA
41088	s	I	IECD	EC		41135	ps	I	IWRR	LA
41089		I	ICCT	LA		41136	s	I	IWRR	LA
41090		I	IECD	EC		41137	ps	I	IWRR	PM
41091		I	IECD	EC		41138	s	I	IWRR	PM
41092		I	IECD	EC		41139	p	I	IWRR	LA
41093		I	IWCW	LA		41140		I	IWRR	LA
41094		I	IWCW	LA		41141	p	I	IWRR	LA
41095	s	I	ICCE	EC		41142		I	IWRR	LA
41096	s	I	ICCE	EC		41143	p	I	IWRR	LA
41097		I	IECD	EC		41144		I	IWRR	LA
41098		I	IECD	EC		41145	p	I	IWRR	PM
41099	s	I	IECD	EC		41146		I	IWRR	PM
41100		I	IECD	EC		41147	s	I	ICCE	EC
41101		I	IWRR	LA		41148	s	I	ICCE	EC
41102		I	IWRR	LA		41149	s	I	ICCE	EC
41103	s	I	IWRR	LA		41150		I	IECD	NL
41104	s	I	IWRR	LA		41151		I	IECD	EC
41105		I	IECD	EC		41152		I	IECD	EC
41106		I	IECD	EC		41153	s	I	IMLR	NL
41107	s	I	ICCE	EC		41154	s	I	IMLR	NL
41108		I	IECD	EC		41155		I	IMLR	NL
41109	s	I	ICCT	LA		41156		I	IMLR	NL
41110		I	IWRR	PM		41157	s	I	IECD	NL
41111	s	I	IMLR	NL		41158	s	I	IECD	NL
41112		I	IMLR	NL		41159		I	ICCT	PM
41113		I	IMLR	NL		41160		I	ICCT	PM
41114	s	I	ICCE	EC		41161	s	I	ICCT	PM
41115		I	IMLR	NL		41162	s	I	ICCT	PM
41116		I	IECD	NL		41163	s	I	ICCT	PM
41117		I	IMLR	NL		41164	ps	I	IWRR	PM
41118		I	IECD	EC		41165		I	ICCT	LA
41119	s	I	ICCE	EC		41166		I	ICCT	LA
41120		I	IECD	EC		41167		I	ICCT	LA
41121	ps	I	IWRR	LA		41168		I	ICCT	LA
41122		I	IWRR	LA		41169	s	I	ICCT	LA
41123	p	I	IWRR	PM		41170 (41001)		I	IECD	EC
41124		I	IWRR	PM		41171 (42001)	s	I	ICCT	LA
41125		I	IWRR	LA		41172 (42000)	s	I	IWRR	LA
41126	p	I	IWRR	LA		41173 (42002)		I	IWRR	PM
41127	p	I	IWRR	PM		41174 (41002)	s	I	IWRR	LA
41128	s	I	IWRR	PM		41175 (42114)	s	I	IECD	NL
41129	p	I	IWRR	PM		41176 (42142)		I	IMLR	NL

GH2G (TS)   TRAILER STANDARD

Dia. GH202 (GH203*). pa. 72S 2L. (76S 2L*)

42003–42090. Lot No. 30882 Derby 1976–7. 33.60 t.
42091–42250. Lot No. 30897 Derby 1977–9. 33.60 t.
42251–42305. Lot No. 30939 Derby 1979–80. 33.60 t.
42306–42322. Lot No. 30969 Derby 1982. 33.60 t.
42323–42341. Lot No. 30983 Derby 1984–5. 33.60 t.
42342. Lot No. 30949 Derby 1982. 33.47 t. Converted from TGS.
42343/5. Lot No. 30970 Derby 1982. 33.47 t. Converted from TGS.
42344. Lot No. 30964 Derby 1982. 33.47 t. Converted from TGS.
42346/7/50/1. Lot No. 30881 Derby 1976–7. 33.66 t. Converted from TF.
42348/9. Lot No. 30896 Derby 1977–8. 33.66 t. Converted from TF.

42158 was converted to TF and numbered 41177 for a time.
42342–45 were converted TGS.
42346–51 were converted from TF.

42003	I	IWRR	PM	42041 s	I	IWRR	LA
42004	I	IWRR	PM	42042	I	IWRR	LA
42005	I	IWRR	PM	42043 s	I	IWRR	LA
42006	I	IWRR	PM	42044	I	IWRR	LA
42007	I	IWRR	PM	42045 s	I	IWRR	LA
42008	I	IWRR	PM	42046 s	I	IWRR	LA
42009	I	IWRR	PM	42047 s	I	IWRR	LA
42010	I	IWRR	PM	42048	I	IWRR	LA
42011	I	IWRR	PM	42049 s	I	IWRR	LA
42012 s	I	IWRR	PM	42050 s	I	IWRR	LA
42013	I	IWRR	PM	42051	I	IWRR	LA
42014	I	IWRR	PM	42052	I	IWRR	LA
42015 s	I	IWRR	PM	42053	I	IWRR	LA
42016 s	I	IWRR	PM	42054	I	IWRR	LA
42017 s	I	IWRR	PM	42055	I	IWRR	LA
42018 s	I	IWRR	PM	42056	I	IWRR	LA
42019	I	IWRR	PM	42057 s	I	IECD	NL
42020	I	IWRR	PM	42058	I	IECD	NL
42021	I	IWRR	PM	42059	I	IECD	NL
42022 s	I	IWRR	PM	42060 s	I	IWRR	PM
42023 s	I	IWRR	PM	42061 s	I	IWRR	PM
42024	I	IWRR	PM	42062 s	I	IWCW	LA
42025	I	IWRR	PM	42063	I	IECD	NL
42026	I	IWRR	PM	42064	I	IECD	NL
42027	I	IWRR	PM	42065	I	IECD	NL
42028	I	IWRR	PM	42066	I	IWCW	LA
42029	I	IWRR	PM	42067 s	I	IWCW	LA
42030	I	IWRR	PM	42068 s	I	IWCW	LA
42031	I	IWRR	PM	42069	I	IWRR	PM
42032	I	IWRR	PM	42070	I	IWRR	PM
42033	I	IWRR	LA	42071	I	IWRR	PM
42034 s	I	IWRR	LA	42072 s	I	IWRR	PM
42035 s	I	IWRR	LA	42073	I	IWRR	PM
42036 s	I	IWRR	LA	42074 s	I	IWRR	PM
42037	I	IWRR	LA	42075	I	IWRR	LA
42038	I	IWRR	LA	42076	I	IWRR	LA
42039	I	IWRR	LA	42077	I	IWRR	LA
42040	I	IWRR	LA	42078	I	IWRR	LA

42079	I	IWRR	PM	42132 s	I	IMLR	NL
42080	I	IWRR	PM	42133	I	IMLR	NL
42081 s	I	IWCW	LA	42134	I	IWRR	LA
42082	I	IWCW	LA	42135 s	I	IMLR	NL
42083	I	IWCW	LA	42136	I	IMLR	NL
42084	I	ICCT	PM	42137	I	IMLR	NL
42085	I	ICCT	PM	42138 s	I	IWRR	LA
42086	I	ICCT	PM	42139 s	I	IMLR	NL
42087	I	ICCT	PM	42140	I	IMLR	NL
42088 s	I	ICCT	PM	42141	I	IMLR	NL
42089 s	I	ICCT	PM	42143	I	IWRR	PM
42090 s	I	ICCT	PM	42144	I	IWRR	PM
42091 s	I	ICCT	PM	42145	I	IWRR	PM
42092 s	I	ICCT	PM	42146 s	I	IECD	NL
42093 s	I	ICCT	PM	42147	I	IMLR	NL
42094 s	I	ICCT	PM	42148	I	IMLR	NL
42095 s	I	ICCT	PM	42149 s	I	IMLR	NL
42096	I	IWRR	LA	42150 s	I	IECD	NL
42097	I	IWRR	LA	42151 s	I	IMLR	NL
42098	I	IWRR	LA	42152 s	I	IMLR	NL
42099 s	I	IWRR	LA	42153 s	I	IMLR	NL
42100 s	I	IMLR	NL	42154 s	I	IECD	NL
42101 s	I	IMLR	NL	42155 s	I	IMLR	NL
42102 s	I	IMLR	NL	42156 s	I	IMLR	NL
42103 s	I	ICCE	EC	42157 s	I	IMLR	NL
42104 s	I	IECD	EC	42158	I	IECD	EC
42105 s	I	ICCT	LA	42159	I	IMLR	NL
42106	I	IECD	EC	42160 s	I	IMLR	NL
42107 s	I	IWCW	LA	42161 s	I	IMLR	NL
42108	I	ICCT	LA	42162 s	I	ICCE	EC
42109	I	ICCT	LA	42163 s	I	IMLR	NL
42110	I	ICCT	LA	42164 s	I	IMLR	NL
42111 s	I	IMLR	NL	42165 s	I	IMLR	NL
42112 s	I	IMLR	NL	42166 s	I	ICCE	EC
42113 s	I	IMLR	NL	42167 s	I	ICCE	EC
42115	I	ICCE	EC	42168 s	I	ICCE	EC
42116 s	I	ICCE	EC	42169 s	I	ICCE	EC
42117 s	I	ICCE	EC	42170 s	I	ICCE	EC
42118	I	IWRR	PM	42171 s	I	IECD	EC
42119 s	I	IMLR	NL	42172 s	I	IECD	EC
42120 s	I	IMLR	NL	42173 s	I	ICCE	EC
42121 s	I	IMLR	NL	42174 s	I	ICCE	EC
42122 s	I	IWRR	LA	42175 s	I	ICCT	LA
42123	I	IMLR	NL	42176 s	I	ICCT	LA
42124 s	I	IMLR	NL	42177 s	I	ICCT	LA
42125 s	I	IMLR	NL	42178 s	I	ICCE	EC
42126	I	IWCW	LA	42179	I	IECD	EC
42127 s	I	ICCE	EC	42180	I	IECD	EC
42128 s	I	ICCE	EC	42181	I	IECD	EC
42129	I	IECD	NL	42182 s	I	IECD	EC
42130	I	IWRR	LA	42183 s	I	IWCW	LA
42131 s	I	IMLR	NL	42184 s	I	IWCW	LA

42185	s	I	IWCW	LA	42237	s	I	ICCE	EC
42186	s	I	IECD	EC	42238	s	I	ICCE	EC
42187	s	I	ICCE	EC	42239	s	I	ICCE	EC
42188	s	I	ICCE	EC	42240		I	IECD	EC
42189	s	I	ICCE	EC	42241	s	I	IECD	EC
42190	s	I	IECD	EC	42242		I	IECD	EC
42191	s	I	IECD	EC	42243	s	I	IECD	EC
42192		I	IECD	EC	42244		I	IECD	EC
42193		I	IECD	EC	42245	s	I	IECD	NL
42194	s	I	IMLR	NL	42246	s	I	ICCE	EC
42195	s	I	ICCE	EC	42247	s	I	ICCE	EC
42196		I	IWRR	PM	42248	s	I	ICCE	EC
42197		I	IWRR	PM	42249	s	I	ICCE	EC
42198	s	I	IECD	EC	42250		I	IECD	NL
42199		I	IECD	EC	42251		I	IWRR	LA
42200	s	I	IECD	NL	42252	s	I	IWRR	LA
42201	s	I	IWRR	LA	42253		I	IWRR	LA
42202		I	IWRR	LA	42254	s	I	ICCE	EC
42203		I	IWRR	LA	42255	s	I	IWRR	PM
42204		I	IWRR	LA	42256	s	I	IWRR	PM
42205	s	I	IMLR	NL	42257	s	I	IWRR	PM
42206	s	I	IWRR	LA	42258	s	I	ICCE	EC
42207		I	IWRR	LA	42259		I	IWRR	LA
42208		I	IWRR	LA	42260		I	IWRR	LA
42209		I	IWRR	LA	42261		I	IWRR	LA
42210	s	I	IMLR	NL	42262	s	I	ICCE	EC
42211		I	IECD	EC	42263		I	IWRR	PM
42212		I	IECD	EC	42264	s	I	IWRR	LA
42213		I	IECD	EC	42265		I	IWRR	LA
42214		I	IECD	EC	42266	s	I	ICCE	EC
42215		I	IECD	NL	42267		I	IWRR	PM
42216		I	IWRR	LA	42268		I	IWRR	PM
42217	s	I	ICCE	EC	42269		I	IWRR	PM
42218	s	I	ICCE	EC	42270	s	I	ICCE	EC
42219		I	IECD	EC	42271	s	I	IWRR	LA
42220		I	IMLR	NL	42272		I	IWRR	LA
42221	s	I	IWRR	LA	42273		I	IWRR	LA
42222	s	I	ICCT	LA	42274	s	I	ICCE	EC
42223	s	I	ICCT	LA	42275		I	IWRR	LA
42224	s	I	ICCT	LA	42276	s	I	IWRR	LA
42225		I	IMLR	NL	42277		I	IWRR	LA
42226		I	IECD	EC	42278	s	I	ICCE	EC
42227	s	I	IMLR	NL	42279		I	IWRR	LA
42228	s	I	IMLR	NL	42280		I	IWRR	LA
42229	s	I	IMLR	NL	42281		I	IWRR	LA
42230	s	I	IMLR	NL	42282	s	I	ICCE	EC
42231	s	I	ICCE	EC	42283	s	I	IWRR	PM
42232	s	I	ICCE	EC	42284		I	IWRR	PM
42233	s	I	ICCE	EC	42285		I	IWRR	PM
42234	s	I	ICCE	EC	42286		I	ICCT	PM
42235	s	I	IECD	EC	42287		I	IWRR	LA
42236		I	IWRR	PM	42288		I	IWRR	LA

42289	I	IWRR	LA		42321	s I	ICCT	LA
42290	I	ICCT	PM		42322	I	ICCT	LA
42291	I	IWRR	LA		42323	s I	IECD	NL
42292	I	IWRR	LA		42324	s I	IMLR	NL
42293	I	IWRR	LA		42325	s I	IWRR	PM
42294 s	I	ICCT	PM		42326	s I	ICCE	EC
42295	I	IWRR	LA		42327	I	IMLR	NL
42296 s	I	IWRR	LA		42328	s I	IMLR	NL
42297 s	I	IWRR	LA		42329	s I	IMLR	NL
42298	I	ICCT	PM		42330	s I	ICCE	EC
42299 s	I	IWRR	PM		42331	s I	IMLR	NL
42300	I	IWRR	PM		42332	I	IWRR	PM
42301	I	IWRR	PM		42333	I	IWRR	PM
42302	I	ICCT	PM		42334	s I	ICCT	LA
42303 s	I	ICCT	PM		42335	s I	IMLR	NL
42304	I	ICCT	PM		42336	s I	ICCE	EC
42305 s	I	ICCT	PM		42337	s I	IMLR	NL
42306	I	ICCT	LA		42338	s I	ICCE	EC
42307	I	ICCT	LA		42339	I	IMLR	NL
42308	I	ICCT	LA		42340	I	IECD	NL
42309	I	ICCT	LA		42341	s I	IMLR	NL
42310	I	ICCT	LA		42342 (44082)	I	IWRR	LA
42311	I	ICCT	LA		42343 (44085)	I	IWRR	LA
42312	I	ICCT	LA		42344 (44092) s	I	IWRR	LA
42313	I	ICCT	LA		42345 (44096)	I	IWRR	LA
42314	I	ICCT	LA		42346 (41053)	I	IWRR	PM
42315	I	ICCT	LA		42347 (41054)	I	IWRR	LA
42316	I	ICCT	LA		42348 (41073)	I	IWRR	LA
42317	I	ICCT	LA		42349 (41074)	I	IWRR	LA
42318 s	I	ICCT	LA		42350 (41047)	I	IWRR	LA
42319 s	I	ICCT	LA		42351 (41048)	I	IWRR	PM
42320	I	ICCT	LA					

GJ2G (TGS) TRAILER GUARD'S STANDARD

Dia. GJ202. pg. 61S 1L + tip-up seat and wheelchair space.

44000. Lot No. 30953 Derby 1980. 33.47 t.
44001–44090. Lot No. 30949 Derby 1980–2. 33.47 t.
44091–44094. Lot No. 30964 Derby 1982. 33.47 t.
44095–44101. Lot No. 30970 Derby 1982. 33.47 t.

* Two extra seats crammed in. 63S 1L (Dia. GJ205).
† Fitted with side buffers and drophead buckeye couplings.

44000 s	I	ICCE	EC		44008 s	I	IWRR	PM
44001	I	IWRR	LA		44009 s	I	IWRR	PM
44002	I	IWRR	0M		44010	I	IWRR	PM
44003	I	IWRR	PM		44011 *	I	IWRR	LA
44004	I	IWRR	PM		44012	I	IWRR	LA
44005	I	IWRR	PM		44013 *	I	IWRR	LA
44006	I	IWRR	PM		44014 *	I	IWRR	LA
44007	I	IWRR	PM		44015 *s	I	IWRR	LA

44016	*s	I	IWRR	LA
44017	*	I	IWRR	LA
44018		I	IWRR	LA
44019	*	I	IECD	NL
44020	*	I	IWRR	PM
44021	†s	I	ICCE	EC
44022	*s	I	IWCW	LA
44023	*	I	IWRR	PM
44024	*s	I	IWRR	PM
44025	*	I	IWRR	LA
44026	*	I	IWRR	PM
44027	s	I	IMLR	NL
44028	*	I	IWRR	LA
44029	s	I	IWRR	PM
44030	*	I	IWRR	LA
44031		I	IWRR	LA
44032	*	I	IWRR	PM
44033	*s	I	IWRR	LA
44034	*	I	IWRR	LA
44035	*	I	IWRR	LA
44036	*s	I	IWRR	PM
44037	*	I	IWRR	LA
44038		I	IWRR	LA
44039		I	IWRR	LA
44040		I	IWRR	PM
44041	s	I	IMLR	NL
44042	s	I	ICCE	EC
44043	*	I	IWCW	LA
44044	*	I	IMLR	NL
44045		I	IECD	NL
44046	s	I	IMLR	NL
44047	*	I	IMLR	NL
44048	*s	I	IMLR	NL
44049	*	I	IWRR	PM
44050	*	I	IMLR	NL
44051	*	I	IMLR	NL
44052	*s	I	IMLR	NL
44053	*s	I	IMLR	NL
44054	*s	I	IMLR	NL
44055	*s	I	ICCE	EC
44056	*s†	I	IECD	EC
44057	*	I	ICCT	LA
44058	*†	I	IECD	EC
44059	†	I	IWCW	LA
44060	*s	I	ICCE	EC
44061		I	IECD	EC
44062	s	I	ICCE	EC
44063	s	I	IECD	EC
44064	*	I	IWRR	LA
44065		I	ICCT	PM
44066		I	IWRR	LA
44067		I	IECD	EC
44068	*s	I	ICCT	PM
44069		I	ICCT	PM
44070	*s	I	IECD	NL
44071	*	I	IMLR	NL
44072	*s	I	ICCT	PM
44073		I	IMLR	NL
44074	s	I	ICCE	EC
44075	*s	I	ICCE	EC
44076	*	I	ICCT	PM
44077	*s	I	IECD	EC
44078	*	I	ICCE	EC
44079	*s	I	ICCE	EC
44080	*s	I	IECD	EC
44081	s	I	ICCT	LA
44083	*	I	IMLR	NL
44084	s	I	ICCT	LA
44085		I	IMLR	NL
44086	†	I	IECD	NL
44087	*	I	ICCT	LA
44088	*	I	ICCT	LA
44089	*	I	ICCT	LA
44090	*	I	ICCT	LA
44091	*s	I	ICCT	LA
44093	s	I	IWRR	LA
44094	*s	I	IECD	NL
44097	s†	I	ICCE	EC
44098	*†	I	IECD	EC
44099		I	IWRR	LA
44100	*s	I	ICCE	EC
44101	†	I	ICCT	LA

2.3 HST FORMATIONS

WESTERN REGION & WCML UNITS

Unit									Code
PM 1	41093	41094	40707	42183	42184	42185	42107	44001	IWR
PM 2	41101	41102	40712	42201	42202	42203	42204	44064	IWR
PM 3	41103	41104	40713	42206	42207	42208	42209	44066	IWR
PM 4	41009	41010	40204	42012	42004	42013	42014	44004	IWR
PM 5	41011	41012	40205	42015	42005	42016	42017	44005	IWR
PM 6	41013	41014	40206	42018	42006	42019	42020	44006	IWR
PM 7	41015	41016	40207	42021	42007	42022	42023	44007	IWR
PM 8	41017	41018	40208	42024	42008	42025	42026	44008	IWR
PM 9	41019	41020	40211	42027	42009	42028	42029	44009	IWR
PM 10	41021	41022	40210	42030	42010	42031	42032	44010	IWR
LA 11	41023	41024	40755	42096	42033	42034	42035	44011	IWR
LA 12	41025	41026	40723	42097	42036	42037	42038	44012	IWR
LA 13	41027	41028	40725	42098	42039	42040	42041	44013	IWR
LA 14	41029	41030	40726	42099	42042	42043	42044	44014	IWR
LA 15	41031	41032	40727	42216	42045	42046	42047	44015	IWR
LA 16	41033	41034	40731	42221	42048	42049	42050	44016	IWR
LA 17	41035	41036	40732	42051	42342	42052	42053	44017	IWR
LA 18	41037	41038	40757	42054	42343	42055	42056	44018	IWR
PM 19	41003	41004	40752	42333	42143	42144	42145	44049	IWR
PM 20	41127	41128	40717	42196	42197	42060	42061	44020	IWR
LA 22	41045	41065	40738	42062	42066	42067	42068	44022	IWCV
PM 23	41005	41006	40744	42069	42070	42071	42118	44023	IWR
PM 24	41049	41050	40745	42325	42072	42073	42074	44024	IWR
LA 25	41051	41052	40710	42075	42076	42077	42078	44025	IWR
PM 26	41007	41008	40747	42332	42236	42079	42080	44026	IWR
LA 27	41055	41056	40709	42081	42082	42083	42126	44043	IWCV
LA 28	41121	41122	40722	42345	42251	42252	42253	44028	IWR
PM 29	41123	41124	40739	42255	42263	42256	42257	44029	IWR
LA 30	41126	41125	40724	42344	42259	42260	42261	44030	IWR
PM 32	41129	41130	40716	42267	42346	42268	42269	44032	IWR
LA 33	41131	41132	40736	42271	42347	42272	42273	44033	IWR
LA 34	41133	41134	40721	42275	42264	42276	42277	44034	IWR
LA 35	41135	41136	40703	42279	42265	42280	42281	44035	IWR
PM 36	41137	41138	40228	42283	42003	42284	42285	44036	IWR
LA 37	41139	41140	40718	42287	42348	42288	42289	44037	IWR
LA 38	41141	41142	40734	42291	42349	42292	42293	44038	IWR
LA 39	41143	41144	40733	42295	42350	42296	42297	44039	IWR
PM 40	41145	41146	40213	42299	42351	42300	42301	44040	IWR

NORTH EAST–SOUTH WEST ROUTE UNITS

Unit									Code
EC 30	41081		40420	42330	42237	42238	42239	44075	ICC
EC 31	41059		40419	42336	42115	42116	42117	44042	ICC
EC 32	41119		40427	42246	42247	42248	42249	44078	ICC
EC 33	41149		40422	42162	42166	42170	42174	44079	ICC
EC 34	41096		40430	42338	42178	42127	42128	44021	ICC

EC 35	41085		40423	42169	42168	42167	42103	44055	ICCE
EC 36	41095		40435	42326	42187	42188	42189	44060	ICCE
EC 37	41107		40429	42195	42217	42218	42219	44097	ICCE
EC 38	41114		40416	42231	42232	42233	42234	44074	ICCE
EC 39	41147		40401	42254	42258	42262	42266	44000	ICCE
EC 40	41148		40402	42270	42274	42278	42282	44062	ICCE
PM 43	41159		40403	42286	42290	42294	42298	44065	ICCT
PM 44	41160		40425	42302	42303	42304	42305	44068	ICCT
PM 45	41161		40221	42084	42085	42086	42087	44069	ICCT
PM 46	41162		40414	42088	42089	42090	42091	44072	ICCT
PM 47	41163		40415	42092	42093	42094	42095	44076	ICCT
LA 51	41165		40417	42108	42109	42110	42322	44087	ICCT
LA 52	41166		40424	42306	42307	42308	42309	44088	ICCT
LA 53	41167		40436	42310	42311	42312	42313	44089	ICCT
LA 54	41168		40233	42314	42315	42316	42317	44090	ICCT
LA 55	41169		40434	42318	42319	42320	42321	44091	ICCT
LA 56	41109		40418	42334	42222	42223	42224	44101	ICCT
LA 57	41089		40426	42175	42176	42177	42105	44057	ICCT

EAST COAST & MIDLAND LINES UNITS

NL 01	41057	41058	40708	42335	42111	42112	42113	44041	IMLR
NL 02	41112	41111	40749	42194	42229	42227	42228	44073	IMLR
NL 03	41061	41062	40729	42337	42119	42120	42121	44027	IMLR
NL 04	41063	41064	40754	42324	42123	42124	42125	44044	IMLR
NL 05	41153	41154	40741	42327	42147	42205	42210	44083	IMLR
NL 06	41067	41068	40730	42331	42131	42132	42133	44046	IMLR
NL 07	41069	41070	40751	42339	42135	42136	42137	44047	IMLR
NL 08	41071	41072	40728	42329	42139	42140	42141	44048	IMLR
NL 09	41155	41156	41117	40619	42220	42225	42230	44085	IMLR
NL 10	41075	41076	40756	42341	42328	42148	42149	44050	IMLR
NL 11	41077	41078	41046	40753	42151	42152	42153	44051	IMLR
NL 12	41079	41080	40700	42155	42156	42157	42100	44052	IMLR
NL 13	41115	41082	40701	42159	42160	42161	42101	44053	IMLR
NL 14	41083	41084	40702	42163	42164	42165	42102	44054	IMLR
NL 15	41157	41158	40743	42200	42129	42245	42250	44086	IECD
NL 16	41175	41150	40748	42154	42215	42146	42150	44094	IECD
NL 17	41039	41040	40735	42323	42058	42059	42057	44019	IECD
NL 18	41043	41044	40746	42340	42063	42064	42065	44045	IECD
EC 19	41087	41088	40706	42104	42171	42172	42173	44056	IECD
EC 20	41091	41092	40704	42179	42180	42181	42106	44058	IECD
EC 21	41170	41118	40720	42241	42242	42243	42244	44098	IECD
EC 22	41151	41152	40740	42226	42182	42186	42190	44080	IECD
EC 23	41097	41098	40750	42158	42191	42192	42193	44061	IECD
EC 24	41099	41100	40711	42235	42240	42198	42199	44063	IECD
EC 25	41105	41106	40714	42211	42212	42213	42214	44067	IECD

SPARE CARS

The following cars are either spare or not accounted for in sets: in at present:

40209	IWRR	PM	41041	IECD	NL	41176	IMLR	NL
40212	ICCT	LA	41042	IWRR	PM	42011	IWRR	PM
40231	IWRR	LA	41060	IECD	EC	44002	IWRR	OM
40232	ICCT	PM	41066	IECD	NL	44003	IWRR	PM
40437	ICCE	EC	41086	ICCE	EC	44059	IWCW	LA
40501	ICHL	NL	41090	IECD	EC	44070	IECD	NL
40505	IECD	NL	41108	IECD	EC	44071	IMLR	NL
40511	IWRR	OO	41113	IMLR	NL	44077	IECD	EC
40513	IXXH	NL	41116	IECD	NL	44081	ICCT	LA
40705	IECD	EC	41120	IECD	EC	44084	ICCT	LA
40715	IWRR	PM	41164	IWRR	PM	44093	IWRR	LA
40737	IMLR	NL	41171	ICCT	LA	44099	IWRR	LA
40742	IWRR	LA	41173	IWRR	LA	44100	ICCE	EC

3. DIESEL MULTIPLE UNITS

Diesel mechanical and diesel hydraulic multiple unit vehicles are numbered in the series 51000–59999. All vehicles numbered in the 53000–53999 series were originally numbered in the series 50000–50999, and were renumbered by having 3000 added to their original numbers. All vehicles in the series 54000–54504 were originally numbered in the series 56000–56505, and were renumbered by having 2000 subtracted from their original numbers.

Diesel electric multiple unit vehicles are numbered in the series 60108–60999. A number of vehicles which were numbered in the series 60000–60107 were renumbered during 1989 to avoid conficting with Class 60 locomotives. The previous numbers of the remaining vehicle is given in the text.

Regional prefix letters used to be carried preceeding the vehicle number, but these are now no longer used and many have been removed. The prefixes were: E–Eastern Region, M–London Midland Region, S–Southern Region, SC–Scottish Region. Prefixes are not shown in this book as they no longer officially form part of the vehicle number.

ABBREVIATIONS

The codes used by the BR Operating Department to describe the various different types of diesel multiple unit vehicles and quoted in the class headings are as follows:

Diesel Mechanical & Diesel Hydraulic Units.

DMBC   Driving Motor Brake Composite.
DMBS   Driving Motor Brake Standard.
DMCL   Driving Motor Composite with Lavatory.
DMPMV Driving Motor Parcels & Mails Van.
DMS   Driving Motor Standard.
DMSL   Driving Motor Standard with Lavatory.
DTCL   Driving Trailer Composite with Lavatory
DTPMV Driving Trailer Parcels & Mails Van.
DTSL   Driving Trailer Standard with Lavatory.
MS   Motor Standard.
MSL   Motor Standard with Lavatory.
TBSL   Trailer Brake Standard with Lavatory.
TC   Trailer Composite.
TCL   Trailer Composite with Lavatory.
TS   Trailer Standard.
TSL   Trailer Standard with Lavatory.

It should be noted that as all vehicles are of an open configuration the letter 'O' is omitted for all vehicles.

The letters (A) and (B) may be added to the above codes to differentiate between two cars of the same operating type which have differences between them. Note that a consistent system is used, rather than the official operator codes which are sometimes inconsistent.

A composite is a vehicle containing both First and Standard class accommodation, and vehicles are described as such even though most first class accommodation has now been declassified on most vehicles. This is done so as to differentiate between the different styles of seat provided in standard and erstwhile first class areas of a vehicle. At the time of writing only composite vehicles allocated to BY, CA, OO and RG depots retained first class accommodation in use as such.

A brake vehicle is a vehicle containing seperate specific accommodation for the guard (as opposed to the use of spare driving cabs on second generation units).

Diesel Electric Units.

DMBSO Driving Motor Brake Standard (Open).
DTCsoL Driving Trailer Composite with Lavatory (Semi-Open).
DTSOL   Driving Trailer Standard with Lavatory (Open).
DTSO   Driving Trailer Standard (Open).
TCsoL   Trailer Composite with Lavatory (Semi-Open).
TSO   Trailer Standard (Open).
TSOL   Trailer Standard with Lavatory (Open).

The notes as above apply regarding composite and brake vehicles. A semi-open composite vehicle has first class accommodation in compartments with a side corridor and standard class accommodation provided in an open saloon.

DIAGRAMS AND DESIGN CODES

For each type of vehicle, the official design code consists of a seven character code of two letters, four numbers and another letter, e.g. DP2010A. The first five characters of this are the diagram code and are given in the class heading or sub heading. These are explained as follows:

1st Letter

This is always 'D' for a diesel multiple unit vehicle.

2nd Letter

as follows for various vehicle types:

P   Driving motor passenger vehicles without a brake compartment.
Q   Driving motor passenger vehicles with a brake compartment.
R   Non-Driving motor passenger vehicles.
S   Driving trailer passenger vehicles.
T   Trailer passenger vehicles without a brake compartment.
U   Trailer passenger vehicles with a brake compartment.
X   Parcels and Mails vehicles and single unit railcars.

1st Figure

as follows for various vehicle configurations:

2   Standard class accommodation (incl. declassified seats).
3   Composite accommodation.
5   No passenger accommodation.

2nd & 3rd Figures

These denote distinguish between the different designs of vehicle, each different design being allocated a unique two digit number.

Special Note

Where vehicles have been declassified the correct design code for a declassified vehicle is given, even though this may be at variance with official records which do not show the reality of the current position. A declassified composite is still referred to as a composite if it still retains the first class style seats in the erstwhile first class section of the vehicle. Its declassification is denoted by the fact that the first figure of the design code is a '2'.

LOT NUMBERS

Each batch of vehicles is allocated a Lot (or batch) number when ordered and these are quoted in class headings and sub headings.

BUILDERS

These are shown in class headings where the following abbreviations are used:

Alexander	Walter Alexander Ltd., Falkirk.
Barclay	Andrew Barclay Ltd., Kilmarnock.
BRCW	Birmingham Railway Carriage & Wagon Company Ltd.
Derby	BR Derby Carriage Works or British Rail Engineering Limited, Derby Carriage Works. (Now BREL Ltd.)
Gloucester	Gloucester Railway Carriage & Wagon Company Ltd.
Leyland Bus	Leyland Bus Ltd., Workington.
Metro-Cammell	Metropolitan-Cammell Ltd.
Pressed Steel	Pressed Steel Ltd.
York	British Rail Engineering Ltd., York (Now BREL Ltd.)

Where a dual BR works builder is shown (e.g. Ashford/Eastleigh) the first named built the underframe and the last named built the body and assembled the vehicle. For second generation vehicles, the first name is that of the main contractor with the second name being the underframe and final assembly sub-contractor.

ACCOMMODATION

This information is given in class headings and sub headings in the form nF nS nL, where n is the number of seats or lavatories and F, S & L denote first class seats, standard class seats and lavatories respectively. (e.g. 12F 54S 1L denotes 12 first class seats, 54 standard class seats and one lavatory). In declassified vehicles, the capacity is still shown in terms of first and standard class seats to differentiate between the two physically different seat types available, although all seats are officially standard class in such instances.

WEIGHTS

Approximate weights in working order are given in tons for all vehicle types in the class headings and sub headings as appropriate.

DIMENSIONS

The dimensions of each type of vehicle are given in metric units, with length followed by width. All lengths quoted are over buffers (1st generation vehicles) or couplings (2nd generation vehicles). All widths quoted are maxima.

ABBREVIATIONS

The following are used throughout this section:

DEMU	diesel electric multiple unit.
DHMU	diesel hydraulic multiple unit.
DMMU	diesel mechanical multiple unit.
DMU	diesel multiple unit (general term).
F	First class seats.
g	Gangwayed where other members of the class are not.
hp	horsepower.
kW	Kilowatts.
L	Lavatories.
m	metres.
mph	miles per hour.
r	Fitted with radio electronic token block apparatus.
S	Standard class seats.
t	tons.
w	Retains Tungsten lighting.
(S)	Stored servicable. (Not necessarily at allocated depot).
(U)	Stored unservicable. (Not necessarily at allocated depot).
*	Composite vehicle now declassified to standard class only but retaining original seats.
§	Fitted with headlight and radio electronic token block apparatus.

3.1 FIRST GENERATION DMUS

There are three basic types of first generation vehicle as referred to in the class headings as follows:

Standard. (known as 'low density' by BR). Exterior doors are located in entrance vestibules. Largely unidirectional 3+2 seating is provided in standard class, with 2+2 seating in first class. Where no specific type of vehicle is quoted in class headings the vehicle may be assumed to be of this type.

Suburban. (known as 'high density' by BR). Exterior doors to each seating bay. Back to back seating arranged 3+2 in standard class with 2+1 seating in first class.

Cross Country. Exterior doors are located in entrance vestibules. These were originally designed for longer distance services and have 2+2 seating in standard class, with 2+1 in first class.

STANDARD FEATURES.

Transmission: All motor vehicles have mechanical transmission consisting of a cardan shaft and freewheel to a four-speed epicyclic gearbox with a further cardan shaft to the final drive, each engine driving the inner axle of one bogie.

Gangways: Unless stated otherwise, all vehicles are gangwayed at non driving ends with British Standard gangways.

Doors: All units are equipped with slam doors unless otherwise stated.

Lighting: All cars are fitted with fluorescent lighting unless otherwise stated.

Couplings: Screw couplings are used on all vehicles. All remaining first generation vehicles may be coupled together to work in multiple up to a maximum of 6 motor cars or 12 cars in total in a formation. First generation vehicles may not be coupled in multiple with second generation vehicles.

Note: There are many Regional Railways vehicles still officially in capital stock which are now out of use. Vehicles actually in use can be ascertained by reference to the set formations (section 3.2).

CLASS 119   GLOUCESTER CROSS COUNTRY

Engines: Two Leyland 1595 of 112 kW (150 hp).
Bogies: DD10.
Dimensions: 20.45 x 2.82 m.

DMBC. Dia. DQ302. Lot No. 30421 1959. 18F 16S. 37.5 t.

51060	w	**N**	NWXX	RG	51074	w	**N**	NWXX	RG
51065	w	**N**	NWRX	RG	51076	w	**N**	NWXX	RG
51066	w	**N**	NWXX	RG	51079	w	**N**	NWXX	RG
51073	w	**N**	NWXX	RG				

DMSL. Dia. DP203. Lot No. 30422 1958–59. 68S 2L. 38.5 t.

51086 w	**N**	NWXX		RG	51099 w	**N**	NWXX	RG
51088 w	**N**	NWXX		RG	51103 w	**N**	NGBX	OO
51090 w	**N**	NGBX		OO	51104 w	**N**	NWXX	RG
51094 w	**N**	NWXX		RG	51107 w	**N**	NWXX	RG

CLASS 116   DERBY SUBURBAN

Engines: Two Leyland 680/1 of 112 kW (150 hp).
Bogies: DD10.
Dimensions: 20.45 x 2.82 m.

DMBS. Dia. DQ230. Lot No. 30446 1958. 65S. 36.5 t.

51128		PCFX	CF	51134	PCFX	CF
51129		PTSX	TS	51135	PCFX	CF
51130 w		PTSX	TS	51136	PCFX	CF
51131		PTSX	TS	51138	PTSX	TS
51132		PCFX	CF	51140	PCFX	CF
51133		PCFX	CF			

DMS. Dia. DP220. Lot No. 30447 1958. 89S. 36.5 t.

51141		PCFX	CF	51147	PCFX	CF
51142		PTSX	TS	51148	PCFX	CF
51143		PTSX	TS	51149	PTSX	TS
51144		PTSX	TS	51151	PTSX	TS
51145		PCFX	CF	51152	PCFX	CF
51146 w		PTSX	TS	51153	PCFX	CF

CLASS 101   METRO-CAMMELL

Engines: Two Leyland or AEC of 112 kW (150 hp).
Bogies: DD15.
Dimensions: 18.49 x 2.82 m.

DMBS. Dia. DQ202 (†DQ232). Lot No. 30467 1958–59. 52S (†49S with additional luggage rack). 32.5 t.

51175	**RS**	PCAX	CA	51213	**RS**	PNCX	NC
51177		PLOX	LO	51215	**N**	NWRX	RG
51179	**RS**	PLOX	LO	51218		PNCX	NC
51180		PCAX	CA	51220	**N**	NWRX	RG
51184		PLAX	LA	51221	**N**	NWRX	RG
51185		PCAX	CA	51222	**N**	NGEX	CA
51187		PCAX	CA	51224	**S**	PLOX	LO
51188		PCAX	CA	51225	**N**	NWRX	RG
51189		PNCX	NC	51226 †	**N**	NWXX	RG
51190 †	**N**	NNEX		51228		PLOX	LO
51192		PCAX	CA	51230	**RS**	PCAX	CA
51201		PCAX	CA	51231		PLAX	LA
51205	**RS**	PLOX	LO	51245		PLOX	LO
51207	**N**	NNEX	CA	51246		PLAX	LA
51208	**N**	NNEX	CA	51247		PCAX	CA
51210	**RS**	PLOX	LO	51252		PNCX	NC
51211 †	**N**	NNEX	CA	51253		PHAX	HA

CLASS 118   BRCW SUBURBAN

Engines: Two Leyland 680/1 of 112 kW (150 hp).
Bogies: DD10.
Dimensions: 20.45 x 2.82 m.

DMBS. Dia. DQ220. Lot No. 30543 1960. 65S. 36.5 t.

51314 w		PTSX	TS	51316	PTSX	TS
51315 w		PCFX	CF			

DMS. Dia. DP221. Lot No. 30545 1960. 89S. 36.5 t.

51319	N	NGBX	OO	51330 w	PCFX	CF
51329 w		PTSX	TS	51331	PTSX	TS

CLASS 117   PRESSED STEEL SUBURBAN

Engines: Two Leyland 680/1 of 112 kW (150 hp).
Bogies: DD10.
Dimensions: 20.45 x 2.82 m.

DMBS. Dia. DQ220. Lot No. 30546 1959–60. 65S. 36.5 t.

51332	N	NWRX	RG	51353		PTSX	TS
51333	N	NWRX	RG	51354	N	NWRX	RG
51334		PTSX	TS	51355	N	NWRX	RG
51335	N	NWRX	RG	51356	N	NWRX	RG
51336	N	NWRX	RG	51358	N	NWRX	RG
51338		PTSX	TS	51359	N	NWRX	OO
51339		PTSX	TS	51360		PTSX	TS
51340	N	NWRX	RG	51361	N	NWRX	OO
51341	N	NWRX	RG	51362	N	NWRX	OO
51342	N	NWRX	RG	51363	N	NWRX	OO
51343	N	NWRX	RG	51364		PTSX	TS
51344	N	NWRX	RG	51365		PTSX	TS
51345	N	NWRX	RG	51366	N	NWRX	OO
51346	N	NWRX	RG	51367	N	NWRX	RG
51347	N	NWRX	RG	51368	0	PTSX	TS
51348		PXXZ	TS	51369	RS	PTSX	TS
51349	N	NWRX	RG	51370		PTSX	TS
51350	N	NWRX	RG	51371	RS	PTSX	TS
51351	N	NWRX	RG	51372		PTSX	TS
51352		PTSX	TS	51373		PTSX	TS

DMS. Dia. DP221. Lot No. 30548 1959–60. 89S. 36.5 t.

51374	N	NWRX	RG	51382		PTSX	TS
51375	N	NWRX	RG	51383	N	NWRX	RG
51376		PTSX	TS	51384	N	NWRX	RG
51377	N	NWRX	RG	51385	N	NWRX	RG
51378	N	NWRX	RG	51386	N	NWRX	RG
51379	N	NWRX	RG	51387	N	NWRX	RG
51380		PTSX	TS	51388	N	NWRX	RG
51381	N	NWRX	RG	51389	N	NWRX	RG

51390		PXXZ	TS	51404	**N**	NWRX	OO
51391	**N**	NWRX	RG	51405	**N**	NWRX	OO
51392	**N**	NWRX	RG	51406		PTSX	TS
51393	**N**	NWRX	RG	51407		PTSX	TS
51394		PTSX	TS	51408	**N**	NWRX	OO
51395		PTSX	TS	51409	**N**	NWRX	RG
51396	**N**	NWRX	RG	51410	**O**	PTSX	TS
51397	**N**	NWRX	RG	51411		PTSX	TS
51398	**N**	NWRX	RG	51412		PTSX	TS
51399	**N**	NWRX	OO	51413		PTSX	TS
51400	**N**	NWRX	RG	51414		PTSX	TS
51401	**N**	NWRX	OO	51415		PTSX	TS
51402		PTSX	TS				

CLASS 108 DERBY 'LIGHTWEIGHT'

Engines: Two Leyland 680/1 or 680/13 of 112 kW (150 hp).
Bogies: DD7.
Dimensions: 18.49 x 2.82 m.

DMBS. Dia. DQ213. Lot No. 30498 1960. 52S. 29.5 t.

51416		PBRX	BR	51421		PLOX	LO
51417		PLAX	LA	51424		PLOX	LO
51419	w	PLOX	LO				

CLASS 101 METRO-CAMMELL

Engines: Two Leyland or AEC of 112 kW (150 hp).
Bogies: DD15.
Dimensions: 18.49 x 2.82 m.

DMBS. Dia. DQ202 (†DQ232). Lot No. 30500 1959. 52S (†49S with additional luggage rack). 32.5 t.

51425	†	**N**	NWXX	RG	51437	†	**N**	NNEX	CA
51426		**RS**	PCAX	CA	51438		**N**	NNEX	CA
51427			PNCX	NC	51442			PCAX	CA
51428		**RS**	PNCX	NC	51443		**N**	NWXX	RG
51429			PCAX	CA	51444		**N**	NGEX	CA
51431	†	**N**	NWXX	RG	51445		**N**	NWRX	RG
51432	†	**N**	NWXX	RG	51463			PCAX	CA
51434	†	**N**	NWXX	RG	51468			PXXZ	HA
51435			PLAX	LA					

DMCL. Dia. DP317 (DP210*). Lot No. 30501 1959. 12F 46S with additional luggage racks 1L. 32.5t.

Converted to DMSL (dia. DP210)seating 72S 1L.

51496		**RS**	PLOX	LO	51503		**N**	NWXX	RG
51498		**N**	NWXX	RG	51504		**N**	NWXX	RG
51499		**N**	NWXX	RG	51505	*		PTSX	TS
51500	*		PLAX	LA	51506	§*		PNCX	NC
51501		**N**	NWXX	RG	51508	§*		PNCX	NC

51509 w*	PTSX	TS	51530 *	PLAX	LA
51511 *	PTSX	TS	51531 §	PNCX	NC
51512 *	PLAX	LA	51533 *	PTSX	TS

CLASS 108 DERBY 'LIGHTWEIGHT'

Engines: Two Leyland 680/1 or 680/13 of 112 kW (150 hp).
Bogies: DD7.
Dimensions: 18.49 x 2.79 m.

DMCL. Dia. DP311 (*DP226). Lot No. 30461 1959–60. 12F 52S 1L. 28.5 t.

51561 *	PLEX	LE	51567 *	PLEX	LE
51562 w*	PLEX	LE	51568 *	PTSX	TS
51563 *	PLEX	LE	51570 *	PLAX	LA
51565 w*	PLEX	LE	51571 N	NGBX	OO
51566 w*	PTSX	TS	51572 w N	NGBX	OO

CLASS 115 DERBY SUBURBAN

Engines: Two Leyland Albion of 149 kW (200 hp).
Gangways: Non gangwayed except as shown.
Bogies: DD13.
Dimensions: 20.45 x 2.82 m.
Note: All BY allocated cars are fitted with power sanding equipment.

DMBS. Dia. DQ218 (g DQ233). Lot No. 30530 1960. 78S (g 74S). 38.5 t.

51651 g	N	NMYX	BY	51663	N	NMYX	BY
51652 g	N	NMYX	BY	51669	N	NMYX	BY
51653	N	NMYX	BY	51671	N	NMYX	BY
51654 g	N	NMYX	BY	51673	N	NMYX	BY
51656 g	N	NMYX	BY	51674	N	NMYX	BY
51657 g	N	NMYX	BY	51676 g	N	NMYX	BY
51658	N	NMYX	BY	51677	N	NMYX	BY
51659	N	NMYX	BY	51679 g	N	NMYX	BY
51661 g	N	NMYX	BY				

CLASS 101 METRO-CAMMELL

Engines: Two Leyland of 112 kW (150 hp).
Bogies: DD15.
Dimensions: 18.49 x 2.82 m.

DMCL. Dia. DP210. Lot No. 30588 1959. 12F 53S 1L. 32.5 t.

Converted to DMSL. (dia. DP210) seating 72S 1L.

51800	RS PCAX	CA	51808	PTSX	TS
51803	RS PLOX	LO			

153

CLASS 115 DERBY SUBURBAN

Engines: Two Leyland Albion of 149 kW (200 hp).
Gangways: Non gangwayed except as shown.
Bogies: DD13.
Dimensions: 20.45 x 2.82 m.
Note: All BY allocated cars are fitted with power sanding equipment.

51849–51860. DMBS. Dia. DQ218 (g DQ233). Lot No. 30595 1960. 78S (g 74S). 38.5 t.
51862–51900. DMBS. Dia. DQ218 (g DQ233). Lot No. 30598 1960. 78S (g 74S). 38.5 t.

51849 g	**N**	NMYX	BY	51874	**N**	NMYX	BY
51851 g		PTSX	TS	51875	**N**	NMYX	BY
51852 g		PTSX	TS	51876 g		PTSX	TS
51853 g		PTSX	TS	51877 g		PTSX	TS
51854 g		PTSX	TS	51878 g	**N**	NMYX	BY
51855 g	**N**	NMYX	BY	51879	**N**	NMYX	BY
51857	**N**	NMYX	BY	51880 g		PTSX	TS
51858 g		PTSX	TS	51883	**N**	NMYX	BY
51859 g		PTSX	TS	51884 g		PTSX	TS
51860 g		PTSX	TS	51885	**N**	NMYX	BY
51862 g		PTSX	TS	51886	**N**	NMYX	BY
51863	**N**	NMYX	BY	51887	**N**	NMYX	BY
51865 g		PTSX	TS	51888	**N**	NMYX	BY
51866 g	**N**	NMYX	BY	51890	**N**	NMYX	BY
51867 g		PTSX	TS	51891	**N**	NMYX	BY
51868 g		PTSX	TS	51892 g		PTSX	TS
51869 g		PTSX	TS	51897 g		PTSX	TS
51870 g		PTSX	TS	51899	**N**	NMYX	BY
51871	**N**	NMYX	BY	51900	**N**	NMYX	BY
51872	**N**	NMYX	BY				

Name: 51899 Aylesbury College SILVER JUBILEE 1987

CLASS 108 DERBY 'LIGHTWEIGHT'

Engines: Two Leyland 680/1 or 680/13 of 112 kW (150 hp).
Bogies: DD7.
Dimensions: 18.49 x 2.82 m.

DMBS. Dia. DQ213. Lot No. 30601 1960–61. 52S. 29.5 t.

† Fitted with automatic gearbox.

51901		PLOX	LO	51916 w	**N**	NNDX	BY
51903		PLOX	LO	51917		PLOX	LO
51907		PLOX	LO	51919		PLEX	LE
51909	**N**	NNDX	BY	51920 w		PBRX	BR
51911		PLOX	LO	51922		PLEX	LE
51912 w	**N**	NNDX	BY	51924 h		PLEX	LE
51914	**N**	NNDX	BY	51925		PLEX	LE

154

51926		PLEX	LE	51937 §		PLEX	LE
51927 w		PTSX	TS	51938		PLOX	LO
51928		PLEX	LE	51940		PLAX	LA
51930		PLEX	LE	51942	N	NNDX	BY
51931		PLEX	LE	51943		PTSX	TS
51932		PLAX	LA	51945		PBRX	BR
51933		PLAX	LA	51947 w		PTSX	TS
51935		PTSX	TS	51948		PTSX	TS
51936		PLAX	LA				

CLASS 107　　　　　　　　　　DERBY 'HEAVYWEIGHT'

Engines: Two Leyland 1595 of 112 kW (150 hp).
Bogies: DD10.
Dimensions: 18.49 x 2.82 m.

DMBS. Dia. DQ211. Lot No. 30611 1960–61. 52S. 35.0 t.

51985		PHAX	HA	52004		PHAX	HA
51988 w		PHAX	HA	52005	S	PHAX	HA
51990	S	PHAX	HA	52006	S	PHAX	HA
51992		PHAX	HA	52007	S	PHAX	HA
51993	S	PHAX	HA	52008	S	PHAX	HA
51994		PHAX	HA				

DMCL. Dia. DP215. Lot No. 30612 1960–61. 12F 53S 1L. 35.5 t.

52011		PHAX	HA	52026		PHAX	HA
52012 w	S	PHAX	HA	52029	S	PHAX	HA
52015	S	PHAX	HA	52030	S	PHAX	HA
52016		PHAX	HA	52031	S	PHAX	HA
52023	S	PHAX	HA	52033	S	PHAX	HA
52025	S	PHAX	HA				

CLASS 108　　　　　　　　　　DERBY 'LIGHTWEIGHT'

Engines: Two Leyland 680/1 or 680/13 of 112 kW (150 hp).
Bogies: DD7.
Dimensions: 18.49 x 2.82 m.

DMCL. Dia. DP227. Lot No. 30660 1960–61. 12F 53S 1L. 28.5 t.

* Fitted with automatic gearbox.

52038	PLEX	LE	52054		PLAX	LA
52039	PTSX	TS	52055		PLEX	LE
52041	PLEX	LE	52056		PNLX	NL
52042	PTSX	TS	52057		PLAX	LA
52044	PLEX	LE	52058 §		PLEX	LE
52045	PLEX	LE	52059		PLAX	LA
52046 w	PLEX	LE	52060		PLEX	LE
52047	PLAX	LA	52061 w		PLEX	LE
52048	PLEX	LE	52065 w		PTSX	TS
52053	PLAX	LA				

155

CLASS 114   DERBY 'HEAVYWEIGHT'

Engines: Two Leyland Albion of 149 kW (200 hp).
Bogies: DD9.
Dimensions: 20.45 x 2.82 m.

DMBS. Dia. DQ217. Lot No. 30209 1956–57. 62S. 38.0 t.

53019	PTSX	TS	53036	PTSX	TS

CLASS 116   DERBY SUBURBAN

Engines: Two Leyland 680/1 of 112 kW (150 hp).
Bogies: DD10.
Dimensions: 20.45 x 2.82 m.

DMBS. Dia. DQ230. Lot No. 30211 1957. 65S. 36.5 t.

53053		PTSX	TS	53073		PTSX	TS
53054	w	PTSX	TS	53079		PTSX	TS
53055	w	PTSX	TS	53083	N	NWRX	RG
53060	w	PTSX	TS	53090		PTSX	TS
53071	w	PTSX	TS				

DMS. Dia. DP220. Lot No. 30213 1957. 89S. 36.5 t.

53092		PTSX	TS	53114	w	PTSX	TS
53093		PTSX	TS	53116	w	PTSX	TS
53101	w	PTSX	TS	53124		PTSX	TS
53102	w	PTSX	TS	53132		PTSX	TS (S)
53106	w	PTSX	TS				

CLASS 101   METRO-CAMMELL

Engines: Two Leyland or AEC of 112 kW (150 hp).
Bogies: DD15.
Dimensions: 18.49 x 2.82 m.

DMCL. Dia. DP212. Lot No. 30249 1956. 12F 45S 1L. 32.5 t. 2+2 seating.

53139	§*	PNCX	NC	53149	§*	PNCX	NC

DMBS. Dia. DQ202. Lot No. 30252 1956. 52S. 32.5 t.

53155	N	NWRX	RG	

DMCL. Dia. DP214. Lot No. 30253 1956. 12F 53S 1L. 32.5 t.

53160	*	S	PLOX	LO	53163	*	PLAX	LA

DMBS. Dia. DQ202. Lot No. 30254 1957. 52S. 32.5 t.

53164	PLAX	LA	53165	PLAX	LA

53168–53171. DMCL. Dia. DP214. Lot No. 30255 1957. 12F 53S 1L. 32.5 t.
53177–53193. DMCL. Dia. DP214. Lot No. 30256 1957. 12F 53S 1L. 32.5 t.

Converted to DMSL (dia. DP210) seating 72S 1L.

53168	*§	PNCX	NC	53180	§	PHAX	HA
53170	*§	PNCX	NC	53181	§	PNCX	NC
53171	*	PHAX	HA	53193	*§	PNCX	NC
53177	*§	PNCX	NC				

53198–53208. DMBS. Dia. DQ202. Lot No. 30259 1957. 52S. 32.5 t.
53211–53231. DMBS. Dia. DQ202. Lot No. 30261 1957. 52S. 32.5 t.

53198	**RS**	PNCX	NC	53208		PNCX	NC
53200		PLAX	LA	53211	**RS**	PLOX	LO
53201	**RS**	PNCX	NC	53216		PLAX	LA
53202		PNCX	NC	53228		PNCX	NC
53203		PLAX	LA	53231		PNCX	NC
53204		PLAX	LA				

DMCL. Dia. DP213. Lot No. 30263 1957. 12F 45S 1L. 32.5 t. 2+2 seating.

53238	§	PNCX	NC	53243	PLOX	LO
53241	**S**	PLOX	LO	53245	PTSX	TS
53242		PTSX	TS			

DMBS. Dia. DQ202. Lot No. 30266 1957. 52S. 32.5 t.

53250	PLAX	LA	53256	PLAX	LA
53253	PLAX	LA			

DMCL. Dia. DP210 (†DP317). Lot No. 30267 1957. 12F 53S 1L. (†12F 46S with additional luggage racks 1L). 32.5 t.

53265	† **N**	NNEX	CA	53268	*	PTSX	TS
53266	§*	PNCX	NC	53269	*	PLOX	LO
53267	§*	PNCX	NC				

53291–53296. DMBS. Dia. DQ202. Lot No. 30270 1957. 52S. 32.5 t.
53305–53315. DMBS. Dia. DQ202 (†DQ232). Lot No. 30275 1958. 52S. 32.5 t. (†49S with additional luggage rack) 32.5 t.

53291		PLAX	LA	53310	† **N**	NWXX	RG
53293		PNCX	NC	53311	**N**	NWXX	RG
53294		PLAX	LA	53312	† **N**	NWXX	RG
53305	§	PHAX	LA	53314	† **N**	NWXX	RG
53308	† **N**	NWXX	RG	53315		PLAX	LA

DMCL. Dia. DP210 (†DP317). Lot No. 30276 1958. 12F 53S 1L (†12F 46S with additional luggage racks 1L) 32.5 t.

Converted to DMSL (dia. DP210) seating 72S 1L.

53321	§	PNCX	NC	53330		PLAX	LA
53322	† **N**	NWXX	RG	53331	† **N**	NWXX	RG
53326	† **N**	NWXX	RG	53332	† **N**	NWXX	RG
53327	† **N**	NWXX	RG	53333	wt **N**	NNEX	CA

CLASS 104 BRCW

Engines: Two Leyland 680/1 of 112 kW (150 hp).
Bogies: DD14.
Dimensions: 18.49 x 2.82 m.

DMBS. Dia. DQ205. Lot No. 30293 1957–58. 52S 1L. 31.5 t.

53437	N	NGBX	OO	53455	N	NGBX	OO
53447		PXXZ	CH	53477	N	NGBX	OO
53454	B	PDYX	DY	53479	N	NGBX	OO

DMCL. Dia. DP209. Lot No. 30294 1957–58. 12F 54S 1L. 31.5 t.

53528	B	PDYX	DY	53531	B	PXXZ	CH

DMBS. Dia. DQ205. Lot No. 30296 1958. 52S 1L. 31.5 t.

53539	N	NGBX	OO	53540	N	NWRX	OO

CLASS 108 DERBY 'LIGHTWEIGHT'

Engines: Two Leyland 680/1 or 680/13 of 112 kW (150 hp).
Bogies: DD7.
Dimensions: 18.49 x 2.82 m.

53599–53624. DMBS. Dia. DQ212. Lot No. 30406 1958. 52S. 29.5 t.
53625–53629. DMBS. Dia. DQ212. Lot No. 30407 1958–59. 52S. 29.5 t.

53599	N	NGBX	OO	53621		PLEX	LE
53602		PBRX	BR	53622		PLAX	LA
53608		PBRX	BR	53624		PCFX	CF
53612		PBRX	BR	53625		PLEX	LE
53617		PBRX	BR	53627		PLEX	LE
53618		PBRX	BR	53628	N	NWRX	RG
53620		PBRX	BR	53629		PCFX	LA

DMCL. Dia. DP219. Lot No. 30408 1958. 12F 50S 1L. 28.5 t. Luggage rack opposite toilet.
† Converted to DMSL (Dia. DP2??). 71S 1L. No luggage rack.

53631		PLEX	LE	53641		PTSX	TS
53632		PBRX	BR	53642		PLAX	LA
53633		PLEX	LE	53643		PLEX	LE
53634 w		PTSX	TS	53644		PTSX	TS
53635		PBRX	BR	53645		PTSX	TS
53636		PTSX	TS	53646		PLAX	LA
53637		PBRX	BR				

CLASS 101 METRO-CAMMELL

Engines: Two Leyland or AEC of 112 kW (150 hp).
Bogies: DD15.
Dimensions: 18.49 x 2.82 m.

DMCL. Dia. DP304 (*DP210). Lot No. 30271 1957. 12F 53S 1L. 32.5 t.

Converted to DMSL (dia. DP210) seating 72S 1L.

| 53746 | **RS** PLOX | LO | 53751 | **N** NNEX | CA |

CLASS 116 — DERBY SUBURBAN

Engines: Two Leyland 680/1 of 112 kW (150 hp).
Bogies: DD10.
Dimensions: 20.45 x 2.82 m.

DMBS. Dia. DQ230. Lot No. 30363 1957–58. 65S. 36.5 t.

53818		PTSX	TS	53850		PTSX	TS
53820 w	**N**	NGBX	OO	53853		PTSX	TS
53822		PTSX	TS	53854		PTSX	TS (S)
53837		PTSX	TS	53863 w		PTSX	TS
53838 w		PTSX	TS	53865		PTSX	TS

DMS. Dia. DP220. Lot No. 30364 1957–58. 89S. 36.5 t.

53873	PTSX	TS	53897	PTSX	TS
53878	PTSX	TS	53902	PTSX	TS
53881	PTSX	TS	53907	PTSX	TS (S)
53886	PTSX	TS	53916 w	PTSX	TS
53890	PTSX	TS	53919	PTSX	TS
53891	PTSX	TS	53921	PTSX	TS
53894	PTSX	TS			

CLASS 108 — DERBY 'LIGHTWEIGHT'

Engines: Two Leyland 680/1 or 680/13 of 112 kW (150 hp).
Bogies: DD7.
Dimensions: 18.49 x 2.79 m.
Non-standard Livery: Original BR DMU green.

53924–53935. DMBS. Dia. DQ212. Lot No. 30460 1959–60. 52S. 29.5 t.
53938–53987. DMBS. Dia. DQ212. Lot No. 30465 1959. 52S. 29.5 t.

53925 w		PTSX	TS	53951 w		PLOX	LO
53926		PLEX	LE	53956 w		PLOX	LO
53927		PBRX	BR	53958 w		PLOX	LO
53928		PLEX	LE	53960 w		PHTX	HT
53930 w		PTSX	TS	53964 w	**O**	PLOX	LO
53931 w		PBRX	BR	53966 w		PLAX	LA
53933 w		PTSX	TS	53968 w		PLOX	LO
53935		PLEX	LE	53970		PLOX	LO
53938		PLOX	LO	53971		PLOX	LO
53939		PLEX	LE	53973		PBRX	BR
53940		PLOX	LO	53974		PLOX	LO
53941		PBRX	BR	53978		PLOX	LO
53943		PLOX	LO	53980 w		PLOX	LO
53944		PLOX	LO	53981		PLOX	LO
53945		PLEX	LE	53982		PLEX	LE
53947		PLEX	LE	53986		PLOX	LO
53948		PBRX	BR	53987 w		PLOX	LO

159

CLASS 114 DERBY 'HEAVYWEIGHT'

Bogies: DT9a.
Dimensions: 20.45 x 2.82 m.

DTCL. Dia. DS2??. (Shown officially as DS313 but all now declassified). Lot No. 30210 1956–57. 12F 62S 1L. 30.0 t.

54006	PTSX	TS	54027	PTSX	TS

CLASS 101 METRO-CAMMELL

Bogies: DT11.
Dimensions: 18.49 x 2.82 m.

54050–54061. DTCL. Dia. DS302 (*DS206). Lot No. 30260 1957. 12F 53S 1L. 25.5 t.
54062–54091. DTCL. Dia. DS302 (*DS206). Lot No. 30262 1957. 12F 53S 1L. 25.5 t.

Converted to DTSL (dia. DS211) seating 72S 1L.

54050	*		PNCX	NC	54065	*	PNCX	NC
54055	*		PNCX	NC	54068	N	NGEX	CA
54056		**RS**	PCAX	CA	54073	*	PCAX	CA
54060	*		PNCX	NC	54081	N	NWRX	RG
54061	*		PCAX	CA	54085	**RS**	PLOX	LO
54062		**RS**	PNCX	NC	54091	**RS**	PCAX	CA

CLASS 108 DERBY 'LIGHTWEIGHT'

Bogies: DT8.
Dimensions: 18.49 x 2.79 m.

54191–54210. DTCL. Dia. DS314 (*DS207). Lot No. 30409 1958. 12F 53S 1L. 21.5 t.
54212–54214. DTCL. Dia. DS314 (*DS207). Lot No. 30410 1958. 12F 53S 1L. 21.5 t.

54191	*		PBRX	BR	54208	*	PBRX	BR
54194		N	NNDX	BY	54212	*	PLOX	LO
54197	*		PBRX	BR	54214	*	PBRX	BR
54203	*		PLOX	LO				

CLASS 101 METRO-CAMMELL

Bogies: DT11.
Dimensions: 18.49 x 2.82 m.

DTCL. Dia. DS303 (*DS210). Lot No. 30340 1957. 12F 45S 1L. 25.5 t. 2+2 seating.

54220	N	NGEX	CA

CLASS 108   DERBY 'LIGHTWEIGHT'

Bogies: DT8.
Dimensions: 18.49 x 2.79 m. (DS310), 18.49 x 2.82 DS311).

Non-standard Livery: Original BR DMU green.

54221–54270. DTCL. Dia. DS310 (*DS207). Lot No. 30466 1959. 12F 53S 1L. 21.5 t.
54271–54279. DTCL. Dia. DS311 (*DS2??). Lot No. 30499 1960. 12F 53S 1L. 22.5 t.

54221	*		PLOX	LO	54256	w*		PLOX	LO
54223	**N**	NMYX	BY	54257	**N**		NNDX	BY
54224	**N**	NMYX	BY	54260	*		PBRX	BR
54225	*		PLOX	LO	54262	*		PLOX	LO
54228	**N**	NNDX	BY	54263	*		PHTX	HT
54230	*		PBRX	BR	54264	*		PLOX	LO
54232	*		PLOX	LO	54267	w*		PLOX	LO
54235	w*		PLOX	LO	54268	*		PBRX	BR
54238	w*		PLOX	LO	54269	*		PLOX	LO
54239	w*		PLOX	LO	54270	w*		PLOX	LO
54240	w*		PHTX	HT	54271	w	**N**	NNDX	BY
54241	w*		PHTX	HT	54272	w*		PLOX	LO
54242	w*		PBRX	BR	54273	*		PLOX	LO
54246	*		PLOX	LO	54274		**N**	NMYX	BY
54247	w* **0**		PLOX	LO	54275	w*		PLOX	LO
54249	w*		PLOX	LO	54276	w*		PLOX	LO
54253	*		PLOX	LO	54279		**N**	NNDX	RG

CLASS 121   PRESSED STEEL SUBURBAN

Gangways: Not ganywayed except as shown. **Bogies:** DT9.
Dimensions: 20.45 x 2.82 m.

DTS. Dia. DS201 (g DS2??). Lot No. 30519 1960–61. 91S (g 89S). 30.0 t.

54284		**N**	NWRX	OO	54289	g	**N**	NWRX	OO
54287	g	**N**	NWRX	RG					

CLASS 101   METRO-CAMMELL

Bogies: DT11.
Dimensions: 18.49 x 2.82 m.

DTCL. Dia. DS302 (*DS206). Lot No. 30468 1958. 12F 53S 1L. 25.5 t.

54332	*		PCAX	CA	54354	*		PCAX	CA
54340	w*		PNLX	NL	54358	**RS**	PCAX	CA
54343	*		PNCX	NC	54362	**N**	NWRX	RG
54346	§	**RS** PNCX	NC	54365	*		PCAX	CA
54347	*		PCAX	CA	54368	*		PNCX	NC
54352	*		**RS** PNCX	NC	54369	*		PCAX	CA

54371	**N**	NWRX	RG	54388	*	PNCX	NC
54372	**N**	NWRX	RG	54393	*	PCAX	CA
54379	**RS**	PNCX	NC	54396	**N**	NWRX	RG
54380	*	PNCX	NC	54399	*	PNCX	NC
54381	**N**	NWRX	RG	54402	**N**	NNEX	CA
54382	**N**	NNEX	CA	54405	**N**	NNEX	CA
54385	**N**	NWRX	RG	54408 §	**RS**	PCAX	CA
54387	*	PCAX	CA				

CLASS 108   DERBY 'LIGHTWEIGHT'

Bogies: DT8.
Dimensions: 18.49 x 2.82 m.

DTCL. Dia. DS311 (*DS2??). Lot No. 30602 1960. 12F 53S 1L. 22.5 t.

54484	*		PLOX	LO	54496	*	PLOX	LO
54485			PLOX	LO	54499	**N**	NMYX	BY
54488	*		PBRX	BR	54500	**N**	NMYX	BY
54490	*		PLOX	LO	54503	*	PLOX	LO
54491		**N**	NMYX	BY	54504	w*	PLOX	LO
54495	w	**N**	NMYX	BY				

CLASS 122   GLOUCESTER SUBURBAN

Engines: Two AEC 220 of 112 kW (150 hp).

DMBS. Dia. DX202. Lot No. 30419 1958. 65S. 36.5 t.

55000		PLAX	LA	55006		PLAX	LA
55003		PLAX	LA	55009		PLAX	LA
55005		PLAX	LA	55012	**RS**	PLAX	LA

CLASS 121   PRESSED STEEL SUBURBAN

Engines: Two Leyland 1595 of 112 kW (150 hp).
Gangways: Non gangwayed single cars.
Bogies: DD10.
Dimensions: 20.45 x 2.82 m.

DMBS. Dia. DX201. Lot No. 30518 1960. 65S. 38.0 t.

55020	**N**	NWRX	OO	55028	**N**	NWRX	OO
55022	**N**	NWRX	OO	55029	**N**	NWRX	OO
55023	**N**	NWRX	OO	55030	**N**	NWRX	OO
55024	**N**	NWRX	OO	55031	**N**	NWRX	OO
55025	**N**	NWRX	OO	55032		PTSX	TS
55026		PLAX	LA	55033	w	**O**	PTSX	TS
55027	**N**	NWRX	OO	55034		PTSX	TS

CLASS 116   DERBY SUBURBAN

Bogies: DT9b.
Dimensions: 20.45 x 2.82 m.

TS. Dia. DT209. Lot No. 30385 1957. 98S. 29.5 t.

59032	PTSX	TS	

CLASS 101 METRO-CAMMELL

Bogies: DT11.
Dimensions: 18.49 x 2.82 m.

TBSL. Dia. DU202. Lot No. 30251 1956. 45S 1L. 25.5 t. 2+2 seating.

59055	PNCX	NC	

TSL. Dia. DT202. Lot No. 30257 1957. 71S 1L. 25.5 t.

59072	**N** NNEX	CA	

TBSL. Dia. DU203. Lot No. 30258 1957. 53S 1L. 25.5 t.

59077	PNCX	NC	59080	PNCX	NC
59079	PNCX	NC	59084	PNCX	NC

TSL. Dia. DT228. Lot No. 30264 1957. †58S plus additional luggage racks 1L. 25.5 t. 2+2 seating.

59091 †	**N** NWXX	RG	

TBSL. Dia. DU202. Lot No. 30265 1957. 45S 1L. 25.5 t. 2+2 seating.

59092	PNCX	NC	59095	PNCX	NC
59093 w	PNCX	NC			

TSL. Dia. DT202 (†DT228). Lot No. 30269 1957–58. 71S 1L (†58S plus additional luggage racks 1L). 25.5 t.

59110 (59101) †	NWXX	RG	59111 (59105)	**N** NNEX	CA

TCL. Dia. DT220 or †DT228. Lot No. 30277 1958. 12F 53S 1L (†58S 1L) 25.5 t.

59115 †	**N** NWRX	RG	59125 †	**N** NWXX	RG
59117 †	**N** NWXX	RG	59128 w	**N** NNEX	CA
59118 *	PLAX	LA			

CLASS 108 DERBY 'LIGHTWEIGHT'

Bogies: DT8.
Dimensions: 18.49 x 2.79 m.

TBSL. Dia. DU201. Lot No. 30412 1958. 50S 1L. 23.5 t.

59248	PCFX	CF	

CLASS 101 METRO-CAMMELL

Bogies: DT11.
Dimensions: 18.49 x 2.82 m.

TS. Dia. DT202 (†DT228). Lot No. 30273 1957. 71S 1L. (†64S plus additional luggage racks 1L). 25.5 t.

59302		PLOX	LO	59306 †	**N**	NWXX		RG
59303		PLAX	LA					

CLASS 116   DERBY SUBURBAN

Bogies: DT9b.
Dimensions: 20.45 x 2.82 m.

TC. Dia. DT219. Lot No. 30365 1957–58. 20F 68S. 29.0 t.

59335 *	PTSX	TS	59353 *	PTSX	TS
59344 *	PTSX	TS	59367 *	PTSX	TS

CLASS 108   DERBY 'LIGHTWEIGHT'

Bogies: DT8.
Dimensions: 18.49 x 2.79 m.

TSL. Dia. DT205. Lot No. 30411 1958. 68S 1L. 22.5 t. Luggage rack opposite toilet.

59380	PLAX	LA	59383	PCFX	CF
59382	PLAX	LA	59384	PLAX	LA

TSL. Dia. DT206. Lot No. 30493 1958. 68S 1L. 23.5 t. Luggage rack opposite toilet.

59386	PLAX	LA	59387	PCFX	CF

CLASS 119   GLOUCESTER CROSS-COUNTRY

Bogies: DT9.
Dimensions: 20.45 x 2.82 m.
Note: These vehicles were formerly trailer buffet seconds, but the buffets have now been removed and converted into an additional luggage area.

TSL. Dia. DT216. Lot No. 30423 1958–59. 60S 2L. 31.5 t.

59416	**N**	NWXX	RG	59430	**N**	NWXX	RG
59419	**N**	NWXX	RG	59435	**N**	NWXX	RG
59425	**N**	NWXX	RG	59437	**N**	NWXX	RG

CLASS 116   DERBY SUBURBAN

Bogies: DT9b.
Dimensions: 20.45 x 2.82 m.

TC. Dia. DT219. Lot No. 30448 1957–58. 20F 68S. 29.0 t.

59445	PTSX	TS	59446	PTSX	TS

CLASS 118   BRCW SUBURBAN

Bogies: DT9.
Dimensions: 20.45 x 2.82 m.

TCL. Dia. DT230. Lot No. 30544 1960. 22F 48S 2L. 30.5 t.

59481 w		PTSX		TS		59483	PTSX	TS

CLASS 117   PRESSED STEEL SUBURBAN

Bogies: DT9.
Dimensions: 20.45 x 2.82 m.

TCL. Dia. DT305 (*DT230). Lot No. 30547 1959–60. 22F 48S 2L. 30.5 t.

59484	**N**	NWRX	RG	59504	*	PTSX	TS
59485	**N**	NWRX	RG	59505	*	PTSX	TS
59486	*	PTSX	TS	59506	**N**	NWRX	RG
59487	**N**	NWRX	RG	59507	**N**	NWRX	RG
59488	**N**	NWRX	RG	59508	**N**	NWRX	RG
59489	**N**	NWRX	RG	59509	**RS**	PTSX	TS
59490	*	PTSX	TS	59510	**N**	NWRX	RG
59491	**N**	NWRX	RG	59511	**N**	NWRX	OO
59492	*	PTSX	TS	59512	*	PTSX	TS
59493	**N**	NWRX	RG	59513	**N**	NWRX	OO
59494	**N**	NWRX	RG	59514	**N**	NWRX	OO
59495	**N**	NWRX	RG	59515	**N**	NWRX	OO
59496	**N**	NWRX	RG	59516	*	PTSX	TS
59497	**N**	NWRX	RG	59517	*	PTSX	TS
59498	**N**	NWRX	RG	59518	**N**	NWRX	OO
59499	**N**	NWRX	RG	59519	**N**	NWRX	OO
59500	*	PTSX	TS	59520 *	**0**	PTSX	TS
59501	**N**	NWRX	RG	59521	*	PTSX	TS
59502	**N**	NWRX	RG	59522	*	PTSX	TS
59503	**N**	NWRX	RG				

CLASS 101   METRO-CAMMELL

Bogies: DT11.
Dimensions: 18.49 x 2.82 m.

TCL. Dia. DT220 (†DT228). Lot No. 30502 1959. 12F 53S 1L (†58S 1L). 25.5 t.

59526 †	**N**	NWXX	RG	59539		PLAX	LA
59530 †	**N**	NWXX	RG	59540 †	**N**	NWXX	RG
59536		PHAX	HA	59543 †	**N**	NWXX	RG

TSL. Dia. DT228. Lot No. 30510 1959. 58S 1L. 25.5 t.

59570	**N**	NWXX	RG

CLASS 127　　　　　　　　　　　　DERBY SUBURBAN

Bogies: DT9.
Gangways: Lot 30523 are not gangwayed except as shown below.
Dimensions: 20.45 x 2.82 m.

TSL. Dia. DT226. Lot No. 30522 1959. 86S 2L. 30.5 t.

59589	PTSX	TS	59603	PTSX	TS
59590	PTSX	TS	59604	PTSX	TS
59591	PTSX	TS	59607	PTSX	TS
59592	PTSX	TS	59608	PTSX	TS
59594	PTSX	TS	59609	PTSX	TS
59595	PTSX	TS	59611	PTSX	TS
59597	PTSX	TS	59614	PTSX	TS
59598	PTSX	TS	59615	PTSX	TS
59600	PTSX	TS	59617	PTSX	TS
59602	PTSX	TS			

TS. Dia. DT229. Lot No. 30523 1959. 96S. 29.5 t.

59625 g	PTSX	TS	59641 g	PTSX	TS
59629 g	PTSX	TS	59643 g	PTSX	TS
59632 g	PTSX	TS	59648 g	PTSX	TS

CLASS 115　　　　　　　　　　　　DERBY SUBURBAN

Bogies: DT9.
Gangways: Not gangwayed except as shown below.
Dimensions: 20.45 x 2.82 m.

TS. Dia. DT208 (g DT229). Lot No. 30531 1960. 106S (g 96S). 29.5 t.

59651	**N**	NMYX	BY	59659	**N**	NMYX	BY
59655	**N**	NMYX	BY	59661		PTSX	TS
59657	**N**	NMYX	BY	59662	**N**	NMYX	BY
59658		PTSX	TS	59663	**N**	NMYX	BY

TCL. Dia. DT303 (*DT2??). Lot No. 30532 1960. 30F 40S 2L (g 30F 38S 2L). 30.5 t.

59664	**N**	NMYX	BY	59672 g*		PTSX	TS
59667	**N**	NMYX	BY	59673 g*		PTSX	TS
59668 g*		PTSX	TS	59674 g*		PTSX	TS
59669	**N**	NMYX	BY	59676	**N**	NMYX	BY
59670 g*		PTSX	TS	59677 g*		PXXZ	TS
59671	**N**	NMYX	BY	59678		NMYX	BY

CLASS 101　　　　　　　　　　　　　METRO-CAMMELL

Bogies: DT11.
Dimensions: 18.49 x 2.82 m.

TCL. Dia. DT220. Lot No. 30589 1960. 12F 53S 1L. 25.5 t.

59688 *	PLAX	LA	

CLASS 115   DERBY SUBURBAN

Bogies: DT9.
Gangways: Not gangwayed except as shown below.
Dimensions: 20.45 x 2.82 m.

TS. Dia. DT 229. Lot No. 30596 1960. 96S. 29.5 t.

59713 g	PTSX	TS	

TCL. Dia. DT307. Lot No. 30597 1960. 30F 38S 2L. 30.5 t.

59720 g	PTSX	TS	59724 g	PTSX	TS
59721 g	PTSX	TS			

TS. Dia. DT208 (g DT229). Lot No. 30599 1960. 106S (g 96S). 29.5 t.

59726 g		PTSX	TS	59736	**N**	NMYX	BY
59728	**N**	NMYX	BY	59737	**N**	NMYX	BY
59731	**N**	NMYX	BY	59740	**N**	NMYX	BY
59733	**N**	NMYX	BY	59741 g		PTSX	TS
59734 g	**N**	NMYX	BY	59743 g		PTSX	TS
59735 g	**N**	NMYX	BY				

TCL. Dia. DT303 (*g DT2??). Lot No. 30600 1960. 30F 40S 2L. (g 30F 38S 2L). 30.5 t.

59745 g		PTSX	TS	59756 g		PTSX	TS
59747	**N**	NMYX	BY	59757 g		PTSX	TS
59749	**N**	NMYX	BY	59758	**N**	NMYX	BY
59750	**N**	NMYX	BY	59759	**N**	NMYX	BY
59751 g		PTSX	TS	59761	**N**	NMYX	BY
59753 g		PTSX	TS (S)	59764	**N**	NMYX	BY
59754	**N**	NMYX	BY				

CLASS 107   DERBY 'HEAVYWEIGHT'

Bogies: DT9.
Dimensions: 18.49 x 2.82 m.

TSL. Dia. DT204. Lot No. 30613 1960–61. 71S 1L. 28.5 t.

59784	**S**	PHAX	HA	59800		PHAX	HA
59790	**S**	PHAX	HA	59801	**S**	PHAX	HA
59791		PHAX	HA	59804	**S**	PHAX	HA
59792 w	**S**	PHAX	HA	59805		PHAX	HA
59796		PHAX	HA	59806	**S**	PHAX	HA
59797		PHAX	HA				

Note: The following vehicles, though officially shown in stock, have actually been seen in scrapyards!:

51419, 51925/6. 52045. 53631. 54240. 54262/3/9/73. 54496.

FORMATIONS OF FIRST GENERATION DMUS

First generation or "heritage" DMUs have traditionally not been kept in fixed formations by all depots, although in the past the Western Region and certain depots have kept fixed formations. The situation is improving, but reformations often occur, particularly at Tyseley. No fixed formations are kept of first generation units at Bletchley.

Regional Railways are introducing a new series of unit numbers for long-life DMUs and a list of the units, all of which have recently been through works, follows:

101 651	NC	53201	54379		101 691	HA	51293	59536	53171
101 652	NC	53198	54346						
101 653	CA	51426	54358						
101 654	CA	51800	54408						
101 655	NC	51428	54062						
101 656	CA	51230	54056						
101 657	LO	53211	54085						
101 658	CA	51175	54091						
101 659	NC	51213	54352						
					117 301	TS	51353	59505	51395
					117 306	TS	51369	59521	51411
					117 308	TS	51371	59509	51413
					117 310	TS	51373	59486	51415
					117 311	TS	51334	59500	51376
					117 313	TS	51339	59492	51382
101 676	LO	51205	51803		122 112	LA	55012		
101 677	LO	51179	51496						
101 678	LO	51210	53746						

Current formations of other Regional Railways DMUs by depot are as follows:

BRISTOL BATH ROAD DEPOT

896	51945	53941	962	53973	54242
898	51416	53632	963	53620	54230
899	53617	53637	978	53927	54214
960	53602	54197	979	53608	54260
961	51920	54208			

CAMBRIDGE DEPOT

53	51247	54387	63	51185	54365
56	51429	54393	66	51192	54354
59	51442	54061	67	51187	54332
60	51463	54073	72	51201	54347
62	51188	54369			

CARDIFF DEPOT

490	51132		51145	393	51135	51148
491	51128		51141	395	51140	51153
492	51134	59387	51147			

HAYMARKET DEPOT

107 030	51990	59796	52030	107 044	52005	59784	52025
107 033	51993	59790	52012	107 045	52006	59804	52031
107 034	51994	59791	52011	107 047	52008	59792	52029

LAIRA DEPOT

00	55000			829	51246	59382	51500
03	55003			861	53966		51512
05	55005			870	53200		51530
06	55006			871	53256		53646
09	55009			874	53315		53330
26	55026			876	51231		53305
21	53216	59539	53294	879	51435		52059
23	53642	59384	51184	954	51932		52047
24	53291	59688	53203	955	51933		52054
25	53165	59118	53164	956	53629		52053
26	53204	59380	53622	957	51940		52057
28	51936	59386	53163				

LANDORE DEPOT

937	51937	52058	947	53621	51567
940	51919	52048	948	53928	51565
941	51922	51562	949	53945	51563
942	51928	52044	950	53926	53643
943	51930	51561	951	53935	52041
944	51931	52055	952	53627	52060
945	53982	52061	958	51924	52038
946	53939	52046	959	53947	53633

LONGSIGHT DEPOT

253	51421	54275	288	53943	54246	
255	51424	54232	289	53986	54221	
256	51901	54276	290	53987	54270	
257	53970	54264	295	53951	54235	
262	51907	54490	296	53956	54238	
266	51917	54272	297	53958	54239	
275	53980	54256	298	53964	54247	
276	53981	54253	299	53974	54203	
280	53971	54504	601	51177		53269
282	53978	54485	602	51224		53241
283	53940	54503	603	51228		53243
284	53968	54249	604	51245		53160
286	51903	54267				

NORWICH DEPOT

51	51218	54399	88	53208	54060	
55	51427	54055	101	51508	59055	51506
65	51189	54343	102	53168	59084	53139
68	53293	54065	104	53266	59080	53181
70	53202	54050	106	53170	59079	53193
76	51252	54368	107	53177	59077	53321
81	53231	54388	108	53267	59092	53238
86	53228	54380				

12	55032			318	51316	59483	51331
13	55033			319	51129	59756	51149
14	55034			320	51138	59611	53890
27	53019	54006		321	53854	59753	53886
32	53073	53242		322	53071	59751	53132
34	53822	52042		323	53818	59670	53093
35	53850	51533		324	53053	59672	53101
36	53054	53245		325	53060	59757	51142
37	53853	51511		327	53055	59589	53916
38	53838	51808		401	51865	59724	59743 53907
39	53079	51505		402	51851	59614	59658 51146
41	53090	53268		403	51852	59607	59445 53106
42	53863	51509		404	51853	59604	59661 53919
45	51131	53641		405	51854	59615	59726 51143
61	51935	53645		406	51877	59598	59344 53102
63	53925	52039		407	51858	59594	59353 51144
64	51947	53634		408	51859	59617	59643 53902
65	51927	52065		409	51860	59600	59367 53894
66	51943	51568		410	51862	59602	59713 53124
72	53933	51566		411	51869	59597	59625 53873
02	51360	59512	51402	412	51867	59591	59446 53116
03	51364	59516	51406	413	51868	59592	59632 53114
04	51365	59517	51407	414	51880	59641	59674 53921
05	51368	59520	51410	416	51876	59609	59648 53891
07	51370	59522	51412	417	51892	59720	59335 53897
09	51372	59490	51414	419	51884	59608	59629 51151
12	51338	59504	51380	420	51897	59721	59032 53092
15	51352	59590	51394	421	51870	59673	59741 53878
17	51314	59481	51329				

Network SouthEast DMUs are numbered in a common series as follows:

ID	Code			
L120	OO	55020		
L122	OO	55022		
L124	OO	55024		
L125	OO	55025		
L127	OO	55027		
L128	OO	55028		
L129	OO	55029		
L130	OO	55030		
L131	OO	55031		
L200	RG	51215	54081	
L202	RG	51225	54372	
L204	RG	51220	54371	
L205	RG	51367	54385	
L207	RG	51221	54396	
L210	RG	53083	54381	
L211	RG	53155	54287	
L212	RG	53628	54279	
L220	CA	51207	54405	
L221	CA	51208	54402	
L222	CA	51438	54382	
L223	CA	51444	54068	
L224	RG	51445	54362	
L225	CA	51222	54220	
L263	OO	53540	54289	
L284	OO		54284	
L400	RG	51332	59484	51374
L401	RG	51333	59485	51375
L402	RG	51335	59487	51377
L403	RG	51336	59488	51378
L404	RG	51065	59489	51379
L405	RG	51340	59491	51381
L406	RG	51341	59493	51383
L407	RG	51342	59494	51384
L408	RG	51343	59495	51385
L409	RG	51344	59496	51386
L410	RG	51345	59497	51387
L411	RG	51346	59498	51388
L412	RG	51347	59499	51389
L413	RG	51349	59501	51391
L414	RG	51350	59502	51392
L415	RG	51351	59503	51393
L417	RG	51354	59506	51396
L418	RG	51355	59507	51397
L419	RG	51356	59508	51398
L420	RG	51358	59510	51400
L421	OO	51359	59511	51401
L423	OO	51361	59513	51399
L424	OO	51362	59514	51404
L425	OO	51363	59515	51405
L428	OO	51366	59518	51409
L429	OO	55023	59519	51409
L575	RG	51060	59419	51088
L580	RG	51066	59425	51094
L588	RG	51443	59437	51107
L594	RG	51073	59435	51104
L595	RG	51074	59430	51086
L596	RG	51076	59416	51099
L700	CA	51437	59128	53751
L702	OO	53455		51090
L704	OO	53477		51571
L706	OO	53599		51572
L707	OO	53479		53539
L708	OO	53437		51103
L709	BY	51651		51878
L745	OO	53820		51319
L830	CA	51190	59111	53333
L831	CA	51211	59072	53265
L832	RG	51226	59570	51499
L833	RG	51425	59543	51504
L834	RG	51431	59526	51501
L835	RG	51432	59530	51498
L836	RG	51434	59540	51503
L838	RG	53308	59125	53331
L839	RG	53310	59306	53326
L840	RG	53311	59117	53322
L841	RG	53312	59091	53332
L842	RG	53314	59110	53327

3.3 SECOND GENERATION DMUS.

CLASS 141   LEYLAND BUS/BREL RAILBUS

DMS–DMSL. Built form Leyland National bus parts on four-wheeled underframes.

Engine: One Leyland TL11 152 kW (205 hp) (v Cummins LTA 10R).
Transmission: Mechanical. Self Changing Gears. (v Hydraulic. Voith T211r).
Gangways: Within unit only.
Doors: Folding.
Dimensions: 15.45 x 2.50 m.
Seats: 2+2 bus style.
Maximum Speed: 75 mph.

DMS. Dia. DP228 Lot No. 30977 Derby 1984. Modified by Barclay 1988–89. 50S. 26.0 t.
DMSL. Dia. DP229 Lot No. 30978 1984. Modified by Barclay 1988–89.44S 1L. 26.5 t.

141 101	Y	PNLX	NL	55521	55541
141 102	Y	PNLX	NL	55502	55522
141 103	Y	PNLX	NL	55503	55523
141 104	Y	PNLX	NL	55504	55524
141 105	Y	PNLX	NL	55505	55525
141 106	Y	PNLX	NL	55506	55526
141 107	Y	PNLX	NL	55507	55527
141 108	Y	PNLX	NL	55508	55528
141 109	Y	PNLX	NL	55509	55529
141 110	Y	PNLX	NL	55510	55530
141 111	Y	PNLX	NL	55511	55531
141 112	Y	PNLX	NL	55512	55532
141 113 v	Y	PNLX	NL	55513	55533
141 114	Y	PNLX	NL	55514	55534
141 115	Y	PNLX	NL	55515	55535
141 116	Y	PNLX	NL	55516	55536
141 117	Y	PNLX	NL	55517	55537
141 118	Y	PNLX	NL	55518	55538
141 119	Y	PNLX	NL	55519	55539
141 120	Y	PNLX	NL	55520	55540

CLASS 142   LEYLAND BUS/BREL RAILBUS

DMS–DMSL. Development of Class 141 with wider body and improved appearance.

Engine: One Leyland TL11 152 kW (205 hp).
Transmission: Hydraulic. Voith T211r.
Gangways: Within unit only.
Doors: Folding.
Dimensions: 15.55 x 2.80 m.

Seats: 2+3 bus style.
Maximum Speed: 75 mph.
Non-Standard Livery: Chocolate & Cream.

55542–55591. DMS. Dia. DP234 Lot No. 31003 Derby 1985–6. 62S. 24.5 t.
55592–55641. DMSL. Dia. DP235 Lot No. 31004 Derby 1985–6. 59S 1L. 25.0 t.
55701–55746. DMS. Dia. DP234 Lot No. 31013 Derby 1986–7. 62S. 24.5 t.
55747–55792. DMSL. Dia. DP235 Lot No. 31014 Derby 1986–7. 59S 1L. 25.0 t.

142 001	G	PNHX	NH	55542	55592
142 002	G	PNHX	NH	55543	55593
142 003	G	PNHX	NH	55544	55594
142 004	G	PNHX	NH	55545	55595
142 005	G	PNHX	NH	55546	55596
142 006	G	PNHX	NH	55547	55597
142 007	G	PNHX	NH	55548	55598
142 008	G	PNHX	NH	55549	55599
142 009	G	PNHX	NH	55550	55600
142 010	G	PNHX	NH	55551	55601
142 011	G	PNHX	NH	55552	55602
142 012	G	PNHX	NH	55553	55603
142 013	G	PNHX	NH	55554	55604
142 014	G	PNHX	NH	55555	55605
142 015	O	PNHX	NH	55556	55606
142 016	O	PNHX	NH	55557	55607
142 017	O	PNHX	NH	55558	55608
142 018	O	PHTX	HT	55559	55609
142 019	O	PHTX	HT	55560	55610
142 020	O	PHTX	HT	55561	55611
142 021	O	PHTX	HT	55562	55612
142 022	O	PHTX	HT	55563	55613
142 023	RS	PNHX	NH	55564	55614
142 024	O	PNHX	NH	55565	55615
142 025	O	PHTX	HT	55566	55616
142 026	O	PNHX	NH	55567	55617
142 027	O	PNHX	NH	55568	55618
142 028	PR	PNHX	NH	55569	55619
142 029	PR	PNHX	NH	55570	55620
142 030	PR	PNHX	NH	55571	55621
142 031	PR	PNHX	NH	55572	55622
142 032	PR	PNHX	NH	55573	55623
142 033	PR	PNHX	NH	55574	55624
142 034	PR	PNHX	NH	55575	55625
142 035	PR	PNHX	NH	55576	55626
142 036	PR	PNHX	NH	55577	55627
142 037	PR	PNHX	NH	55578	55628
142 038	PR	PNHX	NH	55579	55629
142 039	PR	PNHX	NH	55580	55630
142 040	PR	PNHX	NH	55581	55631
142 041	PR	PNHX	NH	55582	55632
142 042	PR	PNHX	NH	55583	55633
142 043	PR	PNHX	NH	55584	55634
142 044	PR	PNHX	NH	55585	55635

142 045	**PR**	PNHX	NH	55586	55636
142 046	**PR**	PNHX	NH	55587	55637
142 047	**PR**	PNHX	NH	55588	55752
142 048	**PR**	PNHX	NH	55589	55639
142 049	**PR**	PNHX	NH	55590	55640
142 050	**PR**	PHTX	HT	55591	55641
142 051	**PR**	PNHX	NH	55701	55747
142 052	**PR**	PNHX	NH	55702	55748
142 053	**PR**	PNHX	NH	55703	55749
142 054	**PR**	PNHX	NH	55704	55750
142 055	**PR**	PNHX	NH	55705	55751
142 056	**PR**	PNHX	NH	55706	55638
142 057	**PR**	PNHX	NH	55707	55753
142 058	**PR**	PNHX	NH	55708	55754
142 059	**PR**	PNHX	NH	55709	55755
142 060	**PR**	PNHX	NH	55710	55756
142 061	**PR**	PNHX	NH	55711	55757
142 062	**PR**	PNLX	NL	55712	55758
142 063	**PR**	PNLX	NL	55713	55759
142 064	**PR**	PNHX	NH	55714	55760
142 065	**PR**	PHTX	HT	55715	55761
142 066	**PR**	PHTX	HT	55716	55762
142 067	**PR**	PNLX	NL	55717	55763
142 068	**PR**	PNLX	NL	55718	55764
142 069	**PR**	PNHX	NH	55719	55765
142 070	**PR**	PNLX	NL	55720	55766
142 071	**PR**	PNHX	NH	55721	55767
142 072	**PR**	PNLX	NL	55722	55768
142 073	**PR**	PNLX	NL	55723	55769
142 074	**PR**	PNLX	NL	55724	55770
142 075	**PR**	PNLX	NL	55725	55771
142 076	**PR**	PNLX	NL	55726	55772
142 077	**PR**	PNLX	NL	55727	55773
142 078	**PR**	PNLX	NL	55728	55774
142 079	**PR**	PNLX	NL	55729	55775
142 080	**PR**	PNLX	NL	55730	55776
142 081	**PR**	PNLX	NL	55731	55777
142 082	**PR**	PNLX	NL	55732	55778
142 083	**PR**	PNLX	NL	55733	55779
142 084	**PR**	PNLX	NL	55734	55780
142 085	**PR**	PNLX	NL	55735	55781
142 086	**PR**	PNLX	NL	55736	55782
142 087	**PR**	PNLX	NL	55737	55783
142 088	**PR**	PNLX	NL	55738	55784
142 089	**PR**	PNLX	NL	55739	55785
142 090	**PR**	PNLX	NL	55740	55786
142 091	**PR**	PNLX	NL	55741	55787
142 092	**PR**	PNLX	NL	55742	55788
142 093	**PR**	PNLX	NL	55743	55789
142 094	**PR**	PNLX	NL	55744	55790
142 095	**PR**	PNLX	NL	55745	55791
142 096	**PR**	PNLX	NL	55746	55792

CLASS 143   ALEXANDER/BARCLAY RAILBUS

DMS–DMSL. Similar design to Class 142, but bodies built by W. Alexander with Barclay underframes.

Engine: One Leyland TL11 152 kW (205 hp).
Transmission: Hydraulic. Voith T211r.
Gangways: Within unit only.
Doors: Folding.
Dimensions: 15.55 x 2.70 m.
Seats: 2+3 bus style.
Maximum Speed: 75 mph.

DMS. Dia. DP236 Lot No. 31005 Andrew Barclay 1985–6. 62S. 24.5 t.
DMSL. Dia. DP237 Lot No. 31006 Andrew Barclay 1985–6. 60S 1L. 25.0 t.

143 601	**RS**	PCFX	CF	55642	55667
143 602	**RS**	PHTX	HT	55651	55668
143 603	**PR**	PHTX	HT	55658	55669
143 604	**PR**	PCFX	CF	55645	55670
143 605	**PR**	PHTX	HT	55646	55671
143 606	**PR**	PHTX	HT	55647	55672
143 607	**RS**	PHTX	HT	55648	55673
143 608	**PR**	PCFX	CF	55649	55674
143 609	**RS**	PHTX	HT	55650	55675
143 610	**RS**	PCFX	CF	55643	55676
143 611	**PR**	PHTX	HT	55652	55677
143 612	**PR**	PHTX	HT	55653	55678
143 613	**PR**	PHTX	HT	55654	55679
143 614	**RS**	PHTX	HT	55655	55680
143 615	**RS**	PHTX	HT	55656	55681
143 616	**PR**	PHTX	HT	55657	55682
143 617	**PR**	PHTX	HT	55644	55683
143 618	**PR**	PCFX	CF	55659	55684
143 619	**PR**	PHTX	HT	55660	55685
143 620	**T**	PHTX	HT	55661	55686
143 621	**T**	PCFX	CF	55662	55687
143 622	**T**	PHTX	HT	55663	55688
143 623	**T**	PHTX	HT	55664	55689
143 624	**T**	PCFX	CF	55665	55690
143 625	**T**	PHTX	HT	55666	55691

CLASS 144   ALEXANDER/BREL RAILBUS

DMS–DMSL or DMS–MS–DMSL. Similar design to Class 143, but underframes built by BREL as subcontractor to W. Alexander.

Engine: One Leyland TL11 152 kW (205 hp).
Transmission: Hydraulic. Voith T211r.
Gangways: Within unit only.
Doors: Folding.
Dimensions: 15.25 x 2.70 m.
Seats: 2+3 bus style.

Maximum Speed: 75 mph.

DMS. Dia. DP240 Lot No. 31015 Derby 1986–7. 62S and wheelchair space. 24.2 t.
MS. Dia. DR205 Lot No. Derby 31037 1987. 73S. 22.6 t.
DMSL. Dia. DP241 Lot No. Derby 31016 1986–7. 60S 1L. 25.0 t.

144 001	Y	PNLX	NL	55801	55824
144 002	Y	PNLX	NL	55802	55825
144 003	Y	PNLX	NL	55803	55826
144 004	Y	PNLX	NL	55804	55827
144 005	Y	PNLX	NL	55805	55828
144 006	Y	PNLX	NL	55806	55829
144 007	Y	PNLX	NL	55807	55830
144 008	Y	PNLX	NL	55808	55831
144 009	Y	PNLX	NL	55809	55832
144 010	Y	PNLX	NL	55810	55833
144 011	Y	PNLX	NL	55811	55834
144 012	Y	PNLX	NL	55812	55835
144 013	Y	PNLX	NL	55813	55836
144 014	Y	PNLX	NL	55814	55850	55837
144 015	Y	PNLX	NL	55815	55851	55838
144 016	Y	PNLX	NL	55816	55852	55839
144 017	Y	PNLX	NL	55817	55853	55840
144 018	Y	PNLX	NL	55818	55854	55841
144 019	Y	PNLX	NL	55819	55855	55842
144 020	Y	PNLX	NL	55820	55856	55843
144 021	Y	PNLX	NL	55821	55857	55844
144 022	Y	PNLX	NL	55822	55858	55845
144 023	Y	PNLX	NL	55823	55859	55846

CLASS 150/0　　BREL PROTOTYPE SPRINTER

DMSL–MS–DMS. Prototype Sprinter.

Engine: One Cummins NT855R5 of 210 kW (285 hp).
Bogies: One BX8P and one BX8T.
Couplings: BSI at outer end of driving vehicles, bar non-driving ends.
Transmission: Hydraulic. Voith T211r with Gmeinder final drive.
Gangways: Within unit only.
Doors: Sliding.
Seats: Various types now fitted. (2+2*)
Dimensions: 20.06 x 2.82 m (outer cars), 20.18 x 2.82 m (inner car).
Maximum Speed: 75 mph.

DMSL. Dia. DP230. Lot No. 30984 York 1984. 76S 1L (58S 1L*). 35.8 t.
MS. Dia. DR202. Lot No. 30986 York 1984. 84S (72S*). 34.4 t.
DMS. Dia. DP231. Lot No. 30985 York 1984. 79S (60S*). 35.6 t.

Note: 150 002 was converted to 154 002 at RTC Derby in 1986. It is at present being converted back to a Class 150.

150 001	P	PTSX	TS	55200 55300 55400
150 002	P	PDYX	DY	55201 55302 55401

CLASS 150/1
BREL SPRINTER

DMSL–DMS or DMSL–DMSL (Class 150/2)–DMS or DMSL–DMS (Class 150/2)–DMS.

Engine: One Cummins NT855R5 of 210 kW (285 hp).
Bogies: One BP38 and one BT38.
Gangways: Within unit only.
Doors: Sliding.
Seats: 2+3 facing. († Reseated with part unidirectional seating and part facing).
Dimensions: 20.06 x 2.82 m.
Maximum Speed: 75 mph.

DMSL. Dia. DP238. Lot No. 31011 York 1985–6. 68S 1L (72S 1L†). 36.5 t.
DMS. Dia. DP239. Lot No. 31012 York 1985–6. 70S (†76S). 38.45 t.

Note: The centre cars of three-car units are Class 150/2 vehicles. For details see below.

150 101	**PO**	PTSX	TS	52101		57101
150 102	**PO**	PTSX	TS	52102		57102
150 103	**PO**	PTSX	TS	52103		57103
150 104 r†	**CE**	PTSX	TS	52104		57104
150 105	**PO**	PTSX	TS	52105		57105
150 106	**PO**	PTSX	TS	52106		57106
150 107	**PO**	PDYX	DY	52107		57107
150 108 r†	**CE**	PTSX	TS	52108	57226	57108
150 109	**PO**	PDYX	DY	52109		57109
150 110 r†	**CE**	PTSX	TS	52110		57110
150 111 r†	**CE**	PTSX	TS	52111	57206	57111
150 112 r†	**CE**	PTSX	TS	52112	52204	57112
150 113 r†	**CE**	PTSX	TS	52113	52226	57113
150 114 r†	**CE**	PTSX	TS	52114	57204	57114
150 115 r†	**CE**	PTSX	TS	52115	52206	57115
150 116 r†	**CE**	PTSX	TS	52116	52202	57116
150 117 r†	**CE**	PTSX	TS	52117	57209	57117
150 118 r†	**CE**	PTSX	TS	52118	57212	57118
150 119 r†	**CE**	PTSX	TS	52119		57119
150 120 r†	**CE**	PTSX	TS	52120		57120
150 121 r	**PO**	PTSX	TS	52121		57121
150 122 r	**PO**	PTSX	TS	52122		57122
150 123 r†	**CE**	PTSX	TS	52123		57123
150 124 r†	**CE**	PTSX	TS	52124		57124
150 125 r†	**CE**	PTSX	TS	52125		57125
150 126 r†	**CE**	PTSX	TS	52126		57126
150 127 r	**PO**	PTSX	TS	52127		57127
150 128 r†	**CE**	PTSX	TS	52128		57128
150 129 r†	**CE**	PTSX	TS	52129		57129
150 130 r†	**CE**	PTSX	TS	52130	57202	57130
150 131 r†	**CE**	PTSX	TS	52131		57131
150 132 r†	**CE**	PTSX	TS	52132		57132
150 133 r	**GM**	PNHX	NH	52133		57133
150 134 r	**PO**	PNHX	NH	52134		57134

150 135 r	**PO**	PNHX	NH	52135		57135
150 136 r	**PO**	PNHX	NH	52136		57136
150 137 r	**PO**	PNHX	NH	52137		57137
150 138 r	**PO**	PDYX	DY	52138		57138
150 139 r	**PO**	PNHX	NH	52139		57139
150 140 r	**PO**	PNHX	NH	52140	52246	57140
150 141 r	**P**	PNHX	NH	52141	57218	57141
150 142 r	**P**	PNHX	NH	52142	52222	57142
150 143 r	**P**	PNHX	NH	52143	57253	57143
150 144 r	**P**	PNHX	NH	52144	52224	57144
150 145 r	**P**	PNHX	NH	52145	57222	57145
150 146 r	**RS**	PNHX	NH	52146		57146
150 147 r	**P**	PNHX	NH	52147	57224	57147
150 148 r	**P**	PNHX	NH	52148	52253	57148
150 149 r	**P**	PNHX	NH	52149	57246	57149
150 150 r	**P**	PNHX	NH	52150	52218	57150

CLASS 150/2   BREL SPRINTER

DMSL–DMS.

Engine: One Cummins NT855R5 of 210 kW (285 hp).
Bogies: One BP38 and one BT38.
Gangways: Throughout.
Doors: Sliding.
Seats: 2+3 mainly unidirectional.
Dimensions: 20.06 x 2.82 m.
Maximum Speed: 75 mph.

DMSL. Dia. DP242. Lot No. 31017 York 1986–87. 70S 1L. 35.8 t.
DMS. Dia. DP243. Lot No. 31018 York 1986–7. 73S and luggage space. 34.90 t.

150 201	**P**	PNHX	NH	52201	57201
150 203	**P**	PNHX	NH	52203	57203
150 205	**P**	PNHX	NH	52205	57205
150 207	**P**	PNHX	NH	52207	57207
150 208	**P**	PHAX	HA	52208	57208
150 210	**P**	PTSX	TS	57210	57210
150 211	**P**	PNHX	NH	52211	57211
150 213	**P**	PNHX	NH	52213	57213
150 214	**P**	PTSX	TS	52214	57214
150 215	**P**	PNHX	NH	52215	57215
150 216	**P**	PTSX	TS	52216	57216
150 217	**P**	PNHX	NH	52217	57217
150 219	**P**	PNHX	NH	52219	57219
150 220	**CE**	PTSX	TS	52220	57220
150 221	**P**	PNHX	NH	52221	57221
150 223	**P**	PNHX	NH	52223	57223
150 225	**P**	PNHX	NH	52225	57225
150 227	**P**	PDYX	DY	52227	57227
150 228	**P**	PHAX	HA	52228	57228
150 229	**P**	PDYX	DY	52229	57229

150 230	P	PCFX	CF	52230	57230
150 231	P	PDYX	DY	52231	57231
150 232	P	PCFX	CF	52232	57232
150 233	P	PDYX	DY	52233	57233
150 234	P	PCFX	CF	52234	57234
150 235	P	PDYX	DY	52235	57235
150 236	P	PCFX	CF	52236	57236
150 237	P	PDYX	DY	52237	57237
150 238	P	PCFX	CF	52238	57238
150 239	P	PDYX	DY	52239	57239
150 240	P	PCFX	CF	52240	57240
150 241	P	PNHX	NH	52241	57241
150 242	P	PCFX	CF	52242	57242
150 243	P	PNHX	NH	52243	57243
150 244	P	PCFX	CF	52244	57244
150 245	P	PHAX	HA	52245	57245
150 247	P	PCFX	CF	52247	57247
150 248	P	PCFX	CF	52248	57248
150 249	P	PNHX	NH	52249	57249
150 250	P	PHAX	HA	52250	57250
150 251	P	PCFX	CF	52251	57251
150 252	P	PHAX	HA	52252	57252
150 254	P	PCFX	CF	52254	57254
150 255	P	PHAX	HA	52255	57255
150 256	P	PHAX	HA	52256	57256
150 257	P	PHAX	HA	52257	57257
150 258	P	PHAX	HA	52258	57258
150 259	P	PHAX	HA	52259	57259
150 260	P	PHAX	HA	52260	57260
150 261	P	PCFX	CF	52261	57261
150 262	P	PHAX	HA	52262	57262
150 263	P	PCFX	CF	52263	57263
150 264	P	PHAX	HA	52264	57264
150 265	P	PCFX	CF	52265	57265
150 266	P	PCFX	CF	52266	57266
150 267	P	PCFX	CF	52267	57267
150 268	P	PCFX	CF	52268	57268
150 269	P	PCFX	CF	52269	57269
150 270	P	PCFX	CF	52270	57270
150 271	P	PCFX	CF	52271	57271
150 272	P	PCFX	CF	52272	57272
150 273	P	PCFX	CF	52273	57273
150 274	P	PCFX	CF	52274	57274
150 275	P	PCFX	CF	52275	57275
150 276	P	PCFX	CF	52276	57276
150 277	P	PCFX	CF	52277	57277
150 278	P	PCFX	CF	52278	57278
150 279	P	PCFX	CF	52279	57279
150 280	P	PCFX	CF	52280	57280
150 281	P	PCFX	CF	52281	57281
150 282	P	PCFX	CF	52282	57282
150 283	P	PHAX	HA	52283	57283

150 284	**P**	PHAX	HA	52284	57284
150 285	**P**	PHAX	HA	52285	57285

CLASS 153   LEYLAND BUS SUPER SPRINTER

DMSLConverted by Hunslet-Barclay, Kilmarnock from Class 155 two-car units.

Engine: One Cummins NT855R5 of 213 kW (285 hp).
Bogies: One P3-10 and one BT38.
Gangways: Throughout.
Doors: Sliding plug.
Seats: 2+2 facing/unidirectional with wheelchair space.
Dimensions: 23.21 x 2.70 m.
Maximum Speed: 75 mph.

DMSL. Dia. DX203. Lot No. 31026 1987–8. 72S 1L (disabled persons toilet) + 3 tip-up seats. 38.8 t.

153 301	**RS**	PHTX	HT	52301
153 302	**RS**	PCFX	CF	52302
153 303				52303
153 304				52304
153 305				52305
153 306				52306
153 307				52307
153 308				52308
153 309	**RS**	PHTX	HT	52309
153 310				52310
153 311	**RS**	PHTX	HT	52311
153 312				52312
153 313				52313
153 314	**RS**	PHTX	HT	52314
153 315				52315
153 316				52316
153 317	**RS**	PHTX	HT	52317
153 318				52318
153 319	**RS**	PHTX	HT	52319
153 320				52320
153 321				52321
153 322				52322
153 324				52324
153 325				52325
153 326				52326
153 327				52327
153 328				52328
153 329				52329
153 330				52330
153 331	**RS**	PHTX	HT	52331
153 332				52332
153 333				52333
153 334				52334
153 335				52335

153 351	**RS**	PHTX	HT	57301
153 352	**RS**	PHTX	HT	57302
153 353				57303
153 354	**RS**	PHTX	HT	57304
153 355				57305
153 356				57306
153 357				57307
153 358	**RS**	PHTX	HT	57308
153 359	**RS**	PHTX	HT	57309
153 360				57310
153 361	**RS**	PHTX	HT	57311
153 362				57312
153 363				57313
153 364				57314
153 365				57315
153 366				57316
153 367	**RS**	PHTX	HT	57317
153 368				57318
153 369	**RS**	PHTX	HT	57319
153 370				57320
153 371				57321
153 372				57322
153 374				57324
153 375				57325
153 376				57326
153 377				57327
153 378				57328
153 379				57329
153 380				57330
153 381	**RS**	PHTX	HT	57331
153 382				57332
153 383				57333
153 384				57334
153 385				57335

CLASS 155   LEYLAND BUS SUPER SPRINTER

DMSL–DMS.

Engine: One Cummins NT855R5 of 213 kW (285 hp).
Bogies: One P3-10 and one BT38.
Gangways: Throughout.
Doors: Sliding plug.
Seats: 2+2 facing/unidirectional with wheelchair space in DMSL.
Dimensions: 23.21 x 2.70 m.
Maximum Speed: 75 mph.

52301–335. DMSL. Dia. DP248. Lot No. 31026 1987–8. 80S 1L (disabled persons toilet). 38.8 t.
57301–335. DMS. Dia. DP249. Lot No. 31027 1987–8. 80S and parcels area. 38 t.
52341–347. DMSL. Dia. DP248. Lot No. 31057 1988. 80S 1L (disabled persons toilet). 39.0 t.

57341–347. DMS. Dia. DP249. Lot No. 31058 1988. 80S and parcels area. 38.7 t.

155 306	**P**	PCFX	CF	52306	57306
155 307	**P**	PCFX	CF	52307	57307
155 312	**P**	PCFX	CF	52312	57312
155 313	**P**	PCFX	CF	52313	57313
155 315	**P**	PCFX	CF	52315	57315
155 316	**P**	PCFX	CF	52316	57316
155 320	**P**	PCFX	CF	52320	57320
155 321	**P**	PCFX	CF	52321	57321
155 322	**P**	PCFX	CF	52322	57322
155 324	**P**	PCFX	CF	52324	57324
155 325	**P**	PCFX	CF	52325	57325
155 326	**P**	PCFX	CF	52326	57326
155 327	**P**	PCFX	CF	52327	57327
155 328	**P**	PCFX	CF	52328	57328
155 330	**P**	PCFX	CF	52330	57330
155 333	**P**	PCFX	CF	52333	57333
155 334	**P**	PCFX	CF	52334	57334
155 335	**P**	PCFX	CF	52335	57335
155 341	**P**	PNLX	NL	52341	57341
155 342	**P**	PNLX	NL	52342	57342
155 343	**P**	PNLX	NL	52343	57343
155 344	**P**	PNLX	NL	52344	57344
155 345	**P**	PNLX	NL	52345	57345
155 346	**P**	PNLX	NL	52346	57346
155 347	**P**	PNLX	NL	52347	57347

CLASS 156   METRO-CAMMELL SUPER SPRINTER

DMSL–DMS.

Engine: One Cummins NT855R5 of 210 kW (285 hp).
Bogies: One P3-10 and one BT38.
Gangways: Throughout.
Doors: Sliding.
Seats: 2+2 facing/unidirectional with wheelchair space in DMSL.
Dimensions: 23.03 x 2.73 m.
Maximum Speed: 75 mph.

DMSL. Dia. DP244. Lot No. 31028 1988–9. 74S (72S†) 1L (disabled persons toilet). 36.1 t.
DMS. Dia. DP245. Lot No. 31029 1987–9. 35.5 t. 76S (74S†) + parcels area.

156 401	**P**	PNCX	NC	52401	57401
156 402 r	**P**	PNCX	NC	52402	57402
156 403	**P**	PNCX	NC	52403	57403
156 404	**P**	PNCX	NC	52404	57404
156 405	**P**	PNCX	NC	52405	57405
156 406	**P**	PNCX	NC	52406	57406
156 407	**P**	PNCX	NC	52407	57407
156 408	**P**	PNCX	NC	52408	57408
156 409	**P**	PNCX	NC	52409	57409

156 410	**P**	PNCX	NC	52410		57410
156 411 r	**P**	PNCX	NC	52411		57411
156 412	**P**	PNCX	NC	52412		57412
156 413	**P**	PNCX	NC	52413		57413
156 414	**P**	PNCX	NC	52414		57414
156 415	**P**	PNCX	NC	52415		57415
156 416	**P**	PNCX	NC	52416		57416
156 417	**P**	PNCX	NC	52417		57417
156 418	**P**	PNCX	NC	52418		57418
156 419	**P**	PDYX	DY	52419		57419
156 420	**P**	PDYX	DY	52420		57420
156 421	**P**	PDYX	DY	52421		57421
156 422	**P**	PDYX	DY	52422		57422
156 423	**P**	PDYX	DY	52423		57423
156 424	**P**	PDYX	DY	52424		57424
156 425	**P**	PDYX	DY	52425		57425
156 426	**P**	PDYX	DY	52426		57426
156 427	**P**	PDYX	DY	52427		57427
156 428	**P**	PDYX	DY	52428		57428
156 429	**P**	PDYX	DY	52429		57429
156 430	**P**	PCKX	CK	52430		57430
156 431	**P**	PCKX	CK	52431		57431
156 432	**P**	PCKX	CK	52432		57432
156 433	**P**	PCKX	CK	52433		57433
156 434	**P**	PCKX	CK	52434		57434
156 435	**P**	PCKX	CK	52435		57435
156 436 r†	**P**	PHAX	HA	52436		57436
156 437	**P**	PCKX	CK	52437		57437
156 438	**P**	PNLX	NL	52438	52470	57438
156 439	**P**	PCKX	CK	52439		57439
156 440	**P**	PNCX	NC	52440		57440
156 441	**P**	PNLX	NL	52441		57441
156 442	**P**	PCKX	CK	52442		57442
156 443	**P**	PNLX	NL	52443		57443
156 444	**P**	PNLX	NL	52444		57444
156 445 r†	**P**	PHAX	HA	52445		57445
156 446 r†	**P**	PISX	IS	52446		57446
156 447 r†	**P**	PHAX	HA	52447		57447
156 448	**P**	PNLX	NL	52448		57448
156 449 r†	**P**	PHAX	HA	52449		57449
156 450 r†	**P**	PHAX	HA	52450		57450
156 451	**P**	PNLX	NL	52451		57451
156 452	**P**	PNCX	NC	52452		57452
156 453 r†	**P**	PHAX	HA	52453		57453
156 454	**P**	PNLX	NL	52454		57454
156 455	**P**	PNLX	NL	52455	57491	57455
156 456 r†	**P**	PHAX	HA	52456		57456
156 457 r†	**P**	PISX	IS	52457		57457
156 458 r†	**P**	PISX	IS	52458		57458
156 459	**P**	PNLX	NL	52459		57459
156 460	**P**	PNLX	NL	52460		57460
156 461	**P**	PNLX	NL	52461		57461

156 462	**P**	PNLX	NL	52462 57470	57462
156 463	**P**	PNLX	NL	52463	57463
156 464	**P**	PNCX	NC	52464	57464
156 465 r†	**P**	PHAX	HA	52465	57465
156 466	**P**	PNCX	NC	52466	57466
156 467	**P**	PNLX	NL	52467	57467
156 468	**P**	PNLX	NL	52468	57468
156 469	**P**	PNLX	NL	52469	57469
156 471	**P**	PHAX	HA	52471	57471
156 472	**P**	PNLX	NL	52472	57472
156 473	**P**	PNLX	NL	52473	57473
156 474 r†	**P**	PISX	IS	52474	57474
156 475	**P**	PNLX	NL	52475	57475
156 476	**P**	PNLX	NL	52476	57476
156 477 r†	**P**	PISX	IS	52477	57477
156 478 r†	**P**	PISX	IS	52478	57478
156 479	**P**	PNLX	NL	52479	57479
156 480	**P**	PNLX	NL	52480	57480
156 481	**P**	PNLX	NL	52481	57481
156 482	**P**	PNLX	NL	52482	57482
156 483	**P**	PNLX	NL	52483	57483
156 484	**P**	PNLX	NL	52484	57484
156 485 r†	**P**	PISX	IS	52485	57485
156 486	**P**	PNLX	NL	52486	57486
156 487	**P**	PNLX	NL	52487	57487
156 488	**P**	PNLX	NL	52488	57488
156 489	**P**	PNLX	NL	52489	57489
156 490	**P**	PNLX	NL	52490	57490
156 491	**P**	PNLX	NL (U)	52491	
156 492 r†	**P**	PISX	IS	52492	57492
156 493 r†	**P**	PISX	IS	52493	57493
156 494 r†	**P**	PISX	IS	52494	57494
156 495 r†	**P**	PISX	IS	52495	57495
156 496 r†	**P**	PISX	IS	52496	57496
156 497	**P**	PNLX	NL	52497	57497
156 498	**P**	PNLX	NL	52498	57498
156 499 r†	**P**	PISX	IS	52499	57499
156 500 r†	**P**	PISX	IS	52500	57500
156 501	**S**	PCKX	CK	52501	57501
156 502	**S**	PCKX	CK	52502	57502
156 503	**S**	PHAX	HA	52503	57503
156 504	**S**	PHAX	HA	52504	57504
156 505	**S**	PHAX	HA	52505	57505
156 506	**S**	PCKX	CK	52506	57506
156 507	**S**	PCKX	CK	52507	57507
156 508	**S**	PCKX	CK	52508	57508
156 509	**S**	PCKX	CK	52509	57509
156 510	**S**	PCKX	CK	52510	57510
156 511	**S**	PCKX	CK	52511	57511
156 512	**S**	PCKX	CK	52512	57512
156 513	**S**	PCKX	CK	52513	57513
156 514	**S**	PCKX	CK	52514	57514

CLASS 158/0   BREL EXPRESS

DMSL (B)–DMSL (A) or DMCL–DMSL* or DMSL (B)–MSL–DMSL (A).

Engine: One Cummins NTA855R of 260 kW (350 hp) [One Perkins 2006-TWH of 260 kW (350 hp)† or 300 kW (400 hp)§].
Bogies: One BREL P4 and one BREL T4 per car.
Gangways: Throughout.
Doors: Sliding plug.
Seats: 2+2 facing/unidirectional (first & standard classes).
Dimensions: 23.21 x 2.70 m.
Maximum Speed: 90 mph.

DMSL (B).. Dia. DP252. Lot No. 31051 Derby 1990–2. 68S + wheelchair space 1L (disabled persons toilet). Public telephone and trolley space. 38.5 t.
DMCL.. Dia. DP252. Lot No. 31051 Derby 1989–90. 15F 51S + wheelchair space 1L (disabled persons toilet). Public telephone and trolley space. 38.5 t.
MSL. Dia. DR207. Lot No. 31050 Derby 1991.   t. 70S 2L.
DMSL (A). Dia. DP251. Lot No. 31052 Derby 1990–92. 70S 1L and parcels area. 37.8 t.

158 701	*	RE	PHAX	HA	52701	57701
158 702	*	RE	PHAX	HA	52702	57702
158 703	*	RE	PHAX	HA	52703	57703
158 704	*	RE	PHAX	HA	52704	57704
158 705	*	RE	PHAX	HA	52705	57705
158 706	*	RE	PHAX	HA	52706	57706
158 707	*	RE	PHAX	HA	52707	57707
158 708	*	RE	PHAX	HA	52708	57708
158 709	*	RE	PHAX	HA	52709	57709
158 710	*	RE	PHAX	HA	52710	57710
158 711	*	RE	PHAX	HA	52711	57711
158 712	*	RE	PHAX	HA	52712	57712
158 713	*	RE	PHAX	HA	52713	57713
158 714	*	RE	PHAX	HA	52714	57714
158 715	*	RE	PHAX	HA	52715	57715
158 716	*	RE	PHAX	HA	52716	57716
158 717	*	RE	PHAX	HA	52717	57717
158 718	*	RE	PHAX	HA	52718	57718
158 719	*	RE	PHAX	HA	52719	57719
158 720	*	RE	PHAX	HA	52720	57720
158 721	*	RE	PHAX	HA	52721	57721
158 722	*	RE	PHAX	HA	52722	57722
158 723	*	RE	PHAX	HA	52723	57723
158 724	*	RE	PHAX	HA	52724	57724
158 725	*	RE	PHAX	HA	52725	57725
158 726	*	RE	PHAX	HA	52726	57726
158 727	*	RE	PHAX	HA	52727	57727
158 728	*	RE	PHAX	HA	52728	57728
158 729	*	RE	PHAX	HA	52729	57729

158 730	*	RE	PHAX	HA	52730	57730
158 731	*	RE	PHAX	HA	52731	57731
158 732	*	RE	PHAX	HA	52732	57732
158 733	*	RE	PHAX	HA	52733	57733
158 734		RE	PHAX	HA	52734	57734
158 735		RE	PHAX	HA	52735	57735
158 736		RE	PHAX	HA	52736	57736
158 737		RE	PHAX	HA	52737	57737
158 738		RE	PHAX	HA	52738	57738
158 739		RE	PHAX	HA	52739	57739
158 740		RE	PHAX	HA	52740	57740
158 741		RE	PHAX	HA	52741	57741
158 742		RE	PHAX	HA	52742	57742
158 743		RE	PHAX	HA	52743	57743
158 744		RE	PHAX	HA	52744	57744
158 745		RE	PHAX	HA	52745	57745
158 746		RE	PNLX	NL	52746	57746
158 747		RE	PNLX	NL	52747	57747
158 748		RE	PNLX	NL	52748	57748
158 749		RE	PNLX	NL	52749	57749
158 750		RE	PNLX	NL	52750	57750
158 751		RE	PNLX	NL	52751	57751
158 752		RE	PNLX	NC	52752	57752
158 753		RE	PNLX	NL	52753	57753
158 754		RE	PNLX	NL	52754	57754
158 755		RE	PNLX	NL	52755	57755
158 756		RE	PNLX	NL	52756	57756
158 757		RE	PNLX	NL	52757	57757
158 758		RE	PNLX	NL	52758	57758
158 759		RE	PNLX	NL	52759	57759
158 760		RE	PNLX	NL	52760	57760
158 761		RE	PNCX	NC	52761	57761
158 762		RE	PNCX	NC	52762	57762
158 763		RE	PNCX	NC	52763	57763
158 764		RE	PNCX	NC	52764	57764
158 765		RE	PNCX	NC	52765	57765
158 766		RE	PNCX	NC	52766	57766
158 767		RE	PCFX	CF	52767	57767
158 768		RE	PNCX	NC	52768	57768
158 769		RE	PCFX	CF	52769	57769
158 770		RE	PNCX	NC	52770	57770
158 771		RE	PCFX	CF	52771	57771
158 772		RE	PNCX	NC	52772	57772
158 773		RE	PNCX	NC	52773	57773
158 774		RE	PNCX	NC	52774	57774
158 775		RE	PNCX	NC	52775	57775
158 776		RE	PNCX	NC	52776	57776
158 777		RE	PNCX	NC	52777	57777
158 778		RE	PNCX	NC	52778	57778
158 779		RE	PNCX	NC	52779	57779
158 780		RE	PNCX	NC	52780	57780
158 781		RE	PNCX	NC	52781	57781

158 782	**RE**	PNCX	NC	52782		57782
158 783	**RE**	PCFX	CF	52783		57783
158 784	**RE**	PNCX	NC	52784		57784
158 785	**RE**	PNCX	NC	52785		57785
158 786	**RE**	PNCX	NC	52786		57786
158 787	**RE**	PCFX	CF	52787		57787
158 788	**RE**	PCFX	CF	52788		57788
158 789	**RE**	PCFX	CF	52789		57789
158 790	**RE**	PNCX	NC	52790		57790
158 791	**RE**	PCFX	CF	52791		57791
158 792	**RE**	PCFX	CF	52792		57792
158 793	**RE**	PCFX	CF	52793		57793
158 794	**RE**	PCFX	CF	52794		57794
158 795	**RE**	PCFX	CF	52795		57795
158 796	**RE**	PCFX	CF	52796		57796
158 797	**RE**	PCFX	CF	52797		57797
158 798	**RE**	PHTX	HT	52798	58715	57798
158 799	**RE**	PHTX	HT	52799	58716	57799
158 800	**RE**	PHTX	HT	52800	58717	57800
158 801	**RE**	PHTX	HT	52801	58701	57801
158 802	**RE**	PHTX	HT	52802	58702	57802
158 803	**RE**	PHTX	HT	52803	58703	57803
158 804	**RE**	PHTX	HT	52804	58704	57804
158 805	**RE**	PHTX	HT	52805	58705	57805
158 806	**RE**	PHTX	HT	52806	58706	57806
158 807	**RE**	PHTX	HT	52807	58707	57807
158 808	**RE**	PHTX	HT	52808	58708	57808
158 809	**RE**	PHTX	HT	52809	58709	57809
158 810	**RE**	PHTX	HT	52810	58710	57810
158 811	**RE**	PHTX	HT	52811	58711	57811
158 812	**RE**	PHTX	HT	52812	58712	57812
158 813	**RE**	PHTX	HT	52813	58713	57813
158 814	**RE**	PHTX	HT	52814	58714	57814
158 815 †	**RE**	PCFX	CF	52815		57815
158 816 †	**RE**	PCFX	CF	52816		57816
158 817 †	**RE**	PCFX	CF	52817		57817
158 818 †	**RE**			52818		57818
158 819 †	**RE**	PCFX	CF	52819		57819
158 820 †	**RE**	PCFX	CF	52820		57820
158 821 †	**RE**	PCFX	CF	52821		57821
158 822 †	**RE**	PCFX	CF	52822		57822
158 823 †	**RE**	PCFX	CF	52823		57823
158 824 †	**RE**	PCFX	CF	52824		57824
158 825 †	**RE**	PCFX	CF	52825		57825
158 826 †	**RE**	PCFX	CF	52826		57826
158 827 †	**RE**			52827		57827
158 828 †	**RE**	PCFX	CF	52828		57828
158 829 †	**RE**	PCFX	CF	52829		57829
158 830 †	**RE**	PCFX	CF	52830		57830
158 831 †	**RE**	PCFX	CF	52831		57831
158 832 †	**RE**			52832		57832
158 833 †	**RE**			52833		57833

158 834 †	**RE**		52834	57834
158 835 †	**RE**		52835	57835
158 836 †	**RE**		52836	57836
158 837 †	**RE**		52837	57837
158 838 †	**RE**		52838	57838
158 839 †	**RE**		52839	57839
158 840 †	**RE**		52840	57840
158 841 †	**RE**		52841	57841
158 842 †	**RE**		52842	57842
158 843 †	**RE**		52843	57843
158 844 †	**RE**		52844	57844
158 845 †	**RE**		52845	57845
158 846 †	**RE**		52846	57846
158 847 †	**RE**		52847	57847
158 848 †	**RE**		52848	57848
158 849 †	**RE**		52849	57849
158 850 †	**RE**		52850	57850
158 851 †	**RE**		52851	57851
158 852 †	**RE**		52852	57852
158 853 †	**RE**		52853	57853
158 854 †	**RE**		52854	57854
158 855 †	**RE**		52855	57855
158 856 †	**RE**		52856	57856
158 857 †	**RE**		52857	57857
158 858 †	**RE**		52858	57858
158 859 †	**RE**		52859	57859
158 860 †	**RE**		52860	57860
158 861 †	**RE**		52861	57861
158 862 §	**RE**		52862	57862
158 863 §	**RE**		52863	57864
158 864 §	**RE**		52864	57864
158 865 §	**RE**		52865	57865
158 866 §	**RE**		52866	57866
158 867 §	**RE**		52867	57867
158 868 §	**RE**		52868	57868
158 869 §	**RE**		52869	57869
158 870 §	**RE**		52870	57870
158 871 §	**RE**		52871	57871
158 872 §	**RE**		52872	57872

CLASS 158/9   BREL EXPRESS

DMSL–DMS. Units leased by West Yorkshire PTE. Details as for Class 158/0 except for seating layout and toilets.

DMSL.. Dia. DP252. Lot No. 31051 Derby 1990–2. 70S + wheelchair space 1L (disabled persons toilet). Public telephone and trolley space. 38.1 t.
DMS. Dia. DP251. Lot No. 31052 Derby 1990–92. 72S and parcels area. 37.8 t.

158 901	**Y**	**PNLX**	NL	52901	57901
158 902	**Y**	**PNLX**	NL	52902	57902

158 903	Y	PNLX	NL	52903	57903
158 904	Y	PNLX	NL	52904	57904
158 905	Y	PNLX	NL	52905	57905
158 906	Y	PNLX	NL	52906	57906
158 907	Y	PNLX	NL	52907	57907
158 908	Y	PNLX	NL	52908	57908
158 909	Y	PNLX	NL	52909	57908
158 910	Y	PNLX	NL	52910	57910

CLASS 159   BREL EXPRESS

DMCL–TSL–DMSL. Built as Class 158 by BREL and converted before entering passenger service to Class 159 by Rosyth Dockyard.

Engine: One Perkins 2006-TWH of 300 kW (400 hp).
Bogies: One BREL P4 and one BREL T4 per car.
Gangways: Throughout.
Doors: Sliding plug.
Seats: 2+2 facing/unidirectional (standard class), 2+1 facing (first class).
Dimensions: 23.21 x 2.82 m.
Maximum Speed: 90 mph.

DMCL. Dia. DP252. Lot No. 31051 Derby 1992. 24F 35S 1L (disabled persons toilet). 38.5 t.
MSL. Dia. DR207. Lot No. 31050 Derby 1992.   t. 70S 1L.
DMSL. Dia. DP251. Lot No. 31052 Derby 1992. 70S 1L and parcels area. 37.8 t.

159 001	52873	58718	57873
159 002	52874	58719	57874
159 003	52875	58720	57875
159 004	52876	58721	57876
159 005	52877	58722	57877
159 006	52878	58723	57878
159 007	52879	58724	57879
159 008	52880	58725	57880
159 009	52881	58726	57881
159 010	52882	58727	57882
159 011	52883	58728	57883
159 012	52884	58729	57884
159 013	52885	58730	57885
159 014	52886	58731	57886
159 015	52887	58732	57887
159 016	52888	58733	57888
159 017	52889	58734	57889
159 018	52890	58735	57890
159 019	52891	58736	57891
159 020	52892	58737	57892
159 021	52893	58738	57893
159 022	52894	58739	57894

CLASS 165/0   BREL NETWORK TURBO

DMCL–DMS or DMC–MS–DMS. Network SouthEast Units for Chiltern Line
(Marylebone) services

Engine: One Perkins 2006-TWH of 260 kW (350 hp).
Bogies: One BREL P3 and one BREL T3 per car.
Transmission: Hydraulic. Voith T211r with Gmeinder final drive.
Gangways: Within unit only.
Doors: Sliding plug.
Seats: 2+3.
Dimensions: 23.50 x 2.85 t.
Maximum Speed: 75 mph.

58801–58822. 58873–58878. DMCL. Dia. DP319. Lot No. 31087 York 1990. 16F
72S 1L. 37.0 t.
58823–58833. DMCL. Dia. DP320. Lot No. 31089 York 1990. 24F 60S 1L. 37.0 t.
MS. Dia. DR208. Lot No. 31090 York 1990. 106S. 37.0 t.
DMS. Dia. DP253. Lot No. 31088 York 1990. 98S. 37.0 t.

165 001	**N**	NMYX	AL	58801		58834
165 002	**N**	NMYX	AL	58802		58835
165 003	**N**	NMYX	AL	58803		58836
165 004	**N**	NMYX	AL	58804		58837
165 005	**N**	NMYX	AL	58805		58838
165 006	**N**	NMYX	AL	58806		58839
165 007	**N**	NMYX	AL	58807		58840
165 008	**N**	NMYX	AL	58808		58841
165 009	**N**	NMYX	AL	58809		58842
165 010	**N**	NMYX	AL	58810		58843
165 011	**N**	NMYX	AL	58811		58844
165 012				58812		58845
165 013				58813		58846
165 014				58814		58847
165 015				58815		58848
165 016				58816		58849
165 017				58817		58850
165 018				58818		58851
165 019				58819		58852
165 020				58820		58853
165 021				58821		58854
165 022				58822		58855
165 023				58873		58867
165 024				58874		58868
165 025				58875		58869
165 026				58876		58870
165 027				58877		58871
165 028				58878		58872
165 029				58823	55404	58856
165 030				58824	55405	58857
165 031				58825	55406	58858

165 032	58826	55407	58859
165 033	58827	55408	58860
165 034	58828	55409	58861
165 035	58829	55410	58862
165 036	58830	55411	58863
165 037	58831	55412	58864
165 038	58832	55413	58865
165 039	58833	55414	58866

CLASS 165/1   BREL NETWORK TURBO

DMC–DMS or DMC–MS–DMS. Network SouthEast Units for Thames Line (Paddington) services

Engine: One Perkins 2006-TWH of 260 kW (350 hp).
Bogies: One BREL P3 and one BREL T3 per car.
Transmission: Hydraulic. Voith T211r with Gmeinder final drive.
Gangways: Within unit only.
Doors: Sliding plug.
Seats: 2+3.
Dimensions: 23.50 x 2.85 t.
Maximum Speed: 90 mph.

58953–58969. DMC. Dia. DP320. Lot No. 31098 York 1992. 24F 60S. 37.0 t.
58879–58898. DMC. Dia. DP319. Lot No. 31096 York 1992. 16F 72S. 37.0 t.
MS. Dia. DR208. Lot No. 31099 York 1992. 106S. 37.0 t.
DMS. Dia. DP253. Lot No. 31097 York 1992. 98S. 37.0 t.

165 101	58916	55415	58953
165 102	58917	55416	58954
165 103	58918	55417	58955
165 104	58919	55418	58956
165 105	58920	55419	58957
165 106	58921	55420	58958
165 107	58922	55421	58959
165 108	58923	55422	58960
165 109	58924	55423	58961
165 110	58925	55424	58962
165 111	58926	55425	58963
165 112	58927	55426	58964
165 113	58928	55427	58965
165 114	58929	55428	58966
165 115	58930	55429	58967
165 116	58931	55430	58968
165 117	58932	55431	58969
165 118	58879		58933
165 119	58880		58934
165 120	58881		58935
165 121	58882		58936
165 122	58883		58937
165 123	58884		58938
165 124	58885		58939
165 125	58886		58940

Class 101 2-car unit 101 651 in the new 'Regional stripes' livery (code 'RS') leaves Cambridge with the 12.13 to Norwich on 13th September 1991.   *John Augustson*

Class 101 3-car unit No. LA832 with an Exmouth–Paignton service at Kingswell on 15th September 1991.   *Nic Joynson*

▲ Class 104 units are now operated only by Network SouthEast. 53477 + 535 approach Acton Main Line on an e.c.s. working to Old Oak Common on 1 April 1990.   *Paul D Shann*

▼ Only six Class 107s remain in service, all at Haymarket. Set 107 040 (52001/5978 52024) in Strathclyde PTE livery was photographed at Stepps with a Glasgo Queen Street–Cumbernauld service on 1st August 1990. This set has since be withdrawn.   *John Augusts*

A pair of Class 108 2-car units Nos. Lo 266 (51913/54497) and LO 276 (53981/54253) pass Blackrod with a Manchester–Barrow service on 8th August 1991.

Paul Senior

One of the two remaining Class 114 "Derby Heavyweight" sets No. T027 (53019/54027) at Shirley on a snowy 14th

Class 117 suburban set T305 has been painted in the chocolate and cream ~ry of the former Great Western railway for a few years now. It was seen on ~h April 1991 leaving Birmingham Moor Street for Dorridge.   *Chris Morrison*

Gloucester RCW Co. Class 119 'cross-country' set L575 (51060/59419/51088) ~ves Workingham with a Reading–Gatwick service on 2nd August 1991.
                                                                    Chris Morrison

▲ Class 121 No. 55121 in Network SouthEast livery on 26th March 1991.
Norman Barring

▼ Class 122 No. 55012, the first "bubble car" to be painted in the new 'Regio stripes' livery at Laira on 14th September 1991.
Colin J Marsd

Class 141 set No. 141 109 in Metro (West Yorkshire PTE) livery at Stourton on
d August 1990 forming the 13.35 Castleford–Leeds.   *Hugh Ballantyne*

Class 142 set No. 142 002 in Greater Manchester PTE livery passes Westh-
ghton on 14th July 1991 with the 08.55 Southport–Stockport.   *Paul Senior*

Exworks in Regional stripes livery, Class 143 No. 143 604 runs through Durham station on 21st August 1991.

Another Class 143, this time in the yellow livery of Tyne & Wear PTE, unit No.
̶3 624 approaches Cargo Fleet, Middlesbrough with a Saltburn–Darlington ser-
̶e on 16th January 1991. *John Augustson*

Another 'Metro'-liveried unit 3-car Class 144 No. 144 022 forming the 15.08
̶orecambe–Leeds during July 1990. *L A Nixon*

▲ Prototype Class 150 3-car unit No. 150 001 at Henley-in-Arden on 30th Aug 1991. *Chris Morris*

▼ This 2-car Class 150/1 is painted in Centro (West Midlands PTE) livery and seen ex-works travelling from Eastleigh to Tyseley on 7th September 1991. Unl earlier units in this livery, it carries the 'REGIONAL RAILWAYS' branding.
David C Warw

Class 150/2 2-car set 150 203 in Network NorthWest livery leaves Bolton with 10.25 Southport–Hazel Grove on 30th October 1990.   *Hugh Ballantyne*

Car 52317 was formerly part of a Class 155 2-car unit. It has since been converted a single unit of Class 153 and is seen on a crew-training run on 11th September)1 passing Hartlepool. Unfortunately, the new cabs are so cramped that they /e been 'blacked' by the Heaton drivers.   *John Augustson*

'Metro'-liveried Class 155 No. 155 345 is seen passing Sowerby Bridge on Calder Valley line on 20th July 1990.

Paul D Shanr

Class 156 No. 156 497 passes the site of the new Walsden station with the 12.23 York-Liverpool Lime St. on 21st February 1990.
Paul D Shannon

Class 158 No. 158 756 at Saddleworth on 16th February 1991 with the 09.56 Scarborough–Liverpool. At the time of ... ... on the line alone because they would not operate the track circuits.

'Metro'-liveried Class 158 No. 158 901 calls at Newton-le-Willows with a Liver-
pol Lime St.-York via the Calder Valley service on 17th September 1991.

Paul Senior

The first two Class 165s Nos. 165 002 and 165 001 outside the new Aylesbury
depot on 14th May 1991.   *Colin C Marsden*

▲ DEMU 205 033 climbs past Ponton with the 09.40 Salisbury–Basingstoke 23rd April 1991. *David Warw*

▼ One of the few remaining Class 207 DEMUs in service No. 207 010 pas Alderley with the 16.32 Southampton–Salisbury service on 17th April 1991. *Phil Mars*

65 126	58887	58941
65 127	58888	58942
65 128	58889	58943
65 129	58890	58944
65 130	58891	58945
65 131	58892	58946
65 132	58893	58947
65 133	58894	58948
65 134	58895	58949
65 135	58896	58950
65 136	58897	58951
65 137	58898	58952

3.4 DIESEL ELECTRIC MULTIPLE UNITS

All SR diesel-electric multiple unit power cars have above-floor-mounted engines and all vehicles are equipped with buckeye couplings and were buil at Eastleigh with frames laid at Ashford.

CLASS 205   3H

DMBSO–TSOL–DTCsoL. Buckeye couplings.

Engine: English Electric 4SRKT engines of 450 kW (600 hp).
Transmission: Two EE 507 traction motors on the inner bogie.
Gangways: Non-gangwayed.
Dimensions: 20.28 x 2.82 m.
Maximum Speed: 75 mph.

60108–117/154. DMBSO. Dia DB203. Lot No. 30332 1957. 52S. 56 t.
60120. DMBSO. Dia DB203. Lot No. 30398 1957. 52S. 56 t.
60122–125. DMBSO. Dia DB203. Lot No. 30540 1958–59. 52S. 56 t.
60145–151. DMBSO. Dia DB204. Lot No. 30671 1960–62. 42S. 56 t.
60650–670. TSO. Dia DH203. Lot No. 30542 1958–59. 104S. 30 t.
60672–678. TSO. Dia DH203. Lot No. 30672 1960–62. 104S. 30 t.
60800–817. DTCsoL. Dia DE302 (†DE301). Lot No. 30333 1956–57. 19F 50S 2|
†–One compartment converted to luggage compartment. 13F 50S 2L.
60822–824. DTCsoL. Dia DE302 (†DE301). Lot No. 30541 1958–59. 19F 50S 2|
†–One compartment converted to luggage compartment. 13F 50S 2L.
60826–832. DTCsoL. Dia DE303. Lot No. 30673 1960–62. 13F 62S 2L. 32 t

60154 was renumbered from 60100.

205 001	(1101)	†	**N**	NSLX	SU	60154	60650	60800
205 008	(1108)			NSLX	SU	60120	60651	60814
205 009	(1109)		**N**	NSLX	SU	60108	60658	60808
205 012	(1112)		**N**	NSLX	SU	60111	60661	60811
205 015	(1115)		**N**	NSLX	SU	60114	60664	60801
205 016	(1116)		**N**	NSLX	SU	60115	60665	60815
205 018	(1118)		**N**	NSLX	SU	60117	60667	60817
205 023	(1123)		**N**	NSLX	SU	60122	60668	60822
205 024	(1124)	†	**N**	NSLX	SU	60123	60669	60823
205 025	(1125)	†	**N**	NSLX	SU	60124	60670	60824
205 027	(1127)			NSLX	SU	60145	60672	60826
205 028	(1128)		**N**	NSLX	SU	60146	60673	60827
205 029	(1129)		**N**	NWXX	EH	60147	60674	60828
205 030	(1130)		**N**	NWXX	EH	60148	60675	60829
205 031	(1131)			NSLX	SU	60149	60676	60830
205 032	(1132)		**N**	NWXX	EH	60150	60677	60831
205 033	(1133)		**N**	NWXX	EH	60151	60678	60832
Spare	( )		**N**	NSLX	SU	60125		

CLASS 205/1   3H

DMBSO–TSO–DTSOL. Refurbished 1980. Fluorescent lighting. PA.

Engine: English Electric 4SRKT engines of 450 kW (600 hp).
Transmission: Two EE 507 traction motors on the inner bogie.
Gangways: Within unit only.
Dimensions: 20.28 x 2.82 m.
Maximum Speed: 75 mph.

DMBSO. Dia DB203. Lot No. 30332 1957. 39S. 57 t.
TSO. Dia DH203. Lot No. 30542 1959. 98S. 30 t.
DTSOL. Dia DE204. Lot No. 30333 1957. 76S 2L. 32 t.

205 101 (1111)	**N**	NKCX	SU	60110	60660	60810

CLASS 207   3D

DMBSO–TCsoL–DTSO. Buckeye couplings.

Engine: English Electric 4SRKT engines of 450 kW (600 hp).
Transmission: Two EE 507 traction motors on the inner bogie.
Gangways: Non-gangwayed.
Dimensions: 20.34 x 2.74 m. (DMBSO), 20.32 x 2.74 m. (DTS), 20.34 x 2.74 m. (TCsoL).
Maximum Speed: 75 mph.

DMBSO. Dia DB205. Lot No. 30625 1962. 42S. 56 t.
TCsoL. Dia DH301. Lot No. 30626 1962. 24F 42S 1L. 31 t.
DTSO. Dia DE201. Lot No. 30627 1962. 76S. 32 t.

207 001 (1301)	**N**	NWXX	EH	60126	60600	60900
207 002 (1302)	**N**	NKCX	SU	60127	60601	60901
207 010 (1310)	**N**	NWXX	EH	60135	60609	60909
207 013 (1313)	**N**	NWXX	EH	60138	60612	60912
207 017 (1317)	**N**	NWXX	EH	60142	60616	60916
207 101 (1304)		NKCX	SU	60129		60903
207 102 (1305)		NKCX	SU	60130		60904

3.5 DEPARTMENTAL DMU CARS

For information in this section we wish to thank Roger Butcher.

Conversions:

DB 975007	(79018)	RG	Ultrasonic test train coach (out of use).
DB 975008	(79612)	RG	Ultrasonic test train coach (out of use).
RDB 975010	(79900)	RTC	Lab Coach 19 (Iris).
TDB 975023	(55001)	OO	Route learning car. (L101).
TDB 975025	(60755)	SL	NSE inspection saloon.
ADB 975042	(55019)	BY	Sandite car.
DB 975349	(51116)	HT	Inspection saloon.
DB 975539	(56101)	HT	Inspection saloon.
TDB 975540	(55016)	TS	Sandite car. (T008).
TDB 975659	(55035)	OO	Route learning car. (L135).
ADB 977376	(60002)	SU	Sandite unit 1066.
ADB 977377	(60003)	SU	Sandite unit 1066.
ADB 977379	(60504)	SU	Sandite unit 1066.
DB 977391	(51433)	RTC	Ultrasonic test train car.
DB 977392	(53167)	RTC	Ultrasonic test train car.
DB 977393	(53246)	Radyr	Pending conversion to UTT car.
TDB 977466	(54286)	LA	Sandite vehicle.
TDB 977486	(54285)	CF	Sandite vehicle.
TDB 977535	(53259)	HT	Sandite vehicle.
TDB 977536	(53295)	HT	Sandite vehicle.
ADB 977554	(54182)	BX	Sandite vehicle.
ADB 977555	(54183)	CL	Sandite vehicle.
TDB 977607	(51464)	ED	Route learning & sandite vehicle.
TDB 977608	(51525)	ED	Route learning & sandite vehicle.
RDB 977645	(60450)	RTC	Lab Coach.
ADB 977649	(60200)	RTC	De-icing & Sandite Coach (not converted).
ADB 977650	(60201)	RTC	De-icing & Sandite Coach (not converted).
TDB 977651	(53290)	ED	Sandite & Route Learning Car.
TDB 977652	(53197)	ED	Sandite & Route Learning Car.
RDB 977693	(53222)	RTC	Lab Coach 19 (Iris 2).
RDB 977694	(53338)	RTC	Lab Coach.19 (Iris 2).
ADB 977696	(60522)	EH	Sandite unit 068.
ADB 977697	(60523)	SU	Sandite unit 067.
ADB 977698	(60152)	SU	Sandite unit 067.
ADB 977699	(60153)	SU	Sandite unit 067.
ADB 977700	(60139)	EH	Sandite unit 068.
ADB 977701	(60910)	EH	Sandite unit 068.
ADB 977722	(55020)	OC	Route learning & Sandite vehicle.
ADB 977723	(55021)	BY	Route learning & Sandite vehicle.
977744	(51906)	LO	Sandite vehicle.
977745	(53626)	LO	Sandite vehicle.
977746	(53929)	LO	Sandite vehicle.
977748	(53950)	LO	Sandite vehicle.
977752	(51306)	TS	Sandite vehicle.*
977753	(51321)	TS	Sandite vehicle.*

* Departmental numbers not carried.

977756	(51985)	ED	Sandite vehicle.
977757	(52028)	ED	Sandite vehicle.
977758	(51992)	ED	Sandite vehicle.
977762	(52023)	ED	Sandite vehicle.

New Build:

RDB 999507	RTC	Wickham self propelled laboratory.
DB 999600	RTC	Civil Engineer's track recording unit.
DB 999601	RTC	Civil Engineer's track recording unit.

4. ELECTRIC MULTIPLE UNITS

GENERAL

BR design electric multiple unit vehicles are numbered in the series 61000–78999. SR vehicles carry numbers in the SR 14000–15999 number series, and there is one unit kept for special duties with vehicles numbered in the LNER 6xxxx number series.

Regional prefix letters used to be carried preceeding the vehicle number, but these are now no longer used and many have been removed. The prefixes were: E–Eastern Region, M–London Midland Region, S–Southern Region, SC–Scottish Region. Prefixes are not shown in this book as they no longer officially form part of the vehicle number. In addition, SR number series vehicles carry the suffix S (also being removed).

NOTES

Unless stated otherwise, all multiple unit vehicles are of BR design, or designed by contractors for BR and have buckeye couplings and tread brakes. Seating is 3+2 in standard class open vehicles, 2+2 in first class open vehicles, 12 to a non-corridor standard class compartment, 8 to a corridor standard class compartment and 6 to a corridor first class compartment. In express stock, open standards have 2+2 seating and open firsts have 2+1 seating.

ABBREVIATIONS

The following abbreviations are used in this book:

Operator Codes:

Each vehicle is referred to by an operator code as follows:

M	Motor
DM	Driving Motor
BDM	Battery Driving Motor
	Trailer
DT	Driving Trailer
BDT	Battery Driving Trailer
	Brake, i.e. vehicle with luggage space and guards compartment.
	First
	Standard
	Composite
	Unclassified
B	Buffet Car
	handbrake fitted.
BSM	Buffet Standard (Modular)
PMV	Parcels and Mails Van
V	Luggage Van
	Open vehicle
	Side corridor with lavatory
O	Semi-open vehicle.
	Open or semi-open Vehicle with lavatory
MLS	Motor Luggage Standard (an MBS minus the guards equipment)

The letters (A) and (B) may be added to the above codes to differentiate between two cars of the same operating type which have differences between them. Note that a consistent system is used, rather than the official operator codes which are sometimes inconsistent.

Notes:

1) Compartment Stock (non-corridor) has no suffix.
2) Semi-open composites generally have the first class accommodation in compartments and the standard class in open saloons.
3) Unless stated otherwise, it is assumed that motor vehicles are fitted with pantographs. If the pantograph is on a trailer, then the trailer has the prefix 'P', e.g. PTSO – Pantograph trailer open standard.

Builder Codes:

AEI	Associated Electrical Industries Ltd.
BRCW	The Birmingham Railway Carriage & Wagon Co. Ltd.
BTH	The British Thomson Houston Electrical Co. Ltd.
CP	Crompton-Parkinson Ltd.
EE	The English Electric Co. Ltd.
GEC	The General Electric Company Ltd.
Gloucester	The Gloucester Railway Carriage and Wagon Co. Ltd.
Hunslet	Hunslet Transportation Projects Ltd.
Metro-Cammell	The Metropolitan Cammell Railway Carriage and Wagon Co. Ltd.

Other Abbreviations:

(S)	Stored Serviceable
(U)	Stored Unserviceable
LNER	London & North Eastern Railway
SR	Southern Railway

DIAGRAMS AND DESIGN CODES

For each type of vehicle, the official design code consists of a seven character code of two letters, four numbers and another letter, e.g. EC2040B. The first five characters of this are the diagram code and are given in the class heading or sub heading. These are explained as follows:

1st Letter

This is always 'E' for an electric multiple unit vehicle.

2nd Letter

as follows for various vehicle types:

A	Driving motor passenger vehicles.
B	Driving motor passenger vehicles with a brake compartment.
C	Non-Driving motor passenger vehicles.
D	Non-Driving trailer passenger vehicles with a brake compartment.
E	Driving Trailer passenger vehicles.
F	Battery Driving Trailer passenger vehicles.
G	Driving Trailer passenger vehicles with a brake compartment.
H	Trailer passenger vehicles.
I	Battery Driving Motor passenger vehicles.
J	Trailer passenger vehicles with a brake compartment.
N	Trailer passenger vehicles with a buffet compartment.
O	Battery Driving Trailer passenger vehicles with a brake compartment.
P	Trailer passenger vehicles with a handbrake.
X	Driving Motor Luggage Vans.
Y	Non-driving Motor Luggage Van.

1st Figure

1	First class accommodation.
2	Standard class accommodation (incl. declassified seats).
3	Composite accommodation.
5	No passenger accommodation.

4.1. 25 kV a.c. OVERHEAD EMUs.

Note: All units are 25 kV overhead only except where stated otherwise.

CLASS 302

BDTCOL–MBSO–TSOL–DTSO. All remaining units refurbished with new seats, fluorescent lighting and pa.
Gangways: Within unit.
Traction Motors: Four EE536A 143.5 kW.
Dimensions: 19.50 x 2.82 m (outer cars), 19.36 x 2.82 m (inner cars).
Maximum Speed: 75 mph.

75084–75205. BDTCOL. Lot No. 30436. York/Doncaster 1958–59.
75311–75358. BDTCOL. Lot No. 30440. York/Doncaster 1959.
61060–61091. MBSO. Lot No. 30434. York 1958–59.
61122–61226. MBSO. Lot No. 30438. York 1960.
70060–70091. TSOL. Lot No. 30437. York/Doncaster 1958–59.
70122–70226. TSOL. Lot No. 30441. York 1959–61.
75033–75079. DTSO. Lot No. 30435. York 1958–59.
75236–75283. DTSO. Lot No. 30439. York 1959–60.

BDTCOL. Dia. EF303. 24F 52S 1L. 39.5 t. B5 bogies.
MBSO. Dia. ED216. 76S. 55.3 t. Gresley Bogies.
TSOL. Dia. EH223. 86S 1L. 34.4 t. B4 bogies.
DTSO. Dia. EE219. 88S. 33.4 t. B4 or B5 bogies.

302 201	N	NNEX	EM	75085	61060	70060	75033
302 202		NNEX	EM	75086	61061	70061	75034
302 203 (302 263)		NNEX	EM	75311	61122	70122	75236
302 204		NNEX	EM	75088	61063	70063	75036
302 205	N	NNEX	EM	75089	61064	70064	75037
302 206	N	NNEX	EM	75090	61065	70065	75038
302 207 (302 310)		NNEX	EM	75358	61226	70226	75283
302 208 (302 308)	N	NNEX	EM	75356	61224	70224	75281
302 209	N	NNEX	EM	75093	61068	70068	75041
302 210		NNEX	EM	75094	61069	70069	75042
302 211		NTSX	EM	75095	61070	70070	75043
302 212		NTSX	EM	75096	61071	70071	75044
302 213		NTSX	EM	75097	61072	70072	75060
302 214 (302 304)	N	NTSX	EM	75352	61220	70220	75277
302 215		NTSX	EM	75099	61074		75062
302 216	N	NTSX	EM	75100	61075		75063
302 217	N	NTSX	EM	75190	61076	70076	75064
302 218		NTSX	EM	75191	61077		75065
302 219		NTSX	EM	75192	61078		75066
302 220	N	NTSX	EM	75193	61079		75067
302 221		NTSX	EM	75194	61080		75068
302 222	N	NTSX	EM	75195	61081		75069
302 223 (302 293)		NTSX	EM	75341	61209		75266
302 224	N	NTSX	EM	75197	61083		75071
302 225		NTSX	EM	75198	61084		75072

302 226		NNEX	EM	75199	61085		75073
302 227 (302 277)	**N**	NNEX	EM	75325	61193	70193	75250
302 228		NNEX	EM	75201	61087	70087	75075
302 229		NNEX	EM	75202	61088	70088	75076
302 230 (302 232)		NNEX	EM	75205	61091	70091	75079

Class 302/9. Parcels Units. BDTPMV–MPMV–DTPMV.

68100/5. BDTPMV. Dia. EF501. Lot No. 30435. York 1959.
68101–2. BDTPMV. Dia. EF501. Lot No. 30439. York 1959.
68020–1. MPMV. Dia. ED501. Lot No. 30434. York 1959.
68022–3. MPMV. Dia. ED501. Lot No. 30438. York 1960.
68207/13. DTPMV. Dia. EE501. Lot No. 30435. York 1959.
68208–9. DTPMV. Dia. EE501. Lot No. 30439. York 1959.

302 990	**R**	RPMA	IL	68100	68020	68207
302 991	**R**	RPMA	IL	68101	68021	68208
302 992	**R**	RPMA	IL	68102	68022	68209
302 993	**R**	RPMA	IL	68105	68023	68213

Former numbers of converted vehicles:

68020 (61090)	68023 (61222)	68102 (?????)	68208 (75217)
68021 (61067)	68100 (75084)	68105 (75078)	68209 (75218)
68022 (61227)	68101 (75221)	68207 (75082)	68213 (75074)

Spare TSOL:

70074	70077	70079	70081	70083	70084	70085	70209
70075	70078	70080					

CLASS 303

DTSO–MBSO–BDTSO. Sliding doors.
Bogies: Gresley.
Gangways: None [Gangwayed within units only (r)].
Traction Motors: Four MV 155 kW.
Dimensions: 19.50 x 2.82 m (outer cars), 19.36 x 2.82 m (inner cars).
Maximum Speed: 75 mph.

Class 303/0. Unrefurbished sets.

DTSO. Dia. EE206. 83S. 34.4 t.
MBSO. Dia. ED201. 70S. 56.4 t.
BDTSO. Dia. EF202. 83S. 38.4 t.

Class 303/1. Refurbished with 2+2 seating and hopper-type window vents).
Denoted by 'r'

DTSO. Dia. EE241. 56S. 34.4 t.
MBSO. Dia. ED220. 48S. 56.4 t.
BDTSO. Dia. EF217. 56S. 38.4 t.

75566–75599. DTSO. Lot No. 30579 Pressed Steel 1959–60.
75747–75801. DTSO. Lot No. 30629 Pressed Steel 1960–61.
61481–61514. MBSO. Lot No. 30580 Pressed Steel 1959–60.
61813–61867. MBSO. Lot No. 30630 Pressed Steel 1960–61.
75601–75634. BDTSO. Lot No. 30581 Pressed Steel 1959–60.

75803–75857. BDTSO. Lot No. 30631 Pressed Steel 1960–61.

303 001 r	S	PGWX	GW	75566	61481	75601
303 003 r	S	PGWX	GW	75568	61483	75603
303 004 r	S	PGWX	GW	75569	61484	75604
303 006 r	S	PGWX	GW	75571	61486	75606
303 008 r	S	PGWX	GW	75573	61488	75608
303 009 r	S	PGWX	GW	75574	61489	75609
303 010 r	S	PGWX	GW	75575	61490	75610
303 011 r	S	PGWX	GW	75576	61491	75611
303 012 r	S	PGWX	GW	75577	61492	75612
303 013 r	S	PGWX	GW	75578	61493	75613
303 014 r	S	PGWX	GW	75579	61494	75614
303 016 r	S	PGWX	GW	75581	61496	75616
303 019 r	S	PGWX	GW	75584	61499	75619
303 020 r	S	PGWX	GW	75585	61500	75620
303 021 r	S	PGWX	GW	75586	61501	75621
303 023 r	S	PGWX	GW	75588	61503	75623
303 024 r	S	PGWX	GW	75589	61504	75624
303 025 r	S	PGWX	GW	75590	61505	75625
303 027 r	S	PGWX	GW	75592	61507	75627
303 028 r	S	PGWX	GW	75600	61508	75635
303 032 r	S	PGWX	GW	75597	61512	75632
303 034 r	S	PGWX	GW	75599	61514	75634
303 035 r	S	PGWX	GW	75595	61860	75817
303 038 r	S	PGWX	GW	75748	61814	75804
303 040 r	S	PGWX	GW	75750	61816	75806
303 043 r	S	PGWX	GW	75572	61819	75809
303 045 r	S	PGWX	GW	75755	61821	75811
303 047 r	S	PGWX	GW	75757	61823	75813
303 048	O	PGWX	GW	75752	61839	75808
303 049	G	PLGX	LG	75759	61825	75815
303 052		PGWX	GW	75773		75829
303 054 r	S	PGWX	GW	75764	61830	75820
303 055 r	S	PGWX	GW	75765	61831	75821
303 056 r	S	PGWX	GW	75766	61832	75822
303 058 r	S	PGWX	GW	75768	61834	75824
303 060	G	PLGX	LG	75770	61836	75826
303 061 r	S	PGWX	GW	75771	61837	75827
303 062	S	PXXZ	GW	75772	61838	75828
303 063	S	PGWX	GW	75773	61824	75829
303 065 r	S	PGWX	GW	75775	61841	75831
303 070 r	S	PGWX	GW	75780	61846	75836
303 073	S	PXXZ	GW	75783	61849	75839
303 077 r	S	PGWX	GW	75787	61853	75843
303 079 r	S	PGWX	GW	75789	61855	75845
303 080 r	S	PGWX	GW	75790	61856	75846
303 082	G	PXXZ	LG	75792	61858	75848
303 083 r	S	PGWX	GW	75793	61859	75849
303 084	S	PXXZ	GW	75785		75841
303 085 r	S	PGWX	GW	75795	61861	75851
303 087 r	S	PGWX	GW	75797	61863	75853

303 088	r	**S**	PGWX	GW	75798	61864	75854
303 089	r	**S**	PGWX	GW	75799	61865	75855
303 090	r	**S**	PGWX	GW	75800	61866	75856
303 091	r	**S**	PGWX	GW	75801	61867	75857
Spare	r	**S**	PGWX	GW		61813	75803
Spare	r	**S**	PGWX	GW		61822	75812

CLASS 304

BDTSOL–MBSO–DTBSO. Originally 4 cars.
Bogies: Gresley.
Gangways: None.
Traction Motors: Four BTH 155 kW.
Maximum Speed: 75 mph.
Dimensions: 19.53 x 2.82 m (outer cars), 19.36 x 2.82 m (inner cars).

Class 304/1. These cars have pairs of narrow windows instead of wide windows and the MBSOs were formerly MBS and were refurbished with new seats etc.

BDTSOL. Dia. EF203. Lot No. 30429 Wolverton 1960. 80S 2L. 36.8 t.
MBSO. Dia. ED215. Lot No. 30428 Wolverton 1960. 72S. 54.5 t.
DTBSO. Dia. EG202. Lot No. 30430 Wolverton 1960. 82S. 32.5 t.

304 001	PLGX	LG	75045	61045	75645
304 002	PLGX	LG	75046	61046	75646
304 003	PLGX	LG	75047	61047	75647
304 004	PLGX	LG	75048	61048	75648
304 005	PLGX	LG	75049	61049	75649
304 006	PLGX	LG	75050	61050	75650
304 007	PLGX	LG	75051	61051	75651
304 008	PLGX	LG	75052	61052	75652
304 009	PLGX	LG	75053	61053	75653
304 010	PLGX	LG	75054	61054	75654
304 012	PLGX	LG	75056	61056	75656
304 013	PLGX	LG	75057	61057	75657
304 014	PLGX	LG	75058	61058	75658
304 015	PLGX	LG	75059	61059	75659

Class 304/2. Standard design with wide windows.

75680–75699. BDTSOL. Dia. EF204. Lot No. 30610 Wolverton 1960–61. 80S 2L. 36.8 t.
75868–75877. BDTSOL. Dia. EF204. Lot No. 30645 Wolverton 1961. 80S 2L. 36.8 t.
61628–61647. MBSO. Dia. ED203. Lot No. 30607 Wolverton 1960–61. 72S. 54.5 t.
61873–61882. MBSO. Dia. ED203. Lot No. 30642 Wolverton 1961. 72S. 54.5 t.
75660–75679. DTBSO. Dia. EG203. Lot No. 30608 Wolverton 1960–61. 82S. 32.5 t.
75858–75867. DTBSO. Dia. EG203. Lot No. 30643 Wolverton 1961. 82S. 32.5 t.

304 016	PLGX	LG	75680	61628	75660
304 017	PLGX	LG	75681	61629	75661

304 019	PLGX	LG		75683	61631	75663
304 020	PLGX	LG		75684	61632	75664
304 021	PLGX	LG		75685	61633	75665
304 024	PLGX	LG		75688	61636	75668
304 027	PLGX	LG		75691	61639	75671
304 028	PLGX	LG		75692	61640	75672
304 029	PLGX	LG		75693	61641	75673
304 030	PLGX	LG		75694	61642	75674
304 032	PLGX	LG		75696	61644	75676
304 033	PLGX	LG		75697	61645	75677
304 034	PLGX	LG		75698	61646	75678
304 036	PLGX	LG		75868	61873	75858
304 037	PLGX	LG		75869	61874	75859
304 039	PLGX	LG		75871	61876	75861
304 040	PLGX	LG		75872	61877	75862
304 041	PLGX	LG		75873	61878	75863
304 042	PLGX	LG		75874	61879	75864
304 043	PLGX	LG		75875	61880	75865
304 045	PLGX	LG		75877	61882	75867

CLASS 305/1

BDTSO–MBSO–DTSO. All facelifted with fluorescent lighting and PA.
Bogies: Gresley.
Gangways: None.
Traction Motors: Four GEC WT380 of 153 kW.
Dimensions: 19.53 x 2.82 m (outer cars), 19.34 x 2.82 m (inner cars).
Maximum Speed: 75 mph.

BDTSO. Dia. EF205. Lot No. 30570 York 1960. 34.9 t. 92S.
MBSO. Dia. ED204. Lot No. 30571 York 1960. 56.4 t. 84S.
DTSO. Dia. EE209. Lot No. 30572 York 1960. 31.5 t. 92S.

305 401	**N**	NNEX	IL	75462	61429	75514
305 402		NNEX	EM	75463	61430	75515
305 403 (305 445)		NNEX	EM	75506	61473	75558
305 404 (305 447)		NNEX	EM	75508	61475	75560
305 405		NNEX	EM	75466	61433	75518
305 406		NNEX	EM	75467	61434	75519
305 407		NNEX	EM	75468	61435	75520
305 409		NNEX	EM	75470	61437	75522
305 410	**N**	NNEX	EM	75471	61438	75523
305 411 (305 448)		NNEX	EM	75509	61476	75561
305 412		NNEX	EM	75473	61440	75525
305 413		NNEX	EM	75474	61441	75526
305 414 (305 449)		NNEX	EM	75510	61477	75562
305 415		NNEX	EM	75476	61443	75528
305 416		NNEX	EM	75477	61444	75529
305 417		NNEX	EM	75478	61445	75530
305 418		NNEX	EM	75479	61446	75531
305 419 (305 450)		NNEX	EM	75511	61478	75563
305 420		NNEX	EM	75481	61448	75533
305 421		NNEX	EM	75482	61449	75534

305 422 (305 452)   NNEX   EM   75513 61480 75565

CLASS 305/2

BDTCOL–MBSO–TSOL–DTSO. All facelifted with fluorescent lighting, new seats and PA.
Bogies: Gresley.
Gangways: Originally non-gangwayed, but now gangwayed within unit.
Traction Motors: Four GEC WT380 of 153 kW.
Dimensions: 19.53 x 2.82 m (outer cars), 19.36 x 2.82 m (inner cars).
Maximum Speed: 75 mph.

BDTCOL. Dia. EF304. Lot No. 30566 York/Doncaster 1960.24F 52S 1L. 36.5 t.
MBSO. Dia. ED216. Lot No. 30567 York/Doncaster 1960. 76S. 56.5 t.
TSOL. Dia. EH223. Lot No. 30568 York/Doncaster 1960. 86S 1L. 31.5 t.
DTSO. Dia. EE220. Lot No. 30569 York/Doncaster 1960. 88S. 32.7 t.

305 501	**RS**	PGWX	GW	75424	61410	70356	75443
305 502	**RS**	PGWX	GW	75425	61421	70357	75444
305 503	**N**	NTSX	IL	75426	61412	70358	75445
305 504		NTSX	IL	75427	61413	70359	75446
305 506	**N**	NTSX	LG	75429	61415	70361	75448
305 507		NTSX	LG	75430	61416	70362	75449
305 508	**RS**	PGWX	GW	75431	61417	70363	75450
305 509	**N**	NTSX	EM	75432	61418	70364	75451
305 510	**N**	NTSX	EM	75433	61419	70365	75452
305 511	**N**	NTSX	LG	75434	61420	70366	75453
305 513	**N**	NTSX	LG	75436	61422	70368	75455
305 514	**N**	NTSX	LG	75437	61423	70369	75456
305 515	**N**	NTSX	EM	75438	61424	70370	75457
305 516	**N**	NTSX	LG	75439	61425	70371	75458
305 517	**RS**	PGWX	GW	75440	61426	70372	75459
305 518	**N**	PGWX	EM	75441	61427	70373	75460
305 519	**RS**	PGWX	GW	75442	61428	70374	75461
Spare		NTSX	EM			70360	75447

CLASS 305/3

BDTSO–MBSO–TCsoL–DTSO. New batch formed by strengthening class 305/1 with Class 302 TCsoL. All facelifted with fluorescent lighting, new seats and PA.
Bogies: Gresley.
Gangways: None.
Traction Motors: Four GEC WT380 of 153 kW.
Dimensions: 19.53 x 2.82 m (outer cars), 19.36 x 2.82 m (inner cars).
Maximum Speed: 75 mph.

BDTSO. Dia. EF205. Lot No. 30570 York 1960. 34.9 t. 92S.
MBSO. Dia. ED204. Lot No. 30571 York 1960. 56.4 t. 84S.
70093. TCsoL. Lot No. 30437. York/Doncaster 1958–59.
70098–70221. TCsoL. Lot No. 30441. York 1959–61.
DTSO. Dia. EE209. Lot No. 30572 York 1960. 31.5 t. 92S.

305 521 (305 403)		NNEX	EM	75464	61431	70098	75516
305 522 (305 404)	N	NNEX	EM	75465	61432	70099	75517
305 523 (305 411)	N	NNEX	EM	75472	61439	70221	75524
305 524 (305 414)		NNEX	EM	75475	61442	70118	75527
305 525 (305 419)	N	NNEX	EM	75480	61447	70213	75532
305 526 (305 422)		NNEX	EM	75483	61450	70093	75535
305 527 (305 446)	N	NNEX	EM	75507	61474	70204	75559
305 528 (305 451)	N	NNEX	EM	75512	61479	70210	75564

CLASS 306

DMSO–TBSO–DTSO. Converted 1960–1 from 1500 V d.c. Kept for special workings. LNER design. Sliding doors. Screw couplings.
Bogies: LNER bogies.
Gangways: None.
Traction Motors: Four Crompton Parkinson of 155 kW.
Dimensions: 18.41 x 2.90 m (DMSO), 16.78 x 2.90 m (TBSO), 16.87 x 2.90 m (DTSO).
Maximum Speed: 65 mph.
Non-standard Livery: Original BR multiple unit green.

DMSO. Dia. EA217. Lot No. 363 Metro-Cammell. 1949. 51.7 t. 62S.
TBSO. Dia. EJ201. Lot No. 364 1949. Metro-Cammell. 26.4 t. 46S.
DTSO. Dia. EE211. Lot No. 365 1949. BRCW. 27.9 t. 60S.

306 017	**0**	NGEX	IL	65217	65417	65617

CLASS 307

BDTBSO–MSO–TSO–DTCOL. 25 kV a.c. overhead. Converted 1960–1 from 1500 V d.c. All refurbished with new seats, fluorescent lighting, PA.
Bogies: Gresley (MSO), B4 (TSO and DTCO) B5 (BDTBSO).
Gangways: Originally non-gangwayed, but now gangwayed within unit.
Traction Motors: Four GEC WT344 of 130 kW.
Dimensions: 19.50 x 2.83 m.
Maximum Speed: 75 mph.

BDTBSO. Dia. EO202. Lot No. 30205 Ashford/Eastleigh 1954–6. 66S. 43 t.
MSO. Dia. EC204. Lot No. 30203 Ashford/Eastleigh 1954–6. 86S. 47.5 t.
TSOL. Dia. EH222. Lot No. 30204 Ashford/Eastleigh 1954–6. 86S 1L. 31 t.
DTCOL. Dia. EE307. Lot No. 30206 Afd./Elh 1954–6. 24F 52S 1L. 33 t.

307 102	N	PNLX	NL	75002	61002	70002	75102
307 103		RPMB	KM	75003	61003	70003	75103
307 104		RPMB	KM	75004	61004	70004	75104
307 105	Y	PNLX	NL	75005	61005	70005	75105
307 107		RPMB	KM	75007	61007	70007	75107
307 108		RPMB	KM	75008	61008	70008	75108
307 109		RPMB	KM	75009	61009	70009	75109
307 110		RPMB	KM	75010	61010	70010	75110
307 111	Y	PNLX	NL	75011	61011	70011	75111
307 112		RPMB	KM	75012	61012	70012	75112
307 113		RPMB	KM	75013	61013	70013	75113
307 114		RPMB	KM	75014	61014	70014	75114

307 115		RPMB	KM	75015	61015	70015	75115
307 116		PNLX	NL	75016	61016	70016	75116
307 117	N	RPMB	KM	75017	61017	70017	75117
307 118		PNLX	NL	75018	61018	70018	75118
307 119		RPMB	KM	75019	61019	70019	75119
307 120	Y	RPMB	NL	75020	61030	70020	75130
307 122	Y	PNLX	NL	75022	61022	70022	75122
307 123		RPMB	KM	75023	61023	70023	75123
307 124	N	RPMB	KM	75024	61024	70024	75124
307 125		RPMB	KM	75025	61025	70025	75125
307 126	N	RPMB	KM	75026	61026	70026	75126
307 127		RPMB	KM	75027	61027	70027	75127
307 128		RPMB	KM	75028	61028	70028	75128
307 129		RPMB	KM	75029	61029	70029	75129
307 130	Y	RPMB	NL	75030	61020	70030	75120
307 131		RPMB	KM	75031	61031	70031	75131
307 132	N	RPMB	KM	75032	61032	70032	75132

CLASS 308/1

Bogies: Gresley.
Gangways: Originally non-gangwayed, but now gangwayed within unit.
Traction Motors: Four English Electric 536A of 143.5 kW.
Dimensions: 19.36 x 2.82 m (outer cars), 19.35 x 2.82 m (inner cars).
Maximum Speed: 75 mph.

75878–75886. BDTCOL. Dia. EF304. Lot No. 30652 Yk 1961. 24F 52S 1L. 36.3 t.
75896–75919. BDTCOL. Dia. EF304. Lot No. 30656 Yk 1961. 24F 52S 1L. 36.3 t.
75435. BDTCOL. Dia. EF304. Lot No. 30566 York/Doncaster 1960.24F 52S 1L. 36.5 t. Class 305/1 car.
61883–61891. MBSO. Dia. ED216. Lot No. 30653 York 1961. 76S. 55.0 t.
61892–61915. MBSO. Dia. ED216. Lot No. 30657 York 1961. 76S. 55.0 t.
70367. TSOL. Dia. EH223. Lot No. 30568 York/Doncaster 1960. 86S 1L. 31.4 t.
70611–70619. TSOL. Dia. EH223. Lot No. 30654 York 1961. 86S 1L. 31.4 t.
70620–70643. TSOL. Dia. EH223. Lot No. 30658 York 1961. 86S 1L. 31.4 t.
75887–75895. DTSO. Dia. EE220. Lot No. 30655 York 1961. 88S. 33 t.
75929–75952. DTSO. Dia. EE220. Lot No. 30659 York 1961. 88S. 33 t.

308 133		NTSX	EM	75878	61883	70611	75887
308 134		NTSX	EM	75879	61884	70612	75888
308 135	N	NTSX	EM	75880	61885	70613	75889
308 136	N	NTSX	EM	75881	61886	70614	75890
308 137		NTSX	EM	75882	61887	70615	75891
308 138		NTSX	EM	75883	61888	70367	75892
308 139	N	NTSX	EM	75884	61889	70617	75893
308 140	N	NTSX	EM	75885	61890	70618	75894
308 141		NTSX	EM	75886	61891	70619	75895
308 142		NTSX	EM	75896	61892	70620	75929
308 143	N	NTSX	EM	75897	61893	70621	75930
308 144 *	N	NTSX	EM	75435	61894	70622	75931
308 145	N	NTSX	EM	75899	61895	70623	75932
308 146	N	NTSX	EM	75900	61896	70624	75933
308 147	N	NTSX	EM	75901	61897	70625	75934

308 148		NTSX	EM		75902	61898	70626	75935
308 149	N	NTSX	EM		75903	61899	70627	75936
308 150		NTSX	EM		75904	61900	70628	75937
308 151	N	NTSX	EM		75905	61901	70629	75938
308 152	N	NTSX	EM		75906	61902	70630	75939
308 153		NTSX	EM		75907	61903	70631	75940
308 154		NTSX	EM		75908	61904	70632	75941
308 155		NTSX	EM		75909	61905	70633	75942
308 156	N	NTSX	EM		75910	61906	70634	75943
308 157		NTSX	EM		75911	61907	70635	75944
308 158	N	NTSX	EM		75912	61908	70636	75945
308 159	N	NTSX	EM		75913	61909	70637	75946
308 160	N	NTSX	EM		75914	61910	70638	75947
308 161	N	NTSX	EM		75915	61911	70639	75948
308 162	N	NTSX	EM		75916	61912	70640	75949
308 163	N	NTSX	EM		75917	61913	70641	75950
308 164	N	NTSX	EM		75918	61914	70642	75951
308 165		NTSX	EM		75919	61915	70643	75952
Spare		NTSX	EM	(U)	75898			

CLASS 309/1　　　　　　　ESSEX EXPRESS STOCK

DMBSO(T)–TSOL–TCsoL–BDTSOL. Built 1962–3 as 2 car units. Made up to
four cars by the conversion of loco-hauled stock in 1973/80–1. All now
refurbished with fluorescent lighting, hopper ventilators, new seating, PA.
Bogies: Commonwealth.
Gangways: Throughout.
Traction Motors: Four GEC of 210 kW.
Dimensions: 19.76 x 2.82 m (outer cars), 19.67 x 2.82 m (inner cars).
Maximum Speed: 100 mph.

DMBSO(T). Dia. EB206. Lot No. 30684 York 1962–63. 44S. 60 t.
71107–71110. TSOL. Dia. EH227. Lot No. 30871 W'ton 1973–74. 64S 2L. 35 t.
71569–71572. TSOL. Dia. EH227. Lot No. 30954 W'ton 1978–81. 64S 2L. 35 t.
71111–71114. TCsoL. Dia. EH309. Lot No. 30872 Wolverton 1973–74.
24F 28S 1L. 36 t.
71573–71576. TCsoL. Dia. EH309. Lot No. 30954 Wolverton 1978–81.
24F 28S 1L. 36 t.
BDTSOL. Dia. EF213. Lot No. 30683 York 1960–62. 60S 1L. 40 t.

Note: 61940/2 are DMBSO and seat 52S.

309 601	N	NGEX	CC	61940	71569	71573	75984
309 602	N	NGEX	CC	61941	71570	71574	75985
309 603	N	NGEX	CC	61942	71571	71575	75986
309 604	N	NGEX	CC	61943	71572	71576	75987
309 605	N	NGEX	CC	61944	71108	71113	75988
309 606	N	NGEX	CC	61945	71109	71112	75989
309 607	N	NGEX	CC	61946	71107	71111	75990
309 608	N	NGEX	CC	61947	71110	71114	75991

CLASS 309/2   ESSEX EXPRESS STOCK

BDTCsoL–MBSOL(T)–TSO–DTSOL. Built 1962–3 as 2 car units. Units 309 611–309 618 formerly contained griddle cars, but these were withdrawn and their place has been taken by the conversion of loco-hauled TSOs on refurbishment. All refurbished with fluorescent lighting, hopper ventilators, new seating, PA.
Bogies: Commonwealth.
Gangways: Throughout.
Traction Motors: Four GEC of 210 kW.
Dimensions: 19.76 x 2.82 m (outer cars), 19.67 x 2.82 m (inner cars).
Maximum Speed: 100 mph.

75637–44. BDTCsoL. Dia. EF301. Lot No. 30679 York 1962. 18F 32S 2L. 40 t.
75962–68. BDTCsoL. Dia. EF213. Lot No. 30675 York 1962. 18F 32S 2L. 40 t.
61925–31. MBSO(T). Dia. ED209. Lot No. 30676 York 1962. 44S 2L. 58 t.
61932–39. MBSO(T). Dia. ED209. Lot No. 30680 York 1962. 44S 2L. 58 t.
70253–59. TSO. Dia. EH229. Lot No. 30677 York 1962. 68S 35 t.
71754–61. TSO. Dia. EH228. Lot No. 31001 Wolverton 1984–87. 68S. 35 t.
75969 75. DTSOL. Dia. EF213. Lot No. 30678 York 1962. 56S 2L 37 t.
75976–83. DTSOL. Dia. EF213. Lot No. 30682 York 1962–1963. 56S 2L. 37 t.

61933/29/30/31 are MBSO and seat 48S 2L.
p MBSO(T) is fitted with public telephone. 42S 2L.

309 612		**N**	NGEX	CC	75638	61933	71755	75977
309 613	p	**N**	NGEX	CC	75639	61934	71756	75978
309 614		**N**	NXXZ	CC	75640	61935	71757	75979
309 615		**N**	NGEX	CC	75641	61936	71758	75980
309 616	p	**N**	NGEX	CC	75642	61937	71759	75981
309 617	p	**N**	NGEX	CC	75643	61938	71760	75982
309 618	p	**N**	NGEX	CC	75966	61939	71761	75983
309 621		**N**	NGEX	CC	75962	61925	70253	75969
309 622		**N**	NGEX	CC	75963	61926	70254	75970
309 623		**N**	NXXZ	CC	75964	61927	70255	75971
309 624		**N**	NGEX	CC	75965	61928	70256	75972
309 626		**N**	NGEX	CC	75967	61930	70258	75974
309 627		**N**	NGEX	CC	75968	61931	70259	75975
Spare		**N**	NXXZ	CC (U)	75644			

Former numbers of converted hauled stock:

71107 (26203)	71113 (16244)	71573 (16264)	71757 (5069)
71108 (26189)	71114 (16252)	71574 (16257)	71758 (5058)
71109 (26196)	71569 (5047)	71575 (16242)	71759 (5062)
71110 (26204)	71570 (5050)	71576 (16259)	71760 (5056)
71111 (16246)	71571 (5059)	71755 (5051)	71761 (5066)
71112 (16249)	71572 (5061)	71758 (5068)	

CLASS 310

Disc brakes. All facelifted. with new panels and PA.
Bogies: B4.

Gangways: Within unit.
Traction Motors: Four EE546 of 201.5 kW.
Dimensions: 19.86 x 2.82 m (outer cars), 19.93 x 2.82 m (inner cars).
Maximum Speed: 75 mph.

BDTSOL. Dia. EF211. Lot No. 30745 Derby 1965–67. 80S 2L. 37.3 t.
76228. BDTSOL. Formerly a DTCOL to Lot 39748. Dia. EF210. Seats 68S 2L.
76998. BDTSOL. Rebuilt from TSO 70756 to Lot 30747. Dia. EF214. Seats 75S 2L.
MBSO. Dia. ED219. Lot No. 30746 Derby 1965–67. 68S. 57.2 t.
TSO. Dia. EH232. Lot No. 30747 Derby 1965–67. 98S. 31.7 t.
DTCOL (310/0). Dia. EE306. Lot No. 30748 Derby 1965–67. 25F 43S 2L. 34.4 t.
DTSOL (310/1). Dia. EE237. Lot No. 30748 Derby 1965–67. 75S 2L. 34.4 t.

Class 310/0. BDTSOL–MBSO–TSO–DTCOL.

310 046	**N**	NTSX	EM	76130	62071	70731	76180
310 047	**N**	NTSX	EM	76131	62072	70732	76181
310 049	**N**	NTSX	EM	76133	62074	70734	76183
310 050	**N**	NTSX	EM	76134	62075	70735	76184
310 051	**N**	NTSX	EM	76135	62076	70736	76185
310 052	**N**	NTSX	EM	76136	62077	70737	76186
310 056	**N**	NTSX	EM	76140	62081	70741	76190
310 057	**N**	NTSX	EM	76141	62082	70742	76191
310 058	**N**	NTSX	EM	76142	62083	70743	76192
310 059	**N**	NTSX	EM	76143	62084	70744	76205
310 060	**N**	NTSX	EM	76144	62085	70745	76194
310 061	**N**	NTSX	EM	76145	62086	70746	76195
310 064	**N**	NTSX	EM	76148	62089	70749	76198
310 065	**N**	NTSX	EM	76149	62090	70750	76199
310 066	**N**	NTSX	EM	76228	62091	70751	76200
310 067	**N**	NTSX	EM	76151	62092	70752	76201
310 068	**N**	NTSX	EM	76152	62093	70753	76202
310 069	**N**	NTSX	EM	76153	62094	70754	76203
310 070	**N**	NTSX	EM	76154	62095	70755	76204
310 074	**N**	NNEX	EM	76158	62099	70759	76208
310 075	**N**	NNEX	EM	76159	62100	70760	76209
310 077	**N**	NNEX	EM	76161	62102	70762	76211
310 079	**N**	NNEX	EM	76163	62104	70764	76213
310 080	**N**	NTSX	EM	76164	62105	70765	76214
310 081	**N**	NTSX	EM	76165	62106	70766	76215
310 082	**N**	NTSX	EM	76166	62107	70767	76216
310 083	**N**	NTSX	EM	76167	62108	70768	76217
310 084	**N**	NTSX	EM	76168	62109	70769	76218
310 085	**N**	NTSX	EM	76169	62110	70770	76219
310 086	**N**	NTSX	EM	76170	62111	70771	76220
310 087	**N**	NTSX	EM	76171	62112	70772	76221
310 088	**N**	NTSX	EM	76172	62113	70773	76222
310 089	**N**	NTSX	EM	76173	62114	70774	76223
310 091	**N**	NTSX	EM	76175	62116	70776	76225
310 092	**N**	NTSX	EM	76176	62117	70777	76226
310 093	**N**	NTSX	EM	76177	62118	70778	76227

310 094	**N**	NTSX	EM	76998	62119	70780	76193
310 095	**N**	NTSX	EM	76179	62120	70779	76229

Class 310/1. BDTSOL–MBSO–TSO–DTSOL.

310 101 (310 073)	**PM**	PBYX	BY	76157	62098	70758	76207
310 102 (310 055)	**PM**	PBYX	BY	76139	62080	70740	76189
310 103 (310 076)	**PM**	PBYX	BY	76160	62101	70761	76210
310 104 (310 078)	**PM**	PBYX	BY	76162	62103	70763	76212
310 105 (310 090)	**PM**	PBYX	BY	76174	62115	70775	76224
310 106 (310 072)	**PM**	PBYX	BY	76156	62097	70757	76206
310 107 (310 062)	**PM**	PBYX	BY	76146	62087	70747	76196
310 108 (310 048)	**PM**	PBYX	BY	76132	62073	70733	76182
310 109 (310 053)	**PM**	PBYX	BY	76137	62078	70738	76187
310 110 (310 054)	**PM**	PBYX	BY	76138	62079	70739	76188
310 111 (310 063)	**PM**	PBYX	BY	76147	62088	70748	76197

CLASS 311

DTSO–MBSO–BDTSO. Sliding doors.
Bogies: Gresley.
Gangways: Non-gangwayed.
Traction Motors: Four AEI 165 kW.
Dimensions: 19.50 x 2.82 m (outer cars), 19.36 x 2.82 m (inner cars).
Maximum Speed: 75 mph.

DTSO. Dia. EE214. Lot No. 30767 Cravens 1967. 83S. 34.4 t.
MBSO. Dia. ED211. Lot No. 30768 Cravens 1967. 70S. 56.4 t.
BDTSO. Dia. EF212. Lot No. 30769 Cravens 1967. 83S. 38.4 t.

311 104		PGWX	GW	76415	62175	76434

CLASS 312

BDTSOL–MBSO–TSO–DTCOL. Disc brakes PA.
Bogies: B4.
Gangways: Within unit.
Traction Motors: Four EE546 of 201.5 kW.
Dimensions: 19.86 x 2.82 m (outer cars), 19.93 x 2.82 m (inner cars).
Maximum Speed: 90 mph.

Class 312/0. Standard design.

76994–97 BDTSOL. Dia. EF213. Lot No. 30891 York 1976. 84S 1L. 34.9 t.
62657–60 MBSO. Dia. ED214. Lot No. 30892 York 1976. 68S. 56 t.
71277–80 TSO. Dia. EH209. Lot No. 30893 York 1976. 98S. 30.5 t.
78045–48 DTCOL. Dia. EE305. Lot No. 30894 York 1976. 25F 47S 2L.
76949–74 BDTSOL. Dia. EF213. Lot No. 30863 York 1977–78. 84S 1L. 34.9 t.
62484–509 MBSO. Dia. ED212. Lot No. 30864 York 1977–78. 68S. 56 t.
71168–93 TSO. Dia. EH209. Lot No. 30865 York 1977–78. 98S. 30.5 t.
78000–25 DTCOL. Dia. EE305. Lot No. 30866 York 1977–78. 25F 47S 2L.

Notes: 312 727–730 were formerly numbered 312 201–204.

312 701	**N**	NGEX	CC	76949	62484	71168	78000
312 702	**N**	NGEX	CC	76950	62485	71169	78001

312 703	**N**	NGEX	CC	76951	62486	71170	78002
312 704	**N**	NGEX	CC	76952	62487	71171	78003
312 705	**N**	NGEX	CC	76953	62488	71172	78004
312 706	**N**	NGEX	CC	76954	62489	71173	78005
312 707	**N**	NGEX	CC	76955	62490	71174	78006
312 708	**N**	NGEX	CC	76956	62491	71175	78007
312 709	**N**	NGEX	CC	76957	62492	71176	78008
312 710	**N**	NGEX	CC	76958	62493	71177	78009
312 711	**N**	NGEX	CC	76959	62494	71178	78010
312 712	**N**	NGEX	CC	76960	62495	71179	78011
312 713	**N**	NGEX	CC	76961	62496	71180	78012
312 714	**N**	NGEX	CC	76962	62497	71181	78013
312 715	**N**	NGEX	CC	76963	62498	71182	78014
312 716	**N**	NGEX	CC	76964	62499	71183	78015
312 717	**N**	NGEX	CC	76965	62500	71184	78016
312 718	**N**	NGEX	CC	76966	62501	71185	78017
312 719	**N**	NGEX	CC	76967	62502	71186	78018
312 720	**N**	NGEX	CC	76968	62503	71187	78019
312 721	**N**	NGEX	CC	76969	62504	71188	78020
312 722	**N**	NGEX	CC	76970	62505	71189	78021
312 723	**N**	NGEX	CC	76971	62506	71190	78022
312 724	**N**	NGEX	CC	76972	62507	71191	78023
312 725	**N**	NGEX	CC	76973	62508	71192	78024
312 726	**N**	NGEX	CC	76974	62509	71193	78025
312 727	**N**	NGEX	CC	76994	62657	71277	78045
312 728	**N**	NGEX	CC	76995	62658	71278	78046
312 729	**N**	NGEX	CC	76996	62659	71279	78047
312 730	**N**	NGEX	CC	76997	62660	71280	78048

Class 312/1. Can also operate on 6.25 kV a.c. overhead.

BDTSOL. Dia. EF213. Lot No. 30867 York 1975–76. 84S 2L. 34.9 t.
MBSO. Dia. ED213. Lot No. 30868 York 1975–76. 68S. 56 t.
TSO. Dia. EH209. Lot No. 30869 York 1975–76. 98S. 30.5 t.
DTCOL. Dia. EE305. Lot No. 30870 York 1975–76. 25F 47S 2L.

312 781	**N**	NGEX	CC	76975	62510	71194	78026
312 782	**N**	NGEX	CC	76976	62511	71195	78027
312 783	**N**	NGEX	CC	76977	62512	71196	78028
312 784	**N**	NGEX	CC	76978	62513	71197	78029
312 785	**N**	NGEX	CC	76979	62514	71198	78030
312 786	**N**	NTSX	EM	76980	62515	71199	78031
312 787	**N**	NTSX	EM	76981	62516	71200	78032
312 788	**N**	NTSX	EM	76982	62517	71201	78033
312 789	**N**	NTSX	EM	76983	62518	71202	78034
312 790	**N**	NTSX	EM	76984	62519	71203	78035
312 791	**N**	NTSX	EM	76985	62520	71204	78036
312 792	**N**	NTSX	EM	76986	62521	71205	78037
312 793	**N**	NTSX	EM	76987	62522	71206	78038
312 794	**N**	NTSX	EM	76988	62523	71207	78039
312 795	**N**	NTSX	EM	76989	62524	71208	78040
312 796	**N**	NTSX	EM	76990	62525	71209	78041
312 797	**N**	NTSX	EM	76991	62526	71210	78042

| 312 798 | N | NTSX | EM | 76992 | 62527 | 71211 | 78043 |
| 312 799 | N | NTSX | EM | 76993 | 62528 | 71212 | 78044 |

CLASS 313

DMSO–PTSO–BDMSO. Tightlock couplers. Sliding doors. Disc and rheostatic brakes. PA. Cab to shore radio.
System: 25 kV a.c. overhead/750 V d.c. third rail.
Bogies: BX1.
Gangways: Within unit. End doors.
Traction Motors: Four GEC G310AZ of 82.125 kW.
Dimensions: 19.80 x 2.82 m (outer cars), 19.92 x 2.82 m (inner cars).
Maximum Speed: 75 mph.

DMSO (A). Dia. EA204. Lot No. 30879 York 1976–77. 74S. 36.4 t.
PTSO. Dia. EH210. Lot No. 30880 York 1976–77. 84S. 30.5 t.
DMSO (B). Dia. EI201. Lot No. 30885 York 1976–77. 74S. 37.6 t.

*–Extra shoegear for Euston–Watford line services. Class 313/1.

313 001	*	N	NNLX	BY	62529	71213	62593
313 002	*	N	NNLX	BY	62530	71214	62594
313 003	*	N	NNLX	BY	62531	71215	62595
313 004	*	N	NNLX	BY	62532	71216	62596
313 005	*	N	NNLX	BY	62533	71217	62597
313 006	*	N	NNLX	BY	62534	71218	62598
313 007	*	N	NNLX	BY	62535	71219	62599
313 008	*	N	NNLX	BY	62536	71220	62600
313 009	*	N	NNLX	BY	62537	71221	62601
313 010	*	N	NNLX	BY	62538	71222	62602
313 011	*	N	NNLX	BY	62539	71223	62603
313 012	*	N	NNLX	BY	62540	71224	62604
313 013	*	N	NNLX	BY	62541	71225	62605
313 014	*	N	NNLX	BY	62542	71226	62606
313 015	*	N	NNLX	BY	62543	71227	62607
313 016	*	N	NNLX	BY	62544	71228	62608
313 017	*	N	NNLX	BY	62545	71229	62609
313 018	*	N	NGNX	HE	62546	71230	62610
313 019	*	N	NGNX	HE	62547	71231	62611
313 020	*	N	NGNX	HE	62548	71232	62612
313 021	*	N	NNLX	BY	62549	71233	62613
313 022	*	N	NNLX	BY	62550	71234	62614
313 023	*	N	NGNX	HE	62551	71235	62615
313 024		N	NGNX	HE	62552	71236	62616
313 025		N	NGNX	HE	62553	71237	62617
313 026		N	NGNX	HE	62554	71238	62618
313 027		N	NGNX	HE	62555	71239	62619
313 028		N	NGNX	HE	62556	71240	62620
313 029		N	NGNX	HE	62557	71241	62621
313 030			NGNX	HE	62558	71242	62622
313 031		N	NGNX	HE	62559	71243	62623
313 032		N	NGNX	HE	62560	71244	62624
313 033		N	NGNX	HE	62561	71245	62625

313 034	*	N	NNLX	BY	62562		62626
313 035		N	NGNX	HE	62563	71247	62627
313 036		N	NGNX	HE	62564	71248	62628
313 037		N	NGNX	HE	62565	71249	62629
313 038		N	NGNX	HE	62566	71250	62630
313 039		N	NGNX	HE	62567	71251	62631
313 040		N	NGNX	HE	62568	71252	62632
313 041		N	NGNX	HE	62569	71253	62633
313 042		N	NGNX	HE	62570	71254	62634
313 043			NGNX	HE	62571	71255	62635
313 044		N	NGNX	HE	62572	71256	62636
313 045		N	NGNX	HE	62573	71257	62637
313 046		N	NGNX	HE	62574	71258	62638
313 047		N	NGNX	HE	62575	71259	62639
313 048		N	NGNX	HE	62576	71260	62640
313 049			NGNX	HE	62577	71261	62641
313 050		N	NGNX	HE	62578	71262	62642
313 051		N	NGNX	HE	62579	71263	62643
313 052		N	NGNX	HE	62580	71264	62644
313 053		N	NGNX	HE	62581	71265	62645
313 054		N	NGNX	HE	62582	71266	62646
313 055		N	NGNX	HE	62583	71267	62647
313 056		N	NGNX	HE	62584	71268	62648
313 057		N	NGNX	HE	62585	71269	62649
313 058			NGNX	HE	62586	71270	62650
313 059		N	NGNX	HE	62587	71271	62651
313 060		N	NGNX	HE	62588	71272	62652
313 061		N	NGNX	HE	62589	71273	62653
313 062		N	NGNX	HE	62590	71274	62654
313 063		N	NGNX	HE	62591	71275	62655
313 064		N	NGNX	HE	62592	71276	62656

CLASS 314

DMSO–PTSO–DMSO. Thyristor control. Tightlock couplers. Sliding doors.
Disc and rheostatic brakes. PA. Cab to shore radio.
Bogies: BX1.
Gangways: Within unit. End doors.
Traction Motors: Four GEC G310AZ (Brush TM61-53*) of 82.125 kW.
Dimensions: 19.80 x 2.82 m (outer cars), 19.92 x 2.82 m (inner cars).
Maximum Speed: 75 mph.

DMSO. Dia. EA206. Lot No. 30912 York 1979. 68S. 34.5 t.
PTSO. Dia. EH211. Lot No. 30913 York 1979. 76S. 33.0 t.

314 201	*	S	PGWX	GW	64583	71450	64584
314 202	*	S	PGWX	GW	64585	71451	64586
314 204	*	S	PGWX	GW	64589	71453	64590
314 205	*	S	PGWX	GW	64591	71454	64592
314 206	*	S	PGWX	GW	64593	71455	64594
314 207		S	PGWX	GW	64595	71456	64596
314 208		S	PGWX	GW	64597	71457	64598
314 209		S	PGWX	GW	64599	71458	64600

314 210	S	PGWX	GW	64601	71459	64602
314 211	S	PGWX	GW	64603	71460	64604
314 212	S	PGWX	GW	64605	71461	64606
314 213	S	PGWX	GW	64607	71462	64608
314 214	S	PGWX	GW	64609	71463	64610
314 215	S	PGWX	GW	64611	71464	64612
314 216	S	PGWX	GW	64613	71465	64614
Spare *	S	PGWX	GW (S)	64587	71452	

CLASS 315

DMSO–TSO–PTSO–DMSO. Thyristor control. Tightlock couplers. Sliding doors. Disc and rheostatic brakes. PA.
Bogies: BX1.
Gangways: Within unit. End doors.
Traction Motors: Four Brush TM61-53 (GEC G310AZ*) of 82.125 kW.
Dimensions: 19.80 x 2.82 m (outer cars), 19.92 x 2.82 m (inner cars).
Maximum Speed: 75 mph.

64461–64582. DMSO. Dia. EA207. Lot No. 30902 York 1980–81. 74S. 35 t
71281–71341. TSO. Dia. EH216. Lot No. 30904 York 1980–81. 86S. 25.5 t
71389–71449. PTSO. Dia. EH217. Lot No. 30903 York 1980–81. 84S. 32 t

315 801	N	NGEX	IL	64461	71281	71389	64462
315 802	N	NGEX	IL	64463	71282	71390	64464
315 803	N	NGEX	IL	64465	71283	71391	64466
315 804	N	NGEX	IL	64467	71284	71392	64468
315 805	N	NGEX	IL	64469	71285	71393	64470
315 806	N	NGEX	IL	64471	71286	71394	64472
315 807	N	NGEX	IL	64473	71287	71395	64474
315 808	N	NGEX	IL	64475	71288	71396	64476
315 809	N	NGEX	IL	64477	71289	71397	64478
315 810	N	NGEX	IL	64479	71290	71398	64480
315 811	N	NGEX	IL	64481	71291	71399	64482
315 812	N	NGEX	IL	64483	71292	71400	64484
315 813	N	NGEX	IL	64485	71293	71401	64486
315 814	N	NGEX	IL	64487	71294	71402	64488
315 815	N	NGEX	IL	64489	71295	71403	64490
315 816	N	NGEX	IL	64491	71296	71404	64492
315 817	N	NGEX	IL	64493	71297	71405	64494
315 818	N	NGEX	IL	64495	71298	71406	64496
315 819	N	NGEX	IL	64497	71299	71407	64498
315 820	N	NGEX	IL	64499	71300	71408	64500
315 821	N	NGEX	IL	64501	71301	71409	64502
315 822	N	NGEX	IL	64503	71302	71410	64504
315 823	N	NGEX	IL	64505	71303	71411	64506
315 824	N	NGEX	IL	64507	71304	71412	64508
315 825	N	NGEX	IL	64509	71305	71413	64510
315 826	N	NGEX	IL	64511	71306	71414	64512
315 827	N	NGEX	IL	64513	71307	71415	64514
315 828	N	NGEX	IL	64515	71308	71416	64516
315 829	N	NGEX	IL	64517	71309	71417	64518

315 830		**N**	NGEX	IL	64519	71310	71418	64520
315 831		**N**	NGEX	IL	64521	71311	71419	64522
315 832		**N**	NGEX	IL	64523	71312	71420	64524
315 833		**N**	NGEX	IL	64525	71313	71421	64526
315 834		**N**	NGEX	IL	64527	71314	71422	64528
315 835		**N**	NGEX	IL	64529	71315	71423	64530
315 836		**N**	NGEX	IL	64531	71316	71424	64532
315 837		**N**	NGEX	IL	64533	71317	71425	64534
315 838		**N**	NGEX	IL	64535	71318	71426	64536
315 839		**N**	NGEX	IL	64537	71319	71427	64538
315 840		**N**	NGEX	IL	64539	71320	71428	64540
315 841		**N**	NGEX	IL	64541	71321	71429	64542
315 842	*	**N**	NGEX	IL	64543	71322	71430	64544
315 843	*	**N**	NGEX	IL	64545	71323	71431	64546
315 844	*	**N**	NGEX	IL	64547	71324	71432	64548
315 845	*	**N**	NGEX	IL	64549	71325	71433	64550
315 846	*	**N**	NGEX	IL	64551	71326	71434	64552
315 847	*	**N**	NGEX	IL	64553	71327	71435	64554
315 848	*	**N**	NGEX	IL	64555	71328	71436	64556
315 849	*	**N**	NGEX	IL	64557	71329	71437	64558
315 850	*	**N**	NGEX	IL	64559	71330	71438	64560
315 851	*	**N**	NGEX	IL	64561	71331	71439	64562
315 852	*	**N**	NGEX	IL	64563	71332	71440	64564
315 853	*	**N**	NGEX	IL	64565	71333	71441	64566
315 854	*	**N**	NGEX	IL	64567	71334	71442	64568
315 855	*	**N**	NGEX	IL	64569	71335	71443	64570
315 856	*	**N**	NGEX	IL	64571	71336	71444	64572
315 857	*	**N**	NGEX	IL	64573	71337	71445	64574
315 858	*	**N**	NGEX	IL	64575	71338	71446	64576
315 859	*	**N**	NGEX	IL	64577	71339	71447	64578
315 860	*	**N**	NGEX	IL	64579	71340	71448	64580
315 861	*	**N**	NGEX	IL	64581	71341	71449	64582

CLASS 316   NETWORKER PROTOTYPE

DMSO–TSO–PTSO–DMSO. Sliding doors. Disc brakes. Fluorescent lighting. PA. The DMSOs and TSO were converted from class 210 vehicles with 7000 being added to the former numbers. The power cars have three-phase motors.

Bogies:
Gangways: Throughout.
Traction Motors:
Dimensions: 19.83 x 2.82 m. (outer cars), 19.92 x 2.82 m (inner cars).
Maximum Speed: 90 mph.

DMSO. Dia. EA209. Lot No. 30934 Derby 1981. 74S. 45 t.
TSO(A). Dia. EH236. Lot No. 30932 York 1981. 84S. 26.5 t.
TSO(B). Dia. EH210. Lot No. 30880 York 1976–77. 84S. 31.0 t.

316 999	**N**	NXXX	CC		67300	67401	71246	67301

CLASS 317

DTSO–MSO–TCOL–DTSO. Thyristor control. Tightlock couplers. Sliding doors. Disc brakes. PA.
Bogies: BP20 (MSO), BT13 (others).
Gangways: Throughout.
Traction Motors: Four GEC G315BZ of 247.5 kW.
Dimensions: 19.83 x 2.82 m (outer cars), 19.92 x 2.82 m (inner cars).
Maximum Speed: 100 mph.

Class 317/1. Pressure ventilated.

DTSO(A) Dia. EE216. Lot No. 30955 York 1981–82. 74S. 29.44 t.
MSO. Dia. EC202. Lot No. 30958 York 1981–82. 79S. 49.76 t.
TCOL. Dia. EH307. Lot No. 30957 Derby 1981–82. 22F 46S 2L. 28.80 t.
Controlled emission toilets (but decommisioned except for units allocated to NMLX).
DTSO(B) Dia. EE235 (EE232†). Lot No. 30956 York 1981–82. 70S. (71S†). 29.28 t.

317 301	N	NNEX	HE	77024	62661	71577	77048
317 302	N	NNEX	HE	77001	62662	71578	77049
317 303	N	NNEX	HE	77002	62663	71579	77050
317 304	N	NNEX	HE	77003	62664	71580	77051
317 305	N	NNEX	HE	77004	62665	71581	77052
317 306	N	NNEX	HE	77005	62666	71582	77053
317 307	N	NNEX	HE	77006	62667	71583	77054
317 308	N	NNEX	HE	77007	62668	71584	77055
317 309	N	NNEX	HE	77008	62669	71585	77056
317 310	N	NNEX	HE	77009	62670	71586	77057
317 311	N	NNEX	HE	77010	62671	71587	77058
317 312	N	NNEX	HE	77011	62672	71588	77059
317 313	N	NNEX	HE	77012	62673	71589	77060
317 314	N	NNEX	HE	77013	62674	71590	77061
317 315	N	NNEX	HE	77014	62675	71591	77062
317 316	N	NNEX	HE	77015	62676	71592	77063
317 317	N	NNEX	HE	77016	62677	71593	77064
317 318	N	NNEX	HE	77017	62678	71594	77065
317 319	N	NNEX	HE	77018	62679	71595	77066
317 320	N	NNEX	HE	77019	62680	71596	77067
317 321	N	NNEX	HE	77020	62681	71597	77068
317 322	N	NNEX	HE	77021	62682	71598	77069
317 323	N	NNEX	HE	77022	62683	71599	77070
317 324	N	NGNX	HE	77023	62684	71600	77071
317 325	N	NGNX	HE	77000	62685	71601	77072
317 326	N	NGNX	HE	77025	62686	71602	77073
317 327	N	NGNX	HE	77026	62687	71603	77074
317 328	N	NGNX	HE	77027	62688	71604	77075
317 329	N	NGNX	HE	77028	62689	71605	77076
317 330	N	NGNX	HE	77029	62690	71606	77077
317 331	N	NGNX	HE	77030	62691	71607	77078
317 332	N	NGNX	HE	77031	62692	71608	77079
317 333	N	NGNX	HE	77032	62693	71609	77080

317 334		N	NGNX	HE	77033	62694	71610	77081
317 335		N	NGNX	HE	77034	62695	71611	77082
317 336		N	NGNX	HE	77035	62696	71612	77083
317 337	†	N	NGNX	HE	77036	62697	71613	77084
317 338	†	N	NGNX	HE	77037	62698	71614	77085
317 339	†	N	NGNX	HE	77038	62699	71615	77086
317 340	†	N	NGNX	HE	77039	62700	71616	77087
317 341	†	N	NGNX	HE	77040	62701	71617	77088
317 342	†	N	NGNX	HE	77041	62702	71618	77089
317 343	†	N	NGNX	HE	77042	62703	71619	77090
317 344	†	N	NGNX	HE	77043	62704	71620	77091
317 345	†	N	NGNX	HE	77044	62705	71621	77092
317 346	†	N	NGNX	HE	77045	62706	71622	77093
317 347	†	N	NGNX	HE	77046	62707	71623	77094
317 348	†	N	NGNX	HE	77047	62708	71624	77095

Class 317/2. Convection heating.

77200–19. DTSO(A). Dia..EE224. Lot No. 30994 York 1985–86. 74S. 29.31 t.
77280–83. DTSO(A). Dia. EE224. Lot No. 31007 York 1987. 74S. 29.31 t.
62846–65. MSO. Dia. EC205. Lot No. 30996 York 1985–86. 79S. 50.08 t.
62886–89. MSO. Dia. EC205. Lot No. 31009 York 1987. 79S. 50.08 t.
71734–53. TCOL. Dia. EH308. Lot No. 30997 Yk 1985–86. 22F 46S 2L. 28.28 t.
71762–65. TCOL. Dia. EH308. Lot No. 31010 York 1987. 22F 46S 2L. 28.28 t.
77220–39. DTSO(B). Dia. EE225. Lot No. 30995 York 1985–86. 29.28 t. 71S.
77284–87. DTSO(B). Dia. EE225. Lot No. 31008 York 1987. 29.28 t. 71S.

317 349	N	NGNX	HE	77200	62846	71734	77220
317 350	N	NGNX	HE	77201	62847	71735	77221
317 351	N	NGNX	HE	77202	62848	71736	77222
317 352	N	NGNX	HE	77203	62849	71739	77223
317 353	N	NGNX	HE	77204	62850	71738	77224
317 354	N	NGNX	HE	77205	62851	71737	77225
317 355	N	NGNX	HE	77206	62852	71740	77226
317 356	N	NGNX	HE	77207	62853	71742	77227
317 357	N	NGNX	HE	77208	62854	71741	77228
317 358	N	NGNX	HE	77209	62855	71743	77229
317 359	N	NGNX	HE	77210	62856	71744	77230
317 360	N	NGNX	HE	77211	62857	71745	77231
317 361	N	NGNX	HE	77212	62858	71746	77232
317 362	N	NGNX	HE	77213	62859	71747	77233
317 363	N	NGNX	HE	77214	62860	71748	77234
317 364	N	NGNX	HE	77215	62861	71749	77235
317 365	N	NNEX	HE	77216	62862	71750	77236
317 366	N	NNEX	HE	77217	62863	71752	77237
317 367	N	NNEX	HE	77218	62864	71751	77238
317 368	N	NNEX	HE	77219	62865	71753	77239
317 369	N	NNEX	HE	77280	62886	71762	77284
317 370	N	NNEX	HE	77281	62887	71763	77285
317 371	N	NNEX	HE	77282	62888	71764	77286
317 372	N	NNEX	HE	77283	62889	71765	77287

CLASS 318

DTSOL–MSO–DTSO. Thyristor control. Tightlock couplers. Sliding doors. Disc brakes. PA. Cab to shore radio.
Bogies: BP20 (MSO), BT13 (others).
Gangways: Throughout.
Traction Motors: Four Brush TM 2141 of 268 kW.
Dimensions: 19.83 x 2.82 m (outer cars), 19.92 x 2.82 m (inner cars).
Maximum Speed: 90 mph.

77240–59. DTSOL. Dia. EE227. Lot No. 30999 York 1985–86. 66S 1L. 30.01 t.
77288. DTSOL. Dia. EE227. Lot No. 31020 York 1986–87. 66S 1L. 30.01 t.
62866–85. MSO. Dia. EC207. Lot No. 30998 York 1985–86. 79S. 50.90 t.
62890. MSO. Dia. EC207. Lot No. 31019 York 1987. 79S. 50.90 t.
77260–79. DTSO. Dia. EE228. Lot No. 31000 York 1985–86. 71S. 26.60 t.
77289. DTSO. Dia. EE228. Lot No. 31021 York 1987. 71S. 26.60 t.

318 250	S	PGWX	GW	77260	62866	77240
318 251	S	PGWX	GW	77261	62867	77241
318 252	S	PGWX	GW	77262	62868	77242
318 253	S	PGWX	GW	77263	62869	77243
318 254	S	PGWX	GW	77264	62870	77244
318 255	S	PGWX	GW	77265	62871	77245
318 256	S	PGWX	GW	77266	62872	77246
318 257	S	PGWX	GW	77267	62873	77247
318 258	S	PGWX	GW	77268	62874	77248
318 259	S	PGWX	GW	77269	62875	77249
318 260	S	PGWX	GW	77270	62876	77250
318 261	S	PGWX	GW	77271	62877	77251
318 262	S	PGWX	GW	77272	62878	77252
318 263	S	PGWX	GW	77273	62879	77253
318 264	S	PGWX	GW	77274	62880	77254
318 265	S	PGWX	GW	77275	62881	77255
318 266	S	PGWX	GW	77276	62882	77256
318 267	S	PGWX	GW	77277	62883	77257
318 268	S	PGWX	GW	77278	62884	77258
318 269	S	PGWX	GW	77279	62885	77259
318 270	S	PGWX	GW	77289	62890	77288

Name: DTSOL No. 77240 of set 318 250 is named 'GEOFF SHAW'.

CLASS 319

Thyristor control. Tightlock couplers. Sliding doors. Disc brakes. PA. Cab to shore radio.
System: 25 kV a.c. overhead/750 V d.c. third rail.
Bogies: P7-4 (MSO), T3-7 (others).
Gangways: Within unit. End doors.
Traction Motors: Four GEC G315BZ of 247.5 kW.
Dimensions: 19.83 x 2.82 m (outer cars), 19.92 x 2.82 m (inner cars).
Maximum Speed: 100 mph.

Class 319/0. DTSO–MSO–TSOL–DTSO.

77291–381. DTSO. Dia. EE233. Lot No. 31022 (odd nos.) York 1987–8. 82S. 30 t.
77431–457. DTSO. Dia. EE233. Lot No. 31038 (odd nos.) York 1988. 82S. 30 t.
62891–936. MSO. Dia. EC209. Lot No. 31023 York 1987–8. 82S. 51 t.
62961–974. MSO. Dia. EC209. Lot No. 31039 York 1988. 82S. 51 t.
71772–817. TSOL. Dia. EH234. Lot No. 31024 York 1987–8. 77S 2L. 51 t.
71866–879. TSOL. Dia. EH234. Lot No. 31040 York 1988. 77S 2L. 51 t.
77290–380. DTSO. Dia. EE234. Lot No. 31025 (even nos.) York 1987–8. 78S. 30 t.
77430–456. DTSO. Dia. EE234. Lot No. 31041 (even nos.) York 1988. 78S. 30 t.

319 001	**N**	NSLX	SU	77291	62891	71772	77290
319 002	**N**	NSLX	SU	77293	62892	71773	77292
319 003	**N**	NSLX	SU	77295	62893	71774	77294
319 004	**N**	NSLX	SU	77297	62894	71775	77296
319 005	**N**	NSLX	SU	77299	62895	71776	77298
319 006	**N**	NSLX	SU	77301	62896	71777	77300
319 007	**N**	NSLX	SU	77303	62897	71778	77302
319 008	**N**	NSLX	SU	77305	62898	71779	77304
319 009	**N**	NSLX	SU	77307	62899	71780	77306
319 010	**N**	NSLX	SU	77309	62900	71781	77308
319 011	**N**	NSLX	SU	77311	62901	71782	77310
319 012	**N**	NSLX	SU	77313	62902	71783	77312
319 013	**N**	NSLX	SU	77315	62903	71784	77314
319 014	**N**	NSLX	SU	77317	62904	71785	77316
319 015	**N**	NSLX	SU	77319	62905	71786	77318
319 016	**N**	NSLX	SU	77321	62906	71787	77320
319 017	**N**	NSLX	SU	77323	62907	71788	77322
319 018	**N**	NMLX	SU	77325	62908	71789	77324
319 019	**N**	NMLX	SU	77327	62909	71790	77326
319 020	**N**	NMLX	SU	77329	62910	71791	77328
319 021	**N**	NMLX	SU	77331	62911	71792	77330
319 022	**N**	NMLX	SU	77333	62912	71793	77332
319 023	**N**	NMLX	SU	77335	62913	71794	77334
319 024	**N**	NMLX	SU	77337	62914	71795	77336
319 025	**N**	NMLX	SU	77339	62915	71796	77338
319 026	**N**	NMLX	SU	77341	62916	71797	77340
319 027	**N**	NMLX	SU	77343	62917	71798	77342
319 028	**N**	NMLX	SU	77345	62918	71799	77344
319 029	**N**	NMLX	SU	77347	62919	71800	77346
319 030	**N**	NMLX	SU	77349	62920	71801	77348
319 031	**N**	NMLX	SU	77351	62921	71802	77350
319 032	**N**	NMLX	SU	77353	62922	71803	77352
319 033	**N**	NMLX	SU	77355	62923	71804	77354
319 034	**N**	NMLX	SU	77357	62924	71805	77356
319 035	**N**	NMLX	SU	77359	62925	71806	77358
319 036	**N**	NMLX	SU	77361	62926	71807	77360
319 037	**N**	NMLX	SU	77363	62927	71808	77362
319 038	**N**	NMLX	SU	77365	62928	71809	77364

319 039	**N**	NMLX	SU	77367	62929	71810	77366
319 040	**N**	NMLX	SU	77369	62930	71811	77368
319 041	**N**	NMLX	SU	77371	62931	71812	77370
319 042	**N**	NMLX	SU	77373	62932	71813	77372
319 043	**N**	NMLX	SU	77375	62933	71814	77374
319 044	**N**	NMLX	SU	77377	62934	71815	77376
319 045	**N**	NMLX	SU	77379	62935	71816	77378
319 046	**N**	NMLX	SU	77381	62936	71817	77380
319 047	**N**	NMLX	SU	77431	62961	71866	77430
319 048	**N**	NMLX	SU	77433	62962	71867	77432
319 049	**N**	NMLX	SU	77435	62963	71868	77434
319 050	**N**	NMLX	SU	77437	62964	71869	77436
319 051	**N**	NMLX	SU	77439	62965	71870	77438
319 052	**N**	NMLX	SU	77441	62966	71871	77440
319 053	**N**	NMLX	SU	77443	62967	71872	77442
319 054	**N**	NMLX	SU	77445	62968	71873	77444
319 055	**N**	NMLX	SU	77447	62969	71874	77446
319 056	**N**	NMLX	SU	77449	62970	71875	77448
319 057	**N**	NMLX	SU	77451	62971	71876	77450
319 058	**N**	NMLX	SU	77453	62972	71877	77452
319 059	**N**	NMLX	SU	77455	62973	71878	77454
319 060	**N**	NMLX	SU	77457	62974	71879	77456

Class 319/1. DTCO–MSO–TSOL–DTSO.

DTCO. Dia. EE310. Lot No. 31063 York 1990. 16F 54S. 29 t.
MSO. Dia. EC214. Lot No. 31064 York 1990. 79S. 50.6 t.
TSOL. Dia. EH238. Lot No. 31065 York 1990. 74S 2L. 31 t.
DTSO. Dia. EE240. Lot No. 31066 York 1990. 78S. 29.7 t.

319 161	**N**	NMLX	SU	77459	63043	71929	77458
319 162	**N**	NMLX	SU	77461	63044	71930	77460
319 163	**N**	NMLX	SU	77463	63045	71931	77462
319 164	**N**	NMLX	SU	77465	63046	71932	77464
319 165	**N**	NMLX	SU	77467	63047	71933	77466
319 166	**N**	NMLX	SU	77469	63048	71934	77468
319 167	**N**	NMLX	SU	77471	63049	71935	77470
319 168	**N**	NMLX	SU	77473	63050	71936	77472
319 169	**N**	NMLX	SU	77475	63051	71937	77474
319 170	**N**	NMLX	SU	77477	63052	71938	77476
319 171	**N**	NMLX	SU	77479	63053	71939	77478
319 172	**N**	NMLX	SU	77481	63054	71940	77480
319 173	**N**	NMLX	SU	77483	63055	71941	77482
319 174	**N**	NMLX	SU	77485	63056	71942	77484
319 175	**N**	NMLX	SU	77487	63057	71943	77486
319 176	**N**	NMLX	SU	77489	63058	71944	77488
319 177	**N**	NMLX	SU	77491	63059	71945	77490
319 178	**N**	NMLX	SU	77493	63060	71946	77492
319 179	**N**	NMLX	SU	77495	63061	71947	77494
319 180	**N**	NMLX	SU	77497	63062	71948	77496
319 181	**N**	NMLX	SU	77973	63093	71979	77974
319 182	**N**	NMLX	SU	77975	63094	71980	77976
319 183	**N**	NMLX	SU	77977	63095	71981	77978

319 184	**N**	NMLX	SU	77979	63096	71982	77980
319 185	**N**	NMLX	SU	77981	63097	71983	77982
319 186	**N**	NMLX	SU	77983	63098	71984	77984

CLASS 320

DTSO–MSO–DTSO. Thyristor control. Tightlock couplers. Sliding doors. Disc brakes. PA.
Bogies: P7-4 (MSO), T3-7 (others).
Gangways: Within unit.
Traction Motors: Brush TM2141B of 268 kW.
Dimensions: 19.83 x 2.82 m (outer cars), 19.92 x 2.82 m (inner car).
Maximum Speed: 75 mph.

DTSO (A). Dia. EE238. Lot No. 31060 York 1990. 77S. 30.7 t.
MSO. Dia. EC212. Lot No. 31062 York 1990. 77S. 52.1 t.
DTSO (B). Dia. EE239. Lot No. 31061 York 1990. 76S 31.7 t.

320 301	**S**	PGWX	GW	77899	63021	77921
320 302	**S**	PGWX	GW	77900	63022	77922
320 303	**S**	PGWX	GW	77901	63023	77923
320 304	**S**	PGWX	GW	77902	63024	77924
320 305	**S**	PGWX	GW	77903	63025	77925
320 306	**S**	PGWX	GW	77904	63026	77926
320 307	**S**	PGWX	GW	77905	63027	77927
320 308	**S**	PGWX	GW	77906	63028	77928
320 309	**S**	PGWX	GW	77907	63029	77929
320 310	**S**	PGWX	GW	77908	63030	77930
320 311	**S**	PGWX	GW	77909	63031	77931
320 312	**S**	PGWX	GW	77910	63032	77932
320 313	**S**	PGWX	GW	77911	63033	77933
320 314	**S**	PGWX	GW	77912	63034	77934
320 315	**S**	PGWX	GW	77913	63035	77935
320 316	**S**	PGWX	GW	77914	63036	77936
320 317	**S**	PGWX	GW	77915	63037	77937
320 318	**S**	PGWX	GW	77916	63038	77938
320 319	**S**	PGWX	GW	77917	63039	77939
320 320	**S**	PGWX	GW	77918	63040	77940
320 321	**S**	PGWX	GW	77919	63041	77941
320 322	**S**	PGWX	GW	77920	63042	77942

CLASS 321

DTCO (DTSO on Class 321/9)–MSO–TSOL–DTSO. Thyristor control. Tightlock couplers. Sliding doors. Disc brakes. PA.
Bogies: P7-4 (MSO), T3-7 (others).
Gangways: Within unit.
Traction Motors: Brush TM2141B (268 kW).
Dimensions: 19.83 x 2.82 m (outer cars), 19.92 x 2.82 m (inner cars).
Maximum Speed: 100 mph.

Note: Lot numbers and diagrams were officially changed on 09/02/90.

Class 321/3. Units built for Liverpool Street workings.
DTCO. Dia. EE308. Lot No. 31053 York 1988–90. 12F 56S. 29.3 t.
MSO. Dia. EC210. Lot No. 31054 York 1988–90. 79S. 51.5 t.
TSOL. Dia. EH235. Lot No. 31055 York 1988–90. 74S 2L. 28 t.
DTSO. Dia. EE236. Lot No. 31056 York 1988–90. 78S. 29.1 t.

321 301	**N**	NGEX	IL	78049	62975	71880	77853
321 302	**N**	NGEX	IL	78050	62976	71881	77854
321 303	**N**	NGEX	IL	78051	62977	71882	77855
321 304	**N**	NGEX	IL	78052	62978	71883	77856
321 305	**N**	NGEX	IL	78053	62979	71884	77857
321 306	**N**	NGEX	IL	78054	62980	71885	77858
321 307	**N**	NGEX	IL	78055	62981	71886	77859
321 308	**N**	NGEX	IL	78056	62982	71887	77860
321 309	**N**	NGEX	IL	78057	62983	71888	77861
321 310	**N**	NGEX	IL	78058	62984	71889	77862
321 311	**N**	NGEX	IL	78059	62985	71890	77863
321 312	**N**	NGEX	IL	78060	62986	71891	77864
321 313	**N**	NGEX	IL	78061	62987	71892	77865
321 314	**N**	NGEX	IL	78062	62988	71893	77866
321 315	**N**	NGEX	IL	78063	62989	71894	77867
321 316	**N**	NGEX	IL	78064	62990	71895	77868
321 317	**N**	NGEX	IL	78065	62991	71896	77869
321 318	**N**	NGEX	IL	78066	62992	71897	77870
321 319	**N**	NGEX	IL	78067	62993	71898	77871
321 320	**N**	NGEX	IL	78068	62994	71899	77872
321 321	**N**	NGEX	IL	78069	62995	71900	77873
321 322	**N**	NGEX	IL	78070	62996	71901	77874
321 323	**N**	NGEX	IL	78071	62997	71902	77875
321 324	**N**	NGEX	IL	78072	62998	71903	77876
321 325	**N**	NGEX	IL	78073	62999	71904	77877
321 326	**N**	NGEX	IL	78074	63000	71905	77878
321 327	**N**	NGEX	IL	78075	63001	71906	77879
321 328	**N**	NGEX	IL	78076	63002	71907	77880
321 329	**N**	NGEX	IL	78077	63003	71908	77881
321 330	**N**	NGEX	IL	78078	63004	71909	77882
321 331	**N**	NGEX	IL	78079	63005	71910	77883
321 332	**N**	NGEX	IL	78080	63006	71911	77884
321 333	**N**	NGEX	IL	78081	63007	71912	77885
321 334	**N**	NGEX	IL	78082	63008	71913	77886
321 335	**N**	NGEX	IL	78083	63009	71914	77887
321 336	**N**	NGEX	IL	78084	63010	71915	77888
321 337	**N**	NGEX	IL	78085	63011	71916	77889
321 338	**N**	NGEX	IL	78086	63012	71917	77890
321 339	**N**	NGEX	IL	78087	63013	71918	77891
321 340	**N**	NGEX	IL	78088	63014	71919	77892
321 341	**N**	NGEX	IL	78089	63015	71920	77893
321 342	**N**	NGEX	IL	78090	63016	71921	77894
321 343	**N**	NGEX	IL	78091	63017	71922	77895
321 344	**N**	NGEX	IL	78092	63018	71923	77896
321 345	**N**	NGEX	IL	78093	63019	71924	77897
321 346	**N**	NGEX	IL	78094	63020	71925	77898

321 347	**N**	NGEX	IL	78131	63105	71991	78280
321 348	**N**	NGEX	IL	78132	63106	71992	78281
321 349	**N**	NGEX	IL	78133	63107	71993	78282
321 350	**N**	NGEX	IL	78134	63108	71994	78283
321 351	**N**	NGEX	IL	78135	63109	71995	78284
321 352	**N**	NGEX	IL	78136	63110	71996	78285
321 353	**N**	NGEX	IL	78137	63111	71997	78286
321 354	**N**	NGEX	IL	78138	63112	71998	78287
321 355	**N**	NGEX	IL	78139	63113	71999	78288
321 356	**N**	NGEX	IL	78140	63114	72000	78289
321 357	**N**	NGEX	IL	78141	63115	72001	78290
321 358	**N**	NGEX	IL	78142	63116	72002	78291
321 359	**N**	NGEX	IL	78143	63117	72003	78292
321 360	**N**	NGEX	IL	78144	63118	72004	78293
321 361	**N**	NGEX	IL	78145	63119	72005	78294
321 362	**N**	NGEX	IL	78146	63120	72006	78295
321 363	**N**	NGEX	IL	78147	63121	72007	78296
321 364	**N**	NGEX	IL	78148	63122	72008	78297
321 365	**N**	NGEX	IL	78149	63123	72009	78298
321 366	**N**	NGEX	IL	78150	63124	72010	78299

Name: DTSOL No. 71891 of set 321 312 is named 'Southend-on-Sea'.

Class 321/4. Units built for WCML workings.

DTCO. Dia. EE309. Lot No. 31067 York 1989–90. 28F 40S. 29.3 t.
MSO. Dia. EC210. Lot No. 31068 York 1989–90. 79S. 51.5 t.
TSOL. Dia. EH235. Lot No. 31069 York 1989–90. 74S 2L. 28 t.
DTSO. Dia. EE236. Lot No. 31070 York 1989–90. 78S. 29.1 t.

321 401	**N**	NNWX	BY	78095	63063	71949	77943
321 402	**N**	NNWX	BY	78096	63064	71950	77944
321 403	**N**	NNWX	BY	78097	63065	71951	77945
321 404	**N**	NNWX	BY	78098	63066	71952	77946
321 405	**N**	NNWX	BY	78099	63067	71953	77947
321 406	**N**	NNWX	BY	78100	63068	71954	77948
321 407	**N**	NNWX	BY	78101	63069	71955	77949
321 408	**N**	NNWX	BY	78102	63070	71956	77950
321 409	**N**	NNWX	BY	78103	63071	71957	77951
321 410	**N**	NNWX	BY	78104	63072	71958	77952
321 411	**N**	NNWX	BY	78105	63073	71959	77953
321 412	**N**	NNWX	BY	78106	63074	71960	77954
321 413	**N**	NNWX	BY	78107	63075	71961	77955
321 414	**N**	NNWX	BY	78108	63076	71962	77956
321 415	**N**	NNWX	BY	78109	63077	71963	77957
321 416	**N**	NNWX	BY	78110	63078	71964	77958
321 417	**N**	NNWX	BY	78111	63079	71965	77959
321 418	**N**	NNWX	BY	78112	63080	71966	77960
321 419	**N**	NNWX	BY	78113	63081	71967	77961
321 420	**N**	NNWX	BY	78114	63082	71968	77962
321 421	**N**	NNWX	BY	78115	63083	71969	77963
321 422	**N**	NNWX	BY	78116	63084	71970	77964
321 423	**N**	NNWX	BY	78117	63085	71971	77965
321 424	**N**	NNWX	BY	78118	63086	71972	77966

321 425	N	NNWX	BY	78119	63087	71973	77967
321 426	N	NNWX	BY	78120	63088	71974	77968
321 427	N	NNWX	BY	78121	63089	71975	77969
321 428	N	NNWX	BY	78122	63090	71976	77970
321 429	N	NNWX	BY	78123	63091	71977	77971
321 430	N	NNWX	BY	78124	63092	71978	77972
321 431	N	NNWX	BY	78151	63125	72011	78300
321 432	N	NNWX	BY	78152	63126	72012	78301
321 433	N	NNWX	BY	78153	63127	72013	78302
321 434	N	NNWX	BY	78154	63128	72014	78303
321 435	N	NNWX	BY	78155	63129	72015	78304
321 436	N	NNWX	BY	78156	63130	72016	78305
321 437	N	NNWX	BY	78157	63131	72017	78306
321 438	N	NNWX	BY	78158	63132	72018	78307
321 439	N	NNWX	BY	78159	63133	72019	78308
321 440	N	NNWX	BY	78160	63134	72020	78309
321 441	N	NNEX	IL	78161	63135	72021	78310
321 442	N	NNEX	IL	78162	63136	72022	78311
321 443	N	NNEX	IL	78125	63099	71985	78274
321 444	N	NNEX	IL	78126	63100	71986	78275
321 445	N	NNEX	IL	78127	63101	71987	78276
321 446	N	NNEX	IL	78128	63102	71988	78277
321 447	N	NNEX	IL	78129	63103	71989	78278
321 448	N	NNEX	IL	78130	63104	71990	78279

Class 321/9. West Yorkshire PTE Units. DTSO(A)–MSO–TSOL–DTSO(B).

DTSO (A). Dia. EE277. Lot No. 31108 York 1991. 78S. 29.3 t.
MSO. Dia. EC216. Lot No. 31109 York 1991. 79S. 51.5 t.
TSOL. Dia. EH240. Lot No. 31110 York 1991. 74S 2L. 28 t.
DTSO (B). Dia. EE277. Lot No. 31111 York 1991. 78S. 29.1 t.

321 901	Y	PNLX	NL	77990	63153	72128	77993
321 902	Y	PNLX	NL	77991	63154	72129	77994
321 903	Y	PNLX	NL	77992	63155	72130	77995

CLASS 322   STANSTED EXPRESS STOCK

DTCO–MSO–TSOL–DTSO. Units dedicated for use on Stansted Airport services. Thyristor control. Tightlock couplers. Sliding doors. Disc brakes. PA.

Bogies: P7-4 (MSO), T3-7 (others).
Gangways: Within unit.
Traction Motors: Brush TM2141B (268 kW).
Dimensions: 19.83 x 2.82 m (outer cars), 19.92 x 2.82 m (inner cars).
Maximum Speed: 100 mph.
Non-Standard Livery: Light grey with broad green band and narrow white and dark grey bands. White at cantrail level and on outer ends of end cars. 'Stansted Express' lettering.

DTCO. Dia. EE313. Lot No. 31094 York 1990. 35F 22S. 30.43 t.
MSO. Dia. EC215. Lot No. 31092 York 1990. 70S. 52.27 t.
TSOL. Dia. EH239. Lot No. 31093 York 1990. 60S 2L. 29.51 t.
DTSO. Dia. EE242. Lot No. 31091 York 1990. 65S. 29.77 t.

322 481	0	NNEX	IL	78163	63137	72023	77985
322 482	0	NNEX	IL	78164	63138	72024	77986
322 483	0	NNEX	IL	78165	63139	72025	77987
322 484	0	NNEX	IL	78166	63140	72026	77988
322 485	0	NNEX	IL	78167	63141	72027	77989

CLASS 323

DMSO(A)–TSO–DMSO(B). New units under construction for West Midlands PTE and Greater Manchester PTE areas. Aluminium alloy bodies. Thyristor control. Tightlock couplers. Sliding doors. Disc brakes. PA.
Bogies:
Gangways: Within unit.
Traction Motors:
Dimensions:
Maximum Speed: 75 mph.

DMSO(A). Dia. EA2 . Lot No. 31 Hunslet 1990. 98S. . t.
TSO. Dia. EH2 . Lot No. 31 Hunslet 1990. 88S 1L. . t.
DMSO(B). Dia. EA2 . Lot No. 31 Hunslet 1990. 98S. . t.

323 201	P		64001	72201	65001
323 202	P		64002	72202	65002
323 203	P		64003	72203	65003
323 204	P		64004	72204	65004
323 205	P		64005	72205	65005
323 206	P		64006	72206	65006
323 207	P		64007	72207	65007
323 208	P		64008	72208	65008
323 209	P		64009	72209	65009
323 210	P		64010	72210	65010
323 211	P		64011	72211	65011
323 212	P		64012	72212	65012
323 213	P		64013	72213	65013
323 214	P		64014	72214	65014
323 215	P		64015	72215	65015
323 216	P		64016	72216	65016
323 217	P		64017	72217	65017
323 218	P		64018	72218	65018
323 219	P		64019	72219	65019
323 220	P		64020	72220	65020
323 221	P		64021	72221	65021
323 222	P		64022	72222	65022
323 223	P		64023	72223	65023
323 224	P		64024	72224	65024
323 225	P		64025	72225	65025
323 226	P		64026	72226	65026
323 227	P		64027	72227	65027
323 228	P		64028	72228	65028
323 229	P		64029	72229	65029
323 230	P		64030	72230	65030
323 231	P		64031	72231	65031
323 232	P		64032	72232	65032

323 233	P	64033	72233	65033
323 234	P	64034	72234	65034
323 235	P	64035	72235	65035
323 236	P	64036	72236	65036
323 237	P	64037	72237	65037

4.2. SOUTHERN REGION 750 V d.c. EMUs

These classes are all allocated to the Southern Region and operate on the third rail system at 750–850 V d.c. Except where stated otherwise, all multiple units can run in multiple with one another. Buffet cars have electric cooking. In addition to the class number, the old SR designations e.g. 2 Hap are quoted together with the year of introduction of their type of control gear. Whilst outer couplings are buckeyes on all units, 1951 and 1957-type suburban units have centre buffers and three link couplings within a unit.

CLASS 438   4 TC

DTSO–TFK–TBSK–DTSO or DTSO–TBSK–DTSO. Converted from loco-hauled stock. Unpowered units which worked push & pull with class 431/2 tractor units and class 33/1 and 73 locos. Express stock. Two units remain and have regained their original numbers for use on charter and special services. Another has been reinstated temporarily for working the Kensington Olympia–Clapham Junction service.

Electrical Equipment: 1966-type.
Bogies: B5 (SR) bogies.
Gangways: Throughout.
Dimensions: 19.66 x 2.82 m.
Maximum Speed: 90 mph.

DTSO. Dia. EE266. Lot No. 30764 York 1966–67. 64S. 32 t.
TCK. Dia. EH363. Lot No. 30766 York 1966–67. 42F 2L. 33.5 t.
70812–70843. TBSK. Dia. EJ260. Lot No. 30765 York 1966–67. 32S 1L. 35.5 t.
TBSK. Dia. EJ260. Lot No. 30855 York 1974. 32S 1L. 35.5 t.

410	(8010)	pa **B**	NSSX	BM	76288	70859	70812	76287
417	(8017)	pa **B**	NSSX	BM	76302	70860	70826	76301
8001		pa **N**	NSLX	CJ	76270		70821	76332
Spare				BM	76327			

Former numbers of converted Class 431 and 438 vehicles converted from hauled stock:

70812 (34987)	70839 (34978)	76275 (3929)	76321 (3930)
70821 (34985)	70845 (13008)	76287 (4379)	76322 (3936)
70824 (34984)	70859 (13040)	76288 (4391)	76324 (4009)
70826 (34980)	70860 (13019)	76301 (4375)	76327 (4018)
70830 (34976)	71163 (13097)	76302 (4382)	76328 (4044)
70838 (34979)	76270 (4043)	76321 (3930)	76332 (3937)

CLASS 421/1   4 Cig (PHASE 1)

DTCsoL (A)–MBSO–TSO–DTCsoL (B). Express stock. Fitted with electric parking brake.

Electrical Equipment: 1963-type.
Bogies: Two Mk. 4 motor bogies (MBSO). B5 (SR) bogies (trailer cars).
Gangways: Throughout.
Traction Motors: Four EE507 of 185 kW.

Dimensions: 19.75 x 2.82 m.
Maximum Speed: 90 mph.

DTCsoL(A). Dia. EE364. Lot No. 30741 York 1964–65. 18F 36S 2L. 35.5 t.
MBSO. Dia. ED260. Lot No. 30742 York 1964–65. 56S. 49 t.
70699–70721. TSO. Dia. EH275. Lot No. 30730 York 1964–65. 72S. 31.5 t.
71051. TSO. Dia. EH275. Lot No. 30817 York 1971. 72S. 31.5 t. (ex 421/2).
DTCsoL(B). Dia. EE363. Lot No. 30740 York 1964–65. 24F 28S 2L. (* 18F 36S 2L) 35 t.

Renumbered from 7300–7327.

1100		N	NSXX	BI	76125	62066	71051	76071
1105		N	NSXX	BI	76080	62021	70699	76039
1110	*	N	NSXX	BI	76085	62026	70704	76031
1116		N	NSXX	BI	76091	62032	70710	76037
1118		N	NSXX	BI	76026	62034	70712	76093
1123		N	NSXX	BI	76119	62060	70717	76065
1127		N	NSXX	BI	76102	62043	70721	76048

CLASS 421/2   4 Cig (PHASE 2)

DTCsoL (A)–MBSO–TSO–DTCsoL (B). Express stock.

Electrical Equipment: 1963-type.
Bogies: Two Mk. 6 motor bogies (MBSO). B5 (SR) bogies (trailer cars).
Gangways: Throughout.
Traction Motors: Four EE507 of 185 kW.
Dimensions: 19.75 x 2.82 m.
Maximum Speed: 90 mph.

76581–76610. DTCsoL(A). Dia. EE364. Lot No. 30806 York 1970. 35.5 t.
76717–76787. DTCsoL(A). Dia. EE364. Lot No. 30814 York 1970–72. 35.5 t.
62282. MBSO. Dia. ED260. Lot No. 30804 York 1970. 56S. 49t.
62287–62316. MBSO. Dia. ED260. Lot No. 30808 York 1970. 56S. 49t.
62355–62425. MBSO. Dia. ED260. Lot No. 30816 York 1970. 56S. 49t.
70967–70996. TSO. Dia. EH275. Lot No. 30809 York 1970–71. 72S. 31.5t.
71035–71105. TSO. Dia. EH275. Lot No. 30817 York 1970. 72S. 31.5t.
76611–76640. DTCsoL(B). Dia. EE363. Lot No. 30807 York 1970. 35 t.
76788–76858. DTCsoL(B). Dia. EE363. Lot No. 30815 York 1970–72. 35 t.

DTCsoL (A) seat 18F 36S 2L. DTCsoL (B) seat 24F 28S 2L. 76812 has hopper ventilators.

Renumbered from the series 7401–7426 and 7337–7400.

1204	N	NSXX	BI	76754	62392	71072	76825
1205	N	NSXX	BI	76755	62393	71073	76826
1206	N	NSSX	EH	76756	62394	71074	76827
1208	N	NSSX	EH	76771	62396	71076	76829
1209	N	NSSX	EH	76759	62397	71077	76830
1210	N	NSSX	EH	76760	62398	71078	76831
1211	N	NSSX	EH	76761	62399	71079	76832
1212	N	NSSX	EH	76762	62400	71080	76833

1213	**N**	NSSX	EH		76763	62401	71081	76834
1214	**N**	NSSX	EH		76764	62402	71082	76835
1215	**N**	NSSX	EH		76765	62403	71083	76836
1216	**N**	NSSX	EH		76766	62404	71084	76837
1217	**N**	NSSX	EH		76767	62405	71085	76838
1218	**N**	NSSX	EH		76768	62406	71086	76839
1219	**N**	NSSX	EH		76769	62407	71087	76840
1220	**N**	NSSX	EH		76770	62408	71088	76841
1221	**N**	NSSX	EH	(U)	76758	62409	71089	76842
1222	**N**	NSSX	EH		76772	62410	71090	76843
1223	**N**	NSSX	EH		76773	62411	71091	76844
1224	**N**	NSSX	EH		76774	62412	71092	76845
1225	**N**	NSSX	EH		76775	62413	71093	76846
1226	**N**	NSSX	EH		76776	62414	71094	76847
Spare	**N**	NSXX	BI		76816		70995	76824

CLASS 421/5   'GREYHOUND' 4 Cig (PHASE 2)

DTCsoL–MBSO–TSO–DTCsoL. Express stock. Facelifted with new trim, fluorescent lighting in saloons, PA. Fitted with an additional stage of field weakening to improve the maximum attainable speed.

Electrical Equipment: 1963-type.
Bogies: Two Mk. 6 motor bogies (MBSO). B5 (SR) bogies (trailer cars).
Gangways: Throughout.
Traction Motors: Four EE507 of 185 kW.
Dimensions: 19.75 x 2.82 m.
Maximum Speed: 90 mph.

DTCsoL. Dia. EE369. 18F 36S 2L. 35 t.
MBSO. Dia. ED264. 56S. 49 t.
TSO. Dia. EH287. 72S. 31.5 t.

For lot numbers see classes 421/2 or 422/2.

1301	(1814)	**N**	NSSX	EH	76595	62301	70981	76625
1302	(1815)	**N**	NSSX	EH	76584	62290	70970	76614
1303	(1816)	**N**	NSSX	EH	76581	62287	70967	76611
1304	(1817)	**N**	NSSX	EH	76583	62289	70969	76613
1305	(1818)	**N**	NSSX	EH	76717	62355	71035	76788
1306	(1819)	**N**	NSSX	EH	76723	62361	71041	76794
1307	(1820)	**N**	NSSX	EH	76586	62292	70972	76616
1308	(1821)	**N**	NSSX	EH	76627	62298	70978	76622
1309	(1822)	**N**	NSSX	EH	76594	62300	70980	76624
1310	(1823)	**N**	NSSX	EH	76567	62283	71926	76577
1311	(1824)	**N**	NSSX	EH	76561	62277	71927	76571
1312	(1825)	**N**	NSSX	EH	76562	62278	71928	76572
1313	(1252)	**N**	NSSX	EH	76596	62302	70982	76626
1314	(1244)	**N**	NSSX	EH	76588	62294	70974	76618
1315	(1264)	**N**	NSSX	EH	76608	62314	70994	76638
1316	(1241)	**N**	NSSX	EH	76585	62291	70971	76615
1317	(1253)	**N**	NSSX	EH	76597	62303	70983	76592

Former numbers of converted buffet cars:

71926 (69315) │71927 (69330) │71928 (69331) │

Note: No new Lot Nos were issued for the above conversions.

CLASS 411/4* & 411/5   REFURBISHED 4 Cep

DMSO (A)–TBCK–TSOL–DMSO (B). Kent Coast Express Stock. Refurbished and renumbered from the 71/72xx series. Fitted with hopper ventilators, Inter-City 70 seats, fluorescent lighting and PA.

Electrical Equipment: 1957-type (*1951-type).
Bogies: One Mk. 4 (Mk 3B†) motor bogie (DMSO). Commonwealth trailer bogies.
Gangways: Throughout.
Traction Motors: Two EE507 of 185 kW.
Dimensions: 19.75 x 2.82 m.
Maximum Speed: 90 mph.

§–70345 is a TBFK with one compartment declassified. it is from the original refurbished unit (1500), has a different interior colour scheme and does not have hopper ventilators.

61305 has four seats at inner vestibule end replaced by luggage racks.

DMSO (A). Dia. EA263. 64S. 44.15 t.
TBCK. Dia. EJ361. 24F 6S 2L. 36.17 t.
TSOL. Dia. EH282. 64S 2L. 33.78 t.
DMSO (B). Dia. EA264. 64S. 43.54 t.

Lot numbers are as follows, all cars being built at Ashford/Eastleigh:

61033–61040. Lot No. 30108 1956. │**70043–70044.** Lot No. 30639 1961.
61041–61044. Lot No. 30111 1956. │**70229–70234.** Lot No. 30450 1958.
61229–61240. Lot No. 30449 1958. │**70235–70240.** Lot No. 30451 1958.
61304–61409. Lot No. 30454 1958–59.│**70241.** Lot No. 30640 1961.
61694–61811. Lot No. 30619 1960–61.│**70260–70302.** Lot No. 30455 1958–59.
61868–61870. Lot No. 30638 1960–61.│**70303–70355.** Lot No. 30456 1958–59.
61948–61961. Lot No. 30708 1963. │**70503–70551.** Lot No. 30620 1960–61.
70033–70036. Lot No. 30109 1956. │**70552–70610.** Lot No. 30621 1960–61.
70037–70040. Lot No. 30110 1956. │**70653–70659.** Lot No. 30709 1963.
70041–70042. Lot No. 30112 1956. │**70660–70666.** Lot No. 30710 1963.

1501	*	N	NKCX	RE	61041	70041	70034	61042
1502	*	N	NKCX	RE	61040	70040	70036	61039
1503	*	N	NKCX	RE	61033	70037	70033	61034
1504	*	N	NKCX	RE	61043	70042	71712	61037
1505	*	N	NKCX	RE	61044	70039	70035	61038
1506		N	NKCX	RE	61349	70325	70282	61348
1507		N	NKCX	RE	61363	70332	70289	61362
1508		N	NKCX	RE	61305	70303	70260	61304
1509		N	NKCX	RE	61335	70318	70275	61334
1510		N	NKCX	RE	61365	70333	70290	61366
1511		N	NKCX	RE	61367	70334	70291	61366
1512		N	NKCX	RE	61321	70311	70268	61320

1513		**N**	NKCX	RE	61796	70321	70278	61340
1514		**N**	NKCX	RE	61327	70314	70271	61326
1515		**N**	NKCX	RE	61345	70323	70280	61344
1516		**N**	NKCX	RE	61319	70310	70267	61318
1517		**N**	NKCX	RE	61317	70309	70266	61316
1518		**N**	NKCX	RE	61333	70317	70274	61332
1519		**N**	NKCX	RE	61403	70352	70516	61402
1520		**N**	NKCX	RE	61343	70327	70284	61380
1521		**N**	NKCX	RE	61353	70324	70281	61352
1522		**N**	NKCX	RE	61347	70341	70665	61346
1523		**N**	NKCX	RE	61383	70342	70299	61382
1524		**N**	NKCX	RE	61309	70305	70262	61308
1525		**N**	NKCX	RE	61235	70238	70232	61236
1526		**N**	NKCX	RE	61239	70240	70234	61240
1527		**N**	NKCX	RE	61237	70239	70233	61238
1528		**N**	NKCX	RE	61379	70340	70297	61378
1529		**N**	NKCX	RE	61355	70328	70285	61354
1530		**N**	NKCX	RE	61331	70316	70273	61330
1531		**N**	NKCX	RE	61233	70237	70231	61234
1532		**N**	NKCX	RE	61391	70346	71626	61390
1533		**N**	NKCX	RE	61393	70347	71627	61385
1534		**N**	NKCX	RE	61405	70353	71628	61404
1535		**N**	NKCX	RE	61397	70349	71629	61396
1536		**N**	NKCX	RE	61399	70350	71631	61398
1537		**N**	NKCX	RE	61229	70235	70229	61230
1538		**N**	NKCX	RE	61307	70304	70261	61306
1539		**N**	NKCX	RE	61401	70351	71632	61400
1540		**N**	NKCX	RE	61870	70343	70300	61384
1541		**N**	NKCX	RE	61409	70355	71633	61408
1542		**N**	NKCX	RE	61395	70348	71634	61394
1543		**N**	NKCX	RE	61323	70312	70269	61322
1544		**N**	NKCX	RE	61315	70308	70265	61314
1545		**N**	NKCX	RE	61359	70330	70287	61358
1546		**N**	NKCX	RE	61357	70329	70286	61356
1547	§	**N**	NKCX	RE	61329	70345	70272	61328
1548		**N**	NKCX	RE	61375	70338	70295	61374
1549		**N**	NKCX	RE	61339	70320	70277	61338
1550		**N**	NKCX	RE	61313	70307	70264	61312
551		**N**	NKCX	RE	61325	70313	70270	61324
552		**N**	NKCX	RE	61373	70337	70294	61372
553		**N**	NKCX	RE	61351	70306	70263	61350
554		**N**	NKCX	RE	61369	70335	70292	61368
555		**N**	NKCX	RE	61311	70326	70283	61310
556		**N**	NKCX	RE	61371	70336	70293	61370
557		**N**	NKCX	RE	61337	70331	70288	61360
558		**N**	NKCX	RE	61361	70319	70276	61336
559		**N**	NKCX	RE	61377	70339	70296	61376
560		**N**	NKCX	RE	61387	70344	70301	61386
561		**N**	NKCX	RE	61231	70604	70230	61232
562		**N**	NKCX	RE	61407	70236	70241	61406
563	†	**N**	NKCX	RE	61740	70575	70526	61741
564	†	**N**	NKCX	RE	61788	70599	70550	61789

1565	†	N	NKCX	RE	61762	70586	71711	61763
1566	†	N	NKCX	RE	61722	70566	70517	61723
1567	†	N	NKCX	RE	61786	70598	70549	61787
1568	†	N	NKCX	RE	61766	70588	70539	61767
1569	†	N	NKCX	RE	61782	70596	70547	61783
1570	†	N	NKCX	RE	61738	70574	70525	61739
1571	†	N	NKCX	RE	61806	70608	71636	61807
1572	†	N	NKCX	RE	61734	70572	70523	61735
1573	†	N	NKCX	RE	61726	70568	70519	61727
1574	†	N	NKCX	RE	61792	70601	71635	61793
1575	†	N	NKCX	RE	61768	70583	70540	61769
1576	†	N	NKCX	RE	61770	70590	70541	61771
1577	†	N	NKCX	RE	61718	70564	70515	61719
1578	†	N	NKCX	RE	61700	70555	70506	61701
1579	†	N	NKCX	RE	61772	70591	70542	61773
1580	†	N	NKCX	RE	61756	70589	70534	61757
1581	†	N	NKCX	RE	61784	70597	70548	61785
1582	†	N	NKCX	RE	61748	70603	71630	61797
1583	†	N	NKCX	RE	61746	70578	70529	61747
1584	†	N	NKCX	RE	61752	70581	70532	61753
1585	†	N	NKCX	RE	61710	70560	70511	61711
1586	†	N	NKCX	RE	61714	70562	70513	61715
1587	†	N	NKCX	RE	61764	70587	71625	61765
1588	†	N	NKCX	RE	61720	70044	70520	61721
1589	†	J	NKCX	RE	61742	70576	70527	61743
1590	†	N	NKCX	RE	61696	70553	70504	61697
1591	†	N	NKCX	RE	61790	70600	70551	61791
1592	†	N	NKCX	RE	61778	70594	70545	61779
1593	†	N	NKCX	RE	61730	70570	70521	61731
1594	†	N	NKCX	RE	61754	70582	70533	61755
1595	†	N	NKCX	RE	61704	70557	70508	61705
1596	†	N	NKCX	RE	61716	70563	70514	61717
1597	†	N	NKCX	RE	61708	70559	70510	61709
1598	†	N	NKCX	RE	61780	70595	70546	61781
1599	†	N	NKCX	RE	61706	70558	70509	61707
1600	†	N	NKCX	RE	61724	70567	70518	61725
1601	†	N	NKCX	RE	61776	70593	70544	61777
1602	†	N	NKCX	RE	61958	70565	70279	61959
1603	†	N	NKCX	RE	61728	70569	70298	61729
1604	†	N	NKCX	RE	61732	70571	70522	61733
1605	†	N	NKCX	RE	61712	70561	70512	61713
1606	†	N	NKCX	RE	61694	70552	70503	61695
1607	†	N	NKCX	RE	61698	70554	70505	61699
1608	†	N	NKCX	RE	61960	70659	70666	61961
1609	†	N	NKCX	RE	61744	70577	70528	61745
1610	†	N	NKCX	RE	61750	70580	70531	61751
1611	†	N	NKCX	RE	61758	70584	70537	61759
1612	†	N	NKCX	RE	61794	70602	70535	61795
1613	†	N	NKCX	RE	61760	70585	70536	61761
1614	†	N	NKCX	RE	61702	70556	70507	61703
1615	†	N	NKCX	RE	61956	70657	70664	61957
1616	†	N	NKCX	RE	61950	70654	70543	61951

1617	†	**N**	NKCX	RE	61800	70605	70661	61801
1618	†	**N**	NKCX	RE	61868	70043	70663	61869
1619	†	**N**	NKCX	RE	61952	70655	70662	61953
1620	†	**N**	NKCX	RE	61948	70653	70660	61949
1621	†	**N**	NKCX	RE	61810	70610	70524	61811

Former numbers of converted hauled stock:

71625 (4381)	71629 (3992)	71633 (4072)	71636 (4065)
71626 (3916)	71630 (3988)	71634 (4059)	71711 (3994)
71627 (3921)	71631 (4436)	71635 (3990)	71712 (4062)
71628 (3844)	71632 (4063)		

CLASS 421/3 & 421/6   FACELIFTED 4 Cig (PHASE 1)

DTCsoL–MBSO–TSO–DTCsoL. Express stock. Fitted with electric parking brake. Facelifted with new trim, fluorescent lighting in saloons, PA.

Electrical Equipment: 1963-type.
Bogies: Two Mk. 4 motor bogies (MBSO). B5 (SR) bogies (trailer cars).
Gangways: Throughout.
Traction Motors: Four EE507 of 185 kW.
Dimensions: 19.75 x 2.82 m.
Maximum Speed: 90 mph.

76022–75. DTCsoL. Dia. EE369. Lot 30740 Yk 1964–66. 18F 36S 2L. 35.5 t.
76076–129. DTCsoL. Dia. EE369. Lot. 30741 Yk 1964–66. 18F 36S 2L. 35 t.
62017–70. MBSO. Dia. ED264. Lot No. 30742 York 1964–66. 56S. 49 t.
70695–730. TSO. Dia. EH287. Lot No. 30743 York 1964–66. 72S. 31.5 t.
71044–97. TSO. Dia. EH287. Lot No. 30817 York 1970. 72S. 31.5 t. **71766–70.
TSO.** Dia. EH287. Lot No. 30744 York 1965–66. 72S. 31.5 t.

* Units reformed from Class 422 to enable all Class 422 power cars to have Mk. 6 motor bogies. Phase 1 units with phase 2 TSOs.
† As above, but not facelifted.

1701	(7312)	**N**	NSXX	BI	76087	62028	70706	76033
1702	(7326)	**N**	NSXX	BI	76101	62042	70720	76047
1703	(7322)	**N**	NSXX	BI	76097	62038	70716	76043
1704	(7317)	**N**	NSXX	BI	76092	62033	70711	76038
1705	(7301)	**N**	NSXX	BI	76076	62017	70695	76022
1706	(7319)	**N**	NSXX	BI	76094	62035	70713	76040
1707	(7309)	**N**	NSXX	BI	76084	62025	70703	76030
1708	(7335)	**N**	NSXX	BI	76110	62051	70729	76056
1709	(7328)	**N**	NSXX	BI	76103	62044	70722	76049
1710	(7303)	**N**	NSXX	BI	76078	62019	70697	76024
1711	(7033)	**N**	NSXX	BI	76114	62055	71766	76060
1712	(7304)	**N**	NSXX	BI	76079	62020	70698	76025
1713	(7047)	**N**	NSXX	BI	76128	62069	71767	76074
1714	(7302)	**N**	NSXX	BI	76077	62018	70696	76023
1715	(7307)	**N**	NSXX	BI	76082	62023	70701	76028
1716	(7325)	**N**	NSXX	BI	76100	62041	71768	76046
1717	(7308)	**N**	NSXX	BI	76083	62024	70702	76029
1718	(7306)	**N**	NSXX	BI	76081	62022	70700	76027
1719	(7035)	**N**	NSXX	BI	76116	62057	70719	76062

1720	(7038)		**N**	NSXX	BI	76098	62039	71769	76044
1721	(7315)		**N**	NSXX	BI	76090	62031	71709	76036
1722	(7331)		**N**	NSXX	BI	76106	62047	70725	76052
1723	(7332)		**N**	NSXX	BI	76107	62048	70726	76053
1724	(7039)		**N**	NSXX	BI	76120	62061	71770	76066
1725	(7313)		**N**	NSXX	BI	76088	62029	70707	76034
1726	(7334)		**N**	NSXX	BI	76109	62050	70728	76055
1727	(7336)		**N**	NSXX	BI	76111	62052	70730	76057
1728	(7324)		**N**	NSXX	BI	76099	62040	70718	76045
1729	(7329)		**N**	NSXX	BI	76104	62045	70723	76050
1730	(7330)		**N**	NSXX	BI	76105	62046	70724	76113
1731	(7320)		**N**	NSXX	BI	76095	62036	70714	76041
1732	(7321)		**N**	NSXX	BI	76096	62037	70715	76042
1733	(1757)	*	**N**	NSXX	BI	76122	62063	71047	76068
1734	(1751)	*	**N**	NSXX	BI	76063	62054	71044	76059
1735	(1754)	*	**N**	NSXX	BI	76117	62058	71050	76051
1736	(1753)	*	**N**	NSXX	BI	76124	62065	71052	76070
1737	(1755)	*	**N**	NSXX	BI	76121	62062	71058	76067
1738	(1752)	*	**N**	NSXX	BI	76129	62064	71046	76069
1739	(1759)	*	**N**	NSXX	BI	76123	62070	71066	76075
1740	(1762)	*	**N**	NSXX	BI	76126	62067	71097	76072
1741	(1114)		**N**	NSXX	BI	76089	62030	70708	76035
1742	(1111)		**N**	NSXX	BI	76086	62027	70705	76032
1743	(1756)	†	**N**	NSXX	BI	76118	62059	71065	76064
1744	(1758)	†	**N**	NSXX	BI	76127	62068	71064	76073
1760	(2110)	†	**N**	NSXX	BI	76115	62056	71067	76061
1761	(2111)	†	**N**	NSXX	BI	76112	62053	71068	76058

Former numbers of converted buffet cars:

| 71766 (69303) | 71768 (69317) | 71769 (69305) | 71770 (69308) |
| 71767 (69314) | | | |

CLASS 421/4   FACELIFTED 4 Cig (PHASE 2)

DTCsoL–MBSO–TSO–DTCsoL. Express stock. Facelifted with new trim, fluorescent lighting in saloons, PA.

Electrical Equipment: 1963-type.
Bogies: Two Mk. 6 motor bogies (MBSO). B5 (SR) bogies (trailer cars).
Gangways: Throughout.
Traction Motors: Four EE507 of 185 kW.
Dimensions: 19.75 x 2.82 m.
Maximum Speed: 90 mph.

DTCsoL. Dia. EE369. 18F 36S 2L. 35 t.
MBSO. Dia. ED264. 56S. 49t.
TSO. Dia. EH287. 72S. 31.5t.

For lot numbers see classes 421/2 or 422/2 except for:

76859. DTCsoL. Lot No. 30827 York 1972.
76860. DTCsoL. Lot No. 30828 York 1972.
62430. MBSO. Lot No. 30829 York 1972.

71106. TSO. Lot No. 30830 York 1972.

1800	(3515)	N	NSXX	BI	76599	62319	70958	76543
1801	(7427)	N	NSXX	BI	76777	62415	71095	76848
1803	(7430)	N	NSXX	BI	76780	62418	71098	76851
1804	(7428)	N	NSXX	BI	76778	62416	71096	76849
1805	(7432)	N	NSXX	BI	76782	62420	71100	76853
1806	(7433)	N	NKCX	RE	76783	62421	71101	76854
1807	(7434)	N	NKCX	RE	76784	62422	71102	76855
1808	(7435)	N	NKCX	RE	76785	62423	71103	76856
1809	(7436)	N	NKCX	RE	76786	62424	71104	76857
1810	(7437)	N	NKCX	RE	76787	62425	71105	76858
1811	(7431)	N	NKCX	RE	76781	62419	71099	76852
1812	(7407)	N	NKCX	RE	76757	62395	71075	76828
1813	(7438)	N	NKCX	RE	76859	62430	71106	76860
1831	(1254)	N	NSXX	BI	76598	62304	70984	76628
1832	(1269)	N	NSXX	BI	76719	62357	71037	76790
1833	(1238)	N	NSXX	BI	76582	62288	70968	76612
1834	(1258)	N	NSXX	BI	76566	62282	70988	76576
1835	(1257)	N	NSXX	BI	76601	62307	70987	76631
1836	(1249)	N	NSSX	EH	76593	62299	70979	76623
1837	(1272)	N	NSXX	BI	76722	62360	71040	76793
1838	(1243)	N	NSSX	EH	76587	62293	70973	76617
1839	(1263)	N	NKCX	RE	76607	62313	70993	76637
1840	(1274)	N	NKCX	RE	76724	62362	71042	76795
1841	(1259)	N	NKCX	RE	76603	62309	70989	76633
1842	(1275)	N	NKCX	RE	76725	62363	71043	76796
1843	(1281)	N	NKCX	RE	76731	62369	71049	76802
1844	(1245)	N	NSSX	EH	76589	62295	70975	76619
1845	(1255)	N	NSXX	BI	76544	62305	70985	76573
1846	(1287)	N	NSXX	BI	76737	62375	71055	76808
1847	(1256)	N	NSXX	BI	76600	62306	70986	76630
1848	(1261)	N	NSXX	BI	76605	62311	70991	76635
1849	(1246)	N	NSSX	EH	76590	62296	70976	76620
1850	(1268)	N	NSXX	BI	76718	62356	71036	76789
1851	(1271)	N	NSXX	BI	76721	62359	71039	76792
1852	(1247)	N	NSSX	EH	76591	62297	70977	76621
1853	(1262)	N	NSXX	BI	76606	62312	70992	76636
1854	(1288)	N	NSXX	BI	76738	62376	71056	76809
1855	(1270)	N	NSXX	BI	76720	62358	71038	76791
1856	(1289)	N	NSXX	BI	76739	62377	71057	76810
1857	(1266)	N	NSXX	BI	76610	62316	70996	76640
1858	(1260)	N	NSXX	BI	76604	62310	70990	76634
1859	(1277)	N	NSXX	BI	76727	62365	71045	76798
1860	(1202)	N	NSXX	BI	76752	62390	71070	76823
1861	(1285)	N	NSXX	BI	76735	62373	71053	76806
1862	(1286)	N	NSXX	BI	76736	62374	71054	76807
1863	(1292)	N	NSXX	BI	76742	62380	71060	76813
1864	(1291)	N	NSXX	BI	76741	62379	71059	76812
1865	(1295)	N	NSXX	BI	76745	62383	71063	76639
1866	(1293)	N	NSXX	BI	76743	62381	71061	76814
1867	(1294)	N	NSXX	BI	76744	62382	71062	76815

1868	(1201)	**N**	NSXX	BI	76751	62389	71069	76822
1869	(1203)	**N**	NSXX	BI	76753	62391	71071	76804
1870								
1871								
1872								
1873								
1874								
1875								
1876								
1877								
1878								
1879								
1880								
1881								
1882								
1883								
1884								
1885								
1886								
1887								
1888								
1889								
1890								

CLASS 431   MODIFIED 4 Rep.

DTSO–TBSK–TFK–DMSO–TBSK–DTSO. Express stock. New 6-car units formed from Class 438 cars with a Class 432 power car. The Class 438 cars were rebuilt from loco-hauled FKs TSOs and BSKs.

Electrical Equipment: 1966-type.
Bogies: Two Mk. 6 motor bogies (DMSO). B5(SR) bogies on driving ends. B4 bogies (others).
Gangways: Throughout.
Traction Motors: Four EE546 of 300 kW.
Dimensions: 19.66 × 2.82 m.
Maximum Speed: 90 mph.

DTSO. Dia. EE266. Lot No. 30764 York 1966–67. 64S. 32 t.
DMSO. Dia. EA260. Lot No. 30761 York 1967. 64S. 52.5 t.
70845. TCK. Dia. EH362. Lot No. 30856 York 1974. 30F 12S 2L. 33.5 t.
71163. TCK. Dia. EH362. Lot No. 30856 York 1974. 30F 12S 2L. 33.5 t.
TBSK. Dia. EJ260. Lot No. 30765 York 1966–67. 32S 1L. 35.5 t.

1901	**N**	NSSX	BM	76324	70830	71163	62142	70824	76322
1904	**N**	NSSX	BM	76321	70838	70845	62141	70839	76275

CLASS 422/2   4 Big (PHASE 2)

DTCsoL (A)–MBSO–TSRB–DTCsoL (B). Express stock.

Electrical Equipment: 1963-type.
Bogies: Two Mk. 6 motor bogies (MBSO). B5 (SR) bogies (trailer cars).
Gangways: Throughout.

Traction Motors: Four EE507 of 185 kW.
Dimensions: 19.75 x 2.82 m.
Maximum Speed: 90 mph.

76561–76570. DTCsoL(A). Dia. EE364. Lot No. 30802 York 1970. 18F 36S 2L. 35.5 t.
62279–62286. MBSO. Dia. ED260. Lot No. 30804 York 1970–71. 56S. 49 t.
62308. MBSO. Dia. ED260. Lot No. 30808 York 1971. 56S. 49 t.
69332–69339. TSRB. Dia. EN260. Lot No. 30805 York 1970. 40S. 35 t.
76573–76580. DTCsoL(B). Dia. EE363. Lot No. 30803 York 1970. 24F 28S 2L. 35.5 t.
76602. DTCsoL(A). Dia. EE363. Lot No. 30806 York 1970. 18F 36S 2L. 35.5 t.
76632. DTCsoL(B). Dia. EE363. Lot No. 30807 York 1970. 24F 28S 2L. 35.5 t.

2203	(7051)	N	NSXX	BI	76563	62279	69332	76629
2204	(7052)	N	NSXX	BI	76564	62280	69336	76574
2205	(7053)	N	NSXX	BI	76565	62281	69339	76575
2206	(7054)	N	NSXX	BI	76602	62308	69338	76632
2208	(7056)	N	NSXX	BI	76568	62284	69334	76578
2209	(7057)	N	NSXX	BI	76569	62285	69335	76575
2210	(7058)	N	NSXX	BI	76570	62286	69337	76580

CLASS 422/3 & 422/4(f)   4 Big (PHASE 2/1)

DTCsoL (A)–MBSO–TSRB–DTCsoL (B). Express stock. Units reformed from Class 421 to ensure that all Class 422 power cars have Mk. 6 motor bogies. Phase 2 units with phase 1 TSRBs (except for 69333 which is a phase 2 TSRB).

Electrical Equipment: 1963-type.
Bogies: Two Mk. 6 motor bogies (MBSO). B5 (SR) bogies (trailer cars).
Gangways: Throughout.
Traction Motors: Four EE507 of 185 kW.
Dimensions: 19.75 x 2.82 m.
Maximum Speed: 90 mph.

76726–76779. DTCsoL. Dia. EE364. Lot No. 30814 York 1970–72. 18F 36S 2L. 35.5 t.
62364–62417. MBSO. Dia. ED260. Lot No. 30816 York 1970. 56S. 49 t.
69301–69318. TSRB. Dia. EN260. Lot No. 30744 York 1966. 40S. 35 t.
69333. TSRB. Dia. EN260. Lot No. 30805 York 1970. 40S. 35 t.
76797–76850. DTCsoL. Dia. EE363. Lot No. 30815 York 1970–72. 24F 28S 2L. 35.5 t.

f Facelifted unit (except for 69333).

2251	(1276)	N	NSXX	BI	76726	62364	69302	76797
2252	(1278)	N	NSXX	BI	76728	62366	69312	76799
2253	(1284)	N	NSXX	BI	76734	62372	69313	76805
2254	(1282)	N	NSXX	BI	76732	62370	69306	76803
2255	(1290)	N	NSXX	BI	76740	62378	69310	76811
2256	(1297)	N	NSXX	BI	76747	62385	69307	76818
2257	(1279)	N	NSXX	BI	76729	62367	69311	76800
2258	(1296)	N	NSXX	BI	76746	62384	69316	76817
2259	(1298)	N	NSXX	BI	76748	62386	69318	76819
2260	(1299)	N	NSXX	BI	76749	62387	69304	76820

| 2261 | (1300) | N | NSXX | BI | 76750 | 62388 | 69301 | 76821 |
| 2262 | (1802) | N | NSXX | BI | 76779 | 62417 | 69333 | 76850 |

CLASS 412 REFURBISHED 4 Bep

DMSO (A)–TBCK–TRB–DMSO (B). Kent Coast Express Stock. Refurbished and renumbered from the 70xx series. Fitted with hopper ventilators, Inter-City 70 seats, fluorescent lighting and PA.

Electrical Equipment: 1957-type.
Bogies: One Mk 3B motor bogie (DMSO). Commonwealth trailer bogies.
§ Rebogied with Mk 6 motor bogies and B5(SR) trailer bogies.
* Rebogied with B5(SR) trailer bogies.
Gangways: Throughout.
Traction Motors: Four EE507 of 185 kW.
Dimensions: 19.75 x 2.82 m.
Maximum Speed: 90 mph.

DMSO (A). Dia. EA263. 64S. 44.15 t.
TBCK. Dia. EJ361. 24F 6S 2L. 36.17 t.
TRSB. Dia. EN261. 24S 1L + 9 longitudinal buffet chairs. 35.5 t.
DMSO (B). Dia. EA264. 64S. 43.54 t.
Lot numbers are as follows, all cars being built at Ashford/Eastleigh:

61736–61809. Lot No. 30619 1960–61.		**70354.** Lot No. 30456 1959.	
61954–61955. Lot No. 30708 1963.		**70573–70609.** Lot No. 30621 1960–61.	
69341–69347. Lot No. 30622 1961.		**70656.** Lot No. 30709 1963.	

2301	(7019)	N	NSSX	EH	61804	70607	69341	61805
2302	(7194)	N	NSSX	EH	61774	70592	69342	61809
2303	(7208)	N	NSSX	EH	61954	70606	69347	61955
2304	(7175)	N	NSSX	EH	61736	70573	69344	61737
2305		N	NSSX	EH	61798	70354	69345	61799
2306	(7021)	N	NSSX	EH	61808	70609	69346	61775
2307	(7018)	N	NSSX	EH	61802	70656	69343	61803

Former numbers of converted buffet cars:

69341 (69014)	69343 (69018)	69345 (69013)	69347 (69015)
69342 (69019)	69344 (69012)	69346 (69016)	

CLASS 442 WESSEX EXPRESS STOCK

DTFsoL–TSOL(A)–MBRSM–TSOL(B)–DTSOL. New express stock for Waterloo–Bournemouth–Weymouth service. Air conditioned (heat pump system). Power-operated sliding plug doors. PA. Can be hauled and heated by any BR ETH fitted locomotive. Multiple working with class 33/1 and 73 locomotives.

Electrical Equipment: 1986-type.
Bogies: Mk 6 motor bogies (MBRSM). T4 trailer bogies.
Gangways: Throughout.
Traction Motors: Four EE546 of 300 kW recovered from class 432.
Dimensions: 22.57 x 2.74 m.
Maximum Speed: 100 mph.

DTFsoL. Dia. EE160. Lot No. 31030 Derby 1988–89. 48F 1L. Public Telephone.

30.06 t.
TSOL (A). Dia. EH288. Lot No. 31032 Derby 1988–89. 80S 2L. 35.26 t.
MBRSM. Dia. ED265. Lot No. 31034 Derby 1988–89. 14S. 54.10 t.
TSOL (B). Dia. EH289. Lot No. 31033 Derby 1988–89. 76S 2L + wheelchair space. + 2 tip-up seats. 35.36 t.
DTSOL. Dia. EE273. Lot No. 31031 Derby 1988–89. 78S 1L. 39.06 t.

2401	N	NSSX	BM	77382	71818	62937	71842	77406
2402	N	NSSX	BM	77383	71819	62938	71843	77407
2403	N	NSSX	BM	77384	71820	62941	71844	77408
2404	N	NSSX	BM	77385	71821	62939	71845	77409
2405	N	NSSX	BM	77386	71822	62944	71846	77410
2406	N	NSSX	BM	77389	71823	62942	71847	77411
2407	N	NSSX	BM	77388	71824	62943	71848	77412
2408	N	NSSX	BM	77387	71825	62945	71849	77413
2409	N	NSSX	BM	77390	71826	62946	71850	77414
2410	N	NSSX	BM	77391	71827	62948	71851	77415
2411	N	NSSX	BM	77392	71828	62940	71858	77422
2412	N	NSSX	BM	77393	71829	62947	71853	77417
2413	N	NSSX	BM	77394	71830	62949	71854	77418
2414	N	NSSX	BM	77395	71831	62950	71855	77419
2415	N	NSSX	BM	77396	71832	62951	71856	77420
2416	N	NSSX	BM	77397	71833	62952	71857	77421
2417	N	NSSX	BM	77398	71834	62953	71852	77416
2418	N	NSSX	BM	77399	71835	62954	71859	77423
2419	N	NSSX	BM	77400	71836	62955	71860	77424
2420	N	NSSX	BM	77401	71837	62956	71861	77425
2421	N	NSSX	BM	77402	71838	62957	71862	77426
2422	N	NSSX	BM	77403	71839	62958	71863	77427
2423	N	NSSX	BM	77404	71840	62959	71864	77428
2424	N	NSSX	BM	77405	71841	62960	71865	77429

Names:

62937 BEAULIEU	62943 THOMAS HARDY
62938 COUNTY OF HAMPSHIRE	62945 COUNTY OF DORSET
62941 THE NEW FOREST	62955 BBC SOUTH TODAY

CLASS 423   4 Vep

DTCsoL–MBSO–TSO–DTCsoL. Outer suburban stock.

Electrical Equipment: 1963-type.
Bogies: Two Mk. 4 motor bogies (MBSO). B5 (SR) bogies (trailer cars).
Gangways: Throughout.
Traction Motors: Four EE507 of 185 kW.
Dimensions: 19.75 x 2.82 m.
Maximum Speed: 90 mph.

62121–40. MBSO. Dia. ED261. Lot No. 30760 Derby 1967. 58S. 49 t.
62182–216. MBSO. Dia. ED261. Lot No. 30773 York 1967–68. 58S. 49 t.
62217–66. MBSO. Dia. ED263. Lot No. 30794 York 1968–69. 58S. 49 t.
62267–76. MBSO. Dia. ED263. Lot No. 30800 York 1970. 58S. 49 t.
62317–54. MBSO. Dia. ED263. Lot No. 30813 York 1970–73. 58S. 49 t.

62435–75. MBSO. Dia. ED263. Lot No. 30851 York 1973–74. 58S. 49 t.
70781–800. TSO. Dia. EH276. Lot No. 30759 Derby 1967. 98S. 31.5 t.
70872–906. TSO. Dia. EH276. Lot No. 30772 York 1967–68. 98S. 31.5 t.
70907–56. TSO. Dia. EH283. Lot No. 30793 York 1968–69. 98S. 31.5 t.
70957–66. TSO. Dia. EH283. Lot No. 30801 York 1970. 98S. 31.5 t.
70997–71034. TSO. Dia. EH283. Lot No. 30812 York 1970–73. 98S. 31.5 t.
71115–55. TSO. Dia. EH283. Lot No. 30852 York 1973–74. 98S. 31.5 t.
76230–69. DTCsoL. Dia. EE365. Lot No. 30758 York 1967. 18F 46S 1L. 35 t.
76333–402. DTCsoL. Dia. EE365. Lot No. 30771 Yk 1967–68. 18F 46S 1L. 35 t.
76441–540. DTCsoL. Dia. EE367. Lot No. 30792 Yk 1968–69. 18F 46S 1L. 35 t.
76541–60. DTCsoL. Dia. EE367. Lot No. 30799 York 1970. 18F 46S 1L. 35 t.
76641–716. DTCsoL. Dia. EE367. Lot No. 30811 Yk 1970–73. 18F 46S 1L. 35 t.
76861–942. DTCsoL. Dia. EE368. Lot No. 30853 Yk 1973–74. 18F 46S 1L. 35 t.
Renumbered from 7700–7894 respectively with the last three digits unchanged.

3001	*	**N**	NSBX	WD	76230	62121	70781	76231
3002		**N**	NSBX	WD	76233	62122	70782	76232
3003		**N**	NSBX	WD	76234	62123	70783	76235
3006	*	**N**	NSBX	WD	76241	62126	70786	76240
3007		**N**	NSBX	WD	76243	62127	70787	76242
3008	*	**N**	NSBX	WD	76244	62128	70788	76245
3009	*	**N**	NSBX	WD	76246	62129	70789	76247
3010	*	**N**	NSBX	WD	76369	62130	70790	76249
3012	*	**N**	NSBX	WD	76252	62132	70792	76253
3013	*	**N**	NSBX	WD	76255	62133	70793	76254
3014	*	**N**	NSBX	WD	76257	62134	70794	76248
3015		**N**	NSBX	WD	76258	62135	70795	76259
3016	*	**N**	NSBX	WD	76261	62339	70796	76260
3017		**N**	NSBX	WD	76262	62137	70797	76263
3018	*	**N**	NSBX	WD	76265	62138	70875	76264
3019	*	**N**	NSBX	WD	76267	62349	70799	76266
3020	*	**N**	NSBX	WD	76269	62140	70800	76268
3026	*	**N**	NSBX	WD	76344	62187	70877	76343
3030	*	**N**	NSBX	WD	76352	62191	70881	76351
3032		**N**	NSBX	WD	76356	62193	70883	76355
3034		**N**	NSBX	WD	76360	62195	70885	76359
3035		**N**	NSBX	WD	76362	62196	70890	76361
3037		**N**	NSBX	WD	76366	62198	70888	76365
3046		**N**	NSBX	WD	76384	62207	70897	76383
3075		**N**	NSBX	WD	76480	62236	70926	76479
3078	*	**N**	NSBX	WD	76486	62229	70929	76485
3080	*	**N**	NSXX	BI	76490	62241	70931	76489
3088		**N**	NSXX	BI	76506	62249	70939	76505
3092		**N**	NSXX	BI	76514	62253	70943	76513
3093		**N**	NSXX	BI	76516	62254	70944	76515
3098		**N**	NSXX	BI	76364	62259	70949	76525
3099		**N**	NSXX	BI	76528	62260	70950	76527
3120		**N**	NSBX	WD	76649	62321	71001	76650
3134		**N**	NSXX	BI	76677	62335	71015	76678
3139	*	**N**	NSXX	BI	76687	62340	71020	76688
3147	*	**N**	NSXX	BI	76703	62348	71028	76704
3149	*	**N**	NSXX	BI	76707	62350	71030	76708

3152	*	**N**	NSXX	BI	76465	62353	71033	76714
3153	*	**N**	NSBX	WD	76715	62354	71034	76716
3154	*	**N**	NSBX	WD	76861	62435	71115	76862
3155	*	**N**	NSBX	WD	76863	62238	71116	76864
3156	*	**N**	NSBX	WD	76865	62437	71117	76866
3157	*	**N**	NSBX	WD	76867	62438	71118	76868
3158	*	**N**	NSBX	WD	76869	62439	71119	76870
3159		**N**	NSBX	WD	76871	62440	71120	76872
3160	*	**N**	NSBX	WD	76873	62441	71121	76874
3161	*	**N**	NKCX	RE	76875	62442	71122	76876
3162	*	**N**	NKCX	RE	76877	62443	71123	76878
3163		**N**	NKCX	RE	76879	62444	71124	76880
3164		**N**	NKCX	RE	76881	62445	71125	76882
3165	*	**N**	NKCX	RE	76883	62446	71126	76884
3166	*	**N**	NKCX	RE	76885	62447	71127	76886
3167	*	**N**	NKCX	RE	76887	62448	71128	76888
3169		**N**	NKCX	RE	76891	62450	71130	76892
3170	*	**N**	NKCX	RE	76893	62451	71131	76894
3171	*	**N**	NKCX	RE	76895	62452	71132	76896
3172	*	**N**	NKCX	RE	76899	62453	71133	76898
3173	*	**N**	NKCX	RE	76899	62454	71134	76900
3175	*	**N**	NKCX	RE	76903	62456	71136	76904
3176	*	**N**	NKCX	RE	76905	62457	71137	76906
3177	*	**N**	NKCX	RE	76907	62458	71138	76908
3178	*	**N**	NKCX	RE	76909	62463	71139	76910
3179		**N**	NKCX	RE	76911	62460	71140	76912
3180	*	**N**	NKCX	RE	76913	62461	71141	76914
3181		**N**	NKCX	RE	76915	62462	71142	76916
3182	*	**N**	NKCX	RE	76917	62459	71143	76918
3183	*	**N**	NKCX	RE	76919	62464	71144	76920
3184		**N**	NKCX	RE	76921	62465	71145	76922
3185		**N**	NKCX	RE	76923	62466	71146	76924
3186		**N**	NKCX	RE	76925	62467	71147	76926
3187	*	**N**	NKCX	RE	76927	62468	71148	76928
3188	*	**N**	NKCX	RE	76929	62469	71149	76930
3189	*	**N**	NKCX	RE	76931	62470	71150	76932
3190	*	**N**	NKCX	RE	76933	62471	71151	76934
3191		**N**	NKCX	RE	76935	62472	71152	76936
3192		**N**	NKCX	RE	76937	62473	71153	76938
3193		**N**	NKCX	RE	76939	62474	71154	76940
3194		**N**	NKCX	RE	76941	62475	71155	76942

CLASS 413/2   4 Cap

DTCsoL–MBSO–MLSO–DTSsoL. Formed 1982 by the combination of pairs of class 414 (2 Hap) units. Driving equipment removed from motor cars, plus one set of guard's equipment. Driving trailers all declassified.

Electrical Equipment: 1951-type.
Bogies: Mk. 4.
Gangways: Non-gangwayed.
Traction Motors: Two EE507 of 185 kW.

Dimensions: 19.49 x 2.82 m.
Maximum Speed: 90 mph.

All built at Eastleigh on frames laid at Ashford.

65393–65396. MBSO/MLSO. Dia. EB269. Lot No. 30314 1957. 84S. 42 t.
65398–65401. MBSO/MLSO. Dia. EB269. Lot No. 30319 1957. 84S. 42 t.
65404–65429. MBSO/MLSO. Dia. EB269. Lot No. 30388 1958. 84S. 42 t.
77115–77118. DTCsoL. Dia. EE221. Lot No. 30316 1957. 19F 50S 2L. 32.5 t.
77123. DTCsoL. Dia. EE221. Lot No. 30320 1957. 19F 50S 2L. 32.5 t.
77126–77150. DTCsoL. Dia. EE221. Lot No. 30389 1958. 19F 50S 2L. 32.5 t.

3201	**N**	NKSX	GI	77120	65398	65401	77123
3202	**N**	NKSX	GI	77118	65396	65412	77134
3203	**N**	NKSX	GI	77117	65395	65424	77146
3204	**N**	NKCX	GI	77132	65410	65420	77142
3205	**N**	NKCX	GI	77135	65413	65422	77144
3207	**N**	NKCX	GI	77126	65404	65428	77150
3208	**N**	NKCX	GI	77147	65425	65429	77537
3211	**N**	NKCX	GI	77115	65393	65427	77149

CLASS 413/3   4 Cap

DTCsoL–MBSO–MLSO–DTCsoL. Formed 1982 by the combination of pairs of class 414 (2 Hap) units. Driving equipment removed from motor cars, plus one set of guard's equipment. Driving trailers all declassified.

Electrical Equipment: 1957-type.
Bogies: Mk. 4.
Gangways: Non-gangwayed.
Traction Motors: Two EE507 of 185 kW.
Dimensions: 19.49 x 2.82 m.
Maximum Speed: 90 mph.

MBSO/MLSO. Dia. EB270. Lot No. 30452 Afd/Elh 1958–59. 84S. 42 t.
DTCsoL. Dia. EE222. Lot No. 30453 Afd/Elh 1958–59. 19F 50S 2L. 32.5 t.

3301	**N**	NKSX	GI	75373	61253	61255	75375
3302	**N**	NKSX	GI	75361	61241	61244	75364
3303	**N**	NKSX	GI	75370	61250	61252	75372
3304	**N**	NKSX	GI	75402	61282	61283	75403
3305	**N**	NKSX	GI	75399	61279	61302	75422
3306	**N**	NKSX	GI	75374	61254	61256	75376
3307	**N**	NKSX	GI	75378	61258	61271	75391
3311	**N**	NKCX	GI	75411	61291	61297	75417

New batch being formed with the motor cars as outer vehicles. MBSO–2DTCsoL–MBSO.

3321	**N**	NKSX	GI	61268	75388	75398	61278
3322	**N**	NKSX	GI	61295	75415	75420	61300
3323	**N**	NKSX	GI	61262	75382	75393	61273
3324	**N**	NKSX	GI	61270	75390	75423	61303
3325	**N**	NKSX	GI	61261	75381	75418	61298
3333	**N**	NSBX	WD (S)	65405	77127	75735	61683

CLASS 423/1   Facelifted 4 Vep.

DTCsoL–MBSO–TSO–DTCsoL. For details see 3000 series. Facelifted with fluorescent lighting, PA. The MBSO has been modified to seat 76S.

3404	(3441)	N	NSBX	WD	76378	62261	70894	76236
3405	(3005)	N	NSBX	WD	76239	62271	70785	76238
3411	(3011)	N	NSBX	WD	76251	62342	70791	76250
3421	(3168)	N	NKCX	RE	76889	62449	71129	76890
3422	(3040)	N	NKCX	RE	76372	62201	70891	76371
3423	(3061)	N	NKCX	RE	76452	62222	70912	76451
3424	(3031)	N	NKCX	RE	76354	62185	70882	76353
3425	(3023)	N	NSBX	WD	76338	62192	70874	76358
3426	(3047)	N	NSBX	WD	76386	62208	70898	76385
3427	(3041)	N	NSBX	WD	76374	62184	70892	76373
3428	(3062)	N	NSBX	WD	76454	62223	70913	76453
3429	(3021)	N	NSBX	WD	76334	62202	70872	76333
3430	(3028)	N	NSBX	WD	76348	62189	70879	76347
3431	(3064)	N	NSBX	WD	76458	62182	70915	76457
3432	(3054)	N	NSBX	WD	76400	62225	70905	76399
3433	(3057)	N	NSBX	WD	76444	62215	70908	76443
3434	(3066)	N	NSBX	WD	76462	62218	70917	76461
3435	(3025)	N	NSXX	BI	76342	62228	70876	76341
3436	(3029)	N	NSXX	BI	76350	62190	70880	76349
3437	(3027)	N	NSXX	BI	76346	62186	70878	76345
3438	(3100)	N	NSXX	BI	76530	62262	70951	76529
3439	(3055)	N	NSXX	BI	76402	62227	70906	76401
3440	(3102)	N	NSXX	BI	76534	62188	70953	76533
3442	(3081)	N	NSXX	BI	76492	62216	70932	76491
3443	(3082)	N	NSXX	BI	76494	62263	70933	76493
3444	(3038)	N	NSXX	BI	76368	62204	70889	76367
3445	(3060)	N	NKCX	RE	76450	62242	70911	76449
3446	(3101)	N	NKCX	RE	76532	62243	70952	76531
3447	(3044)	N	NKCX	RE	76380	62199	70895	76379
3448	(3042)	N	NKCX	RE	76376	62221	70886	76375
3449	(3022)	N	NKCX	RE	76336	62205	70873	76335
3450	(3060)	N	NKCX	RE	76460	62203	70916	76459
3451	(3079)	N	NKCX	RE	76488	62240	70930	76487
3452		N	NKCX	RE	76340	62183	71021	76690
3453	(3045)	N	NKCX	RE	76382	62226	70896	76381
3454		N	NKCX	RE	76390	62200	70798	76389
3455	(3048)	N	NSBX	WD	76388	62206	70899	76387
3456	(3063)	N	NSBX	WD	76456	62210	70914	76455
3457	(3050)	N	NSBX	WD	76392	62197	70901	76391
3458	(3051)	N	NSBX	WD	76394	62209	70902	76393
3459	(3052)	N	NSBX	WD	76396	62224	70903	76370
3460	(3105)	N	NSXX	BI	76540	62211	70956	76539
3461	(3104)	N	NSXX	BI	76538	62212	70955	76537
3462	(3103)	N	NSXX	BI	76536	62213	70954	76535
3463	(3053)	N	NSXX	BI	76398	62266	70904	76397
3464	(3056)	N	NSXX	BI	76442	62265	70907	76441

3465	(3106)	**N**	NSXX	BI	76542	62264	70957	76541
3466	(3067)	**N**	NSBX	WD	76464	62214	70918	76463
3467	(3058)	**N**	NSBX	WD	76446	62217	70909	76445
3468	(3059)	**N**	NSBX	WD	76448	62267	70910	76447
3469	(3108)	**N**	NSBX	WD	76546	62220	70959	76545
3470	(3083)	**N**	NSBX	WD	76496	62220	70934	76495
3471	(3084)	**N**	NKCX	RE	76498	62269	70935	76497
3472	(3085)	**N**	NKCX	RE	76500	62244	70936	76499
3473	(3086)	**N**	NKCX	RE	76502	62245	70937	76339
3474	(3087)	**N**	NKCX	RE	76504	62246	70938	76503
3475	(3111)	**N**	NKCX	RE	76552	62270	70962	76551
3476	(3109)	**N**	NSXX	BI	76548	62247	70960	76547
3477	(3110)	**N**	NSXX	BI	76550	62248	70961	76549
3478	(3122)	**N**	NSXX	BI	76653	62125	71003	76654
3479	(3123)	**N**	NSBX	WD	76655	62272	71004	76656
3480	(3072)	**N**	NSBX	WD	76474	62323	70923	76473
3481	(3119)	**N**	NSBX	WD	76647	62324	70900	76648
3482	(3124)	**N**	NSBX	WD	76657	62320	71005	76658
3483	(3126)	**N**	NSBX	WD	76661	62233	71007	76662
3484	(3073)	**N**	NSBX	WD	76476	62325	70924	76475
3485	(3089)	**N**	NSBX	WD	76508	62327	70940	76507
3486	(3074)	**N**	NSBX	WD	76478	62234	70925	76477
3487	(3090)	**N**	NSBX	WD	76510	62250	70941	76509
3488	(3127)	**N**	NSBX	WD	76663	62235	71008	76664
3489	(3128)	**N**	NSBX	WD	76665	62251	71009	76666
3490	(3143)	**N**	NSBX	WD	76695	62238	71024	76696
3491	(3076)	**N**	NKCX	RE	76337	62436	70927	76481
3492	(3129)	**N**	NKCX	RE	76667	62344	71010	76668
3493	(3130)	**N**	NKCX	RE	76669	62237	71011	76670
3494	(3133)	**N**	NKCX	RE	76675	62330	71014	76676
3495	(3145)	**N**	NKCX	RE	76699	62331	71026	76700
3496	(3132)	**N**	NKCX	RE	76673	62334	71013	76674
3497	(3131)	**N**	NKCX	RE	76671	62346	71012	76672
3498	(3146)	**N**	NKCX	RE	76701	62333	71027	76702
3499	(3174)	**N**	NKCX	RE	76901	62347	71135	76902
3500	(3070)	**N**	NKCX	RE	76470	62455	70921	76469
3501	(3091)	**N**	NSXX	BI	76512	62332	70942	76511
3502	(3150)	**N**	NSXX	BI	76709	62252	71031	76710
3503	(3136)	**N**	NSXX	BI	76681	62231	71017	76682
3504	(3151)	**N**	NSXX	BI	76711	62351	71032	76712
3505	(3071)	**N**	NSXX	BI	76472	62352	70922	76471
3506	(3112)	**N**	NSXX	BI	76554	62317	70963	76553
3507	(3114)	**N**	NSXX	BI	76558	62232	70965	76557
3508	(3117)	**N**	NSBX	WD	76643	62273	70998	76644
3509	(3115)	**N**	NSBX	WD	76560	62275	70966	76559
3510	(3116)	**N**	NSBX	WD	76641	62210	70997	76642
3511	(3118)	**N**	NSBX	WD	76645	62276	70999	76646
3512	(3135)	**N**	NSXX	BI	76679	62337	71016	76680
3513	(3141)	**N**	NSXX	BI	76691	62136	71022	76692
3514	(3137)	**N**	NSXX	BI	76683	62136	71018	76684
3516	(3142)	**N**	NSBX	WD	76693	62268	71023	76694
3517	(3138)	**N**	NSXX	BI	76685	62338	71019	76686

3518	(3140)	**N**	NSXX	BI	76689	62343	70887	76363
3519	(3113)	**N**	NSBX	WD	76556	62274	70964	76555
3520	(3144)	**N**	NSBX	WD	76697	62131	71025	76698
3521	(3077)	**N**	NSBX	WD	76484	62345	70928	76483
3522	(3148)	**N**	NSXX	BI	76705	62341	71029	76706
3523	(3121)	**N**	NSBX	WD	76651	62139	71002	76652
3524	(3068)	**N**	NSBX	WD	76466	62322	70919	76395
3525	(3096)	**N**	NSXX	BI	76522	62229	70947	76521
3526	(3097)	**N**	NSXX	BI	76524	62326	70948	76523
3527	(3095)	**N**	NSXX	BI	76520	62258	70946	76519
3528	(3094)	**N**	NSXX	BI	76518	62256	70945	76517
3529	(3125)	**N**	NSBX	WD	76659	62257	71006	76660
3530	(3069)	**N**	NSBX	WD	76468	62230	70920	76467

3531
3532
3533
3534
3535
3536
3537
3538
3539
3540
3541
3542
3543
3544
3545
3546
3547
3548
3549
3550
3551
Spare   (S)   62194

CLASS 414/3   2 Hap

DMBSO–DTCsoL.

Electrical Equipment: 1957-type.
Bogies: Mk. 4.
Gangways: Non-gangwayed.
Traction Motors: Two EE507 of 185 kW.
Dimensions: 19.49 x 2.82 m.
Maximum Speed: 90 mph.

DMBSO. Dia. EB270. Lot No. 30452 Ashford/Eastleigh 1959. 84S. 42 t.
DTCsoL. Dia. EE362. Lot No. 30453 Ashford/Eastleigh 1959. 19F 60S 1L. 32.5 t.

4308	**N**	NKCX	RE	61275	75395
4309	**N**	NKCX	RE	61276	75396

4311	**N**	NKCX	RE	61287	75407
4313	**N**	NKCX	RE	61290	75410
4314	**N**	NKCX	RE	61294	75414

CLASS 405 1936 type 4 Sub

DMBSO–TS–TSO–DMBSO. This unit is kept for special workings and is not compatible electrically with other SR EMUs. It has automatic air brakes, but no electro-pneumatic brakes.

Electrical Equipment: 1936-type.
Bogies: Central 43" motor bogies and SR standard trailer bogies.
Gangways: Non-gangwayed.
Traction Motors: Two EE507 of 185 kW.
Dimensions: 19.05 x 2.82 m. (outer cars), 18.90 x 2.82 m (inner cars).
Maximum Speed: 75 mph.

DMBSO. Dia. EB265. Lot No. 3638 Eastleigh 1951. 82S. 42 t.
TS. Dia. EH262. Lot No. 3351 Eastleigh 1947. 120S. 27 t.
TSO. Dia. EH266. Lot No. 3384 Eastleigh 1948. 102S. 26 t.

| 4732 | **SG** NSXX | BI | 12795 10239 12354 12796 |

CLASS 415/1 SR DESIGN 4 EPB

DMBSO–2TSO–DMBSO. Originally formed with a TS and a TSO, but all except 5001 now have 2TSO.

Electrical Equipment: 1951-type.
Bogies: Central 40" motor bogies and SR standard trailer bogies.
Gangways: Non-gangwayed.
Traction Motors: Two EE507 of 185 kW.
Dimensions: 19.05 x 2.82 m. (outer cars), 18.90 x 2.82 m (inner cars).
Maximum Speed: 75 mph (90 mph e).
Non-standard livery: Southern Region green.

Built to various SR lots as shown, all at Lancing/Eastleigh.

† Converted from class 405 (4 Sub) TS.

14001–14026. DMBSO. Dia. EB266. Lot No. 3638 1952. 82S. 40 t.
14039–14053. DMBSO. Dia. EB266. Lot No. 3756 1953. 82S. 40 t.
14069–14208. DMBSO. Dia. EB266. Lot No. 3757 1953–4. 82S. 40 t.
14221–14310. DMBSO. Dia. EB266. Lot No. 4016 1954–5. 82S. 40 t.
14311–14405. DMBSO. Dia. EB266. Lot No. 4099 1955–6. 82S. 40 t.
14413–14426. DMBSO. Dia. EB266. Lot No. 4172 1956. 82S. 40 t.
14433–14510. DMBSO. Dia. EB266. Lot No. 4173 1956–7. 82S. 40 t.
14522–14523. DMBSO. Dia. EB267. Lot No. 4281 1957. 84S. 40 t. Former class 418/0 vehicles.

15015. TSO†. Lot No. 3463 1948. 102S. 27 t.
15101–15113. TSO. Dia. EH270. Lot No. 3638 1951–2. 102S. 27 t.
15118–15127. TSO. Dia. EH270. Lot No. 3756 1953. 102S. 27 t.
15135–15158. TSO. Dia. EH270. Lot No. 3757 1953–4. 102S. 27 t.
15207. TS. Dia. EH268. Lot No. 4016 1954–55. 120S. 28 t.
15234–15277/279–283. TSO. Dia. EH270. Lot No. 4016 1954–5. 102S. 27 t.

15334–15382. TSO. Dia. EH270. Lot No. 4099 1955–6. 102S. 27 t.
15395–15401. TSO. Dia. EH270. Lot No. 4172 1956. 102S. 27 t.
15405–15444. TSO. Dia. EH270. Lot No. 4173 1956–7. 102S. 27 t.

BR design DMBSOs (ex class 416/2):

65300–65310. DMBSO. Dia. EB269. Lot No. 30114 Ashford/Eastleigh 1954. 84S. 42 t.
65383. DMBSO. Dia. EB269. Lot No. 30314 Ashford/Eastleigh 1956. 84S. 42 t.

5001		**SG**	NKSX	SG	14001	15207	15101	14002
5104			NKSX	SG	14207	15409	15157	14208
5114			NKSX	SG (S)	14227	15426	15242	14228
5115			NKSX	SG	14229	15350	15243	14230
5121			NKSX	SG	14413	15247	15249	14241
5124			NKSX	SG	14248	15248	15252	14247
5126			NKSX	SG	14252	15244	15254	14376
5131			NKSX	SG	14261	15412	15259	14262
5134			NKSX	SG	65383	15444	15262	14268
5138			NKSX	SG	14275	15423	15266	14276
5139			NKSX	SG	14277	15442	15267	14278
5145			NKSX	SG	14290	15158	15273	14289
5153			NKSX	SG	14305	15256	15281	14306
5154			NKSX	SG	14308	15279	15282	14307
5155			NKSX	SG	14309	15107	15283	14310
5156			NKSX	SG	14311	15272	15334	14312
5157			NKSX	SG	14313	15381	15335	14314
5159			NKSX	SG	14317	15105	15337	14318
5160			NKSX	SG	14319	15268	15338	14320
5169			NKSX	SG	65303	15109	15347	14338
5170			NKSX	SG	14339	15245	15348	14340
5176			NKSX	SG	14352	15396	15354	14351
5177			NKSX	SG	14354	15257	15355	14353
5185			NKSX	SG	14369	15277	15363	14370
5190			NKSX	SG	14380	15361	15368	14379
5194			NKSX	SG	14388	15275	15372	14387
5195			NKSX	SG	14389	15239	15373	14390
5196			NKSX	SG	14392	15399	15374	14391
5209			NKSX	SG	14039	15395	15397	14417
5210			NKSX	SG	14420	15263	15398	14419
5213			NKSX	SG	14425	15353	15401	14426
5217			NKSX	SG	14434	15366	15405	14433
5220			NKSX	SG	14439	15349	15408	14260
5226			NKSX	SG	14451	15280	15414	14452
5232			NKSX	SG	14464	15422	15420	14463
5240			NKSX	SG	14103	15425	15428	14480
5243			NKSX	SG	14405	15375	15356	14485
5248			NKSX	SG	14492	15443	15346	14510
5261			NKSX	SG	65300	15154	15413	65310
5264		e	NKSX	SG	14522	15258	15147	14523
5266	(5020)		NKSX	SG	14418	15234	15382	14040
5267	(5027)		NKSX	SG	14053	15123	15127	14042
268	(5035)		NKSX	SG	14069	15113	15135	14070

5269	(5039)	NKSX	SG	14078	15118	15139	14094
5270	(5040)	NKSX	SG	14080	15122	15140	14079
5275	(5049)	NKSX	SG	14098	15271	15149	14097
5276	(5051)	NKSX	SG	14101	15143	15151	14102
5277	(5052)	NKSX	SG	14104	15103	15152	14495
5279		NKSX	SG	14257	15429	15380	14258
5280		NKSX	SG	14232	15421	15410	14231
5281		NKSX	SG	14274	15427	15411	14414
Spare		NKSX	SG (S)	14242	15015		14026
Spare		NKSX	SG (S)	14294			14293
Spare		NKSX	SG (S)				14383
Spare		NKSX	SG (S)	14221			14222
Spare		NKSX	SG (S)	14373			14336

CLASS 415/4   FACELIFTED SR DESIGN 4 EPB

DMBSO–2TSO–DMBSO. Facelifted with new trim, fluorescent lighting, PA.

Electrical Equipment: 1951-type.
Bogies: Central 40″ motor bogies and SR standard trailer bogies.
Gangways: Non-gangwayed.
Traction Motors: Two EE507 of 185 kW.
Dimensions: 19.05 x 2.82 m. (outer cars), 18.90 x 2.82 m (inner cars).
Maximum Speed: 75 mph. (90 mph e).

Built to various SR lots as shown, all at Lancing/Eastleigh.
† Converted from class 405 (4 Sub) TS. Vehicles in the 154xx series were converted on facelifting.
§ Converted from class 415 TS.

14003–14030. DMBSO. Dia. EB277. Lot No. 3638 1952. 82S. 40 t.
14037–14066. DMBSO. Dia. EB277. Lot No. 3756 1953. 82S. 40 t.
14071–14206. DMBSO. Dia. EB277. Lot No. 3757 1953–4. 82S. 40 t.
14211–14304. DMBSO. Dia. EB277. Lot No. 4016 1954–5. 82S. 40 t.
14315–14410. DMBSO. Dia. EB277. Lot No. 4099 1955–6. 82S. 40 t.
14411–14430. DMBSO. Dia. EB277. Lot No. 4172 1956. 82S. 40 t.
14431–14520. DMBSO. Dia. EB277. Lot No. 4173 1956–7. 82S. 40 t.
14521–14570. DMBSO. Dia. EB278. Lot No. 4281 1957. 82S. 40 t. Former class 418/0 vehicle or 416/3 vehicles.

15001/10. 15466/67/71/74/75. TSO†. Dia. EH270. Lot No. 1094 1946. 102S 27 t.
15002/19/23/27/30/39–42/48/50. 15450. TSO†. Lot No. 3351 1947. 102S 27 t.
15011/20/29/37/44/51/52/56–58/61–62/65/66/68–71/73/75–78. TSO†. Lot No. 3463 1948. 102S. 27 t.
15012/54/74. TSO†. Lot No. 3386 1948. 102S. 27 t.
15033/34/36/45–47/53/55/59/60/67. TSO†. Lot No. 3231 1947. 102S. 27 t
15104–15115. TSO. Lot No. 3638 1951–2. 102S. 27 t.
15119–15128. TSO. Lot No. 3756 1953. 102S. 27 t.
15136–15182. TSO§. Lot No. 3757 1953–4. 102S. 27 t.
15184–15227/230–265. TSO§. Lot No. 4016 1954–5. 102S. 27 t.
15285–15383. TSO§. Lot No. 4099 1955–6. 102S. 27 t.

15384–15403. TSO§. Lot No. 4172 1956. 102S. 27 t.
15404–15448. TSO. Lot No. 4173 1956–7. 102S. 27 t.
15449/65/79/80. TSO†. Lot No. 3384 1948. 102S. 27 t.
15451. TSO†. Lot No. 3617 1948. 102S. 27 t.
15452/59/61/64/69/73. TSO†. Lot No. 3504 1949. 102S. 27 t.
15453/63. TSO†. Lot No. 3385 1948. 102S. 27 t.
15454/56/57/58/60/62/68/70/72/76/78. TSO†. Lot No. 3464 1949. 102S. 27 t.
15481. TSO†. Lot No. 3505 1950. 102S. 27 t.
15455/77. TSO†. Lot No. 3506 1950. 102S. 27 t.

e—Express gear ratio.

5401	e	**N**	NKSX	SG		14556	15449	15450	14521
5402			NKSX	SG		14449	15464	15465	14407
5403		**N**	NSLX	SU		14286	15174	15221	14285
5404			NKSX	SG		14435	15036	15406	14436
5405		**N**	NSLX	SU		14470	15053	15216	14469
5406			NKSX	SG		14303	15230	15285	14356
5407		**N**	NKSX	SG		14428	15392	15060	14427
5408		**N**	NSLX	SU		14297	15227	15313	14298
5409		**N**	NKSX	SG		14494	15065	15047	14206
5410	e	**N**	NKSX	SG		14540	15386	15304	14528
5411		**N**	NSLX	SU		14475	15056	15192	14476
5412			NKSX	SG		14415	15451	15452	14304
5413		**N**	NSLX	SU		14396	15326	15191	14395
5414		**N**	NSLX	SU		14441	15039	15182	14442
5415		**N**	NSLX	SU		14465	15040	15051	14466
5416		**N**	NSLX	SU		14421	15389	15324	14422
5419		**N**	NKSX	SG		14473	15055	15058	14474
5420		**N**	NSLX	SU		14240	15198	15202	14239
5421		**N**	NSLX	SU		14500	15068	15073	14499
5422		**N**	NSLX	SU		14467	15209	15050	14468
5423		**N**	NKSX	SG		14511	15074	15212	14512
5424		**N**	NKSX	SG		14447	15042	15052	14448
5425	e	**N**	NSLX	SU		14538	15453	15454	14570
5426		**N**	NKSX	SG		14517	15077	15066	14518
5427		**N**	NKSX	SG		14453	15045	15046	14454
5428		**N**	NKSX	SG		14430	15393	15061	14429
5429		**N**	NKSX	SG		14410	15333	15383	14409
5430		**N**	NKSX	SG		14496	15438	15437	14509
5431		**N**	NKSX	SG		14423	15390	15400	14424
5432		**N**	NKSX	SG		14416	15044	15447	14486
5433		**N**	NKSX	SG		14472	15054	15424	14471
5434		**N**	NKSX	SG		14497	15067	15455	14498
5435		**N**	NKSX	SG		14491	15403	15431	14267
5436		**N**	NKSX	SG		14534	15456	15457	14543
5437		**N**	NKSX	SG		14411	15384	15394	14412
5438		**N**	NKSX	SG		14530	15459	15458	14547
5440			NKSX	SG	(S)	14514	15075	15445	14513
5441		**N**	NKSX	SG		14397	15327	15377	14398
5442		**N**	NKSX	SG		14537	15460	15461	14554
5443		**N**	NKSX	SG		14504	15070	15440	14503
5444		**N**	NKSX	SG		14535	15463	15462	14553

5445		**N**	NKSX	SG	14527	15020	15351	14529
5446		**N**	NKSX	SG	14531	15466	15467	14541
5447		**N**	NKSX	SG	14532	15468	15469	14550
5448		**N**	NKSX	SG	14539	15470	15471	14548
5449			NKSX	SG	14438	15037	15407	14437
5450			NKSX	SG	14533	15472	15473	14552
5451	e		NKSX	SG (S)	14526	15474	15475	14551
5452	e	**N**	NKSX	SG	14536	15477	15476	14563
5453	e		NKSX	SG	14545	15479	15478	14525
5454	e	**N**	NKSX	SG	14264	15481	15480	14524
5455		**N**	NKSX	SG	14062	15023	15027	14054
5456		**N**	NKSX	SG	14482	15059	15001	14481
5457		**N**	NKSX	SG	14502	15069	15439	14501
5458		**N**	NKSX	SG	14431	15034	15404	14432
5459		**N**	NKSX	SG	14505	15071	15441	14506
5460		**N**	NKSX	SG	14515	15076	15446	14516
5461		**N**	NKSX	SG	14519	15078	15448	14520
5462		**N**	NKSX	SG	14021	15011	15111	14022
5463		**N**	NKSX	SG	14037	15019	15119	14038
5464		**N**	NKSX	SG	14081	15166	15159	14082
5465			NKSX	SG	14236	15196	15208	14350
5466			NKSX	SG	14004	15002	15220	14003
5467		**N**	NKSX	SG	14006	15062	15177	14005
5468			NKSX	SG	14212	15184	15332	14211
5470			NKSX	SG	14315	15286	15215	14316
5471		**N**	NKSX	SG	14255	15206	15231	14256
5472			NKSX	SG	14508	15295	15169	14458
5473			NKSX	SG	14493	15029	15170	14058
5474			NKSX	SG	14065	15033	15224	14066
5475			NKSX	SG	14019	15010	15048	14020
5476			NKSX	SG	14016	15316	15319	14015
5477			NKSX	SG	14013	15180	15233	14057
5478			NKSX	SG	14059	15030	15167	14060
5479			NKSX	SG	14322	15289	15317	14321
5480			NKSX	SG	14555	15210	15291	14263
5481			NKSX	SG	14330	15293	15226	14329
5482			NKSX	SG	14017	15009	15297	14018
5483			NKSX	SG	14052	15175	15329	14051
5485		**N**	NKSX	SG	14105	15178	15185	14106
5486		**N**	NKSX	SG	14071	15161	15125	14072
5487		**N**	NKSX	SG	14361	15309	15359	14362
5488		**N**	NKSX	SG	14386	15321	15371	14385
5489		**N**	NKSX	SG	14024	15012	15112	14023
5490		**N**	NKSX	SG	14056	15433	15128	14205
5491		**N**	NKSX	SG	14029	15136	15115	14030
5492		**N**	NKSX	SG	14223	15246	15240	14224
5493		**N**	NKSX	SG	14028	15237	15114	14027
5494		**N**	NKSX	SG	14073	15236	15137	14074
5495		**N**	NKSX	SG	14095	15265	15148	14096
5496		**N**	NKSX	SG	14400	15336	15378	14399
5497		**N**	NKSX	SG	14246	15104	15251	14245
Spare	*	**N**	NSLX	SU (U)			15432	14025

Old numbers of cars converted from class 405:

	0	1	2	3	4	5	6	7	8	9
15000–9		10398	10345	10333	10203	11454	10253	10228	10335	10201
15010–9	10391	10174	10169	10189	10184	10277	10251	10292	10238	10332
15020–9	10177	10254	10175	10309	10266	10456	10298	10281	10272	10202
15030–9	10278	10192	10280	10460	10470	10229	10459	10222	11451	10246
15040–9	10285	10322	10283	10275	10224	10452	10466	10468	10299	10176
15050–9	10260	10211	10223	10471	10167	10451	10190	10193	10188	10450
15060–9	10467	10226	10178	10194	10469	10212	10186	10453	10183	10225
15070–9	10180	10191	10179	10185	10168	10187	10227	10204	10182	10195
15080–4	11456	10208	10207	10395	11485					
15450–9	10337	8980	12361	12360	10139	12404	10133	10143	10132	12381
15460–9	10125	12393	10131	12359	12389	12355	10444	10448	10128	12390
15470–9	10124	10439	12391	10137	10446	10445	10129	12402	10141	12353
15480–1	12358	12398								
15449:	10480									

CLASSES 415/6 & 415/7   BR DESIGN 4 EPB

DMBSO(A)–2TSO–DMBSO(B). All remaining units have been facelifted with new trim, fluorescent lighting and PA. Units with express gear ratio (e) are classified Class 415/7.

Electrical Equipment: 1951-type.
Bogies: Mark 3C (Mk 3D*) bogies. † Mk 3C motor bogie and Mk 3D trailer bogies.
Gangways: Non-gangwayed.
Traction Motors: Two EE507 of 185 kW.
Dimensions: 19.50 x 2.82 m. (outer cars), 19.35 x 2.82 m (inner cars).
Maximum Speed: 75 mph (90 mph e).

DMBSO(A). Dia. EB271. Lot No. 30582 Eastleigh 1959–61. 82S. 41 t.
DMBSO(B). Dia. EB272. Lot No. 30582 Eastleigh 1959–61. 82S. 41 t.
TSO. Dia. EH271. Lot No. 30583 Eastleigh 1959–61. 102S. 29.5 t.

e Express gear ratio.

5601	*		NKSX	SG	61550	70409	70410	61551
5602		N	NKSX	SG	61582	70441	70442	61583
5603	*		NKSX	SG	61538	70397	70398	61539
5604		N	NKSX	SG	61588	70447	70448	61589
5605	*	N	NKSX	SG	61540	70399	70400	61541
5606	*	N	NKSX	SG	61536	70395	70396	61537
5610		N	NKSX	SG	61566	70425	70426	61567
5611		N	NKSX	SG	61570	70429	70430	61571
5612	*	N	NKSX	SG	61542	70401	70402	61543
5613	*	N	NKSX	SG	61532	70391	70392	61533
5614	*	N	NKSX	SG	61546	70405	70406	61547
5615		N	NKSX	SG	61612	70471	70472	61613
5616		N	NKSX	SG	61576	70435	70436	61577
5617		N	NKSX	SG	61592	70451	70452	61593
5619		N	NKSX	SG	61562	70421	70422	61563
5620		N	NKSX	SG	61602	70461	70462	61603

5621	*	N	NKSX	SG	61520	70380	70379	61521
5622		N	NKSX	SG	61560	70419	70420	61561
5623	e	N	NKCX	RE	61578	70437	70438	61579
5624	e	N	NKCX	RE	61572	70431	70432	61573
5625	e	N	NKCX	RE	61608	70455	70468	61609
5626	e	N	NKCX	RE	61590	70449	70450	61591
5627	e	N	NKCX	RE	61600	70460	70459	61601
5628	e	N	NKCX	RE	61604	70464	70463	61605

CLASS 455/7

DTSO–MSO–TSO–DTSO. Sliding doors. Disc brakes. Fluorescent lighting
PA. Second series with TSOs originally in class 508. Pressure ventilation.

Bogies: BT13 (DTSO), BP27 (MSO), BX1 (TSO).
Gangways: Through gangwayed.
Traction Motors: Four EE507 of 185 kW.
Dimensions: 19.83 x 2.82 m. (outer cars), 19.92 x 2.82 m (inner cars).
Maximum Speed: 75 mph.

DTSO. Dia. EE218. Lot No. 30976 York 1984–85. 74S. 29.5 t.
MSO. Dia. EC203. Lot No. 30975 York 1984–85. 84S. 45 t.
TSO. Dia. EH219. Lot No. 30944 York 1977–80. 86S. 25.48 t.

5701	N	NSBX	WD	77727	62783	71545	77728
5702	N	NSBX	WD	77729	62784	71547	77730
5703	N	NSBX	WD	77731	62785	71540	77732
5704	N	NSBX	WD	77733	62786	71548	77734
5705	N	NSBX	WD	77735	62787	71565	77736
5706	N	NSBX	WD	77737	62788	71534	77738
5707	N	NSBX	WD	77739	62789	71536	77740
5708	N	NSBX	WD	77741	62790	71560	77742
5709	N	NSBX	WD	77743	62791	71532	77744
5710	N	NSBX	WD	77745	62792	71566	77746
5711	N	NSBX	WD	77747	62793	71542	77748
5712	N	NSBX	WD	77749	62794	71546	77750
5713	N	NSBX	WD	77751	62795	71567	77752
5714	N	NSBX	WD	77753	62796	71539	77754
5715	N	NSBX	WD	77755	62797	71535	77756
5716	N	NSBX	WD	77757	62798	71564	77758
5717	N	NSBX	WD	77759	62799	71528	77760
5718	N	NSBX	WD	77761	62800	71557	77762
5719	N	NSBX	WD	77763	62801	71558	77764
5720	N	NSBX	WD	77765	62802	71568	77766
5721	N	NSBX	WD	77767	62803	71553	77768
5722	N	NSBX	WD	77769	62804	71533	77770
5723	N	NSBX	WD	77771	62805	71526	77772
5724	N	NSBX	WD	77773	62806	71561	77774
5725	N	NSBX	WD	77775	62807	71541	77776
5726	N	NSBX	WD	77777	62808	71556	77778
5727	N	NSBX	WD	77779	62809	71562	77780
5728	N	NSBX	WD	77781	62810	71527	77782
5729	N	NSBX	WD	77783	62811	71550	77784

5730	N	NSBX	WD	77785	62812	71551	77786
5731	N	NSBX	WD	77787	62813	71555	77788
5732	N	NSBX	WD	77789	62814	71552	77790
5733	N	NSBX	WD	77791	62815	71549	77792
5734	N	NSBX	WD	77793	62816	71531	77794
5735	N	NSBX	WD	77795	62817	71563	77796
5736	N	NSBX	WD	77797	62818	71554	77798
5737	N	NSBX	WD	77799	62819	71544	77800
5738	N	NSBX	WD	77801	62820	71529	77802
5739	N	NSBX	WD	77803	62821	71537	77804
5740	N	NSBX	WD	77805	62822	71530	77806
5741	N	NSBX	WD	77807	62823	71559	77808
5742	N	NSBX	WD	77809	62824	71543	77810
5750	N	NSBX	WD	77811	62825	71538	77812

CLASS 455/8

DTSO–MSO–TSO–DTSO. Sliding doors. Disc brakes. Fluorescent lighting. PA. First series. Pressure ventilation.

Bogies: BP20 (MSO), BT13 (trailer cars).
Gangways: Through gangwayed.
Traction Motors: Four EE507 of 185 kW.
Dimensions: 19.83 x 2.82 m. (outer cars), 19.92 x 2.82 m (inner cars).
Maximum Speed: 75 mph.

DTSO. Dia. EE218. Lot No. 30972 York 1982–84. 74S. 29.5 t.
MSO. Dia. EC203. Lot No. 30973 York 1982–84. 84S. 45.6 t.
TSO. Dia. EH221. Lot No. 30974 York 1982–84. 84S. 27.1 t.

5800	N	NSLX	SU	77631	62736		77634
5801	N	NSLX	SU	77579	62709	71637	77580
5802	N	NSLX	SU	77581	62710		77582
5803	N	NSLX	SU	77583	62711	71639	77584
5804	N	NSLX	SU	77585	62712	71640	77586
5805	N	NSLX	SU	77587	62713	71641	77588
5806	N	NSLX	SU	77589	62714	71642	77590
5807	N	NSLX	SU	77591	62715	71643	77592
5808	N	NSLX	SU	77593	62716	71644	77594
5809	N	NSLX	SU	77595	62717	71645	77596
5810	N	NSLX	SU	77597	62718	71646	77598
5811	N	NSLX	SU	77599	62719	71647	77600
5812	N	NSLX	SU	77601	62720	71648	77602
5813	N	NSLX	SU	77603	62721	71649	77604
5814	N	NSLX	SU	77605	62722	71650	77606
5815	N	NSLX	SU	77607	62723	71651	77608
5816	N	NSLX	SU	77609	62724	71652	77633
5817	N	NSLX	SU	77611	62725	71653	77612
5818	N	NSLX	SU	77613	62726	71654	77614
5819	N	NSLX	SU	77615	62727	71655	77616
5820	N	NSLX	SU	77617	62728	71656	77618
5821	N	NSLX	SU	77619	62729	71657	77620

5822	**N**	NSLX	SU	77621	62730	71658	77622
5823	**N**	NSLX	SU	77623	62731	71659	77624
5824	**N**	NSLX	SU	77637	62732	71660	77626
5825	**N**	NSLX	SU	77627	62733	71661	77628
5826	**N**	NSLX	SU	77629	62734	71662	77680
5827	**N**	NSLX	SU	77610	62735	71663	77632
5829	**N**	NSLX	SU	77635	62737	71665	77636
5830	**N**	NSLX	SU	77625	62743	71666	77638
5831	**N**	NSLX	SU	77639	62739	71667	77640
5832	**N**	NSLX	SU	77641	62740	71668	77642
5833	**N**	NSLX	SU	77643	62741	71669	77644
5834	**N**	NSLX	SU	77645	62742	71670	77646
5835	**N**	NSLX	SU	77647	62738	71671	77648
5836	**N**	NSLX	SU	77649	62744	71672	77650
5837	**N**	NSLX	SU	77651	62745	71673	77652
5838	**N**	NSBX	WD	77653	62746	71674	77654
5839	**N**	NSBX	WD	77655	62747	71675	77656
5840	**N**	NSBX	WD	77657	62748	71676	77658
5841	**N**	NSBX	WD	77659	62749	71677	77660
5842	**N**	NSBX	WD	77661	62750	71678	77662
5843	**N**	NSBX	WD	77663	62751	71679	77664
5844	**N**	NSBX	WD	77665	62752	71680	77666
5845	**N**	NSBX	WD	77667	62753	71681	77668
5846	**N**	NSBX	WD	77669	62754	71682	77670
5847	**N**	NSBX	WD	77671	62755	71683	77672
5848	**N**	NSBX	WD	77673	62756	71684	77674
5849	**N**	NSBX	WD	77675	62757	71685	77676
5850	**N**	NSBX	WD	77677	62758	71686	77678
5851	**N**	NSBX	WD	77679	62759	71687	77630
5852	**N**	NSBX	WD	77681	62760	71688	77682
5853	**N**	NSBX	WD	77683	62761	71689	77684
5854	**N**	NSBX	WD	77685	62762	71690	77686
5855	**N**	NSBX	WD	77687	62763	71691	77688
5856	**N**	NSBX	WD	77689	62764	71692	77690
5857	**N**	NSBX	WD	77691	62765	71693	77692
5858	**N**	NSBX	WD	77693	62766	71694	77694
5859	**N**	NSBX	WD	77695	62767	71695	77696
5860	**N**	NSBX	WD	77697	62768	71696	77698
5861	**N**	NSBX	WD	77699	62769	71697	77700
5862	**N**	NSBX	WD	77701	62770	71698	77702
5863	**N**	NSBX	WD	77703	62771	71699	77704
5864	**N**	NSBX	WD	77705	62772	71700	77706
5865	**N**	NSBX	WD	77707	62773	71701	77708
5866	**N**	NSBX	WD	77709	62774	71702	77710
5867	**N**	NSBX	WD	77711	62775	71703	77712
5868	**N**	NSBX	WD	77713	62776	71704	77714
5869	**N**	NSBX	WD	77715	62777	71705	77716
5870	**N**	NSBX	WD	77717	62778	71706	77718
5871	**N**	NSBX	WD	77719	62779	71707	77720
5872	**N**	NSBX	WD	77721	62780	71708	77722
5873	**N**	NSBX	WD	77723	62781	71709	77724
5874	**N**	NSBX	WD	77725	62782	71710	77726

Class 303 No. 303 048 has been repainted in original "blue train livery". It is leaving Cambridge with the 11.25 special to Stansted Airport during the NSE day on 14th September 1991.   *John Augustson*

Class 304 No. 304 010 leaves Altrincham with a service to Alderley Edge on May 1991. The Altrincham service was due to close at the end of December and re-open as part of the 'Metrolink' LRT system.   *L.A. Nixon*

▲ Class 305 No. 305 502 in Regional stripes livery at Prestonpans on 26th
1991 with the 15.35 Haymarket–North Berwick service.   *Alex Fo*

▼ Class 308 No. 308 139 in Network SouthEast livery at Ripple Lane on 7th M
1991 with the 14.20 Southend Central–Fenchurch St. via Tilbury   *Brian Der*

Class 309 'Clacton' unit No. 309 626 on a London Liverpool St.–Ipswich working
Colchester during June 1991.   *Michael J Collins*

Class 310/1 No. 310 104 in Midline livery leaves Birmingham New St. with the
51 service to Coventry.   *Hugh Ballantyne*

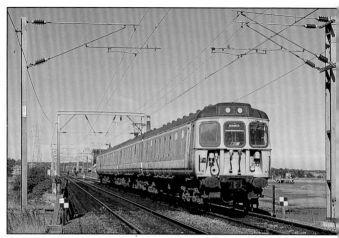

▲ Class 312 No. 312 710 crosses the River Stour at Manningtree on 20th J
1990 with the 16.35 Ipswich–Colchester.   *Hugh Ballant*

▼ Class 313 No. 313 021 at Richmond in the 13.03 North London Line servic
North Woolwich on 17th September 1991. This route is entirely third rail.
                                                            Alex Dasi-Su

Class 314 No. 314 214 leaves Garscadden on 2nd August 1990 with an e.c.s. working to Yoker CS. The unit is in Strathclyde PTE livery. *John Augustson*

Class 317 No. 317 337 with a King's Cross–Cambridge working on 31st July '0. *L A Nixon*

▲ Class 318 No. 318 269 approaches Irvine with the 17.45 Ayr–Glasgow Cen on 2nd August 1990. *John Augus*

▼ Class 320 No. 320 320 at Yoker Yard on 25th May 1991. The destination indic says "GIGGLESWICK"! *Norman Barring*

Class 319 'Thameslink' unit No. 319 055 near South Croydon with the 14.45 London Victoria–Tattenham Corner on 20th April 1991.

Alex Dasi-Sutton

▲ Class 321/9 No. 321 901, the first of the three for West Yorkshire PTE, at Doncaster on a launch special from York to Leeds on 25th July 1991. The unit is in 'Metro' livery.
Colin J Marsh

▼ Class 322 'Stansted Express' Unit No. 322 481 in distinctive livery at Hackney Downs on 25th April 1991 with the 15.30 Stansted Airport–London Liverpool Street.
Chris Wilson

The two remaining Class 438 '4TC' units have been painted in their original in blue livery for use on Network SouthEast special and charter services, and ve regained their original numbers. No. 410 is seen at Bournemouth depot on th October 1991. *Brain Morrison*

A trio of Class 411 (4 Cep) 'Kent Coast' units near Petts Wood on 13th August 91 form the 14.30 London Charing Cross to Ramsgate and Margate. the first o units are 1614 and 1591. *Alex Dasi-Sutton*

The 17.51 London Victoria—Hastings headed by Class 422 /4 Bin] unit 2203 at Southerham Jn near Lewes on 24th

A pair of Class 442 (4 Wes) 'Wessex Express' units Nos. 2419 and 2424 at Raynes Park with the 06.38 Weymouth–London Waterloo on 5th June 1991. *Chris Wilson*

Class 423/1 (refurbished 4 Vep) unit 3510 with Class 414/3 No. 4309 in the rear drive at Byfleet and New Haw station on 21st August 1991. *Hugh Ballantyne*

Class 45 No. 45001 'Royal Signals' at Kettering Research allocation to the 'Cross Country' railway on 12th April 1991

Class 414/3 (2 Hap) No. 4320 at Raynes Park on 5th June 1991 with the 07.28 :smouth–London Waterloo. *Chris Wilson*

Facelifted SR-design Class 415/4 (4-EPB) with 5436 at Selhurst depot on 6th e 1990. *Colin J Marsden*

▲ Class 455/7 unit No. 5707 passes Nine Elms on 13th September 1991. *A J W*

▼ Class 455/9 unit No. 5909 heads for Waterloo near Battersea on 25th May 199?
Dave McAle

The new 2-car units of Class 456 are only just going into service, having been
~ayed because the driver's seats were in the wrong position for viewing platform
~u.s. 456 007 is seen at West Croydon with the 11.36 to Wimbledon on 4th
~ober 1991.   *Chris Wilson*

Class 416/3 (SR design 2 EPB) No. 6321 at Wandsworth Road with the 13.52
~don Victoria–London Bridge on 13th September 1991.   *Chris Wilson*

▲ Class 483 sets Nos. 483 005 and 483 007 leave Sandown, Isle of Wight w the 13.51 Shanklin–Ryde Pier Head on 1st September 1990. *John Augusts*

▼ Merseyside is now the only outpost of third-rail electrification outside Netw SouthEast. Class 508 No. 508 120 approaches Wallasey Village with a N Brighton–Liverpool service on 3rd November 1990. *John Augusts*

CLASS 455/9

DTSO–MSO–TSO–DTSO. Sliding doors. Disc brakes. Fluorescent lighting.
PA. Third series. Convection heating.

Bogies: BP20 (MSO), BT13 (trailer cars).
Gangways: Through gangwayed.
Traction Motors: Four EE507 of 185 kW.
Dimensions: 19.83 x 2.82 m. (outer cars), 19.92 x 2.82 m (inner cars).
Maximum Speed: 75 mph.

DTSO. Dia. EE226. Lot No. 30991 York 1985. 74S. 29.5 t.
MSO. Dia. EC206. Lot No. 30992 York 1985. 84S. 45.6 t.
TSO. Dia. EH224. Lot No. 30993 York 1985. 84S. 27.1 t.
TSO n. Dia. EH224. Lot No. 30932 Derby 1981. 84S. 27.1 t.

*–Chopper control. §–Tread brakes.
n Formerly class 210 No. 60400.

5901		N	NSBX	WD	77813	62826	71714	77814
5902		N	NSBX	WD	77815	62827	71715	77816
5903		N	NSBX	WD	77817	62828	71716	77818
5904		N	NSBX	WD	77819	62829	71717	77820
5905		N	NSBX	WD	77821	62830	71718	77822
5906		N	NSBX	WD	77823	62831	71719	77824
5907		N	NSBX	WD	77825	62832	71720	77826
5908		N	NSBX	WD	77827	62833	71721	77828
5909		N	NSBX	WD	77829	62834	71722	77830
5910		N	NSBX	WD	77831	62835	71723	77832
5911		N	NSBX	WD	77833	62836	71724	77834
5912	*	N	NSBX	WD	77835	62837	71725	77836
5913	§	N	NSBX	WD	77837	62838	71726	77838
5914	§	N	NSBX	WD	77839	62839	71727	77840
5915	§	N	NSBX	WD	77841	62840	71728	77842
5916	*	N	NSBX	WD	77843	62841	71729	77844
5917	*	N	NSBX	WD	77845	62842	71730	77846
5918	*n	N	NSBX	WD	77847	62843	67400	77848
5919	*	N	NSBX	WD	77849	62844	71638	77850
5920	*	N	NSBX	WD	77851	62845	71733	77852
Spare		N	NSBX	WD (S)		71651	71731	71732

CLASS 416/2   BR DESIGN 2 EPB

DMBSO–DTSso.

Electrical Equipment: 1951-type.
Bogies: Mk. 3D.
Gangways: Non-gangwayed.
Traction Motors: Two EE507 of 185 kW.
Dimensions: 19.49 x 2.82 m.
Maximum Speed: 75 mph.

65301–65304. DMBSO. Dia. EB269. Lot No. 30114 Afd/Elh 1954. 84S. 42 t.
65327–65341. DMBSO. Dia. EB269. Lot No. 30119 Afd/Elh 1954. 84S. 42 t.

65344–65365. DMBSO. Dia. EB269. Lot No. 30167 Afd/Elh 1955. 84S. 42 t
65367–65392. DMBSO. Dia. EB269. Lot No. 30314 Afd/Elh 1956–58. 84S. 42 t
77501–77504. DTSso. Dia. EE264. Lot No. 30115 Afd/Elh 1954. 102S. 30.5 t
77512–77526. DTSso. Dia. EE264. Lot No. 30120 Afd/Elh 1954. 102S. 30.5 t
77529–77550. DTSso. Dia. EE264. Lot No. 30168 Afd/Elh 1955. 102S. 30.5 t
77552–77577. DTSso. Dia. EE264. Lot No. 30315 Afd/Elh 1956–58. 102S.
30.5 t.

Note: 77537/9 are DTSO and seat 92S. (Dia. EE275).

6202	NKSX	SG	65301	77501
6203	NKSX	SG	65302	77502
6205	NKSX	SG	65304	77504
6213	NKSX	SG	65327	77512
6217	NKSX	SG	65331	77516
6218	NKSX	SG (S)	65332	77517
6221	NKSX	SG (S)	65335	77520
6222	NKSX	SG (S)	65336	77521
6223	NKSX	SG	65337	77522
6224	NKSX	SG	65338	77523
6225	NKSX	SG	65339	77524
6226	NKSX	SG	65340	77525
6227	NKSX	SG	65341	77526
6230	NKSX	SG	65344	77529
6231	NKSX	SG	65345	77530
6235	NKSX	SG	65349	77534
6236	NKSX	SG	65350	77535
6237	NKSX	SG	65351	77536
6238	NKSX	SG (S)	65352	77151
6239	NKSX	SG	65353	77538
6240	NKSX	SG	65354	77539
6241	NKSX	SG	65355	77540
6243	NKSX	SG (S)	65357	77542
6244	NKSX	SG (S)	65358	77543
6245	NKSX	SG	65359	77544
6247	NKSX	SG	65361	77546
6249	NKSX	SG	65363	77548
6251	NKSX	SG	65365	77550
6253	NKSX	SG	65367	77552
6255	NKSX	SG	65369	77554
6256	NKSX	SG	65370	77555
6259	NKSX	SG	65373	77558
6260	NKSX	SG	65374	77559
6261	NKSX	SG	65375	77560
6262	NKSX	SG	65376	77561
6263	NKSX	SG	65377	77562
6264	NKSX	SG	65378	77563
6265	NKSX	SG	65379	77564
6267	NKSX	SG	65381	77566
6268	NKSX	SG	65382	77567
6270	NKSX	SG	65384	77569
6271	NKSX	SG	65385	77570
6272	NKSX	SG	65386	77571

6273	NKSX	SG	65387	77572
6274	NKSX	SG	65388	77573
6275	NKSX	SG	65389	77574
6277	NKSX	SG (S)	65391	77576
6278	NKSX	SG	65392	77577

CLASS 416/3   SR DESIGN 2 EPB

DMBSO–DTSso. These units were made by producing new bodies for former 2 Nol underframes. All have now been facelifted with new seat trim, fluorescent lighting and PA.

Electrical Equipment: 1951-type.
Bogies: Central 40″ motor bogies and SR standard trailer bogies.
Gangways: Non-gangwayed.
Traction Motors: Two EE507 of 185 kW.
Dimensions: 19.05 x 2.82 m.
Maximum Speed: 75 mph.

14283. DMBSO. Dia. EB269. Lot No. 4016 Eastleigh 1954–5. 82S. 40 t.
14542–14590. DMBSO. Dia. EB269. Lot No. 4281 Eastleigh 1957–9. 82S. 40 t.
DTSO. Dia. EE269. Lot No. 4281 Eastleigh 1957–9. 92S. 30 t.

6301	N	NSLX	SU	14577	16124
6302	N	NSLX	SU	14580	16121
6303	N	NSLX	SU	14576	16120
6304	N	NSLX	SU	14589	16133
6305	N	NSLX	SU	14587	16131
6306	N	NSLX	SU	14571	16115
6307	N	NSLX	SU	14573	16117
6308	N	NSLX	SU	14564	16108
6309	N	NSLX	SU	14562	16106
6310	N	NSLX	SU	14558	16118
6311	N	NSLX	SU	14565	16109
6312	N	NSLX	SU	14579	16123
6313	N	NSLX	SU	14574	16102
6314	N	NSLX	SU	14586	16130
6315	N	NSLX	SU	14590	16134
6316	N	NSLX	SU	14559	16103
6317	N	NSLX	SU	14578	16122
6318	N	NSLX	SU	14566	16110
6319	N	NSLX	SU	14568	16112
6320	N	NSLX	SU	14561	16105
6321	N	NSLX	SU	14283	16128
6322	N	NSLX	SU	14488	16119
6323	N	NSLX	SU	14581	16125
6324	N	NSLX	SU	14560	16104
6325	N	NSLX	SU	14567	16111
6326	N	NSLX	SU	14585	16129
6327	N	NSLX	SU	14572	16116
6328	N	NSLX	SU	14582	16126
6329	N	NSLX	SU	14542	16114
6330	N	NSLX	SU	14588	16132

6331	N	NSLX	SU	14583	16127
6332		NSLX	SU	14569	16113
6333		NSLX	SU	14557	16101
6334		NSLX	SU	14546	16107

CLASS 416/4   FACELIFTED BR DESIGN 2 EPB

DMBSO–DTSO. Facelifted units with new trim, fluorescent lighting and PA.

Electrical Equipment: 1951-type.
Bogies: Mk. 3D.
Gangways: Non-gangwayed.
Traction Motors: Two EE507 of 185 kW.
Dimensions: 19.49 x 2.82 m.
Maximum Speed: 75 mph.

65305–65309. DMBSO. Dia. EB281. Lot No. 30114 Afd/Elh 1954. 82S. 42 t.
65328–65334. DMBSO. Dia. EB281. Lot No. 30119 Afd/Elh 1954. 82S. 42 t.
65342–65366. DMBSO. Dia. EB281. Lot No. 30167 Afd/Elh 1955. 82S. 42 t.
65368–65372. DMBSO. Dia. EB281. Lot No. 30314 Afd/Elh 1956–58. 79S. 42 t.
77113. DTSO. Dia. EE279. Lot No. 30117 Eastleigh 1955. Former South Tyneside trailer. 92s. 30.5 t.
77505. DTSO. Dia. EE274. Lot No. 30115 Afd/Elh 1954. 92S. 30.5 t.
77513–77519. DTSO. Dia. EE274. Lot No. 30120 Afd/Elh 1954. 92S. 30.5 t.
77527–77551. DTSO. Dia. EE274. Lot No. 30168 Afd/Elh 1955. 92S. 30.5 t.
77553–77557. DTSO. Dia. EE274. Lot No. 30315 Afd/Elh 1956–58. 92S. 30.5 t.

*–Modified for working Maidstone service. Doors fitted between saloon and guards compartment in motor car and between saloon and cab in trailer. DMBSO seats 79S (dia. EB280) and DTSO seats 90S (dia. EE271).

6401	*	N	NKSX	SG	65346	77531
6402	*	N	NKSX	SG	65362	77547
6403	*	N	NKSX	SG	65356	77541
6404	*	N	NKSX	SG	65329	77514
6405	*	N	NKSX	SG	65347	77532
6406	*	N	NKSX	SG	65305	77505
6407	*	N	NKSX	SG	65330	77515
6408	*	N	NKSX	SG	65342	77527
6409	*	N	NKSX	SG	65309	77113
6410		N	NKSX	SG	65334	77519
6411		N	NKSX	SG	65333	77518
6412		N	NKSX	SG	65364	77549
6413		N	NKSX	SG	65372	77557
6414		N	NKSX	SG	65368	77553
6415		N	NKSX	SG	65348	77533
6416		N	NKSX	SG	65328	77513
6417		N	NKSX	SG	65366	77551
6418		N	NKSX	SG	65360	77545

CLASS 488   VICTORIA–GATWICK TRAILER SETS

TFOLH–TSOL (Class 488/3 only)–TSOLH. Converted 1983–84 from loco-hauled Mk. 2F FOs and TSOs for Victoria–Gatwick service. Express stock. Air conditioned. Fluorescent lighting. PA. Conversion consisted of a modified seating layout and the removal of one toilet to provide additional luggage space.

Bogies: B4.
Gangways: Throughout.
Dimensions: 20.12 x 2.82 m.
Maximum Speed: 90 mph.

72500–72509. TFOLH. Dia. EP101. Lot No. 30859 Derby 1973–74. 41F 1L. 35 t.
72602–72647. TSOLH. Dia. EP201. Lot No. 30860 Derby 1973–74. 48S 1L. 35 t.
72701–72718. TSOL. Dia. EH285. Lot No. 30860 Derby 1973–74. 48S 1L. 35 t.

CLASS 488/2. Note: TFOLH fitted with public telephone.

8201	I	IVGX	SL	72500 (3413)	72638 (6068)
8202	I	IVGX	SL	72501 (3382)	72617 (6086)
8203	I	IVGX	SL	72502 (3321)	72640 (6097)
8204	I	IVGX	SL	72503 (3407)	72641 (6079)
8205	I	IVGX	SL	72504 (3406)	72628 (6058)
8206	I	IVGX	SL	72505 (3415)	72629 (6048)
8207	I	IVGX	SL	72506 (3335)	72642 (6076)
8208	I	IVGX	SL	72507 (3412)	72643 (6040)
8209	I	IVGX	SL	72508 (3409)	72644 (6039)
8210	I	IVGX	SL	72509 (3398)	72635 (6128)

CLASS 488/3. TSOLH–TSOL–TSOLH.

8302	I	IVGX	SL	72602 (6130)	72701 (6088)	72604 (6087)
8303	I	IVGX	SL	72603 (6093)	72702 (6099)	72608 (6077)
8304	I	IVGX	SL	72606 (6084)	72703 (6075)	72611 (6083)
8305	I	IVGX	SL	72605 (6082)	72704 (6132)	72609 (6080)
8306	I	IVGX	SL	72607 (6020)	72705 (6032)	72610 (6074)
8307	I	IVGX	SL	72612 (6156)	72706 (6143)	72613 (6126)
8308	I	IVGX	SL	72614 (6090)	72707 (6127)	72615 (5938)
8309	I	IVGX	SL	72616 (6007)	72708 (6095)	72639 (6070)
8310	I	IVGX	SL	72618 (6044)	72709 (5982)	72619 (5909)
8311	I	IVGX	SL	72620 (6140)	72710 (6003)	72621 (6108)
8312	I	IVGX	SL	72622 (6004)	72711 (6109)	72623 (6118)
8313	I	IVGX	SL	72624 (5972)	72712 (6091)	72625 (6085)
8314	I	IVGX	SL	72626 (6017)	72713 (6023)	72627 (5974)
8315	I	IVGX	SL	72636 (6071)	72714 (6092)	72645 (5942)
8316	I	IVGX	SL	72630 (6094)	72715 (6019)	72631 (6096)
8317	I	IVGX	SL	72632 (6072)	72716 (6114)	72633 (6129)
8318	I	IVGX	SL	72634 (6089)	72717 (6069)	72637 (6098)
8319	I	IVGX	SL	72646 (6078)	72718 (5979)	72647 (6081)

CLASS 419 1957 type MLV

Built 1959–61. Dual braked.

Electrical Equipment: 1957-type.
Bogies: Mk 3B.
Gangways: Non-gangwayed.
Traction Motors: Two EE507 of 185 kW.
Dimensions: 19.64 x 2.82 m.
Maximum Speed: 90 mph.

68001–2. DMLV. Dia. EX560. Lot No. 30458 Afd./Elh. 1959. 45.5 t.
68003–10. DMLV. Dia. EX560. Lot No. 30623 Afd./Elh. 1960–61. 45.5 t.

9001	**N**	NBTX	RE	68001	9006	**J**	NBTX	RE	68006
9002	**N**	NBTX	RE	68002	9007	**N**	NBTX	RE	68007
9003	**N**	NBTX	RE	68003	9008	**N**	NBTX	RE	68008
9004	**N**	NBTX	RE	68004	9009	**N**	NBTX	RE	68009
9005	**N**	NBTX	RE	68005	9010	**J**	NBTX	RE	68010

CLASS 489 VICTORIA–GATWICK GLV

Converted 1983–84 from class 414/3 (2 Hap) DMBSOs to work with class 488.

Bogies: Mk 4.
Gangways: Gangwayed at inner end only.
Traction Motors: Two EE507 of 185 kW.
Dimensions: 19.49 x 2.82 m.
Maximum Speed: 90 mph.

DMLV. Dia. EX561. Lot No. 30452 Ashford/Eastleigh 1959. 40.5 t.

9101	**I**	IVGX	SL	68500 (61269)	9106	**I**	IVGX	SL	68505 (61299)
9102	**I**	IVGX	SL	68501 (61281)	9107	**I**	IVGX	SL	68506 (61292)
9103	**I**	IVGX	SL	68502 (61274)	9108	**I**	IVGX	SL	68507 (61267)
9104	**I**	IVGX	SL	68503 (61277)	9109	**I**	IVGX	SL	68508 (61272)
9105	**I**	IVGX	SL	68504 (61286)	9110	**I**	IVGX	SL	68509 (61280)

CLASS 456

DMSO–DTSO. Sliding doors. Disc brakes. Fluorescent lighting. PA.

Bogies: P7 (motor) and T3 trailer.
Gangways: Within set.
Traction Motors: Two EE507 of 185 kW.
Dimensions: 19.83 x 2.82 m.
Maximum Speed: 75 mph.

DMSO. Dia. EA267. Lot No. 31073 York 1990–1. 79S. 41.1 t.
DTSO. Dia. EE276. Lot No. 31074 York 1990–1. 51S. 31.4 t.

456 001	**N**	NSLX	SU	64735	78250
456 002	**N**	NSLX	SU	64736	78251
456 003	**N**	NSLX	SU	64737	78252

456 004	**N**	NSLX	SU	64738	78253
456 005	**N**	NSLX	SU	64739	78254
456 006	**N**	NSLX	SU	64740	78255
456 007	**N**	NSLX	SU	64741	78256
456 008	**N**	NSLX	SU	64742	78257
456 009	**N**	NSLX	SU	64743	78258
456 010	**N**	NSLX	SU	64744	78259
456 011	**N**	NSLX	SU	64745	78260
456 012	**N**	NSLX	SU	64746	78261
456 013	**N**	NSLX	SU	64747	78262
456 014	**N**	NSLX	SU	64748	78263
456 015	**N**	NSLX	SU	64749	78264
456 016	**N**	NSLX	SU	64750	78265
456 017	**N**	NSLX	SU	64751	78266
456 018	**N**	NSLX	SU	64752	78267
456 019	**N**	NSLX	SU	64753	78268
456 020	**N**	NSLX	SU	64754	78269
456 021	**N**	NSLX	SU	64755	78270
456 022	**N**	NSLX	SU	64756	78271
456 023	**N**	NSLX	SU	64757	78272
456 024	**N**	NSLX	SU	64758	78273

CLASS 465   NETWORKER

DMSO–TSOL–TSO–DMSO. New units with Aluminium bodies. Sliding doors. Disc and regenerative brakes. PA.

Electrical Equipment: Networker.
Bogies:
Gangways: Within set.
Traction Motors:
Dimensions:
Maximum Speed: 75 mph.

64759–64808. DMSO(A). Dia. EA268. Lot No. 31100 BREL York 1991–2. 86S.

64809–64858. DMSO(B). Dia. EA268. Lot No. 31100 BREL York 1991–2. 86S.

65700–65749. DMSO(A). Dia. EA269. Lot No. 31103 Metro-Cammell 1991–2. 86S.

65750–65799. DMSO(B). Dia. EA269. Lot No. 31103 Metro-Cammell 1991–2. 86S.

72028–72126 (even Nos.). TSO. Dia. EH293. Lot No. 31102 BREL York 1991–2. 86S.

72029–72127 (odd Nos.). TSOL. Dia. EH292. Lot No. 31101 BREL York 1991–2. 86S.

72719–72817 (odd Nos.). TSOL. Dia. EH294. Lot No. 31104 Metro-Cammell 1991–2. 86S.   t.

72720–72818 (even Nos.). TSO. Dia. EH295. Lot No. 31105 Metro-Cammell 1991–2. 86S.   t.

Class 465/0. Built by BREL Ltd.

465 001	**N**		64759	72029 72028	64809
465 002	**N**		64760	72031 72030	64810
465 003	**N**		64761	72033 72032	64811

465 004	N	64762	72035	72034	64812
465 005	N	64763	72037	72036	64813
465 006	N	64764	72039	72038	64814
465 007	N	64765	72041	72040	64815
465 008	N	64766	72043	72042	64816
465 009	N	64767	72045	72044	64817
465 010	N	64768	72047	72046	64818
465 011	N	64769	72049	72048	64819
465 012	N	64770	72051	72050	64820
465 013	N	64771	72053	72052	64821
465 014	N	64772	72055	72054	64822
465 015	N	64773	72057	72056	64823
465 016	N	64774	72059	72058	64824
465 017	N	64775	72061	72060	64825
465 018	N	64776	72063	72062	64826
465 019	N	64777	72065	72064	64827
465 020	N	64778	72067	72066	64828
465 021	N	64779	72069	72068	64829
465 022	N	64780	72071	72070	64830
465 023	N	64781	72073	72072	64831
465 024	N	64782	72075	72074	64832
465 025	N	64783	72077	72076	64833
465 026	N	64784	72079	72078	64834
465 027	N	64785	72081	72080	64835
465 028	N	64786	72083	72082	64836
465 029	N	64787	72085	72084	64837
465 030	N	64788	72087	72086	64838
465 031	N	64789	72089	72088	64839
465 032	N	64790	72091	72090	64840
465 033	N	64791	72093	72092	64841
465 034	N	64792	72095	72094	64842
465 035	N	64793	72097	72096	64843
465 036	N	64794	72099	72098	64844
465 037	N	64795	72101	72100	64845
465 038	N	64796	72103	72102	64846
465 039	N	64797	72105	72104	64847
465 040	N	64798	72107	72106	64848
465 041	N	64799	72109	72108	64849
465 042	N	64800	72111	72110	64850
465 043	N	64801	72113	72112	64851
465 044	N	64802	72115	72114	64852
465 045	N	64803	72117	72116	64853
465 046	N	64804	72119	72118	64854
465 047	N	64805	72121	72120	64855
465 048	N	64806	72123	72122	64856
465 049	N	64807	72125	72124	64857
465 050	N	64808	72127	72126	64858

Class 465/2. Built by Metro-Cammell.

465 201	N	65700	72719	72720	65750
465 202	N	65701	72721	72722	65751
465 203	N	65702	72723	72724	65752

465 204	N		65703	72725	72726	65753
465 205	N		65704	72727	72728	65754
465 206	N		65705	72729	72730	65755
465 207	N		65706	72731	72732	65756
465 208	N		65707	72733	72734	65757
465 209	N		65708	72735	72736	65758
465 210	N		65709	72737	72738	65759
465 211	N		65710	72739	72740	65760
465 212	N		65711	72741	72742	65761
465 213	N		65712	72743	72744	65762
465 214	N		65713	72745	72746	65763
465 215	N		65714	72747	72748	65764
465 216	N		65715	72749	72750	65765
465 217	N		65716	72751	72752	65766
465 218	N		65717	72753	72754	65767
465 219	N		65718	72755	72756	65768
465 220	N		65719	72757	72758	65769
465 221	N		65720	72759	72760	65770
465 222	N		65721	72761	72762	65771
465 223	N		65722	72763	72764	65772
465 224	N		65723	72765	72766	65773
465 225	N		65724	72767	72768	65774
465 226	N		65725	72769	72770	65775
465 227	N		65726	72771	72772	65776
465 228	N		65727	72773	72774	65777
465 229	N		65728	72775	72776	65778
465 230	N		65729	72777	72778	65779
465 231	N		65730	72779	72780	65780
465 232	N		65731	72781	72782	65781
465 233	N		65732	72783	72784	65782
465 234	N		65733	72785	72786	65783
465 235	N		65734	72787	72788	65784
465 236	N		65735	72789	72790	65785
465 237	N		65736	72791	72792	65786
465 238	N		65737	72793	72794	65787
465 239	N		65738	72795	72796	65788
465 240	N		65739	72797	72798	65789
465 241	N		65740	72799	72800	65790
465 242	N		65741	72801	72802	65791
465 243	N		65742	72803	72804	65792
465 244	N		65743	72805	72806	65793
465 245	N		65744	72807	72808	65794
465 246	N		65745	72809	72810	65795
465 247	N		65746	72811	72812	65796
465 248	N		65747	72813	72814	65797
465 249	N		65748	72815	72816	65798
465 250	N		65749	72817	72818	65799

CLASS 466   NETWORKER

MSO–DTSO. New units with Aluminium bodies. Sliding doors. Disc and regenerative brakes. PA.

Electrical Equipment: Networker.
Bogies:
Gangways: Within set.
Traction Motors:
Dimensions:
Maximum Speed: 75 mph.

DMSO. Dia. EA2 . Lot No. 31128 Metro-Cammell 1992–3. 86S. t.
DTSO. Dia. EE277. Lot No. 31129 Metro-Cammell 1991–2. 82S. t.

466 001	N	64860	78312
466 002	N	64861	78313
466 003	N	64862	78314
466 004	N	64863	78315
466 005	N	64864	78316
466 006	N	64865	78317
466 007	N	64866	78318
466 008	N	64867	78319
466 009	N	64868	78320
466 010	N	64869	78321
466 011	N	64870	78322
466 012	N	64871	78323
466 013	N	64872	78324
466 014	N	64873	78325
466 015	N	64874	78326
466 016	N	64875	78327
466 017	N	64876	78328
466 018	N	64877	78329
466 019	N	64878	78330
466 020	N	64879	78331
466 021	N	64880	78332
466 022	N	64881	78333
466 023	N	64882	78334
466 024	N	64883	78335
466 025	N	64884	78336
466 026	N	64885	78337
466 027	N	64886	78338
466 028	N	64887	78339
466 029	N	64888	78340
466 030	N	64889	78341
466 031	N	64890	78342
466 032	N	64891	78343
466 033	N	64892	78344
466 034	N	64893	78345
466 035	N	64894	78346
466 036	N	64895	78347
466 037	N	64896	78348
466 038	N	64897	78349
466 039	N	64898	78350
466 040	N	64899	78351
466 041	N	64900	78352
466 042	N	64901	78353
466 043	N	64902	78354

4.3. SOUTHERN REGION TUBE STOCK

These classes are tube stock used on the Isle of Wight or for the Waterloo and City line in London (known colloquially as the "Drain").

CLASS 483   'NEW' ISLE OF WIGHT STOCK

DMBSO(A)–DMBSO(B). Built 19   for LTE. Converted 1989–90 for Isle of Wight Line. Sliding doors. End doors. dg. pa. Former London Underground numbers are shown in parentheses.

System: 660 V d.c. third rail.
Gangways: Non-gangwayed.
Traction Motors: Two of 130 kW.
Dimensions: 15.95 x 2.69 m.
Maximum Speed: 45 mph.

DMSO (A). Dia. EA265. 42S. 27.5 t.
DMSO (B). Dia. EA266. 42S. 27.5 t.

483 001	N	NSSX	RY	121	(10184)	221	(11184)
483 002	N	NSSX	RY	122	(10221)	222	(11221)
483 003	N	NSSX	RY	123	(10116)	223	(11116)
483 004	N	NSSX	RY	124	(10205)	224	(11205)
483 005	N	NSSX	RY	125	(10142)	225	(11142)
483 006	N	NSSX	RY	126	(10297)	226	(11297)
483 007	N	NSSX	RY	127	(10291)	227	(11291)
483 008	N	NSSX	RY	128	(10255)	228	(11255)
483 009				129	( )	229	( )

CLASSES 485 & 486   ISLE OF WIGHT STOCK

DMBSO–2TSO–DTSO. Built 1923–31 for London Electric Railway (later LT). Converted 1967 for Isle of Wight Line. Sliding doors. End doors. Former London Underground numbers are shown in parentheses.

System: 660 V d.c. third rail.
Gangways: Non-gangwayed.
Traction Motors: Two EE507 of 178 kW.
Dimensions: 15.16 x 2.64 m.
Maximum Speed: 45 mph.

DMBSO. Dia. EB261. Metro-Cammell 1932–5. 26S. 32 t.
DSO. Dia. EH261. Cammell-Laird 1924. 42S. 19 t.
TSO. Dia. EE260. Metro-Cammell 1926–9. 38S. 17 t.

485	N	NXXZ	RY	2	(3706)	49	(7296)	44	(7281)	27	(5279)

CLASS 487 WATERLOO & CITY

Built 1940. Do not run in permanent sets. Run as single motor cars or as pair of motors with up to three trailers in between.

System: 630 V d.c. third rail.
Gangways: Non-gangwayed. End doors.
Traction Motors: Two EE500 of 140 kW.
Dimensions: 14.33 x 2.64 m.
Maximum Speed: 35 mph.

DMBSO. Dia. EB260. English Electric 1940. 40S. 29 t.
TSO. Dia. EH260. English Electric 1940. 52S. 19 t.

DMBSO

51	**N**	NKSX	WC	56	**N**	NKSX	WC	60	**N**	NKSX	WC
53	**N**	NKSX	WC	57	**N**	NKSX	WC	61	**N**	NKSX	WC
54	**N**	NKSX	WC	58	**N**	NKSX	WC	62	**N**	NKSX	WC
59	**N**	NKSX	WC(S)								

TSO

72	**N**	NKSX	WC	77	**N**	NKSX	WC	83	**N**	NKSX	WC
73	**N**	NKSX	WC	78	**N**	NKSX	WC	84	**N**	NKSX	WC
74	**N**	NKSX	WC	80	**N**	NKSX	WC	85	**N**	NKSX	WC
75	**N**	NKSX	WC	81	**N**	NKSX	WC	86	**N**	NKSX	WC
76	**N**	NKSX	WC								

4.4 LONDON MIDLAND REGION d.c. EMUs

CLASS 507   MERSEYRAIL

DMSO–TSO–DMSO. Tightlock couplers. Sliding doors. Disc and rheostatic brakes. PA.

System: 750 V d.c. third rail.
Bogies: BX1.
Gangways: Gangwayed within unit. End doors.
Traction Motors: Four GEC G310AZ of 82.125 kW.
Dimensions: 19.80 x 2.82 m (outer cars), 19.92 x 2.82 m (inner cars).
Maximum Speed: 75 mph.

DMSO. Dia. EI202. Lot No. 30906 York 1978–80. 74S. 37.06 t.
TSO. Dia. EH205. Lot No. 30907 York 1978–80. 82S. 25.60 t.
MSO. Dia. EA201. Lot No. 30908 York 1978–80. 74S. 35.62 t.

507 001		PHRX	HR	64367	71342	64405
507 002		PHRX	HR	64368	71343	64406
507 003		PHRX	HR (S)	64369	71344	64407
507 004		PHRX	HR	64370	71345	64408
507 005		PHRX	HR	64371	71346	64409
507 006		PHRX	HR	64372	71347	64410
507 007		PHRX	HR	64373	71348	64411
507 008		PHRX	HR	64374	71349	64412
507 009		PHRX	HR	64375	71350	64413
507 010		PHRX	HR	64376	71351	64414
507 011		PHRX	HR	64377	71352	64415
507 012		PHRX	HR (S)	64378	71353	64416
507 013	MT	PHRX	HR	64379	71354	64417
507 014		PHRX	HR	64380	71355	64418
507 015		PHRX	HR	64381	71356	64419
507 016		PHRX	HR	64382	71357	64420
507 017		PHRX	HR	64383	71358	64421
507 018		PHRX	HR	64384	71359	64422
507 019		PHRX	HR	64385	71360	64423
507 020		PHRX	HR	64386	71361	64424
507 021		PHRX	HR	64387	71362	64425
507 022		PHRX	HR	64388	71363	64426
507 023		PHRX	HR	64389	71364	64427
507 024		PHRX	HR	64390	71365	64428
507 025		PHRX	HR	64391	71366	64429
507 026		PHRX	HR	64392	71367	64430
507 027		PHRX	HR	64393	71368	64431
507 028		PHRX	HR	64394	71369	64432
507 029		PHRX	HR	64395	71370	64433
507 030		PHRX	HR	64396	71371	64434
507 031		PHRX	HR	64397	71372	64435
507 032		PHRX	HR	64398	71373	64436
507 033		PHRX	HR	64399	71374	64437

CLASS 508   MERSEYRAIL

DMSO–TSO–BDMSO. Tightlock couplers. Sliding doors. Disc and rheostatic brakes. PA. Originally built as four car units and numbered 508 001–043. One trailer removed and used for class 455/7 on transfer from the SR.

System: 750 V d.c. third rail.
Bogies: BX1.
Gangways: Gangwayed within unit. End doors.
Traction Motors: Four GEC G310AZ of 82.125 kW.
Dimensions: 19.80 x 2.82 m (outer cars), 19.92 x 2.82 m (inner cars).
Maximum Speed: 75 mph.

64649–64687. DMSO. Dia. EA208. Lot No. 30942 York 1979–80. 74S. 36.15 t.
64688–64691. DMSO. Dia. EA208. Lot No. 30979 York 1980. 74S. 36.15 t.
71483–71520. TSO. Dia. EH218. Lot No. 30943 York 1979–80. 82S. 26.72 t.
71521–71525. TSO. Dia. EH218. Lot No. 30980 York 1980. 82S. 26.72 t.
64692–64729. BDMSO. Dia. EI203. Lot No. 30945 York 1979–80. 74S. 36.61 t.
64730–64734. BDMSO. Dia. EI203. Lot No. 30981 York 1980. 74S. 36.61 t.

508 101	PBDX	BD	64649	71483	64692
508 102	PBDX	BD	64650	71484	64693
508 103	PBDX	BD	64651	71485	64694
508 104	PBDX	BD	64652	71486	64695
508 105	PBDX	BD	64653	71487	64696
508 106	PBDX	BD	64654	71488	64697
508 107	PBDX	BD	64655	71489	64698
508 108	PBDX	BD	64656	71490	64699
508 109	PBDX	BD	64657	71491	64700
508 110	PBDX	BD	64658	71492	64701
508 111	PBDX	BD	64659	71493	64702
508 112	PBDX	BD	64660	71494	64703
508 113	PBDX	BD	64661	71495	64704
508 114	PBDX	BD	64662	71496	64705
508 115	PBDX	BD	64663	71497	64706
508 116	PBDX	BD	64664	71498	64707
508 117	PBDX	BD	64665	71499	64708
508 118	PBDX	BD	64666	71500	64709
508 119	PBDX	BD	64667	71501	64710
508 120	PBDX	BD	64668	71502	64711
508 121	PBDX	BD	64669	71503	64712
508 122	PBDX	BD	64670	71504	64713
508 123	PBDX	BD	64671	71505	64714
508 124	PBDX	BD	64672	71506	64715
508 125	PBDX	BD	64673	71507	64716
508 126	PBDX	BD	64674	71508	64717
508 127	PBDX	BD	64675	71509	64718
508 128	PBDX	BD	64676	71510	64719
508 129	PBDX	BD	64677	71511	64720
508 130	PBDX	BD	64678	71512	64721
508 131	PBDX	BD	64679	71513	64722
508 132	PBDX	BD	64680	71514	64723

508 133	PBDX	BD	64681	71515	64724
508 134	PBDX	BD	64682	71516	64725
508 135	PBDX	BD	64683	71517	64726
508 136	PBDX	BD	64684	71518	64727
508 137	PBDX	BD	64685	71519	64728
508 138	PBDX	BD	64686	71520	64729
508 139	PHRX	HR	64687	71521	64730
508 140	PHRX	HR	64688	71522	64731
508 141	PHRX	HR	64689	71523	64732
508 142	PHRX	HR	64690	71524	64733
508 143	PHRX	HR	64691	71525	64734

4.5 DEPARTMENTAL EMU CARS

For information in this section we wish to thank Roger Butcher.

Individual vehicles.

ADB 975032	(75165)	SH	SR class 932 experimental stock. 'Mars'.
DB 977335	(76277)	RTC	MTA Pool Generator coach for DB999550.
DB 977336	(76278)	Cathays	MTA Pool Driving trailer for DB999550. (pending conversion).
ADB 977362	(10392)	BI	SR class 930 deicing trailer.
ADB 977363	(10399)	EH	SR Class 930 deicing trailer.
ADB 977364	(10400)	RE	SR class 930 deicing trailer.
ADB 977578	(77101)	HE	Sandite vehicle (work with Class 317/319).
ADB 977579	(77109)	SU	Sandite vehicle (work with Class 317/319).
DB 999602	(62483)	RTC	Ultrasonic test train instrumentation coach. MTA pool.
DB 999603	(62482)	Cathays	Ultrasonic test train coach (pending conversion).

Complete Units

Southern Region Class 930 Deicing and Sandite units.

930 003	SU	ADB 975594 (12658)	ADB 975595 (10994)
930 004	EH	ADB 975586 (10907)	ADB 975587 (10908)
930 005	WD	ADB 975588 (10981)	ADB 975589 (10982)
930 006	WD	ADB 975590 (10833)	ADB 975591 (10834)
930 007	GI	ADB 975592 (10993)	ADB 975593 (12659)
930 008	AF	ADB 975596 (10844)	ADB 975597 (10987)
930 009	BI	ADB 975598 (10989)	ADB 975599 (10990)
930 010	BI	ADB 975600 (10988)	ADB 975601 (10843)
930 011	RE	ADB 975602 (10991)	ADB 975603 (10992)
930 012	BM	ADB 975604 (10939)	ADB 975605 (10940)
930 013	RE	ADB 975896 (11387)	ADB 975897 (11388)
930 014	EH	ADB 977609 (65414)	ADB 977207 (61658)
930 015	WD	ADB 977531 (14047)	ADB 977532 (14048)
930 016	WD	ADB 977533 (14273)	ADB 977534 (14384)
930 017	EH	ADB 977566 (65312)	ADB 977567 (65314)

Southern Region Class 931 Carriage Cleaning Fluid Unit:

| 931 062 | SL | ADB 977559 (65313) | ADB 977560 (65320) |

Southern Region Class 932 Tractor Units:

| 932 021 | WD | ADB 977304 (65317) | ADB 977305 (65322) |
| 932 050 | SH | ADB 977296 (65319) | ADB 977297 (77108) |

Southern Region Test Units:

| 930 053 | SH | ADB 977505 (65321) | ADB 977507 (77110) |
| 930 054 | SH | ADB 977506 (65323) | ADB 977508 (77112) |

Southern Region Emergency Exercise Training Units.

999	ADB 977688 (77111)	ADB 977689 (77106)
	ADB 977690 (77102)	ADB 977691 (77103)

The above unit is used anywhere on the Southern Region.

Southern Region Radio Trials Unit.

	ADB 977731 (61260)	ADB 977732 (75379)

Class 438 4 TC Unit:

8007	SL	ADB 977684 (76282)	ADB 977685 (70818)
		ADB 977686 (70850)	ADB 977687 (76281)

Anglia Region class 302 three-car Sandite Units:

302 996	CC	ADB 977598 (75080)	ADB 977599 (61073)
		ADB 977600 (75061)	
302 997	IL	ADB 977601 (75211)	ADB 977602 (61228)
		ADB 977603 (75035)	
302 998	EM	ADB 977604 (75077)	ADB 977605 (61052)
		ADB 977606 (75070)	
305 908	IL	ADB 977741 (75469)	ADB 977742 (61436)
		ADB 977743 (75521)	

Demonstration Unit:

303 999	IL	ADB 977741 (75759)	ADB 977742 (61825)
		ADB 977743 (75815)	

InterCity Instruction Unit:

305 935	HA	ADB 977639 (75548)	ADB 977640 (61463)
		ADB 977641 (75214)	

Note: 977641 of 305 935 is a former Class 302 car.

Crash test units (kept at Old Dalby).

307 101	RTC	75001	61001	70001	75101
307 106	RTC	75006	61006	70006	75106
307 118	RTC	75018	61018	70018	75118
307 121	RTC	75021	61021	70021	75121

The above vehicles have been allocated ADB 977668–679 in the above order, but these numbers are not carried.

Test unit awaiting conversion.

307 118	RTC	75018	61018	70018	75118

London Midland Region Sandite Units:

936 001	BD	ADB 977345 (61178)	ADB 977346 (75178)
936 002	BD	ADB 977347 (61180)	ADB 977348 (75180)
936 003	BD	ADB 977349 (61183)	ADB 977350 (75183)
936 501	SH	ADB 977385 (61148)	ADB 977386 (75189)

Note: Most units do not carry '93x' numbers.

5. NON-PASSENGER-CARRYING COACHING STOCK

AK51 (RK)   KITCHEN CAR

Dia. AK503. Mark 1. Gas cooking. Converted from RBR. Fluorescent lighting. xd*. ETH 2X.

Note: Kitchen cars have traditionally been numbered in the NPCCS series, but have passenger coach diagram numbers!

Lot No. 30628 Pressed Steel 1960–61. 39 t.

80041 (1690)   **I**   ICHV   BN |

NN   COURIER VEHICLE

Dia. NN504. Converted 1986–7 from Mark 1 BSKs. One compartment retained for courier use. Roller shutter doors. d. ETH 2.

80200–2/4–6/8/11–14/16–17/21–23/25. Lot No. 30699 Wolverton 1962. Commonwealth bogies. 37 t.
80203/9–10/15/20/24. Lot No. 30573 Gloucester 1960. B4 bogies. 35 t.
80207. Lot No. 30721 Wolverton 1963. Commonwealth bogies. 37 t.
80218. Lot No. 30427 Wolverton 1958–9. B4 bogies. ETH 2. 35 t.
80219. Lot No. 31027 Wolverton 1958. B4 bogies. ETH 2. 35 t.

80200 (35303) v	**B**	RPXG	OM	80213 (35316) x	**R**	RPXG	EN
80201 (35311) v		RPXG	OM	80214 (35323) x	**R**	RPXG	HT
80202 (35462) x	**R**	RPXG	OM	80215 (35292) x	**R**	RPXG	CA
80203 (35287) v		RPXG	OM	80216 (35295) x		RPXG	CA
80204 (35297) x	**R**	RPXG	EN	80217 (35299) x		RPXG	CA
80205 (35312) v	**R**	RPXG	OM	80218 (35197) x		RPXG	HT
80206 (35304) x	**R**	RPXG	EN	80219 (35201) x		RPXG	CA
80207 (35466) x	**I**	RPXG	HT	80220 (35276) x	**R**	RPXG	HT
80208 (35341) x	**R**	RPXG	CA	80221 (35328) x		RPXG	EN
80209 (35279) v	**R**	RPXG	OM	80222 (35315) x	**R**	RPXG	EN
80210 (35282) v	**R**	RPXG	OM	80223 (35331) x	**R**	RPXG	CA
80211 (35296) x	**R**	RPXG	HT	80224 (35291) x		RPXG	HT
80212 (35307) x		RPXG	CA	80225 (35327) x	**R**	RPXG	HT

NPX   POST OFFICE GUV

Dia. NP502. Converted 1991 from newspaper vans. Mark 1. Short frames (57′). Originally converted from GUV. Fluorescent lighting, toilets and gangways fitted. Load 14 t. ETH 3X. These vehicles were originally renumbered 85500–85534. B5 bogies.

Lot No. 30922 Wolverton or Doncaster 1977–8. xe. 31 t (33 t*).

80250 (94008)			OM	80253 (94018)	
80251 (94017)			OM	80254 (94)	
80252 (94022) B5	**R**	RPOW	OM	80255 (94)	

NS (POS) POST OFFICE SORTING VAN

Used in travelling post office (TPO) trains. Mark 1. Various diagrams.

The following lots are vd and have Mark 1 bogies except *-B5 bogies. xd. (subtract 2 t from weight).

80300–80305. Lot No. 30486 Wolverton 1959. Dia. NS501. Originally built with nets for collecting mail bags in motion. Equipment now removed. ETH 3X. 36 t.
80306–80308. Lot No. 30487 Wolverton 1959. Dia. NS502. ETH 3. 36 t.
80309–80314. Lot No. 30661 Wolverton 1961. Dia. NS501. ETH 3. 37 t.
80315–80316. Lot No. 30662 Wolverton 1961. Dia. NS501. ETH 3X. 36 t.
80318. Lot No. 30663 Wolverton 1961. Dia. NS501. ETH 3X. 35 t.

80300	**R**	RPOM	MA	80310	**R**	RPOA	NC
80301	**R**	RPOM	MA	80312	**R**	RPOA	NC
80302	**R**	RPOM	MA	80313	**R**	RPOA	NC
80303 *	**R**	RPHT	HT	80314 *	**R**	RPHT	HT
80305	**R**	RPOA	NC	80315	**R**	RPOA	NC
80306	**R**	RPOA	CA	80316 *	**R**	RPOZ	EC
80308 *	**R**	RPHT	HT	80318 *	**R**	RPHT	HT
80309 *	**R**	RPHT	HT				

The following lots are pressure ventilated and have B5 bogies.

80319–80327. Dia. NS504. Lot No. 30778 York 1968–9. xd. ETH 4. 35 t.
80328–80338. Dia. NS505. Lot No. 30779 York 1968–9. xd. ETH 4. 35 t.
80339–80355. Dia. NS506. Lot No. 30780 York 1968–9. xd. ETH 4. 35 t.

80319		**R**	RPOA	CA	80338	**R**	RPOM	EN
80320		**R**	RPOA	CA	80339	**R**	RPOM	EN
80321	xd	**R**	RPOA	CA	80340	**R**	RPOM	MA
80322		**R**	RPOA	CA	80341	**R**	RPOM	EN
80323		**R**	RPHT	HT	80342	**R**	RPOM	EN
80324		**R**	RPHT	HT	80343	**R**	RPOM	MA
80325		**R**	RPOM	DY	80344	**R**	RPOM	EN
80326		**R**	RPOM	DY	80345	**R**	RPHT	HT
80327		**R**	RPOM	DY	80346	**R**	RPHT	HT
80328		**R**	RPOM	EN	80347	**R**	RPOM	EN
80329		**R**	RPOM	MA	80348	**R**	RPOM	EN
80330		**R**	RPHT	HT	80349	**R**	RPOM	DY
80331		**R**	RPHT	HT	80350	**R**	RPHT	HT
80332		**R**	RPHT	HT	80351	**R**	RPOM	DY
80333		**R**	RPHT	HT	80352	**R**	RPHT	HT
80334		**R**	RPOM	MA	80353	**R**	RPOM	EN
80335		**R**	RPHT	HT	80354	**R**	RPOM	EN
80336		**R**	RPHT	HT	80355	**R**	RPOM	MA
80337		**R**	RPHT	HT				

Name: 80320 The Borders Mail

80356–80380. Lot No. 30839 York 1972–3. Dia. NS501. Pressure ventilated. Fluorescent lighting. B5 bogies. xd. ETH 4X. 37 t.

80356	**R**	RPOM	EN	80357	**R**	RPOM	EN

80358	**R**	RPHT	HT		80370	**R**	RPOM	EN
80359	**R**	RPHT	HT		80371	**R**	RPOM	EN
80360	**R**	RPHT	HT		80372	**R**	RPOM	EN
80361	**R**	RPHT	HT		80373	**R**	RPOM	EN
80362	**R**	RPHT	HT		80374	**R**	RPOM	MA
80363	**R**	RPHT	HT		80375	**R**	RPOM	MA
80364	**R**	RPHT	HT		80376	**R**	RPOM	EN
80365	**R**	RPHT	HT		80377	**R**	RPOM	EN
80366	**R**	RPOM	EN		80378	**R**	RPOM	EN
80367	**R**	RPOM	EN		80379	**R**	RPOW	OM
80368	**R**	RPOM	EN		80380	**R**	RPOM	MA
80369	**R**	RPOM	EN					

80381–80395. Lot No. 30900 Wolverton 1977. Dia NS531. Converted from SK. Pressure ventilated. Fluorescent lighting. B5 bogies. xd. ETH 4X. 38 t.

80381	(25112)	**R**	RPOW	OM	80389	(25103)	**R**	RPOW	OM
80382	(25109)	**R**	RPOW	OM	80390	(25047)	**R**	RPOW	OM
80383	(25033)	**R**	RPOW	OM	80391	(25089)	**R**	RPOW	OM
80384	(25078)	**R**	RPOW	OM	80392	(25082)	**R**	RPOW	OM
80385	(25083)	**R**	RPOW	OM	80393	(25118)	**R**	RPOW	OM
80386	(25099)	**R**	RPOW	OM	80394	(25156)	**R**	RPOW	OM
80387	(25045)	**R**	RPOW	OM	80395	(25056)	**R**	RPOM	MA
80388	(25088)	**R**	RPOW	OM					

NT (POT)   POST OFFICE STOWAGE VAN

Mark 1. Open vans used for stowage of mail bags in conjunction with POS. Various diagrams.

Lot No. 30488 Wolverton 1959. Dia. NT502. Originally built with nets for collecting mail bags in motion. Equipment now removed. B5 bogies. xd. ETH 3. 35 t.

80400	**R**	RPOM	EN		80402	**R**	RPOM	EN
80401	**R**	RPOM	EN					

The following twelve vehicles were converted at York from BSK to lot 30143 (80403) and 30229 (80404–80414). No new lot number was issued. Dia. NT503. B5 bogies. xd. 35 t. (*dia. NT501 BR2 bogies 38 t. ETH 3 (3X*).

80403	(34631)		**R**	RPOM	MA	80409	(35019) §	**R**	RPOW	OM
80404	(35014)		**R**	RPOM	MA	80410	(35001) §	**R**	RPOW	OM
80405	(35009)		**R**	RPOM	MA	80411	(35003) *	**R**	RPOA	CA
80406	(35022)		**R**	RPOM	MA	80412	(35002) *	**R**	RPOA	MA
80407	(35015) §*	**R**	RPOW	OM	80413	(35004) *	**R**	RPOA	CA
80408	(35018) §*	**R**	RPOW	OM	80414	(35005) *	**R**	RPOM	MA

Lot No. 30781 York 1968. Dia. NT505. Pressure ventilated. B5 bogies. xd. ETH 4. 34 t.

80415	**R**	RPOM	EN		80420	**R**	RPHT	HT
80416	**R**	RPOM	EN		80421	**R**	RPHT	HT
80417	**R**	RPOM	EN		80422	**R**	RPHT	HT
80418	**R**	RPOM	EN		80423	**R**	RPOA	CA
80419	**R**	RPOM	EN		80424	**R**	RPOM	EN

Lot No. 30840 York 1973. Dia. NT504. Pressure ventilated. fluorescent lighting. B5 bogies. xd. ETH 4X. 35 t.

80425	R	RPOM	EN	80428	R	RPOM	EN
80426	R	RPHT	HT	80429	R	RPOM	EN
80427	R	RPHT	HT	80430	R	RPOM	EN

Lot No. 30901 Wolverton 1977. converted from SK. Dia. NT521. Pressure ventilated. Fluorescent lighting. B5 bogies. xd. ETH 4X. 35 t.

80431	(25104)	R	RPOM	DY	80436	(25077)	R	RPOW	OM
80432	(25071)	R	RPHT	HT	80437	(25068)	R	RPOW	OM
80433	(25150)	R	RPHT	HT	80438	(25139)	R	RPOM	DY
80434	(25119)	R	RPHT	HT	80439	(25127)	R	RPOM	DY
80435	(25117)	R	RPOW	OM					

NU (BPOT)   BRAKE POST OFFICE STOWAGE VAN

As NT but with brake. Mark 1.

Lot No. 30782 York 1968. Dia. NU502. Pressure ventilated. B5 bogies. xd. ETH 4. 36 t.

80456	R	RPOM	EN	80458	R	RPOM	EN
80457	R	RPOM	EN				

NB/NC/ND (BG)   GANGWAYED BRAKE VAN (90 mph)

These vans are built on short frames (57'). Load 10t. BR1 bogies. There are a number of variants.

NDV or NDX (x) (Dia ND501). BG dual heated. ETH 1 (1X*).
NBV (b) (Dia. NB501). High security letter mail van. Converted at WB from BG 1985. Gangways removed. vd. 84382/7/461/77 formerly renumbered 80460–3, but since given original number to prevent identification by potential train robbers!
NCV (c) (Dia. NC501). Newspaper packing van. Fluorescent lighting. ETH 3X. Not now used for newspapers.

80501–80529. Lot No. 30009 Derby 1952–3. 31 t.
80537–80565. Lot No. 30039 Derby 1954. 31 t.
80570–80596. Lot No. 30040 Wolverton 1954–5. 32 t.
80597–80671. Lot No. 30046 York 1954. 31.5 t.
80672–80724. Lot No. 30136 Metro-Cammell 1955. 31.5 t.
80726–80802. Lot No. 30140 BRCW 1955–6. 31.5 t.
80803–80852. Lot No. 30144 Cravens 1955. 31.5 t.
80855–80962. Lot No. 30162 Pressed Steel 1956–7. 32 t.
80965–80999. Lot No. 30173 York 1956. 31.5 t.

80549	*	RPXX	BJ	80592	*	RPDV	BJ
80554	*	RPDV	BJ	80651	*	RPXX	CA
80565	*	RPXX	BJ	80653	*	RPXX	BJ
80570	*	RPXX	BJ	80654	*	RPDV	BJ
80571	*	RPDV	BJ	80658	*	RPXX	BJ
80576	*	RPXX	BJ	80664	*	RPXT	BJ

80668	*		RPDV	BJ	80780 c*	**B**	RPCV	BJ
80670	*		RPXT	OM	80782 c*	**B**	RPCV	BJ
80671	*		RPXX	BJ	80789 c	**B**	RPCV	BJ
80693	*		RPDV	BJ	80794 c*		RPDV	BJ
80707	*		RPSU	BJ	80804 *		RPXT	BJ
80709	*		RPDV	BJ	80824 *		RPXT	BJ
80710	*		RPXT	BJ	80831 *		RPXT	BJ
80716	*		RPDV	BJ	80885 x*		RPDX	BJ
80720	*	**B**	RPCV	BJ	80886 x*		RPDX	BJ
80730			RPDV	BJ	80889 x*	**R**	RPDX	EC
80754	*		RPXX	BJ	80926 x		RPDX	BJ
80768 c*		**B**	RPCV	BJ	80966 c*	**B**	RPCV	BJ
80775 c*		**B**	RPCV	BJ	80976 *		RPDV	BJ

NZ (DLV) DRIVING BRAKE VAN (110 mph)

Dia. NZ501. Mark 3B. Air conditioned. T4 bogies. ae. dg. Cab to shore communication. ETH 5X.

Lot No. 31042 Derby 1988. 45.18 t.

82101	I	IWCX	MA	82127	I	IWCX	WB
82102	I	IWCX	OY	82128	I	IWCX	MA
82103	I	IWCX	OY	82129	I	IWCX	MA
82104	I	IWCX	MA	82130	I	IWCX	WB
82105	I	IWCX	WB	82131	I	IWCX	WB
82106	I	IWCX	WB	82132	I	IWCX	WB
82107	I	IWCX	WB	82133	I	IWCX	WB
82108	I	IWCX	WB	82134	I	IWCX	WB
82109	I	IWCX	WB	82135	I	IWCX	OY
82110	I	IWCX	WB	82136	I	IWCX	OY
82111	I	IWCX	WB	82137	I	IWCX	WB
82112	I	IWCX	WB	82138	I	IWCX	OY
82113	I	IWCX	OY	82139	I	IWCX	OY
82114	I	IWCX	WB	82140	I	IWCX	OY
82115	I	IWCX	WB	82141	I	IWCX	MA
82116	I	IWCX	WB	82142	I	IWCX	WB
82117	I	IWCX	MA	82143	I	IWCX	MA
82118	I	IWCX	WB	82144	I	IWCX	WB
82119	I	IWCX	WB	82145	I	IWCX	MA
82120	I	IWCX	WB	82146	I	IWCX	OY
82121	I	IWCX	MA	82147	I	IWCX	MA
82122	I	IWCX	MA	82148	I	IWCX	WB
82123	I	IWCX	OY	82149	I	IWCX	OY
82124	I	IWCX	WB	82150	I	IWCX	OY
82125	I	IWCX	WB	82151	I	IWCX	OY
82126	I	IWCX	MA	82152	I	IWCX	OY

NZ (DLV) DRIVING BRAKE VAN (140 mph)

Dia. NZ502. Mark 4. Air conditioned. Swiss-built (SIG) bogies. ae. dg. Cab to shore communication. ETH 6X.

Lot No. 31043 Metro-Cammell 1988. 45.18 t.

82200	I	IECX	BN	82216	I	IECX	BN
82201	I	IECX	BN	82217	I	IECX	BN
82202	I	IECX	BN	82218	I	IECX	BN
82203	I	IECX	BN	82219	I	IECX	BN
82204	I	IECX	BN	82220	I	IECX	BN
82205	I	IECX	BN	82221	I	IECX	BN
82206	I	IECX	BN	82222	I	IECX	BN
82207	I	IECX	BN	82223	I	IECX	BN
82208	I	IECX	BN	82224	I	IECX	BN
82209	I	IECX	BN	82225	I	IECX	BN
82210	I	IECX	BN	82226	I	IECX	BN
82211	I	IECX	BN	82227	I	IECX	BN
82212	I	IECX	BN	82228	I	IECX	BN
82213	I	IECX	BN	82229	I	IECX	BN
82214	I	IECX	BN	82230	I	IECX	BN
82215	I	IECX	BN	82231	I	IECX	BN

NZ (DLV) DRIVING BRAKE VAN (Exptl.)

Dia. NZ503. This is in effect locomotive 33115 with its traction equipment isolated which has been fitted with TGV bogies with third-rail pick-up shoes. It works coupled to a Class 73 locomotive which has its shoegear removed.

83301 (33115) I EPSL SL |

NB/NC/ND (BG) GANGWAYED BRAKE VAN (90 mph)

Class continued from 80994. Note: All 84XXX vehicles were renumbered from the 81XXX series by adding 3000 to the original number.

84000–84014. Lot No. 30173 York 1956. 31.5 t.
84015–84053. Lot No. 30224 Cravens 1956. 31.5 t.
84055–84179. Lot No. 30228 Metro-Cammell 1957–8. 31.5 t.
84180–84204. Lot No. 30234 Cravens 1956–7. 31.5 t.
84205–84265. Lot No. 30163 Pressed Steel 1957. 31.5 t.
84266–84312. Lot No. 30323 Pressed Steel 1957. 32 t.
84313–84497. Lot No. 30400 Pressed Steel 1957–8. 32 t.
84498–84572. Lot No. 30484 Pressed Steel 1958. 32 t.
84573–84592. Lot No. 30715 Gloucester 1962. 31 t.
84594–84612. Lot No. 30716 Gloucester 1962. 31 t.
84613–84628. Lot No. 30725 Gloucester 1962–3. 31 t.

84015	*		RPXX	BJ	84135	c	**B** RPCV	BJ
84016	*		RPEV	OM	84137			RPXX	BJ
84044	x		RPDX	BJ	84181	c*	**B** RPCV	BJ
84057	*		RPXX	BJ	84185			RPDV	BJ
84082	*		RPDV	BJ	84195	*		RPDV	BJ
84100	c	**B** RPCV	BJ	84197			RPXX	BJ
84106	*		RPXX	BJ	84202			RPDV	BJ
84119	c	**B** RPCV	BJ	84203			RPDV	BJ
84129	c	**B** RPCV	BJ	84204			RPDV	BJ
84133			RPDV	BJ	84215	x*		RPDX	BJ

84234	x*	**R**	RPDX	EC	84420 x	**R**	RPDX	BJ
84250	x*	**R**	RPDX	BJ	84428		RPDV	BJ

84234 x*	**R**	RPDX	EC	84420 x	**R**	RPDX	BJ
84250 x*	**R**	RPDX	BJ	84428		RPDV	BJ
84296		RPXT	BJ	84435		RPDV	BJ
84298		RPDV	BJ	84439		RPDV	BJ
84302		RPDV	BJ	84445 x		RPDX	MA
84319		RPSU	BJ	84447		RPDV	BJ
84344		RPEV	OM	84456 x		RPDX	BJ
84347		RPEV	OM	84461 b		RPOM	EN
84350		RPSU	BJ	84467		RPDV	BJ
84356		RPDV	BJ	84477 b		RPOM	EN
84371		RPDV	BJ	84499 x		RPDX	BJ
84382 b		RPOM	EN	84510 x	**R**	RPDX	EC
84386		RPDV	BJ	84512 x		RPDX	BJ
84387 b		RPOM	EN	84519		RPDV	BJ
84388 x		RPDX	BJ	84531 x*		RPDX	BJ
84399 x		RPDX	BJ	84577 x		RPDX	BJ
84406		RPDV	BJ	84619		RPDV	BJ
84419 x		RPDX	BJ	84626		RPXC	CA

NE/NH (BG)   100/110 mph GANGWAYED BRAKE VAN

As ND but rebogied with B4 bogies suitable for 100 mph–NE (110 mph with special maintenance–NH). d. ETH 1 (1X* and NHA). For lot numbers refer to original number series. Deduct 1.5t from weights. All NHA are a*pg.

BGs fitted with cages are denoted by the sector code.

92001	(80855)	NHA I	RPIP	PC	92036 (81158)	NHA I	RPIP	WB
92002	(80858)	x*to I	RPEX	EN	92037 (81165)	NHA I	RPIP	WB
92003	(80864)	x*to R	RPEX	EN	92038 (81173)	NHA I	RPIP	WB
92004	(80867)	x*to I	RPEX	EN	92040 (81186)	a pg I	RPEA	EN
92005	(80876)	x*to I	RPEX	EN	92041 (81205)	a to	RPEA	CA
92006	(80878)	NHA I	RPIP	PC	92042 (81207)	a to R	RPEA	CA
92007	(80880)	x*pg RX	RPEX	CA	92043 (81208)	a to I	RPEA	CA
92009	(80897)	x*to I	RPEX	EN	92044 (81209)	a to I	RPEA	EN
92010	(80900)	x*to I	RPEX	EN	92045 (81210)	a to I	RPEA	EN
92012	(80910)	a*pg I	RPIP	MA	92046 (81214)	NHA I	RPIP	WB
92013	(80916)	x*pg I	RPEX	EN	92047 (81216)	a to	RPEA	CA
92015	(80927)	x*to R	RPEX	CA	92049 (81219)	a to	RPEA	CA
92016	(80930)	x*pg R	RPEX	EN	92050 (81220)	a pg I	RPEA	EN
92017	(80940)	x*to I	RPEX	CA	92051 (81221)	a to R	RPEA	CA
92018	(80941)	x*to	RPEX	CA	92052 (81222)	a to R	RPEA	CA
92021	(80956)	x*to	RPEX	EN	92053 (81223)	a to R	RPEA	CA
92022	(80958)	x*pg	RPEX	EN	92054 (81224)	a to	RPEA	CA
92023	(80971)	a*pg I	RPIP	WB	92055 (81225)	a to I	RPEA	EN
92025	(81023)	NHA I	RPIP	PC	92056 (81226)	a to R	RPEA	EN
92026	(81060)	NHA I	RPIP	PC	92057 (81227)	a to I	RPIP	MA
92028	(81064)	NHA I	RPIP	PC	92058 (81228)	a to P	RPEA	CA
92031	(81102)	NHA I	RPIP	PC	92059 (81229)	a to R	RPEA	EN
92032	(81117)	NHA I	RPIP	PC	92060 (81230)	a to R	RPEA	CA
92033	(81123)	NHA I	RPIP	PC	92062 (81232)	a to	RPEA	CA
92034	(81142)	NHA I	RPIP	PC	92063 (81233)	a*pg I	RPEA	EN
92035	(81150)	a*pg I	RPIP	PC	92064 (81236)	a to	RPEA	CA

92065	(81237) a	RPEA	EN	92121	(81457) x*to	RPEX	EN
92066	(81238) a to I	RPEA	CA	92122	(81459) x*to R	RPEX	EN
92067	(81243) a to I	RPEA	EN	92123	(81460) a to R	RPTS	CA
92068	(81244) a to	RPEA	CA	92124	(81465) x R	RPEX	BJ
92070	(81246) a	RPEA	CA	92125	(81470) a to	RPIC	WB
92071	(81249) a to I	RPEA	CA	92126	(81471) a pg I	RPIP	MA
92072	(81253) a to I	RPEA	CA	92127	(81473) x*pg	RPEX	EN
92073	(81254) a to R	RPEA	EN	92129	(81479) a to R	RPEA	CA
92074	(81255) a to R	RPEA	CA	92130	(81480) a to	RPEA	EN
92075	(81256) a to R	RPEA	CA	92131	(81481) a to I	RPEA	CA
92076	(81257) a to	RPEA	CA	92132	(81482) a to R	RPEA	CA
92077	(81258) a to	RPEA	EN	92133	(81484) a to	RPEA	CA
92078	(81259) a to RX	RPEA	CA	92134	(81485) a to	RPEA	CA
92081	(81264) a to R	RPEA	CA	92135	(81486) a to	RPEA	CA
92082	(81265) a to I	RPTS	CA	92136	(81487) a to R	RPEA	CA
92083	(81266) a to	RPEA	CA	92137	(81488) a to R	RPEA	CA
92084	(81268) a to R	RPEA	CA	92138	(81490) a to	RPEA	EN
92086	(81282) a to	RPIP	NC	92139	(81491) a to R	RPEA	CA
92087	(81283) x*to I	RPEX	EN	92140	(81492) a to	RPEA	EN
92088	(81284) a to I	RPIP	LA	92141	(81493) a to	RPEA	CA
92089	(81303) a to I	RPIP	LA	92142	(81494) a to	RPEA	CA
92090	(81305) a to I	RPEA	CA	92143	(81495) a to R	RPEA	CA
92091	(81308) a to I	RPIP	NC	92144	(81496) a to R	RPEA	CA
92092	(81309) a to I	RPEA	EN	92145	(81497) a to	RPEA	CA
92093	(81312) a*to I	RPEA	EN	92146	(81498) NHA I	RPIP	PC
92094	(81367) a to I	RPIC	MA	92147	(81500) a to I	RPEA	EN
92095	(81375) a to R	RPEA	CA	92148	(81506) a to R	RPIC	MA
92096	(81377) a to	RPIC	WB	92149	(81509) x	RPEX	CA
92097	(81378) a to	RPIC	WB	92150	(81514) x to R	RPEX	EN
92098	(81381) NHA I	RPIP	PC	92151	(81516) a to I	RPIC	MA
92099	(81383) x*pg I	RPEX	EN	92152	(81518) a to	RPEA	CA
92100	(81391) a to	RPIP	LA	92153	(81520) x*to I	RPEX	EN
92101	(81392) a to	RPEA	CA	92154	(81522) x to R	RPEX	CA
92102	(81394) a to	RPIC	WB	92155	(81525) a*pg I	RPIP	MA
92103	(81400) x to	RPEX	BJ	92156	(81529) x*to	RPEX	EN
92104	(81401) a to R	RPEA	CA	92157	(81532) x*pg I	RPEX	EN
92105	(81405) a to R	RPEA	CA	92158	(81533) a to	RPEA	CA
92106	(81409) x to R	RPEA	CA	92159	(81534) NHA I	RPIP	PC
92107	(81410) x to	RPEX	CA	92160	(81537) x to	RPEA	CA
92108	(81411) a to R	RPIC	WB	92161	(81538) a to R	RPEA	CA
92109	(81413) a to	RPEA	CA	92162	(81539) a to R	RPEA	CA
92110	(81426) x*to I	RPEX	EN	92163	(81540) a to	RPEA	CA
92111	(81432) NHA I	RPIP	PC	92164	(81541) a to	RPEA	EN
92112	(81440) x to R	RPEX	EN	92165	(81546) a to	RPIC	MA
92113	(81442) a to I	RPEA	EN	92166	(81550) a to	RPEA	CA
92114	(81443) NHA I	RPIP	PC	92167	(81553) a*pg I	RPIP	PC
92115	(81444) a to	RPIC	WB	92168	(81555) a to R	RPEA	CA
92116	(81450) a to I	RPEA	EN	92169	(81556) x R	RPEX	BJ
92117	(81451) x R	RPEX	CA	92170	(81559) x to	RPEX	BJ
92118	(81452) a to I	RPEA	CA	92172	(81562) a pg I	RPEA	EN
92119	(81454) x to	RPEX	EN	92173	(81565) x to R	RPEX	CA
92120	(81455) x to	RPEX	CA	92174	(81567) NHA I	RPIP	PC

92175 (81568)	a pg l		RPIC	MA	92233 (80890)	x	**R** RPEX	CA
92176 (81569)	x to **R**		RPEX	BJ	92234 (84336)	x	RPEX	CA
92177 (81572)	a to **R**		RPEA	CA	92235 (80908)	x	RPEX	CA
92178 (81574)	x		RPEX	BJ	92236 (80909)	x	**N** RPEX	EN
92179 (81580)	x to **R**		RPEX	CA	92237 (80738)	x	RPEX	EN
92181 (81582)	x to		RPEX	BJ	92238 (84563)	x	**R** RPEX	CA
92182 (81585)	x to **R**		RPEX	BJ	92239 (81170)	x	**R** RPEX	EN
92183 (81588)	a*pg l		RPIP	MA	92240 (80703)	x	**R** RPEX	EN
92184 (81589)	a to **R**		RPEA	CA	92241 (80904)	x	RPEX	EN
92186 (81595)	a to I		RPEA	EN	92242 (80857)	x	**RX** RPEX	CA
92187 (81597)	a to **R**		RPEA	CA	92243 (84489)	x	**R** RPEX	EN
92188 (81598)	a to		RPIC	MA	92244 (84248)	x	**R** RPEX	EN
92189 (81599)	a to		RPXX	CA	92245 (80939)	x	RPEX	EN
92190 (81600)	a to		RPIC	MA	92246 (80929)	x	**I** RPEX	EN
92192 (81602)	x to		RPEX	BJ	92247 (84536)	x	**R** RPEX	CA
92193 (81604)	a pg l		RPEA	EN	92248 (80935)	x	**P** RPEX	EN
92194 (81606)	a to I		RPIP	MA	92249 (84511)	x	**R** RPEX	EN
92195 (81607)	a to I		RPIC	MA	92250 (84563)	x	RPEX	CA
92196 (81609)	a to I		RPIC	MA	92251 (84425)	x	RPEX	CA
92197 (81610)	a to I		RPIC	MA	92252 (80959)	x	**R** RPEX	EN
92198 (81613)	a to		RPEA	CA	92253 (80906)	x	**R** RPEX	EN
92200 (81615)	x to **R**		RPEX	MA	92254 (80894)	x	**R** RPEX	CA
92203 (81621)	a to I		RPEA	EN	92255 (80871)	x	**R** RPEX	CA
92204 (81622)	a to **R**		RPEA	CA	92256 (84424)	x	RPEX	CA
92205 (81623)	a to **R**		RPEA	CA	92257 (80955)	x	**I** RPEX	EN
92206 (81624)	x		RPEX	BJ	92258 (84346)	x	**R** RPEX	CA
92207 (81627)	x to		RPEX	BJ	92259 (84313)	x	**R** RPEX	EN
92208 (84403)	x		RPEX	BJ	92260 (84104)	x	RPHT	HT
92209 (80873)	x		RPEX	BJ	92261 (80988)	x*	**R** RPEX	MA
92210 (84466)	x		RPEX	BJ	92262 (84240)	x*	RPHT	HT
92211 (81267)	x	**R**	RPEX	BJ	92263 (84325)	x	RPEX	CA
92212 (80937)	x	**R**	RPEX	BJ	92264 (84239)	x*	**R** RPHT	HT
92213 (81321)	x		RPEX	CA	92265 (80945)	x	**R** RPEX	CA
92214 (84504)	x		RPEX	CA	92266 (84515)	x	**R** RPHT	HT
92215 (80911)	x		RPEX	CA	92267 (84404)	x	RPEX	CA
92216 (81376)	x	**R**	RPEX	CA	92268 (84352)	x	RPEX	LL
92217 (80877)	x	**R**	RPEX	CA	92269 (84010)	x	RPEX	CA
92218 (84314)	x	**R**	RPEX	CA	92270 (84289)	x	RPEX	CA
92219 (84285)	x		RPEX	CA	92271 (80962)	x*	RPEX	LL
92220 (80924)	x	**R**	RPEX	CA	92272 (84262)	x*	**R** RPXB	MA
92221 (80888)	x	**R**	RPEX	EN	92273 ( )			
92222 (80887)	x		RPEX	CA	92274 ( )			
92223 (80932)	x		RPEX	CA	92275 ( )			
92224 (84277)	x	**R**	RPEX	CA	92276 ( )			
92225 (80891)	x		RPEX	CA	92277 ( )			
92226 (80879)	x	**I**	RPEX	EN	92278 ( )			
92227 (84337)	x		RPEX	CA	92279 ( )			
92228 (80921)	x	**R**	RPEX	CA	92280 ( )			
92229 (80902)	x	**R**	RPEX	CA	92281 ( )			
92230 (81423)	x	**R**	RPEX	CA	92282 ( )			
92231 (80860)	x	**I**	RPEX	CA	92283 ( )			
92232 (80870)	x		RPEX	CA	92284 ( )			

92300–92390

NE (BG)   100 mph GANGWAYED BRAKE VAN

As ND but rebogied with Commonwealth bogies suitable for 100 mph. xe.
ETH 1 (1X*). For lot numbers refer to original number series. Add 1.5 t to
weights to allow for the increased weight of the Commonwealth bogies.

92300 (84200) x		RPEX	EN	92345 (84083) x*	R	RPEX	EN
92301 (80737) x		RPEX	CA	92346 (84091) x	R	RPEX	EN
92302 (84501) x	R	RPEX	CA	92347 (84326) x	RX	RPEX	CA
92303 (84427) x		RPEX	EN	92348 (84075) x*	R	RPEX	CA
92304 (84339) x		RPEX	EN	92349 (84178) x	R	RPEX	EN
92305 (84590) x		RPEX	CA	92350 (84049) x*	R	RPEX	EN
92306 (84217) x*	R	RPEX	EN	92351 (84174) x		RPEX	CA
92307 (80805) *		RPEX	CA	92352 (84182) x		RPEX	EN
92308 (80784) x		RPEX	EN	92353 (84323) x	R	RPEX	EN
92309 (84043) x*		RPEX	EN	92354 (84353) x	R	RPEX	EN
92310 (84105) x	R	RPEX	EN	92355 (84517) x		RPEX	CA
92311 (84453) x	R	RPEX	EN	92356 (84535) x		RPEX	EN
92312 (84548) x		RPEX	EN	92357 (84136) x		RPEX	EN
92313 (80992) x		RPEX	CA	92358 (84393) x		RPEX	EN
92314 (80777) x*	R	RPEX	CA	92359 (84275) x		RPEX	EN
92315 (80848) x*	N	RPEX	EN	92360 (84431) x		RPEX	EN
92316 (80980) x*	R	RPEX	EN	92361 (84463) x	R	RPEX	EN
92317 (80836) x		RPEX	CA	92362 (84188) x	R	RPEX	EN
92318 (80847) x*		RPEX	CA	92363 (84294) x	R	RPEX	EN
92319 (84055) x	I	RPEX	EN	92364 (84030) x*	R	RPEX	EN
92320 (84166) x		RPEX	EN	92365 (84122) x		RPEX	EN
92321 (84566) x	I	RPEX	EN	92366 (84551) x		RPEX	CA
92322 (80771) x*	RX	RPEX	CA	92367 (84293) x pt		RPEX	CA
92323 (80832) x	R	RPEX	CA	92368 (84334) x		RPEX	CA
92324 (84087) x	I	RPEX	EN	92369 (80960) x*		RPEX.	CA
92325 (80791) x	R	RPEX	CA	92370 (84324) x		RPEX	CA
92326 (84270) x		RPEX	CA	92371 (80856) x*		RPEX	CA
92327 (80842) x*		RPEX	EN	92372 (84362) x	R	RPEX	CA
92328 (80999) x*	R	RPEX	CA	92373 (84528) x	R	RPEX	CA
92329 (84001) x*	R	RPEX	CA	92374 (84317) x		RPEX	CA
92330 (80995) x*	R	RPEX	CA	92375 (84335) x		RPEX	CA
92331 (84365) x		RPEX	EN	92376 (84474) x		RPEX	CA
92332 (80845) x*	RX	RPEX	EN	92377 (80928) x*		RPEX	CA
92333 (80982) x*	R	RPEX	CA	92379 (80914) x*	RX	RPEX	CA
92334 (80983) x*	R	RPEX	EN	92380 (84247) x*	R	RPEX	EN
92335 (80973) x*		RPEX	CA	92381 (84476) x	RX	RPEX	CA
92336 (84045) x*		RPEX	EN	92382 (84561) x		RPEX	EN
92337 (84140) x*	RX	RPEX	EN	92383 (84429) x		RPEX	EN
92338 (84524) x		ILAG	LA	92384 (80893) x		RPEX	EN
92339 (84530) x	R	RPEX	EN	92385 (84261) x*	R	RPEX	CA
92340 (84059) x*	R	RPEX	EN	92386 (80843) x		RPEX	EN
92341 (84316) x	R	RPEX	EN	92387 (84380) x		RPEX	CA
92342 (84397) x	R	RPEX	EN	92388 (80868) x*	R	RPEX	EN
92343 (84505) x	R	RPEX	EN	92389 (84026) x		RPHT	HT
92344 (84154) x*	R	RPEX	EN	92390 (80834) x*		RPEX	CA

92391 (80790) x		**R**	RPEX	CA	92411 (84252) x*	**R**	RPEX	EN
92392 (80861) x*		**R**	RPEX	EN	92412 (84354) x	**R**	RPEX	EN
92393 (80701) x		**R**	RPHT	HT	92413 (84472) x	**R**	RPEX	CA
92394 (84322) x			RPEX	EN	92414 (84458) x		RPEX	CA
92395 (84274) x			RPEX	MA	92415 (		)	
92396 (84430) x			RPEX	CA	92416 (		)	
92397 (80700) x*			RPEX	CA	92417 (		)	
92398 (80859) x*		**R**	RPEX	CA	92418 (		)	
92399 (80781) x*		**R**	RPEX	CA	92419 (		)	
92400 (84211) x*			RPEX	LL	92420 (		)	
92401 (84280) x			RPEX	LL	92421 (		)	
92402 (84099) x*		**R**	RPEX	LL	92422 (		)	
92403 (84273) x		**R**	RPEX	CA	92423 (		)	
92404 (84051) x*			RPEX	CA	92424 (		)	
92405 (84320) x			RPEX	EN	92425 (		)	
92406 (84475) x		**R**	RPEX	CA	92426 (		)	
92407 (84363) x			RPEX	CA	92427 (		)	
92408 (84351) x			RPEX	EC	92428 (		)	
92409 (84370) x*			RPEX	CA	92429 (		)	
92410 (84469) x			RPEX	CA	92430 (		)	

NE/NH (BG) 100/110 mph GANGWAYED BRAKE VAN

Renumbered from 92xxx series by adding 900 to number.

92900 (80723) a pg**l**	RPEA	EN	92929 (81077) NHA **l**	RPIP	PC
92908 (80895) NHA **l**	RPIP	PC	92939 (81175) NHA **l**	RPIP	PC
92911 (80903) a*pg**l**	IWCX	EC	92948 (81218) NHA **l**	RPIP	PC
92914 (80923) x*pg**l**	RPEX	EN	92961 (81231) a **l**	RPIP	NC
92919 (80944) x*pg**l**	RPEX	EN	92969 (81245) a to **RX** RPEA	CA
92920 (80950) x*pg**l**	RPEX	CA	92979 (81260) a to **R** RPEA	CA
92927 (81061) NHA **l**	RPIP	WB			

NJ/NK/NX (GUV) GENERAL UTILITY VAN

Mark 1. Short frames. Load 14 t. All vehicles are through steam piped only (Dia. NK501) unless otherwise stated. Screw couplings. Electric wired vehicles or steam piped and electric wired vehicles are Dia. NJ501. All vehicles have BR Mark 2 bogies. ETH 0 or 0X.

93078–93499. Lot No. 30417 Pressed Steel 1958–9. 30 t.
93501–93519. Lot No. 30343 York 1957. 30 t.
93521–93654. Lot No. 30403 York/Glasgow 1958–60. 30 t.
93655–93834. Lot No. 30565 York 1959. 30 t.
93835–93984. Lot No. 30616 Pressed Steel 1959–60. 30 t.

93078	**B**	RPXX	BJ	93105	**B**	RPXX	BJ
93079	**B**	RPKV	BJ	93110 xy*	**B**	RPJX	BJ
93084 xy*	**B**	RPJX	CA	93112 xy*	**B**	RPJX	CA
93086	**B**	RPXX	BJ	93117	**B**	RPKV	BJ
93091 xy*	**R**	RPJX	CA	93122 xy*	**R**	RPJX	CA
93100	**B**	RPSU	BJ	93131 vr*	**R**	RPJV	BJ
93104 xr*	**B**	RPJX	CA	93134 xy*	**RX**	RPOX	CA

93135	vr*	B	RPJV	BJ
93138		B	RPKV	BJ
93160	xy*	B	RPJX	CA
93163	vr*	B	RPJV	BJ
93165	xy*	R	RPJX	CA
93172	vr*	B	RPJX	CA
93176	vr*	B	RPJV	BJ
93180		B	RPKV	BJ
93185	vr*	B	RPJV	BJ
93187		B	RPXX	BJ
93191		B	RPXX	BJ
93192	xy*	B	RPJX	CA
93193		B	RPKV	BJ
93195	vr*	B	RPJV	BJ
93205	xy*	B	RPJX	CA
93207		B	RPJV	BJ
93210	xy*	B	RPJX	BJ
93212	xy*	B	RPJX	BJ
93214		B	RPKV	BJ
93236	vr*	B	RPJV	BJ
93249	xy*	B	RPJX	CA
93251	vr*	B	RPJV	BJ
93255	xr*	B	RPJX	CA
93258	vr*	B	RPJV	BJ
93262	xy*	B	RPJX	CA
93263	xy*	R	RPXE	CA
93265	xy*	B	RPJX	CA
93267	vr*	R	RPJV	BJ
93273	xr*	B	RPJV	BJ
93277	xy*	B	RPJX	CA
93278	vr*	B	RPJV	BJ
93284	vr*	B	RPJV	BJ
93291		B	RPKV	BJ
93292	vr*	B	RPJV	BJ
93293	xy*	B	RPJX	CA
93295		B	RPXX	MA
93319		B	RPKV	BJ
93336		B	RPXX	BJ
93345	vr	B	RPJV	BJ
93348		B	RPXT	BJ
93349	vr		RPJV	BJ
93356		B	RPKV	BJ
93362	xy*	B	RPJX	CA
93367	vr*	B	RPJV	BJ
93370	vr*	R	RPJV	BJ
93375	vr*	B	RPJV	BJ
93379	vr*	B	RPJV	BJ
93386		B	RPXX	BJ
93388	vr*	B	RPJV	BJ
93390		B	RPSU	BJ
93394	vr*	R	RPJV	BJ
93395	xy*	R	RPJX	CA

93396	xy*	B	RPJX	BJ
93401	vr*	B	RPJV	BJ
93407	xy*	B	RPJX	BJ
93411	xy*	B	RPJX	CA
93416	xy*	B	RPJX	CA
93429	xy*	B	RPJX	CA
93431	vr*	B	RPJV	BJ
93446	vr	B	RPJV	BJ
93450	vr*	B	RPJV	BJ
93462	xy*	B	RPOC	BJ
93464		B	RPKV	BJ
93474	vr*	R	RPJV	BJ
93475		B	RPXX	BJ
93478	vr	B	RPJV	BJ
93479		R	RPXT	BJ
93482		B	RPKV	BJ
93485	xr*	B	RPJV	CA
93490	vr	B	RPJV	BJ
93495	vr*		RPJV	BJ
93499	xy*	B	RPJV	BJ
93508	vr*	B	RPJV	BJ
93511	vr*	R	RPJV	BJ
93514	vr*	B	RPJV	BJ
93515	vr*	B	RPJV	BJ
93519		B	RPKV	BJ
93521	xy*	B	RPJX	CA
93523	xy	B	RPJX	BJ
93525	vr*	B	RPJV	BJ
93529	vr*	B	RPJV	BJ
93536	vr*	B	RPJV	CF
93539	xy*	B	RPJX	BJ
93541	vr*	R	RPJV	BJ
93549		B	RPXT	BJ
93556	vr*	B	RPJV	BJ
93557	vr*	B	RPJV	BJ
93560	xy*	R	RPJX	CA
93562	vr*	B	RPJV	BJ
93563	vr*	B	RPJV	BJ
93571	xy*	R	RPJX	BJ
93581	xr*	B	RPJX	CA
93585	vr*	B	RPJV	BJ
93590	xy*	B	RPJX	CA
93596	vr*	B	RPJV	BJ
93604	xy*	RX	RPXE	CA
93606	xy*	B	RPJX	BJ
93610	xy*	B	RPJX	BJ
93617		B	RPKV	BJ
93622	vr*	B	RPJV	BJ
93624	vr*	B	RPJV	BJ
93630	vr*	B	RPJV	BJ
93633	vr*	B	RPJV	BJ
93635		B	RPXX	BJ

93643	vr	**R**	RPJV	BJ	93849	vr*	**R**	RPJV	BJ
93648	xy	**B**	RPJX	CA	93852	xr*	**N**	NWXX	EH
93656			RPJV	BJ	93854	vr*	**B**	RPJV	BJ
93660	vr*	**R**	RPJV	BJ	93855	vr*	**B**	RPJV	BJ
93663		**B**	RPKV	BJ	93857	vr*	**B**	RPJV	BJ
93664		**B**	RPXX	BJ	93858		**B**	RPKV	BJ
93677	vr*	**B**	RPJV	BJ	93859	vr*	**B**	RPJV	BJ
93683	vr*	**B**	RPJV	BJ	93881	vr*	**B**	RPJV	BJ
93694	xy*	**N**	NWXX	EH	93886	vr*	**R**	RPJV	BJ
93701	vr*	**B**	RPJV	BJ	93887	vr*	**B**	RPXX	BJ
93706	vy	**B**	RPJV	BJ	93889	vr*	**B**	RPJV	BJ
93710	vy	**B**	RPJV	BJ	93893	vr*	**B**	RPJV	BJ
93711	vy	**B**	RPJV	BJ	93897	xr*	**R**	RPJX	CA
93713	vy	**R**	RPJV	BJ	93904		**B**	RPXT	BJ
93714	vy	**B**	RPJV	BJ	93905	vr*	**R**	RPJV	BJ
93715	vy	**B**	RPJV	BJ	93907		**B**	RPKV	BJ
93717	vy	**B**	RPJV	BJ	93911	vr*	**B**	RPJV	BJ
93720	vy	**R**	RPJV	BJ	93914	xr*	**B**	RPJX	CA
93722	vy	**R**	RPJV	BJ	93915	vr*	**B**	RPJV	BJ
93725	vy	**R**	RPJV	BJ	93922		**B**	RPXT	BJ
93726	vy	**R**	RPJV	BJ	93930		**B**	RPXX	BJ
93727	vy	**B**	RPJV	BJ	93932		**B**	RPXT	BJ
93728	vy	**B**	RPJV	BJ	93935	vr*	**R**	RPJV	BJ
93775	xy*	**B**	RPJX	BJ	93943		**B**	RPKV	BJ
93791		**B**	RPKV	BJ	93948		**B**	RPXT	BJ
93798	xy*	**B**	RPJX	BJ	93950	vr*	**B**	RPJV	BJ
93801		**B**	RPKV	BJ	93952	vr*	**B**	RPJV	BJ
93811		**B**	RPSU	BJ	93955		**B**	RPJV	BJ
93815		**B**	RPKV	BJ	93957		**B**	RPKV	BJ
93820	xy*	**R**	RPJX	BJ	93962	vr*	**B**	RPJV	BJ
93823	vr	**B**	RPJV	BJ	93969	xy*	**R**	RPJX	CA
93824		**B**	RPKV	BJ	93973	vr*	**B**	RPJV	BJ
93830	vr	**B**	RPJV	BJ	93979	vr*	**B**	RPJV	BJ
93844	xy*	**B**	RPJX	CA	93982	vr*	**R**	RPJV	BJ
93847	vr*	**R**	RPJV	BJ	93999	B5	**RX**	RPEV	CA

NLX   NEWSPAPER VAN

Dia. NL501. Mark 1. Short frames (57'). Converted from GUV. Fluorescent lighting, toilets and gangways fitted. Load 14 t. ETH 3X. These vehicles were originally renumbered 85500–85534. Not now used for News traffic. B5 bogies.

*–Fitted with Mark 1 bogies with roller bearing axleboxes.

Lot No. 30922 Wolverton or Doncaster 1977–8. xe. 31 t (33 t*).

94002	(86651)	B5	**R**	RPLX	OM	94010	(86151)	BR1*	**B**	RPLX	OM
94004	(86156)	B5	**R**	RPLX	OM	94011	(86437)	B5	**B**	RPLX	OM
94005	(86845)	B5	**R**	RPLX	OM	94012	(86082)	B5	**R**	RPLX	OM
94006	(86202)	B5	**B**	RPLX	BJ	94013	(86408)	B5	**R**	RPLX	MA
94007	(86572)	B5	**R**	RPLX	OM	94015	(86484)	B5	**B**	RPLX	BJ
94009	(86144)	B5	**R**	RPLX	OM	94016	(86317)	B5	**B**	RPLX	OM

94018	(86170)	B5	**R**	RPOW	OM	94027	(86732)	BR1***R** RPLX	MA
94019	(86098)	B5	**R**	RPLX	OM	94028	(86733)	BR1***B** RPLX	BJ
94020	(86220)	B5	**R**	RPLX	OM	94029	(86740)	B5 **B** RPLX	BJ
94021	(86204)	B5	**B**	RPLX	OM	94030	(86746)	B5 **B** RPLX	OM
94023	(86221)	B5	**B**	RPLX	BJ	94031	(86747)	B5 **B** RPLX	OM
94024	(86106)	B5	**B**	RPLX	OM	94032	(86730)	B5 **B** RPLX	OM
94025	(86377)	B5	**R**	RPLX	OM	94033	(86731)	B5 **R** RPLX	BJ
94026	(86703)	B5	**R**	RPLX	BJ	94034	(86200)	B5 **B** RPLX	OM

NMV   NEWSPAPER VAN

Dia. NM501/2. Mark 1. Standard GUVs modified as newspaper vans. vd or
vd*. ETH 3 (3X*). For lot numbers see old number series. Formerly NLV. Not
now used for News traffic.

94050	(93771)	d*	**B**	RPJV	BJ	94062	(93803)	d*	**B** RPJV	BJ
94051	(93708)	e	**B**	RPJV	BJ	94068	(93424)	d*	**B** RPJV	BJ
94052	(93709)	e	**B**	RPJV	BJ	94071	(93544)	d*	**B** RPJV	BJ
94056	(93804)	e	**B**	RPJV	BJ	94076	(93842)	d*	**B** RPJV	BJ
94058	(93530)	d*	**B**	RPJV	BJ	94077	(93862)	d*	**B** RPJV	BJ
94061	(93763)	d*	**B**	RPJV	BJ	94078	(93971)	d*	**B** RPJV	BJ

NOX (GUV)   GENERAL UTILITY VAN (100 MPH ETH WIRED)

Dia. NO513. xy. ETH 0 (0X*). Commonwealth bogies. For lot Nos. see BG
section. Add 2 t to weight.

95100	(93668)	xr*	**B**	RPOX	CA	95126	(93692)		**B** RPOX	CA
95101	(93142)	xy*	**B**	RPOX	CA	95127	(93323)		**R** RPOX	CA
95102	(93762)	xy*	**B**	RPOX	CA	95128	(93764)		**R** RPXE	CA
95103	(93956)	xr*	**B**	RPOX	CA	95129	(93347)	xy*	**R** RPXE	CA
95104	(93942)	xr*	**B**	RPOX	CA	95130	(93263)			
95105	(93126)	xy*	**RX**	RPOX	CA	95131	(93860)	xr*	**R** RPXE	CA
95106	(93353)	xy*	**RX**	RPOX	CA	95132	(93607)		**R** RPOX	CA
95107	(93576)	xy*	**B**	RPOX	CA	95133	(93)			
95108	(93600)	xy*	**B**	RPOX	CA	95134	(93462)			
95109	(93269)	xy*	**B**	RPOX	CA					
95110	(93393)	xy*	**B**	RPOX	CA					
95111	(93578)	xy*	**B**	RPOX	CA					
95112	(93673)	xy*	**B**	RPOX	CA					
95113	(93235)	xy*	**B**	RPOX	CA					
95114	(93081)	xy*	**B**	RPOX	CA					
95115	(93174)	xy	**B**	RPOX	CA					
95116	(93426)	xy	**B**	RPOX	CA					
95117	(93534)	xy*	**B**	RPOX	CA					
95118	(93675)	xr	**B**	RPOX	CA					
95119	(93167)	xy*	**R**	RPOX	CA					
95120	(93468)	xy	**R**	RPOX	CA					
95121	(93518)	xy*	**B**	RPOX	CA					
95122	(93864)	xy*	**B**	RPOX	CA					
95123	(93376)	xy*	**B**	RPOX	CA					
95124	(93836)	xr*	**R**	RPOX	CA					
95125	(93143)	xy*	**B**	RPOX	CA	95199	(93141)	xy*	**R** RPOX	CA

NCX   NEWSPAPER VAN (100 mph)

Dia. NC501. BGs modified to carry newspapers. xe. ETH 3 (3X*). Commonwealth bogies. For lot Nos. see BG section. Add 2 t to weight. Not now used
for News traffic. 95229 also carried 95329.

95200 (84019) *	**R**	RPCX	CA	95214 (84360)	**B**	RPCX	CA
95201 (80875) *	**R**	RPCX	CA	95215 (80643) *	**B**	RPCX	CA
95202 (80667) *	**B**	RPCX	CA	95216 (84542)		RPCX	CA
95204 (80947) *	**R**	RPHT	HT	95217 (84385)	**B**	RPCX	CA
95205 (80620) *	**B**	RPCX	CA	95218 (80675) *	**R**	RPCX	CA
95206 (80561)	**R**	RPCX	CA	95219 (80946)	**B**	RPCX	CA
95207 (80560) *	**R**	RPHT	HT	95220 (80717) *	**B**	RPCX	CA
95208 (80660) *	**R**	RPCX	CA	95221 (84153) *		RPCX	CA
95209 (84047)	**B**	RPCX	CA	95222 (80774)	**B**	RPCX	CA
95210 (80731)	**B**	RPCX	CA	95223 (80933) *	**R**	RPCX	CA
95211 (80949)	**R**	RPCX	CA	95229 (84381)	**R**	RPCX	CA
95212 (84179)	**B**	RPCX	CA				

NCV   NEWSPAPER VAN (100 mph)

Dia. NC501. ve. Commonwealth bogies. For lot Nos. see BG section. Add 2t
to weight. Not now used for News traffic.

95300 (80689)	**B**	RPCV	BJ	95308 (84161)	**B**	RPCV	BJ
95303 (80614)	**B**	RPCV	BJ	95310 (84292)	**B**	RPOW	OM
95304 (84345)	**R**	RPOW	OM	95312 (80503)	**B**	RPCV	BJ
95305 (80863)	**B**	RPCV	BJ	95321 (80525)	**B**	RPCV	BJ
95307 (84124)	**B**	RPXX	BJ	95332 (84014)	**B**	RPCV	BJ

NRX   BAA CONTAINER VAN (100 mph)

Dia. NR503. Modified for carriage of British Airports Authority containers
with roller shutter doors and roller floors and gangways removed. xe. ETH 3
(3X*). Commonwealth bogies. For lot Nos. see BG section. Add 2 t to weight.
Also carried 95203/13 respectively.

95400 (80621)	**RX** RPAC	CA	95410 (80826)	**RX** RPAC	CA

NX (GUV)   MOTORAIL VAN

Mark 1. Dia. NX501. Renumbered from 93XXX series. For details and lot
numbers see 93XXX series. BR2 bogies unless stated otherwise. ETH
(0X*).

96100 (93734) a*B5	**I** IWCX	EN	96131 (93737) a*C	**I** IWCX	EN
96101 (93741) a*B5 I	IWCX	EN	96132 (93754) a*C	**I** IWCX	EN
96103 (93744) a*B5	IWCX	EN	96133 (93685) a C	**I** ICCX	EC
96104 (93745) a*B5 I	IWCX	EN	96134 (93691) a C	**I** ICCX	EC
96110 (93738) a*C	**I** IWCX	EN	96135 (93755) a C	**I** ICCX	EC
96111 (93742) a*C	**I** IWCX	EN	96136 (93735) a C	**I** IXXH	EC
96112 (93750) a*C	**I** IWCX	EN	96137 (93748) a C	**I** IXXH	EC
96130 (93736) a*C	**I** IWCX	EN	96138 (93749) a C	**I** IXXH	EC

6139	(93751)	a C		I ICCX	EC	96170	(93159)	x*C	I IWCX	EN
6140	(93752)	a C		IXXH	EC	96171	(93326)	x*C	N IWCX	EN
6141	(93753)	a C		B IXXH	EC	96172	(93363)	x*C	IWCX	EN
6150	(93097)	x*B5	B IWCX		EN	96173	(93440)	x*C	I IWCX	EN
6151	(93286)	x*B5	I IWCX		EN	96174	(93453)	x*C	I ICCX	EC
6152	(93324)	x*B5	IWCX		EN	96175	(93628)	x*C	I IWCX	EN
6153	(93327)	x*B5	B IWCX		EN	96176	(93641)	x*C	I IWCX	EN
6154	(93331)	x*B5	I IWCX		EN	96177	(93980)	a*C	I IWCX	EN
6155	(93334)	x*B5	IWCX		EN	96178	(93782)	a*C	I IWCX	EN
6156	(93337)	x*B5	I IWCX		EN	96179	(93910)	a*C	I IWCX	EN
6157	(93344)	x*B5	IWCX		EN	96181	(93875)	a*C	I IWCX	EN
6158	(93351)	x*B5	IWCX		EN	96182	(93944)	a*C	I IWCX	EN
6159	(93355)	x*B5	I IWCX		EN	96185	(93083)	x*C	I IWCX	EN
6160	(93385)	x*B5	I IWCX		EN	96186	(93087)	x*C	I ICCX	EC
6161	(93443)	x*B5	I IWCX		EN	96187	(93168)	x*C	I ICCX	EC
6162	(93647)	a*C	I IWCX		EN	96188	(93320)	x*C	I IWCX	EN
6163	(93646)	a*C	I IWCX		EN	96189	(93447)	x*C	I IWCX	EN
6164	(93880)	a*C	I IWCX		EN	96190	(93448)	x*C	I IWCX	EN
6165	(93784)	a*C	I IWCX		EN	96191	(93665)	x*C	I IWCX	EN
6166	(93834)	a*C	I IWCX		EN	96192	(93669)	x*C	I IWCX	EN
6167	(93756)	a*C	I IWCX		EN	96193	(93874)	x*C	I IWCX	EN
6168	(93978)	a*C	I IWCX		EN	96194	(93949)	x*C	I IWCX	EN
6169	(93937)	a*C	I IWCX		EN	96195	(93958)	x*C	B IWCX	EN

IY   EXHIBITION VAN

arious interiors. Converted from various vehicle types. Electric heating om shore supply. In some cases new lot numbers have been issued for onversions, but not always. Non-standard livery – varies according to job eing undertaken.

ot 30842 was issued for the conversion of 99621/5.

9621	(34697)	x BR1	O ICHX	?	Swindon	1972–3	NY503	Exhibition Coach.
9625	(34693)	x Mk4	O ICHX	?	Swindon	1972–3	NY503	Generator Van.
9645	(1765)	v C	O ICHE	BN	Salisbury	1981	NY523	Club Car.
9646	(1766)	v C	O ICHE	BN	Salisbury	1981	NY524	Club Car.

6. TRANS-MANCHE SUPER TRAINS

The Trans-Manche Super Trains (TMSTs) are on order for the Channel Tunnel services between London and Paris and Brussels. They are based on the French TGV design concept, and the individual cars are numbered like French TGVs.

Each train consists of two 9-coach sets back-to-back with a power car at the outer end. BR sets will be allocated to North Pole (London), Belgian Railways (SNCB/NMBS) sets will be allocated to Bruxelles Forest/Brussel Vorst and French Railways (SNCF) sets will be allocated to Le Landy (Paris). In addition there are trains for North of London which consist of two 7-coach half-sets.

All sets are articulated with an extra motor bogie on the coach next to the power car. Coaches are numbered R1–R9 (and in traffic R10–R18 in the second set). Coaches R18–R10 are identical to R1–R9.

BR Sets.

3001	730010	730011	730012
3002	730020	730021	730022
3003	730030	730031	730032
3004	730040	730041	730042
3005	730050	730051	730052
3006	730060	730061	730062
3007	730070	730071	730072
3008	730080	730081	730082
3009	730090	730091	730092
3010	730100	730101	730102
3011	730110	730111	730112
3012	730120	730121	730122
3013	730130	730131	730132
3014	730140	730141	730142
3015	730150	730151	730152
3016	730160	730161	730162
3017	730170	730171	730172
3018	730180	730181	730182
3019	730190	730191	730192
3020	730200	730201	730202
3021	730210	730211	730212
3022	730220	730221	730222

SNCB/NMBS Sets.

3101	731010	731011	731012
3102	731020	731021	731022
3103	731030	731031	731032
3104	731040	731041	731042
3105	731050	731051	731052
3106	731060	731061	731062
3107	731070	731071	731072
3108	731080	731081	731082

Systems: 25 kV a.c. overhead, 3000 V d.c. overhead and 750 V d.c. third rail.
Built: 1992–3 by GEC Alsthom at various works.
Wheel Arrangement: Bo–Bo + Bo–2–2–2–2–2–2–2–2–2.
Traction Motors: 6.
Length: 22.15 + 21.845 + [7 x 18.70] + 21.845 m.
Max. Speed: 300 km/h (187.5 mph).
Livery: White with yellow window band.
Details:

Car	Type	Seats	Lot No.	Car	Type	Seats	Lot No.
M	DM		31118	R5	TSOL	60S 2L	31123
R1	MSOL	52S 1L	31119	R6	Kitchen/bar		31124
R2	TSOL	60S 1L	31120	R7	TFOL	39F 1L	31125
R3	TSOL	60S 2L	31121	R8	TFOL	39F 1L	31126
R4	TSOL	60S 1L	31122	R9	TBFOL	27F 1L	31127

730013	730014	730015	730016	730017	730018	730019
730023	730024	730025	730026	730027	730028	730029
730033	730034	730035	730036	730037	730038	730039
730043	730044	730045	730046	730047	730048	730049
730053	730054	730055	730056	730057	730058	730059
730063	730064	730065	730066	730067	730068	730069
730073	730074	730075	730076	730077	730078	730079
730083	730084	730085	730086	730087	730088	730089
730093	730094	730095	730096	730097	730098	730099
730103	730104	730105	730106	730107	730108	730109
730113	730114	730115	730116	730117	730118	730119
730123	730124	730125	730126	730127	730128	730129
730133	730134	730135	730136	730137	730138	730139
730143	730144	730145	730146	730147	730148	730149
730153	730154	730155	730156	730157	730158	730159
730163	730164	730165	730166	730167	730168	730169
730173	730174	730175	730176	730177	730178	730179
730183	730184	730185	730186	730187	730188	730189
730193	730194	730195	730196	730197	730198	730199
730203	730204	730205	730206	730207	730208	730209
730213	730214	730215	730216	730217	730218	730219
730223	730224	730225	730226	730227	730228	730229

731013	731014	731015	731016	731017	731018	731019
731023	731024	731025	731026	731027	731028	731029
731033	731034	731035	731036	731037	731038	731039
731043	731044	731045	731046	731047	731048	731049
731053	731054	731055	731056	731057	731058	731059
731063	731064	731065	731066	731067	731068	731069
731073	731074	731075	731076	731077	731078	731079
731083	731084	731085	731086	731087	731088	731089

SNCF Sets.

3201	732010	732011	732012
3202	732020	732021	732022
3203	732030	732031	732032
3204	732040	732041	732042
3205	732050	732051	732052
3206	732060	732061	732062
3207	732070	732071	732072
3208	732080	732081	732082
3209	732090	732091	732092
3210	732100	732101	732102
3211	732110	732111	732112
3212	732120	732121	732122
3213	732130	732131	732132
3214	732140	732141	732142
3215	732150	732151	732152
3216	732160	732161	732162
3217	732170	732171	732172
3218	732180	732181	732182
3219	732190	732191	732192
3220	732200	732201	732202
3221	732210	732211	732212
3222	732220	732221	732222
3223	732230	732231	732232
3224	732240	732241	732242
3225	732250	732251	732252
3226	732260	732261	732262
3227	732270	732271	732272
3228	732280	732281	732282
3229	732290	732291	732292
3230	732300	732301	732302
3231	732310	732311	732312
3232	732320	732321	732322

BR "North of London" Sets.

These are 7-coach sets consisting of PC + R1/3/2/5/6/7/9 only.

3301	733010	733011	733013
3302	733020	733021	733023
3303	733030	733031	733033
3304	733040	733041	733043
3305	733050	733051	733053
3306	733060	733061	733063
3307	733070	733071	733073
3308	733080	733081	733083
3309	733090	733091	733093
3310	733100	733101	733103
3311	733110	733111	733113
3312	733120	733121	733123
3313	733130	733131	733133
3314	733140	733141	733143

732013	732014	732015	732016	732017	732018	732019
732023	732024	732025	732026	732027	732028	732029
732033	732034	732035	732036	732037	732038	732039
732043	732044	732045	732046	732047	732048	732049
732053	732054	732055	732056	732057	732058	732059
732063	732064	732065	732066	732067	732068	732069
732073	732074	732075	732076	732077	732078	732079
732083	732084	732085	732086	732087	732088	732089
732093	732094	732095	732096	732097	732098	732099
732103	732104	732105	732106	732107	732108	732109
732113	732114	732115	732116	732117	732118	732119
732123	732124	732125	732126	732127	732128	732129
732133	732134	732135	732136	732137	732138	732139
732143	732144	732145	732146	732147	732148	732149
732153	732154	732155	732156	732157	732158	732159
732163	732164	732165	732166	732167	732168	732169
732173	732174	732175	732176	732177	732178	732179
732183	732184	732185	732186	732187	732188	732189
732193	732194	732195	732196	732197	732198	732199
732203	732204	732205	732206	732207	732208	732209
732213	732214	732215	732216	732217	732218	732219
732223	732224	732225	732226	732227	732228	732229
732233	732234	732235	732236	732237	732238	732239
732243	732244	732245	732246	732247	732248	732249
732253	732254	732255	732256	732257	732258	732259
732263	732264	732265	732266	732267	732268	732269
732273	732274	732275	732276	732277	732278	732279
732283	732284	732285	732286	732287	732288	732289
732293	732294	732295	732296	732297	732298	732299
732303	732304	732305	732306	732307	732308	732309
732313	732314	732315	732316	732317	732318	732319
732323	732324	732325	732326	732327	732328	732329

733012	733015	733016	733017	733019
733022	733025	733026	733027	733029
733032	733035	733036	733037	733039
733042	733045	733046	733047	733049
733052	733055	733056	733057	733059
733062	733065	733066	733067	733069
733072	733075	733076	733077	733079
733082	733085	733086	733087	733089
733092	733095	733096	733097	733099
733102	733105	733106	733107	733109
733112	733115	733116	733117	733119
733122	733125	733126	733127	733129
733132	733135	733136	733137	733139
733142	733145	733146	733147	733149

PLATFORM 5
EUROPEAN RAILWAY HANDBOOKS

The Platform 5 European Railway Handbooks are the most comprehensive guides to the rolling stock of selected European railway administrations available. Each book lists all locomotives and multiple units of the country concerned, giving details of number carried, livery and depot allocation, together with a wealth of technical data for each class of vehicle. Lists of preserved locos and MUs are also included, plus a guide to preservation centres. Each book is A5 size, thread sewn and includes at least 16 pages of colour photographs.

The new second edition of French Railways/Chemins de Fer Français and the first edition of Swiss Railways/Chemins de fer Suisses, both contain 32 pages of colour illustrations and are produced in English and French. The full range of overseas titles available is as follows:

French Railways/Chemins de Fer Français 2nd Edition . **£9.95**
Swiss Railways/Chemins de fer Suisses **£9.95**
DB/German Federal Railway 2nd Edition **£6.95**
ÖBB/Austrian Federal Railways 2nd Edition **£6.95**
Benelux Locomotives & Coaching Stock 2nd Edition **£6.95**
A Guide to Portuguese Railways (Fearless) **£4.95**

Other Publishers' Overseas Titles:

Canadian Trackside Guide 1990 .... £9.95
Railways of Southern Africa Locomotive Guide £3.50
Industrial Locomotives of South Africa 1991 .... £6.50

All these publications are available from shops, bookstalls or direct from: Mail Order Department, Platform 5 Publishing Ltd., Lydgate House, Lydgate Lane, Sheffield, S10 5FH. For a full list of titles available by mail order, please send SAE to the above address.

7. PRIVATELY OWNED COACHES

This list comprises privately owned coaches which are "plated" to run on The private owner number is carried on a yellow plate affixed to the solebar. Coaches have to be passed by BR each year and this is denoted by a white equilateral triangle painted on the solebar with the year painted in black. In the following list, the original number is shown in column 2. It should be noted that other numbers may also have been carried. It should be noted that there are other vehicles with PO numbers which are not to be found in the following list. These are vehicles which are not at present registered for running.

Note: All vehicles are assumed to be of BR Mark 1 type unless stated otherwise.

Numbers		Type	Base	Comments
PWDS	99030	34666 BSK	SMC	5407 support coach
MRC	99040	21232 BCK	MRC	80080 support coach
MRC	99041	35476 BSK	MRC	46203 support coach
SGM	99045	34625 BSK	MRC	44932 support coach
MCA	99050	1 GER inspection saloon	GPS	Sir W.H.Mcalpine's sal.
RHE	99052	484 WCJS dining saloon	SMC	'Queen of Scots' train
RFM	99053	9004 GWR first saloon	SMC	Railfilms Ltd saloon
DBA	99070	35123 BSK	BKR	44871 support coach
PES	99090	35131 BSK	SHL	46201 support coach
SGST	99108	14018 BFK	BRM	On loan to SVR for 8233
WDS	99121	3105 FO	SMC	
PULR	99122	3106 FO	FSS	BN91 set
PULR	99123	3109 FO	FSS	BN91 set
PULR	99124	3110 FO	FSS	BN91 set
PULR	99129	21272 BCK	FSS	BN91 set
PULR	99130	14013 BFK	GPS	4472 support coach
GSWR	99131	1531 LNER prototype first	GSW	'Royal Scotsman' train
PULR	99132	1861 RMB	FSS	BN91 set
CHEL	99140	796 GWR third	GWD	Reb. as dynamometer car
CHEL	99141	14041 Mark 2 BFK	GWD	71000 support coach
SU	99180	35333 BSK	GWD	6024 support coach
PULR	99190	3131 FO	FSS	On lease from BR. BN91
PULR	99191	3132 FO	FSS	On lease from BR. BN91
PULR	99192	3133 FO	FSS	On lease from BR. BN91
PULR	99193	4860 TSO	FSS	On lease from BR. BN91
PULR	99194	5032 TSO	FSS	On lease from BR. BN91
PULR	99195	5035 TSO	FSS	On lease from BR. BN91
PULR	99196	35469 BSK (Generator van)	FSS	On lease from BR. BN91
SVR	99241	35449 BSK	SVR	34027 support coach
SVR	99242	35467 BSK	SVR	75069/7819 supp. coach
WDS	99302	13323 FK	SMC	
WDS	99303	13317 FK	SMC	
DS	99304	21256 BCK	SMC	
WDS	99312	35463 BSK	SMC	48151 support coach
DRC	99313	35451 BSK	KWR	45596 support coach

WDS	99314	25729	SK	SMC	
WDS	99315	25955	SK	SMC	
WDS	99316	13321	FK	SMC	
WDS	99317	3766	TSO	SMC	
WDS	99318	4912	TSO	SMC	
PULR	99335	335	Pullman kitchen second	FSS	
PULR	99347	347	Pullman parlour second	FSS	
PULR	99348	348	Pullman parlour second	FSS	
PULR	99349	349	Pullman parlour second	FSS	
PULR	99350	350	Pullman parlour second	FSS	
PULR	99351	351	Pullman parlour second	FSS	
PULR	99352	352	Pullman parlour second	FSS	
PULR	99353	353	Pullman parlour second	FSS	
PULR	99354	354	Pullman parlour second	FSS	
PULR	99356	21245	BCK	FSS	BN 91 set
PULR	99357	3112	FO	FSS	BN 91 set
PULR	99358	3108	FO	FSS	Sold to West Somerset.
GRAM	99371	3128	FO	GRT	
JBC	99405	35486	BSK	MGD	60009 support coach
HLPG	99420	21214	BSK	HLG	5305 support coach
HLPG	99421	14021	BFK	HLG	
HLPG	99422	15644	BCK	HLG	
HLPG	99423	4828	SO	HLG	
HLPG	99424	4823	SO	HLG	
HLPG	99425	4822	SO	HLG	
HLPG	99426	4786	SO	HLG	
HLPG	99427	35204	BSK	HLG	777 support coach
HLPG	99428	5036	TSO	HLG	
GWS	99512	34671	BSK	GWD	5029 support coach
VSOE	99530	301	Pullman parlour first	SCL	'PERSEUS'
VSOE	99531	302	Pullman parlour first	SCL	'PHOENIX'
VSOE	99532	308	Pullman parlour first	SCL	'CYGNUS'
VSOE	99533	70741	LNER BGP	SCL	'BAGGAGE CAR No. 7'
VSOE	99534	245	Pullman kitchen first	SCL	'IBIS'
VSOE	99535	213	Pullman Brake First	SCL	'MINERVA'
VSOE	99536	254	Pullman parlour first	SCL	'ZENA'
VSOE	99537	280	Pullman kitchen first	SCL	'AUDREY'
VSOE	99538	34991	BSK	SCL	'BAGGAGE CAR No. 9'
VSOE	99539	255	Pullman kitchen first	SCL	'IONE'
VSOE	99540	3069	FO	SCL	'SALOON CAR No. 1'
VSOE	99541	243	Pullman kitchen first	SCL	'LUCILLE'
VSOE	99542		Ex Ferry van 889202	SCL	'BAGGAGE CAR No. 8'
VSOE	99543	284	Pullman kitchen first	SCL	'VERA'
MANC	99670	546	Pullman parlour first	MET	'CITY OF MANCHESTER'
MANC	99671	548	Pullman parlour first	MET	'ELIZABETHAN'
MANC	99672	549	Pullman parlour first	MET	'PRINCE RUPERT'
MANC	99673	550	Pullman parlour first	MET	'GOLDEN ARROW'
MANC	99674	551	Pullman parlour first	MET	'CALEDONIAN'
MANC	99675	552	Pullman parlour first	MET	'SOUTHERN BELLE'
MANC	99676	553	Pullman parlour first	MET	'KING ARTHUR'
MANC	99677	586	Pullman brake first	MET	'TALISMAN'
MANC	99678	504	Pullman kitchen first	MET	'WHITE ROSE'

ANC	99679	506	Pullman kitchen first	MET	'RED ROSE'
ANC	99680	14102	Mark 2A BFK	MET	'TRAIN MANAGER'S SALOON'
RTS	99710	25767	SK	TTM	
RTS	99712	25893	SK	TTM	
RTS	99713	26013	SK	TTM	
RTS	99714	16187	CK	TTM	
RTS	99716	25808	SK	TTM	
RTS	99717	25837	SK	TTM	
RTS	99718	25862	SK	TTM	
RTS	99719	16191	CK	TTM	
RTS	99720	35461	BSK	TTM	
RTS	99721	25806	SK	TTM	
RTS	99722	25756	SK	TTM	
RTS	99723	35459	BSK	TTM	
CR	99818	1730	RB	BKR	
CR	99820	1871	TSO	BKR	
CR	99821	9227	BSO	BKR	
CR	99822	1859	RMB	BKR	
CR	99823	4832	TSO	BKR	
CR	99824	4831	TSO	BKR	
CR	99825	13228	FK	BKR	
CR	99826	13229	FK	BKR	
CR	99827	3096	FO	BKR	
E	99880	5159	LNWR dining saloon	SMC	'Queen of Scots' train
E	99881	807	GNR family saloon	SMC	'Queen of Scots' train
E	99882	26169	SK	SMC	'Queen of Scots' train
E	99883	2108	SLF	SMC	'Queen of Scots' train
E	99884	26208	SK	SMC	'Queen of Scots' train
E	99885	2110	SLF	SMC	'Queen of Scots' train
E	99886	35407	BSK	SMC	'Queen of Scots' train
WR	99887	2127	SLF	GSW	'Royal Scotsman' train
E	99888	2442	SLC	SMC	'Queen of Scots' train
MY	99951	10656	SR DMBTK (EMU 2 Bil)	BI	National collection
MY	99952	12123	SR DTCK (EMU 2 Bil)	BI	National collection
MY	99953	35468	BSK	NRM	Loco support coach
WR	99960	23890	LNER Third	GSW	'Royal Scotsman'
WR	99961	324	Pullman parlour first	GSW	'Royal Scotsman'
WR	99962	329	Pullman parlour first	GSW	'Royal Scotsman'
WR	99963	331	Pullman parlour first	GSW	'Royal Scotsman'
WR	99964	313	Pullman kitchen first	GSW	'Royal Scotsman'
WR	99965	319	Pullman kitchen first	GSW	'Royal Scotsman'
WR	99966	34525	BSK	GSW	'Royal Scotsman'

BASE CODES FOR PRIVATE OPERATORS

BKR	Bo'Ness & Kinneil Railway, Bo'Ness Station, West Lothian.
BRM	Birmingham Railway Museum, Tyseley, Birmingham, West Mids.
FSS	Flying Scotsman Services, BR Bounds Green T&RSMD., London.
GPS	Southall Railway Centre, Old Southall Diesel Depot, Southall, Middlesex.
GRT	Grampian Railtours, BR Aberdeen CS, Grampian.
GSW	Great Scottish & Western Railway Company, BR Craigentinny CARMD, Edinburgh, Lothian.
GWD	Great Western Society, Didcot Railway Centre, Didcot, Oxfordshire
HLG	Humberside Locomotive Group, Dairycoates Depot, Hull, Humbs.
KWR	Keighley & Worth Valley Railway, Haworth Station, Keighley, West Yorkshire.
MET	Manchester Executive Travel, BR Crewe Carriage Shed, Crewe, Cheshire (probably to be relocated to BREL Ltd., Crewe Works).
MGD	J.B. Cameron, Thornton Junction, Fife.
MRC	Midland Railway Centre, Butterley Station, Derbyshire.
NRM	National Railway Museum, Leeman Road, York, North Yorkshire.
SCL	Sea Containers Ltd (VSOE), BR Stewarts Lane T&RSMD, London.
SHL	Steam In Hereford Ltd., Bulmers Railway Centre, Hereford, Herefordshire.
SMC	Steamtown Railway Centre, Carnforth, Lancashire.
SVR	Severn Valley Railway, The Railway Station, Bewdley, Worcs.
TTM	Train Tours, BR Edge Hill CARMD, Liverpool.

Note: We would like to thank Mr. P. Hall for information in this section.

CODES

1 LIVERY CODES

LOCOMOTIVES

locomotives are blue unless otherwise indicated. The colour of the lower
lf of the bodyside is stated first. Minor variations to these liveries are ig-
red.

Revised blue (large numbers and full height BR logo)
Blue with red solebar stripe
Civil Engineers (grey and yellow)
Departmental (plain grey with black cab doors)
New Railfreight (two – tone grey sides – no sub-sector markings)
or sub-sector markings unknown.
Trainload Construction – As 'F' with markings as on page 33.
Trainload Coal – As 'F' with markings as on page 33.
Railfreight Distribution – As 'F' with markings as on page 33.
Trainload Metals – As 'F' with markings as on page 33.
Old Railfreight (grey sides, yellow cabsides, red bufferbeams and full
height BR logo)
Trainload Petroleum – As 'F' with markings as on page 33.
As FO but with red solebar stripe
BR or GWR green.
New InterCity (white and dark grey with red stripe and swallow motif)
Old InterCity (light grey and dark grey with red stripe and yellow
lower cab sides.)
As old InterCity but without the yellow cabsides.
Network South East (grey/white/red/white/blue/white)
Other livery (non-Standard – refer to text)
Provincial Services (grey/light blue/white/dark blue).
Scotrail (light grey/light blue/white/dark grey)
Parcels (post office red and dark grey)
Rail Express Systems (post office red with blue/black markings)

COACHING STOCK

coaching stock vehicles are in standard blue & grey livery unless otherwise
icated. The colour of the lower half of the bodyside is stated first.

Plain Blue
Centro (WMPTE) (grey/light blue/white/green)
Inter-City (light grey [white on DVTs]/red stripe/dark grey).
LNER Tourist Green and Cream.
Greater Manchester PTE (orange/brown)
Greater Manchester PTE new (red/cream)
Jaffa Cake (two – tone brown with orange stripe)
BR Maroon
Merseyside PTE (yellow/white)
Network South East (grey/white/red/white/blue/white).
Network South East modified by Scotrail(grey/white/dark grey/
white/blue/white).

O	Other livery (non-Standard – refer to text).
P	Provincial Services (grey/light blue/white/dark blue).
PE	Provincial Express (buff/light grey/dark grey/light grey/buff, with dark blue, white and light blue stripes).
PM	Provincial Midline. As 'P' but with grey and cream stripes.
PN	Provincial Network NorthWest. As 'P' but grey and red stripe.
PO	Provincial Services old livery (grey/dark blue/white/light blue).
PR	Provincial Services railbus variant (dark blue/white/light blue).
PS	Provincial Scotrail (light grey/light blue stripe/dark grey).
RS	Regional Stripes (grey/light blue/white/dark blue with three black and white stripes at end of light blue band).
R	Royal Mail Red
RX	Rail Express Systems (Red and grey with blue/black markings).
S	Strathclyde PTE (orange and black)
SG	Southern green
T	Tyne and Wear PTE (yellow and white)
Y	West Yorkshire PTE (red and cream)

8.2. SECTOR CODES

The following list sector codes for BR locos and rolling stock. The locomoti
sector codes are also known as pool codes. The codes indicate the BR sub-se
tor which owns the vehicle.

LOCOMOTIVES

CYPA	Hunslet-Barclay Class 20/9.
CYPD	Foster-Yeoman Class 59/0.
CYPO	ARC Class 59/1.
DCAA	Civil Engineer Anglia Main Line Locos.
DCAB	Civil Engineer Anglia Main Line Locos (Restricted Use).
DCEA	Civil Engineer Eastern Main Line Locos.
DCEW	Civil Engineer Eastern Class 31/1 Weekend Work Locos.
DCHA	Civil Engineer Scotrail Main Line Locos.
DCHB	Civil Engineer Scotrail Main Line Locos (Restricted Use).
DCMA	Civil Engineer London Midland Class 47 Locos.
DCMB	Civil Engineer London Midland Bescot Class 31 Locos.
DCMC	Civil Engineer London Midland Crewe Class 31 Locos.
DCMN	Civil Engineer London Midland Weekend Work Locos.
DCQA	Civil Engineer BRB Main Line Locos.
DCSA	Civil Engineer Southern Main Line Locos.
DCSB	Selhurst Depot Shunting Locos.
DCSC	Chart Leacon Depot Shunting Locos.
DCSD	Eastleigh & Ryde Depots Shunting Locos.
DCSM	Civil Engineer Southern Meldon Quarry Services Locos.
DCSW	Civil Engineer Southern Weekend Work Locos.
DCWA	Civil Engineer Western Main Line Locos.
DCWC	Civil Engineer Western Class 97/6 Locos.
DCWW	Civil Engineer Western Weekend Work Locos.
DMEA	M & E.E. Main Line Locos.
DMEC	M & E.E. Class 97/7 Locos.
DMEX	M & E.E. Training Locos.

MSA	M & E.E. Southern Region Locos.
MSB	M & E.E. Southern Region Locos (Restricted Use).
OPA	Operations Class 97/8 Locos.
RTC	Research Railway Technical Centre Locos.
XXD	Departmental Stored Locos.
ABI	Trainload Construction – Immingham Locos (based at Buxton).
ALY	Trainload Construction – Thornaby Locos.
AME	Trainload Construction – Eastfield Locos.
ASB	Trainload Construction – Stewarts Lane Locos.
ASN	Trainload Construction – Toton Locos.
AXI	Trainload Construction – Immingham (Anglia) Class 37 Locos.
AXN	Trainload Construction – Toton Locos (based at Leicester).
DTE	Distribution/Trainload Shared Locos.
EAN	Power Station Coal – Class 58 Nottinghamshire Locos
EBN	Power Station Coal – Class 58 Yorkshire Locos.
ECN	Power Station Coal – Class 56 Nottinghamshire Locos
EDN	Power Station Coal – Class 56 Yorkshire Locos.
EEN	Power Station Coal – Class 56 North East Locos.
EFN	Power Station Coal – Class 20 Nottinghamshire Locos.
EGN	Power Station Coal – Class 20 North West Locos.
EHN	Power Station Coal – Class 60 North West Locos.
EJN	Power Station Coal – Class 60 Nottinghamshire Locos.
EKK	Power Station Coal – Class 37 Cardiff Locos.
ENN	Power Station Coal – Class 60 Staffordshire Locos.
EPE	Power Station Coal – Class 37 Eastfield Locos.
EXX	Power Station Coal – Stored Locos.
HAC	Nuclear Flask Traffic – Crewe Diesel Class 31 Locos
HBK	Coal – Class 37 Cardiff Locos.
MAK	Trainload Metals – Cardiff Class 37/0 Locos.
MCK	Trainload Metals – Cardiff Class 56 Locos.
MGM	Trainload Metals – Motherwell Locos.
MHK	Trainload Metals – Cardiff Canton Class 37/7, 37/9 & 60 Locos.
MMY	Trainload Metals – Thornaby Class 60 Locos.
MRY	Trainload Metals – Thornaby Class 20 Locos.
MTY	Trainload Metals – Thornaby Class 20 & 37 Locos.
MYI	Trainload Metals – Immingham Locos.
PAE	Trainload Petroleum – Eastfield Locos.
PBI	Trainload Petroleum – Crewe Diesel Locos.
PCI	Trainload Petroleum – Immingham Locos.
PDI	Trainload Petroleum – Immingham Class 60 Locos.
PEK	Trainload Petroleum – Cardiff Canton Locos.
PFR	Trainload Petroleum – Immingham Locos (Based at Ripple Lane).
PYX	Trainload Petroleum – Stored Locos.
QCK	Coal Distribution Class 37 Locos.
SCB	Blyth Shunters.
SCD	Doncaster Shunters.
SCE	Derby Etches Park Shunters.
SCK	Knottingley Shunters.
SCN	Toton Shunters.
SNH	Heaton Shunters.
SNI	Immingham Shunters.
SNL	Neville Hill Shunters.

FSNT	Tinsley Shunters.
FSNY	Thornaby Shunters.
FSSA	Ayr Shunters.
FSSB	Aberdeen Shunters.
FSSE	Eastfield Shunters.
FSSG	Grangemouth Shunters.
FSSI	Inverness Shunters.
FSSM	Motherwell Shunters.
FSWB	Bristol Bath Road Shunters.
FSWK	Cardiff Canton Shunters.
FSWL	Landore Shunters.
FXXB	New Class 60 Locos.
FXXC	Class 60 ATP Trial Loco
FXXX	General
IANA	InterCity Anglia Services Locos.
IBRA	InterCity Bristol Class 47/4 Locos (Restricted Use).
ICCA	InterCity Cross Country Services Electric Locos.
ICCP	InterCity Cross Country Services Class 43 Locos (LA or PM).
ICCS	InterCity Cross Country Services Class 43 Locos (EC).
ICDA	InterCity Crewe Diesel Class 47/4 locos.
IECA	InterCity ECML Electric Locos.
IECP	InterCity ECML Class 43 Locos.
IEDA	InterCity ECML Class 47/4 Locos.
IERA	InterCity Crewe Diesel Class 47/4 Extended Range locos.
IIHA	InterCity Inverness Class 47/4 ETH
ILRA	InterCity Bristol Class 47/4 Extended Range Locos.
IMLP	InterCity Midland Line Class 43 Locos.
IVGA	InterCity Gatwick Express Services Locos.
IWCA	InterCity WCML Electric Locos.
IWCP	InterCity WCML Class 43 Locos.
IWPA	InterCity Euston – West Midlands Services Locos.
IWRP	InterCity Western Region Services Class 43 Locos (EC).
IXXA	InterCity Stored Unserviceable Locos.
IXXS	InterCity Stored Serviceable Locos.
MDAT	Railfreight Distribution Tinsley Class 47 Locos.
MDCT	Railfreight Distribution Tinsley Class 47 Locos (based at Saltley).
MDDT	Railfreight Distribution Tinsley Class 47 Locos (extended range).
MDIB	Railfreight Distribution Dover Train Ferry Class 33/2 Locos.
MDLC	Railfreight Distribution Class 90/0 Locos.
MDMC	Railfreight Distribution Class 90/1 Locos.
MDNC	Railfreight Distribution Class 86/6 and 87/1 Locos.
MDRL	Railfreight Distribution Laira Refurbished Class 37 Locos.
MDRT	Railfreight Distribution Tinsley Refurbished Class 37 Locos.
MDST	Railfreight Distribution Tinsley Unrefurbished Class 37 Locos.
MDTT	Railfreight Distribution Tinsley Unrefurbished Class 37 Locos (Extended Range).
MDYX	Stored locos.
MSNA	Allerton Shunters.
MSNB	Bescot Shunters.
MSNC	Crewe Shunters.
MSNL	Longsight Shunters.
MSNU	Carlisle Upperby Shunters.

MSNX	Shunters. Stored Unserviceable.
MSSB	Bletchley Shunters.
MSSC	Cambridge Shunters.
MSSL	Laira Shunters.
MSSM	March Shunters.
MSSN	Norwich Shunters.
MSSO	Old Oak Common Shunters.
MSSR	Reading Shunters.
MSSS	Stratford Shunters.
MSSW	Willesden Shunters.
MSSX	Shunters. Stored Unserviceable.
NTWE	Network SouthEast West of England/North Downs Class 47/7 Locos.
NWRA	Network SouthEast Thames & Chiltern Services Locos.
NWXA	Network SouthEast West of England/North Downs Class 50 Locos.
NWXB	Network SouthEast West of England/North Downs Class 73 Locos.
PISA	Regional Railways Inverness 47 Locos.
RXLB	Rail Express Systems Class 31 Locos.
RXLC	Rail Express Systems Crewe Class 47 Locos.
RXLD	Rail Express Systems Reserve and Stored Locos.
RXLE	Rail Express Systems A.C. Electric Locos.
RXXA	Rail Express Systems – Authorised for condemnation.

COACHING STOCK

EPSL	European Passenger Services Ltd.
ANR	Inter-City – Anglia. Refurbished.
ANX	Inter-City – Anglia.
CCE	Inter-City – Cross Country. HST (EC).
CCL	Inter-City – Cross Country. On loan.
CCR	Inter-City – Cross Country. Refurbished.
CCT	Inter-City – Cross Country. HST (LA/PM).
CCX	Inter-City – Cross Country.
CHC	Inter-City – Charter and Special Services (vacuum not refurb).
CHD	Inter-City – Charter and Special Services (air not refurb).
CHH	Inter-City – Charter and Special Services (held for re-use).
CHL	Inter-City – Charter and Special Services (for loan).
CHP	Inter-City – Charter and Special Services (PO loan).
CHS	Inter-City – Charter and Special Services (steam specials).
CHV	Inter-City – Charter and Special Services (VIP).
CHX	Inter-City – Charter and Special Services.
ECD	Inter-City-East Coast Main Line. Class 92 Endurance Testing.
ECG	Inter-City – East Coast Main Line. Barrier Vehicles.
ECX	Inter-City – East Coast Main Line.
LAG	Inter-City – HST Barrier Vehicles LA.
MLR	Inter-City – Midland Main Line Refurbished (HSTs).
MLX	Inter-City – Midland Main Line
VGX	Inter-City – Victoria – Gatwick.
WCD	Inter-City – West Coast Main Line
WCL	Inter-City – West Coast Main Line. On loan.
WCR	Inter-City – West Coast Main Line. Refurbished.
WCW	Inter-City – West Coast Main Line. WR HSTs.
WCX	Inter-City – West Coast Main Line.

IWRG	Inter-City – Great Western Main Line. Barrier Vehicles.
IWRL	Inter-City – Great Western Main Line. On loan.
IWRR	Inter-City – Great Western Main Line.
IWRX	Inter-City – Great Western Main Line.
IXXH	Inter-City – Held for further use.
IXXT	Inter-City – Awaiting transfer to new sector.
IXXX	Inter-City – General.
IXXZ	Inter-City – Authorised for condemnation.
NGBX	Network South East – Gospel Oak – Barking service.
NGEX	Network South East – Great Eastern.
NGNX	Network South East – Great Northern.
NKCX	Network South East – Kent Coast.
NKSX	Network South East – Kent Suburban.
NMLX	Network South East – Midland Line.
NMYX	Network South East – Marylebone Line services.
NNDX	Network South East – North East London DMU services.
NNEX	Network South East – North East London Suburban.
NNLX	Network South East – North London Line.
NNWX	Network South East – London and North Western.
NSBX	Network South East – Surrey and Berkshire Suburban.
NSLX	Network South East – Sussex Local Services.
NSSX	Network South East – Solent and Sarum.
NSXX	Network South East – Sussex.
NTSX	Network South East – London Tilbury & Southend Line.
NWRX	Network South East – Western Region.
NWXX	Network South East – West of England/North Downs services.
NXXX	Network South East – General.
NXXZ	Network South East – Approved for condemnation.
PXXZ	Provincial – Authorised for condemnation.
RPAC	Rail Express Systems – IATA container traffic.
RPCV	Rail Express Systems – Unassigned NCVs.
RPCX	Rail Express Systems – Unassigned NCXs.
RPDV	Rail Express Systems – Unassigned NDVs.
RPDX	Rail Express Systems – Unassigned NDXs.
RPEA	Rail Express Systems – Unassigned NEAs.
RPEV	Rail Express Systems – Unassigned exhibition vehicles.
RPEX	Rail Express Systems – Unassigned NEXs.
RPHT	Rail Express Systems – Allocated to Heaton.
RPIC	Rail Express Systems – BGs with cage.
RPIP	Rail Express Systems – BGs for general use.
RPJV	Rail Express Systems – Unassigned NJVs.
RPJX	Rail Express Systems – Unassigned NJXs.
RPKV	Rail Express Systems – Unassigned NKVs.
RPLX	Rail Express Systems – Unassigned NLXs.
RPMA	Rail Express Systems – EMUs.
RPMB	Rail Express Systems – EMUs held for conversion.
RPOA	Rail Express Systems – Post Office (AR).
RPOC	Rail Express Systems – Post Office central van fleet.
RPOM	Rail Express Systems – Post Office (LMR).
RPOW	Rail Express Systems – Post Office (SR & WR).
RPOX	Rail Express Systems – NOX unallocated.
RPOZ	Rail Express Systems – Post Office (ScR).

RPSU	Rail Express Systems – Stored unserviceable.
RPTS	Rail Express Systems – Unassigned NEXs. Time switch fitted.
RPXB	Rail Express Systems – General (NDX).
RPXC	Rail Express Systems – General (NDV).
RPXE	Rail Express Systems – General (GUV air/dual braked).
RPXG	Rail Express Systems General (Courier vehicles).
RPXT	Rail Express Systems – General. Surplus to requirements.
RPXX	Rail Express Systems – General. Authorised for condemnation.

Note: All other Regional Railways Sector codes for are the letter 'P' followed by the two letter depot code followed by a letter 'X'.

8.3 DEPOT CODES

AB	Aberdeen T&RSMD
AF	Ashford Chart Leacon TMD
AL	Aylesbury TMD
AN	Allerton TMD (Liverpool)
AR	ARC Limited (Whatley)
AY	Ayr TMD
BD	Birkenhead North T&RSMD
BI	Brighton T&RSMD
BJ	Bristol Marsh Junction T&RSMD
BL	Blyth Cambois SD
BM	Bournemouth EMUD
BN	Bounds Green T&RSMD (London)
BR	Bristol Bath Road TMD
BS	Bescot TMD (Walsall)
BX	Buxton TMD
BY	Bletchley TMD
CA	Cambridge T&RSMD
CC	Clacton EMUD
CD	Crewe TMD (D)
CE	Crewe TMD (E)
CE	Crewe TMD (E)
CF	Cardiff Canton T&RSMD
CK	Corkerhill SD (Glasgow)
CL	Carlisle Upperby CWMD
DR	Doncaster TMD
DY	Derby Etches Park T&RSMD
EC	Craigentinny T&RSMD (Edinburgh)
ED	Eastfield TMD (Glasgow)
EH	Eastleigh T&RSMD
EM	East Ham EMUD (London)
EN	Euston Downside CARMD (London)
FF	Bruxelles Forest/Brussel Vorst
FY	Merehead (Foster Yeoman)
GI	Gillingham EMUD
GM	Grangemouth SD
GW	Glasgow Shields TMD
HA	Haymarket TMD (Edinburgh)

HB	Kilmarnock (Hunslet-Barclay)
HE	Hornsey TMD (London)
HR	Hall Road EMUD
HT	Heaton T&RSMD (Newcastle)
IL	Ilford T&RSMD (London)
IM	Immingham TMD (S.Humb'side)
IS	Inverness T&RSMD
KM	Kingmoor Yard (Carlisle)
KY	Knottingley TMD
LA	Laira T&RSMD (Plymouth)
LE	Landore T&RSMD (Swansea)
LG	Longsight TMD (E) (Manchester)
LL	Liverpool Edge Hill CARMD
LO	Longsight TMD (D) (Manchester)
LP	Le Landy (Paris)
MA	Manchester Longsight CARMD
ME	Marylebone TMD (London)
ML	Motherwell TMD
MR	March TMD
NC	Norwich Crown Point T&RSMD
NH	Newton Heath TMD (D)(Manchester)
NL	Neville Hill T&RSMD (Leeds)
NP	North Pole International (London)
OC	Old Oak Common TMD (D) (London)
OM	Old Oak Common CARMD (London)
OO	Old Oak Common TMD (HST) (London)
OY	Oxley CARMD (Wolverhampton)
PC	Polmadie CARMD (Glasgow)
PM	St. Philip's Marsh T&RSMD (Bristol)
RE	Ramsgate T&RSMD
RG	Reading TMD
RTC	Railway Technical Centre (Derby)
RY	Ryde (Isle of Wight) T&RSMD
SA	Salisbury CARMD
SF	Stratford TMD (London)
SG	Slade Green T&RSMD
SH	Strawberry Hill EMUD (London)
SL	Stewarts Lane T&RSMD (London)
SU	Selhurst TMD (London)
TE	Thornaby TMD
TI	Tinsley TMD (Sheffield)
TO	Toton TMD (Notts)
TS	Tyseley TMD (Birmingham)
WB	Wembley InterCity CARMD (London)
WC	Waterloo EMUD (Waterloo & City)
WD	East Wimbledon EMUD (London)
WN	Willesden TMD (London)
ZF	Doncaster Works BRML
ZG	Eastleigh Works BRML
ZH	Springburn Works BRML
ZN	Wolverton Works BRML

OTHER CODES USED

EMUD	Electric Multiple Unit Depot.
T&RSMD	Traction and rolling stock maintenance depot.
TMD	Traction Maintenance Depot.
TMD (E)	Traction Maintenance Depot (Electric).
CWMD	Carriage and wagon maintenance depot.
SD	Servicing depot.
T&RSMD	Traction and rolling stock maintenance depot.
TMD	Traction Maintenance Depot.
TMD (HST)	HST Maintenance Depot.
TMD (D)	Traction Maintenance Depot (Diesel).
BRML	British Rail Maintenance Ltd.
CARMD	Carriage maintenance depot.
CSD	Carriage servicing depot.
CWMD	Carriage and wagon maintenance depot.
T&RSMD	Traction and rolling stock maintenance depot.
GER	Great Eastern Railway.
GWR	Great Western Railway.
LNER	London & North Eastern Railway.
WCJS	West Coast Joint Stock.

9. OTHER RAILWAYS

9.1. BLACKPOOL & FLEETWOOD TRAMWAY

System: 660 V dc overhead.
Depot: Rigby Road.

Note: Numbers in brackets are pre-1968 numbers.

ONE-MAN CARS

Rebuilt 1972–76 from English Electric railcoaches built 1934–5. Radio fitted. 13 converted (1–13).
Seats: 48U.
Traction Motors: Two EE305 of 40 kW.

Note: First numbers in brackets are post 1968 numbers prior to conversion.

5	(609, 221)	10	(614, 267)	11	(615, 268)
8	(612, 265)				

OPEN BOAT CARS

Built 1934–5 by English Electric. 12 built (225–236).
Seats: 56U.
Traction Motors: Two EE327 of 30 kW.

600*	(225)	604§	(230)	606b	(235)
602†	(227)	605	(233)(U)	607	(236)

* On loan to Heaton Park Tramway, Manchester.
† Yellow and black livery.
§ Red and white livery.
b Blue & yellow livery.

REPLICA VANGUARD

Built 1987 by Bolton Trams on underframe of one man car No. 7.(619–282).
Seats: U.
Traction Motors: Two EE327 of 30 kW.

619

BRUSH RAILCOACHES

Built 1937 by Brush. 20 built (284–303).
Seats: 48U.
Traction Motors: Two EE305 of 40 kW. (EE327 of 30 kW*).

621	(284)	627	(290)	633	(296)
622*	(285)	630	(293)	634	(297)
623	(286)	631	(294)	635	(299)
625	(288)	632	(295)	637	(300)
626	(289)				

CENTENARY CLASS

Built 1984–7. Body by East Lancs. Coachbuilders, Blackburn. One man operated. Radio fitted.
Seats: 52U.
Traction Motors: Two EE305 of 40 kW.

* Rebuilt from GEC car 651.

641	644	647
642	645	648*
643	646	

CORONATION CLASS

Built 1953 by Charles Roberts & Co. Resilient wheels. 25 built (304–328).
Seats: 56U.
Traction motors: Four Crompton-Parkinson 92 of 34 kW.

660   (324)

PROGRESS TWIN CARS

Motor cars (671–677) rebuilt 1958–60 from English Electric railcoaches.
Seats: 53U. **Traction Motors:** Two EE305 of 40 kW.
Driving trailers (681–687) built 1960 by Metro-Cammell.
Seats: 53U.

671+681 (281+T1)	674+684 (284+T4)	676+686 (286+T6)
672+682 (282+T2)	675+685 (285+T5)	677+687 (287+T7)
673+683 (283+T1)		

SINGLE CARS

Rebuilt 1958–60 from English Electric railcoaches. Originally ran with trailers.
Seats: 48U.
Traction Motors: Two EE305 of 40 kW.

678 (278)	679 (279)	680 (280)

"BALLOON" DOUBLE DECKERS

Built 1934–5 by English Electric. 700–712 were originally built with open tops, and 706 has now reverted to that condition.
Seats: 94U.
Traction Motors: Two EE305 of 40 kW.
§ Red and white livery.

700§ (237)	706 (243)	711 (248)
701 (238)	707 (244)	712 (249)
702 (239)	708 (245)	713 (250)
703 (240)	709 (246)	715 (252)
704 (241)	710 (247)	716 (253)

717	(254)	720	(257)	723	(260)
718	(255)	721	(258)	724	(261)
719	(256)	722	(259)	726	(263)

ILLUMINATED CARS

732	(168)	Rocket	Seats: 47U
733	(209)	Santa Fe loco. & tender	Seats: 35U
734	(174)	Santa Fe coach	Seats: 60U
735	(222)	Hovertram	Seats: 99U
736	(170)	HMS Blackpool	Seats: 71U

WORKS CARS

259	(748, 624)	PW gang towing car.
260	(751, 628, 291)	Crane car and rail carrier.
749	(S)	Tower wagon trailer.
750		Cable drum trailer.
752	(2, 1)	Rail grinder and snowplough.

JUBILEE CLASS DOUBLE DECKERS

Rebuilt 1979/82 from Balloon cars. Standard bus ends, thyristor control and stairs at each end. 761 has one door per side whereas 762 has two. Radio fitted.
Seats: 100U.
Traction Motors: Two EE305 of 40 kW.

761	(725, 262)	762	(714, 251)	

PRESERVED CARS

Blackpool & Fleetwood 40	Box car. Bogie single decker built 1914
Bolton 66	Bogie double-decker built 1901

In addition, certain other preserved cars may be loaned to Blackpool during 1992.

DEMONSTRATION CAR

The six-axle articulated car built by Tatra of Czechoslovakia which should have been used in Blackpool during 1990 never materialised.

9.2. DOCKLANDS LIGHT RAILWAY

This is a light rail line running in London's East End from Bank and Stratford to Island Gardens. It is being extended to Beckton and Lewisham.

System: 750 V dc third rail (bottom contact).
Depot: Poplar.

CLASS P86   B–2–B

Built 1987 by Linke-Hofmann-Busch. 28.80 x 2.65 m. Inward folding plug doors. Chopper control. Scharfenberg Couplers.
Weight: 39 t. **Seats:** 84U.
Traction Motors: Two GEC of 185 kW.
Max. Speed: 80 km/h.
Electric Brake: Rheostatic.

01 (S)	05 (S)	07 (S)	09 (S)
02 (S)	06 (S)	08 (S)	10 (S)
04 (S)			

This class has been sold to Essen, Germany. Nos. 03/11 have already departed. The vehicles will be converted to driver-operation.

CLASS P89   B–2–B

Built 1990 by BREL Ltd., York Works. 28.00 x 2.65 m. Inward Folding plug doors. Chopper control. Scharfenberg Couplers.
Weight: 39 t. **Seats:** 84U.
Traction Motors: Two GEC of 185 kW.
Max. Speed: 80 km/h.
Electric Brake: Rheostatic.

12	15	18	20
13	16	19	21
14	17		

CLASS B90   B–2–B

Built 1991 by BN Construction, Brugges, Belgium. 28.00 x 2.65 m. Sliding doors. End doors for staff use. Chopper control. Scharfenberg Couplers
Weight: 36 t.
Seats: 66U plus 4 tip-up.
Traction Motors: Two Brush of 140 kW.
Max. Speed: 80 km/h.
Electric Brake: Rheostatic.

22	28	34	40
23	29	35	41
24	30	36	42
25	31	37	43
26	32	38	44
27	33	39	

TODAY'S RAILWAYS REVIEW OF THE YEAR

Today's Railways Review of the Year is a comprehensive review of all the major railway events from 1987 to 1990, both in Great Britain and on the continent of Europe. The introduction of new traction and rolling stock is well documented, as are the withdrawal and disposal of life expired equipment and the many interesting aspects of railway operation. A large section is devoted to British Preservation, concentrating on the operation of steam locomotives in Great Britain but also encompassing diesel and electric operations on preserved lines. Light rail transit systems are also covered in detail, and a diary section of day to day events provides a useful reference section. A4 Casebound. 144 pages.

Volume 1 (events of 1987) 11.95
Volume 2 (events of 1988) 11.95
Volume 3 (events of 1989) 13.95
Volume 4 (events of 1990) 14.95

LIGHT RAIL REVIEW

Over the past 15 years light rail transit has advanced considerably in the UK with the introduction of schemes like Manchester Metrolink, and further important developments are in the pipeline. Light Rail Review takes a comprehensive look at current and future light rail schemes. The editorial content consists of topical articles by recognised authorities in the light rail field, concentrating mainly on UK subjects but also incorporating overseas advances. Much use is made of illustrations, a high proportion of which are in colour making Light Rail Review an informative source of reference which will appeal to both enthusiasts and transport professionals alike. A4 size. Thread sewn.

Light Rail Review 1 .... 6.95
Light Rail Review 2 .... 7.50
Light Rail Review 3 .... 7.50

9.3. GREATER MANCHESTER METROLINK

This new light rail system will initially run from Bury to Altrincham through the streets of Manchester. The first section from Bury to Manchester Victoria is due to open in early March, followed by the street section in early April. The Altrincham line should open in May, with a Royal opening of the spur to Manchester Piccadilly on 2nd June.

System: 750 V dc overhead.
Depot: Cheetham Hill.

SIX-AXLE ARTICULATED CARS   Bo–2–Bo

Built 1991–2 by Firema, Italy. Power operated sliding doors. Chopper control. Scharfenberg Couplers.
Weight: 45 t.
Seats: 84U unidirectional.
Dimensions: 29.00 x 2.65 m.
Traction Motors: Four GEC of 130 kW.
Braking: Rheostatic, regenerative, disc and emergency track brakes.

1001	1008	1015	1021
1002	1009	1016	1022
1003	1010	1017	1023
1004	1011	1018	1024
1005	1012	1019	1025
1006	1013	1020	1026
1007	1014		

Name: 1002 Manchester Arndale Voyager.

SPECIAL PURPOSE VEHICLE

Built 1991 by RFS Industries, Kilnhurst and Brown Root. Used for shunting and track maintenance. Includes a crane.

Unnumbered.

Manchester Metrolink car No. 1005 on 20th December 1991 with a powered trial in Balloon Street. This was the first day of street running on a modern LRT system anywhere in the UK.　　　*David Holt*

9.4. STRATHCLYDE PTE UNDERGROUND

This circular 4' gauge underground line in Glasgow is generally referred t
as the "Subway".
System: 750 V dc third rail.
Depot: Broomloan.

SINGLE CARS   Bo—Bo

Built 1978–9 by Metro-Cammell. Power-operated sliding doors. 12.58 x 2.3
m.
Seats: 36U.
Traction Motors: Two GEC G312AZ.

101	110	118	126
102	111	119	127
103	112	120	128
104	113	121	129
105	114	122	130
106	115	123	131
107	116	124	132
108	117	125	133
109			

9.5. TYNE & WEAR METRO

System: 1500 V d.c. overhead.
Depot: South Gosforth.

BATTERY/OVERHEAD ELECTRIC LOCOS

Built: 1989–90 by Hunslet, Leeds. BSI couplers.
Traction Motors: Hunslet-Greenbat T9-4P.
Weight: 26 t.

BL 1	BL 2	BL 3

SIX-AXLE ARTICULATED UNITS   Bo–2–Bo

Built 1976, 1978–81 by Metro-Cammell. 27.80 x 2.65m. BSI couplers.
Weight: 39 t. **Seats:** 84U. **Traction Motors:** Two 187 kW.

4001	4024	4047	4069
4002	4025	4048	4070
4003	4026	4049	4071
4004	4027	4050	4072
4005	4028	4051	4073
4006	4029	4052	4074
4007	4030	4053	4075
4008	4031	4054	4076
4009	4032	4055	4077
4010	4033	4056	4078
4011	4034	4057	4079
4012	4035	4058	4080
4013	4036	4059	4081
4014	4037	4060	4082
4015	4038	4061	4083
4016	4039	4062	4084
4017	4040	4063	4085
4018	4041	4064	4086
4019	4042	4065	4087
4020	4043	4066	4088
4021	4044	4067	4089
4022	4045	4068	4090
4023	4046		

Names:

4041	HARRY COWANS
4044	Director
4051	Times

Notes:

Standard livery is yellow and white.
4044 is painted yellow.
4051 is painted claret.
4054/5 are painted in 'Metroland' advertising livery..

Front cover: Class 31/4 No. 31422 heads a train of InterCity sector Mk. 2D/E air conditioned stock on the 09.57 Sheffield–Skegness on Saturday 17th August 1992. This loco, now in Mainline livery had been modified to Class 31 and renumbered 31522, but had regained its e.t.h. supply and also its former number during 1991.   *Peter Fo*

Back cover: Inside the new depot at Aylesbury at the official opening on 14 May 1991 with Class 165 'Network Turbo' unit No. 165 002 over the inspection pit.   *Peter Fo*

PLATFORM 5 PUBLISHING LTD.
MAIL ORDER LIST

Modern British Railway Titles

Motive Power Pocket Book Spring 1992	1.75
Coaching Stock Pocket Book 1992	1.75
Diesel Unit Pocket Book 1992	1.75
Electric Unit Pocket Book 1992	1.75
Today's Railways Review of the Year Volume 1	11.95
Today's Railways Review of the Year Volume 2	11.95
Today's Railways Review of the Year Volume 3	13.95
Today's Railways Review of the Year Volume 4	14.95
Preserved Locomotives of British Railways 7th Edition	5.50
Departmental Coaching Stock 4th Edition	4.95
On-Track Plant on British Railways (formerly Track Machines)	5.50
North West Rails in Colour	8.50
British Rail Wagon Fleet – Air Braked Freight Stock (SCTP)	6.95
British Rail Wagon Fleet Volume 4 (SCTP)	3.30
British Rail Wagon Fleet Volume 5 (SCTP)	5.25
Private Owner Wagon Fleet (SCTP)	5.75
British Rail Track Diagrams 3 – Western (Quail) **NEW**	5.00
British Rail Track Diagrams 4 – London Midland (Quail)	6.95
London Railway Map (Quail)	5.95
London Transport Track Map (Quail)	1.30
Miles & Chains Volumes 3/5 – ScR/SR (Milepost) each	1.00
Miles & Chains Volume 2 – London Midland (Milepost)	1.40
Blood, Sweat & Fifties (Class 50 Society)	2.95

Overseas Railways

French Railways/Chemins de Fer Français	9.95
Swiss Railways/Chemins de fer Suisses	9.95
DB/German Federal Railway 2nd Edition	6.95
ÖBB/Austrian Federal Railways 2nd Edition	6.95
Benelux Locomotives & Coaching Stock 2nd Edition	6.95
A Guide to Portuguese Railways (Fearless)	4.95
Railways of Southern Africa Locomotive Guide 1991	3.50
Industrial Locomotives of South Africa 1991	6.50

Historical Railway Titles

Midland Railway Portrait	12.95
The Handbook of British Railways Steam Motive Power Depots	
Volume 1 – Southern England	7.95
Volume 2 – Central England, East Anglia & Wales	8.95
Volume 3 – North Midlands, Lancashire & Yorkshire	8.95
Volume 4 – Northern England & Scotland	9.95
Rails along the Sea Wall (Dawlish–Teignmouth Pictorial History)	4.95
Steam Days on BR 1 – The Midland Line in Sheffield	4.95
Real Steam in Colour 1 – York (Norseman)	4.95
The Railways of Winchester	6.95
Register of Closed Railways 1948–91 (Milepost) **NEW**	5.95

British Railways Mark 1 Coaches (Atlantic) **NEW** 19.95
Along LMS Routes Vol. 1. (Headstock) 14.95
An Illustrated History of the Cheshire Lines Committee (Heyday) ... 10.95
Private Owner Wagons Volume 1 (Headstock) 8.95
Private Owner Wagons Volume 2 (Headstock) 9.95
Private Owner Wagons Volume 3 (Headstock) 6.95
Private Owner Wagons Volume 4 (Headstock) 7.95
Totley & The Tunnel 4.95

Political

The Battle for the Settle & Carlisle 6.95

Rambling

Rambles by Rail 1 – The Hope Valley Line 1.95
Rambles by Rail 2 – Liskeard-Looe **NEW MARCH 30th** 1.95
Buxton Spa Line Rail Rambles 1.20

Light Rail Transit, Trams, Buses & Ships

Light Rail Review 1 (Reprint) 6.95
Light Rail Review 2 .... 7.50
Light Rail Review 3 .... 7.50
UK Light Rail Systems 1:Manchester Metrolink **NEW** 7.50
Blackpool & Fleetwood By Tram 7.50
Bus Review 7 (Bus Enthusiast) **NEW** 4.95
60 Years of A1 Service (Bus Enthusiast) 5.95
London Buses in Exile 2nd Edition (Bus Enthusiast) 4.95
Tramways in and around Stockport (Foxline) 6.95
Edinburgh's Trams & Buses (Bus Enthusiast) 4.95
Tramtracks & Trolleybooms (Chesterfield) 3.95
On The Trams (Gill) 4.95
Speed Bonny Boat (The Story of Caledonian MacBrayne 1969-1990) . 4.95

Scenes from the Past (Foxline Publishing)

Scenes from the Past 9 – The Llangollen Line 7.95
Scenes from the Past 10 – Railways in and around Bolton 7.95
Scenes from the Past 11 – Nottingham (Foxline) 8.95
Scenes from the Past 12 – Conway Valley (Foxline) 7.95
Scenes from the Past 13 – Stockport/Tiviot Dale (Foxline) 5.95

Back Numbers

Locomotives & Coaching Stock 1985 (few left) 2.95
Locomotives & Coaching Stock 1986 .... 3.30
Locomotives & Coaching Stock 1987 .... 3.30
Locomotives & Coaching Stock 1988 .... 3.95
Locomotives & Coaching Stock 1989 .... 4.95
Locomotives & Coaching Stock 1990 .... 5.95
Locomotives & Coaching Stock 1991 .... 6.60

Postage: 20p to £1, 30p to £2, 40p to £3, 50p to £5 then 10% (20% overseas).

All these publications are available from shops, bookstalls or direct from: Mail Order Department, Platform 5 Publishing Ltd., Lydgate House, Lydgate Lane, Sheffield, S10 5FH. For a full list of titles available by mail order, please send SAE to the above address.